PAPUA
NEW GUINEA

BUSINESS LAW HANDBOOK
VOLUME 1
STRATEGIC INFORMATION AND BASIC LAWS

International Business Publications, USA
Washington DC, USA – Papua New Guinea

PAPUA NEW GUINEA

BUSINESS LAW HANDBOOK

VOLUME 1 STRATEGIC INFORMATION AND BASIC LAWS

UPDATED ANNUALLY

We express our sincere appreciation to all government agencies and international organizations which provided information and other materials for this handbook

Cover Design: International Business Publications, USA

2018 Updated Reprint International Business Publications, USA
ISBN

For additional analytical, business and investment opportunities information, please contact Global Investment & Business Center, USA at (703) 370-8082. Fax: (703) 370-8083. E-mail: ibpusa3@gmail.com Global Business and Investment Info Databank - www.ibpus.com

Printed in the USA

For additional analytical, business and investment opportunities information, please contact Global Investment & Business Center, USA at (703) 370-8082. Fax: (703) 370-8083. E-mail: ibpusa3@gmail.com Global Business and Investment Info Databank - www.ibpus.com

PAPUA

NEW GUINEA

BUSINESS LAW HANDBOOK

VOLUME 1

STRATEGIC INFORMATION AND BASIC LAWS

TABLE OF CONTENTS

STRATEGIC AND DEVELOPMENT PROFILES

STRATEGIC PROFILE

Capital and largest city	Port Moresby 9°30′S 147°07′E
Official languages	• Hiri Motu • Tok Pisin • PNG Sign Language • English
Demonym	Papua New Guinean
Government	Unitary parliamentary constitutional monarchy
• Monarch	Elizabeth II
• Governor-General	Bob Dadae
• Prime Minister	Peter O'Neill
Legislature	National Parliament
Independence from Australia	
• Papua and New Guinea Act 1949	1 July 1949
• Declared and recognised	16 September 1975
Area	
• Total	462,840 km^2 (178,700 sq mi) (54th)
• Water (%)	2
Population	
• 2016 census preliminary estimate	8,084,999 [5] (101st)
• 2000 census	5,190,783
• Density	15/km^2 (38.8/sq mi) (201st)
GDP (PPP)	2017 estimate
• Total	$29.481 billion[6] (139th)
• Per capita	$3,635[6]
GDP (nominal)	2017 estimate
• Total	$21.189 billion[6] (115th)
• Per capita	$2,613[6]
Gini (1996)	50.9[7] high
HDI	▲ 0.516[8] low · 154th
Currency	Papua New Guinean kina (PGK)
Time zone	AEST (UTC+10, +11)
Drives on the	left
Calling code	+675
ISO 3166 code	PG
Internet TLD	.pg

Papua New Guinea officially named the **Independent State of Papua New Guinea**, is a country in Oceania that occupies the eastern half of the island of New Guinea (the western portion of the island is a part of the Indonesian provinces of Papua and West Papua) and numerous offshore islands. It is located in the southwestern Pacific Ocean, in a region described since the early 19th century as Melanesia. The capital is Port Moresby.

Papua New Guinea is one of the most culturally diverse countries in the world. According to recent data, 841 different languages are listed for the country, although 11 of these have no known living speakers. There may be at least as many traditional societies, out of a population of about 6.3 million. It is also one of the most rural, as only 18 percent of its people live in urban centres. The country is one of the world's least explored, culturally and geographically, and many undiscovered species of plants and animals are thought to exist in the interior of Papua New Guinea.

Strong growth in Papua New Guinea's mining and resource sector has led to PNG becoming the sixth fastest-growing economy in the world as of 2011. Despite this, many people live in extreme poverty, with about one-third of the population living on less than US$1.25 per day. The majority of the population still live in traditional societies and practice subsistence-based agriculture. These societies and clans have some explicit acknowledgement within the nation's constitutional framework. The PNG Constitution expresses the wish for "traditional villages and communities to remain as viable units of Papua New Guinean society",and for active steps to be taken in their preservation.

After being ruled by three external powers since 1884, Papua New Guinea acquired self-government in 1973 and independence in 1975. It was not strictly speaking "granted" independence by Australia, which had not been its colonist but only administered British New Guinea after federation in 1901 and German New Guinea after 1914 for the League of Nations and for the United Nations after 1945. It became a separate Commonwealth realm upon independence with Her Majesty Queen Elizabeth II reigning as the Queen of Papua New Guinea.

Background:	The eastern half of the island of New Guinea - second largest in the world - was divided between Germany (north) and the UK (south) in 1885. The latter area was transferred to Australia in 1902, which occupied the northern portion during World War I and continued to administer the combined areas until independence in 1975. A nine-year secessionist revolt on the island of Bougainville ended in 1997, after claiming some 20,000 lives.

GEOGRAPHY

Location:	Southeastern Asia, group of islands including the eastern half of the island of New Guinea between the Coral Sea and the South Pacific Ocean, east of Indonesia
Geographic coordinates:	6 00 S, 147 00 E
Map references:	Oceania
Area:	total: 462,840 sq km land: 452,860 sq km water: 9,980 sq km
Area - comparative:	slightly larger than California
Land boundaries:	total: 820 km border countries: Indonesia 820 km

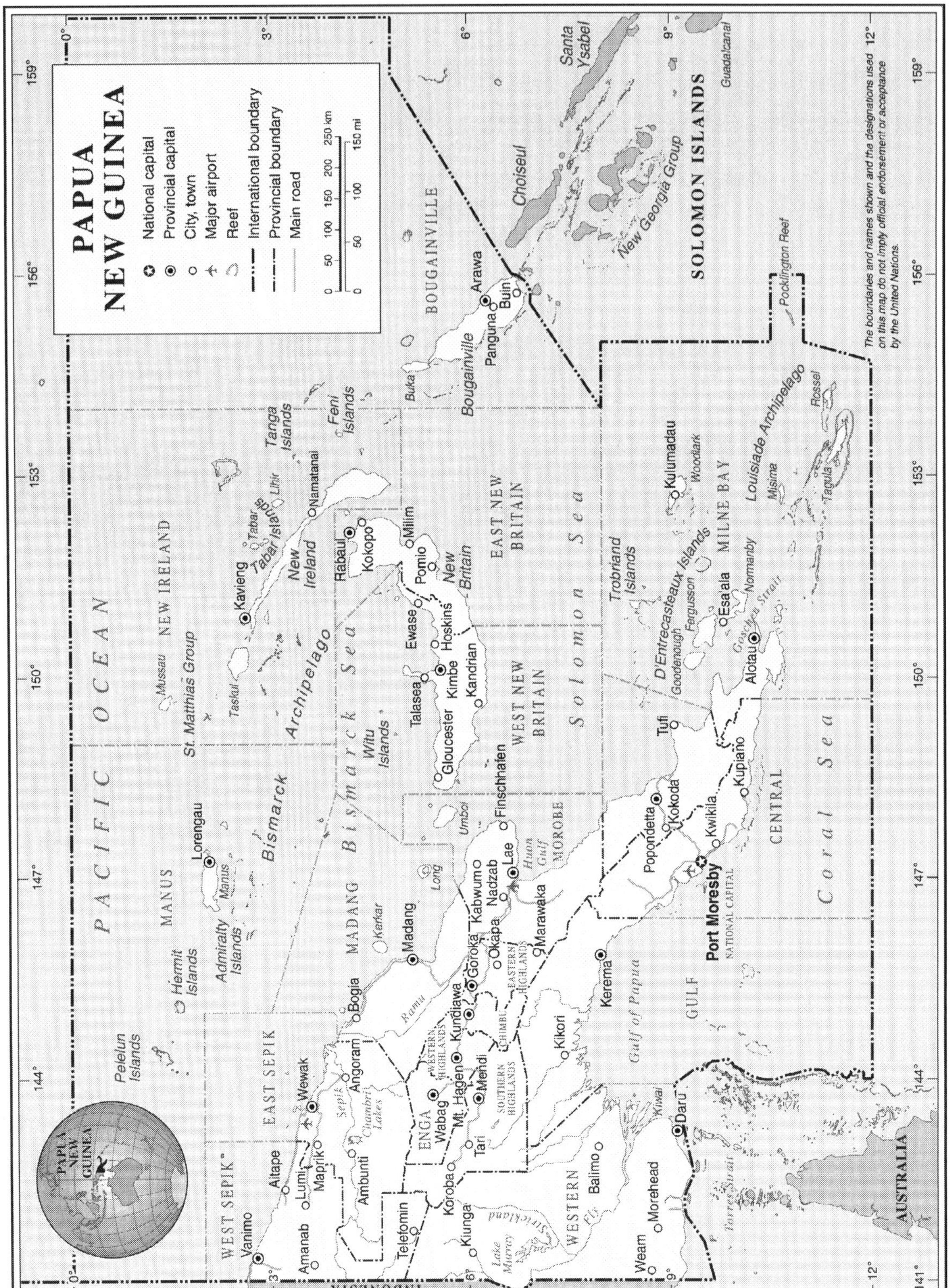

Coastline:	5,152 km

Maritime claims:	measured from claimed archipelagic baselines continental shelf: 200-m depth or to the depth of exploitation exclusive fishing zone: 200 NM territorial sea: 12 NM
Climate:	tropical; northwest monsoon (December to March), southeast monsoon (May to October); slight seasonal temperature variation
Terrain:	mostly mountains with coastal lowlands and rolling foothills
Elevation extremes:	lowest point: Pacific Ocean 0 m highest point: Mount Wilhelm 4,509 m
Natural resources:	gold, copper, silver, natural gas, timber, oil, fisheries
Land use:	arable land: 0.1% permanent crops: 1% permanent pastures: 0% forests and woodland: 92.9% other: 6% (1993 est.)
Irrigated land:	NA sq km
Natural hazards:	active volcanism; situated along the Pacific "Rim of Fire"; the country is subject to frequent and sometimes severe earthquakes; mud slides; tsunamis
ENVIRONMENT - CURRENT ISSUES:	rain forest subject to deforestation as a result of growing commercial demand for tropical timber; pollution from mining projects; severe drought
Environment - international agreements:	party to: Antarctic Treaty, Biodiversity, Climate Change, Desertification, Endangered Species, Environmental Modification, Hazardous Wastes, Law of the Sea, Marine Dumping, Nuclear Test Ban, Ozone Layer Protection, Ship Pollution, Tropical Timber 83, Tropical Timber 94, Wetlands signed, but not ratified: Antarctic-Environmental Protocol, Climate Change-Kyoto Protocol

Geography - note:	shares Island of New Guinea with Indonesia; one of world's largest swamps along southwest coast

PEOPLE

Population:	5,049,055
Age structure:	0-14 years: 38.7% (male 993,248; female 960,647) 15-64 years: 57.63% (male 1,507,064; female 1,402,666) 65 years and over: 3.67% (male 87,779; female 97,651)

Population growth rate:	2.43%

Birth rate:	32.15 births/1,000 population
Death rate:	7.88 deaths/1,000 population
Net migration rate:	0 migrant(s)/1,000 population
Sex ratio:	at birth: 1.05 male(s)/female under 15 years: 1.03 male(s)/female 15-64 years: 1.07 male(s)/female 65 years and over: 0.9 male(s)/female total population: 1.05 male(s)/female
Infant mortality rate:	58.21 deaths/1,000 live births
Life expectancy at birth:	total population: 63.46 years male: 61.39 years female: 65.64 years
Total fertility rate:	4.3 children born/woman
HIV/AIDS - adult prevalence rate:	0.22%
HIV/AIDS - people living with HIV/AIDS:	5,400
HIV/AIDS - deaths:	450
Nationality:	noun: Papua New Guinean(s) adjective: Papua New Guinean
Ethnic groups:	Melanesian, Papuan, Negrito, Micronesian, Polynesian
Religions:	Roman Catholic 22%, Lutheran 16%, Presbyterian/Methodist/London Missionary Society 8%, Anglican 5%, Evangelical Alliance 4%, Seventh-Day Adventist 1%, other Protestant 10%, indigenous beliefs 34%
Languages:	English spoken by 1%-2%, pidgin English widespread, Motu spoken in Papua region note: 715 indigenous languages
Literacy:	definition: age 15 and over can read and write total population: 72.2% male: 81% female: 62.7%

GOVERNMENT

Country name:
conventional long form: Independent State of Papua New Guinea
conventional short form: Papua New Guinea
local short form: Papuaniugini
former: Territory of Papua and New Guinea
abbreviation: PNG
etymology: the word "papua" derives from the Malay "papuah" describing the frizzy hair of the Melanesians; Spanish explorer Ynigo ORTIZ de RETEZ applied the term "Nueva

Guinea" to the island of New Guinea in 1545 after noting the resemblance of the locals to the peoples of the Guinea coast of Africa

Government type:
parliamentary democracy (National Parliament) under a constitutional monarchy; a Commonwealth realm

Capital:
name: Port Moresby
geographic coordinates: 9 27 S, 147 11 E
time difference: UTC+10 (15 hours ahead of Washington, DC, during Standard Time)

Administrative divisions:
20 provinces, 1 autonomous region*, and 1 district**; Bougainville*, Central, Chimbu, Eastern Highlands, East New Britain, East Sepik, Enga, Gulf, Hela, Jiwaka, Madang, Manus, Milne Bay, Morobe, National Capital**, New Ireland, Northern, Southern Highlands, Western, Western Highlands, West New Britain, West Sepik

Independence:
16 September 1975 (from the Australian-administered UN trusteeship)

National holiday:
Independence Day, 16 September (1975)

Constitution:
adopted 15 August 1975, effective at independence 16 September 1975; amended many times, last in 2013; note - in September 2015, the Supreme Court nullified the 2013 constitutional amendment that increased the grace period on motions of no confidence (2016)

Legal system:
mixed legal system of English common law and customary law

International law organization participation:
has not submitted an ICJ jurisdiction declaration; non-party state to the ICCt

Citizenship:
citizenship by birth: no
citizenship by descent only: at least one parent must be a citizen of Papua New Guinea
dual citizenship recognized: no
residency requirement for naturalization: 8 years

Suffrage:
18 years of age; universal

Executive branch:

chief of state: Queen ELIZABETH II (since 6 February 1952); represented by Governor General Grand Chief Sir Bob DADAE (since 28 February 2017)
head of government: Prime Minister Peter Paire O'NEILL (since 2 August 2011); Deputy Prime Minister Charles ABEL (since 4 August 2017)
cabinet: National Executive Council appointed by the governor general on the recommendation of the prime minister

elections/appointments: the monarchy is hereditary; governor general nominated by the National Parliament and appointed by the chief of state; following legislative elections, the leader of the majority party or majority coalition usually appointed prime minister by the governor general pending the outcome of a National Parliament vote
election results: Peter Paire O'NEILL (PNC) reelected prime minister; National Parliament vote - 60 to 46

Legislative branch:
description: unicameral National Parliament (111 seats; members directly elected in single-seat constituencies - 89 local, 20 provinicial, the autonomous province of Bouganville, and the National Capital District - by majority preferential vote; members serve 5-year terms); note - the constitution allows up to 126 seats
elections: last held from 24 June 2017 to 8 July 2017 (next to be held in June 2022)
election results: percent of vote by party - PNC 37%; NA 13%; Pangu 14%; URP 11%; PPP 4%; SDP 4%; Independents 3%; and smaller parties 14%; seats by party - NA

Judicial branch:
highest courts: Supreme Court (consists of the chief justice, deputy chief justice, 35 justices, and 5 activing justices); National Courts (consists of 13 courts located in the province capitals, with a total of 19 resident judges)
judge selection and term of office: Supreme Court chief justice appointed by the governor-general upon advice of the National Executive Council (cabinet) after consultation with the National Justice Administration Minister; deputy chief justice and other justices appointed by the Judicial and Legal Services Commission, a 5-member body to include the Supreme Court chief and deputy chief justices, the chief ombudsman, and a member of the National Parliament; full-time citizen judges appointed for 10-year renewable terms; non-citizen judges initially appointed for 3-year renewable terms and after first renewal until age 70; appointment and tenure of National Court resident judges NA
subordinate courts: district, village, and juvenile courts, military courts, taxation courts, coronial courts, mining warden courts, land courts, traffic courts, committal courts, grade five courts

Political parties and leaders:
National Alliance Party or NAP [Patrick PRUAITCH]
Papua and Niugini Union Party or PANGU [Sam BASIL]
Papua New Guinea Party or PNGP [Belden NAMAH]
People's National Congress Party or PNC [Peter Paire O'NEILL]
People's Party or PP [Peter IPATAS]
People's Progress Party or PPP [Sir Julius CHAN]
Social Democratic Party or SDP [Powes PARKOP]
Triumph Heritage Empowerment Party or THE [Don POLYE]
United Resources Party or URP [William DUMA]
note: as of 8 July 2017, 45 political parties were registered

International organization participation:
ACP, ADB, AOSIS, APEC, ARF, ASEAN (observer), C, CD, CP, EITI (candidate country), FAO, G-77, IAEA, IBRD, ICAO, ICRM, IDA, IFAD, IFC, IFRCS, IHO, ILO, IMF, IMO, Interpol, IOC, IOM, IPU, ISO (correspondent), ITSO, ITU, MIGA, NAM, OPCW, PIF, Sparteca, SPC, UN, UNCTAD, UNESCO, UNIDO, UNMISS, UNWTO, UPU, WCO, WFTU (NGOs), WHO, WIPO, WMO, WTO

Diplomatic representation in the US:
chief of mission: Ambassador (vacant); Charge D'Affaires Elias Rahuromo WOHENGU (since 30 September 2017)

chancery: 1779 Massachusetts Avenue NW, Suite 805, Washington, DC 20036
telephone: [1] (202) 745-3680
FAX: [1] (202) 745-3679

Diplomatic representation from the US:
chief of mission: Ambassador Catherine EBERT-GRAY (since 23 February 2016); note - also accredited to the Solomon Islands and Vanuatu
embassy: P.O. Box 1492, Port Moresby
mailing address: 4240 Port Moresby Place, US Department of State, Washington DC 20521-4240
telephone: [675] 321-1455
FAX: [675] 321-3423

Flag description:
divided diagonally from upper hoist-side corner; the upper triangle is red with a soaring yellow bird of paradise centered; the lower triangle is black with five, white, five-pointed stars of the Southern Cross constellation centered; red, black, and yellow are traditional colors of Papua New Guinea; the bird of paradise - endemic to the island of New Guinea - is an emblem of regional tribal culture and represents the emergence of Papua New Guinea as a nation; the Southern Cross, visible in the night sky, symbolizes Papua New Guinea's connection with Australia and several other countries in the South Pacific

National symbol(s):
bird of paradise; national colors: red, black

National anthem:
name: "O Arise All You Sons"
lyrics/music: Thomas SHACKLADY

ECONOMY

Papua New Guinea (PNG) is richly endowed with natural resources, but exploitation has been hampered by rugged terrain, land tenure issues, and the high cost of developing infrastructure. The economy has a small formal sector, focused mainly on the export of those natural resources, and an informal sector, employing the majority of the population. Agriculture provides a subsistence livelihood for 85% of the people. The global financial crisis had little impact because of continued foreign demand for PNG's commodities.

Mineral deposits, including copper, gold, and oil, account for nearly two-thirds of export earnings. Natural gas reserves amount to an estimated 155 billion cubic meters. Following construction of a $19 billion liquefied natural gas (LNG) project, PNG LNG, a consortium led by ExxonMobil, began exporting liquefied natural gas to Asian markets in May 2014. The project was delivered on time and only slightly above budget. The success of the project has encouraged other companies to look at similar LNG projects. French supermajor Total is expected to begin construction on the Papua LNG project by 2020. Due to lower global commodity prices, resource revenues of all types have fallen dramatically. PNG's government has recently been forced to adjust spending levels downward.

Numerous challenges still face the government of Peter O'NEILL, including providing physical security for foreign investors, regaining investor confidence, restoring integrity to state institutions, promoting economic efficiency by privatizing moribund state institutions, and maintaining good relations with Australia, its former colonial ruler. Other socio-cultural challenges could upend the economy including chronic law and order and land tenure issues.

GDP (purchasing power parity):

$28.02 billion (est.)
$27.33 billion (2015 est.)
$25.63 billion (2014 est.)
note: data are in 2016 dollars
country comparison to the world: 134

GDP (official exchange rate):
$19.92 billion (est.)

GDP - real growth rate:
2.5% (est.)
6.6% (2015 est.)
7.4% (2014 est.)
country comparison to the world: 112

GDP - per capita (PPP):
$3,500 (est.)
$3,500 (2015 est.)
$3,400 (2014 est.)
note: data are in 2016 dollars
country comparison to the world: 183
Gross national saving:
38.1% of GDP (est.)
24% of GDP (2015 est.)
-11.7% of GDP (2014 est.)
country comparison to the world: 8

GDP - composition, by end use:
household consumption: 49.4%
government consumption: 7.8%
investment in fixed capital: 9.9%
investment in inventories: 0.4%
exports of goods and services: 68.7%
imports of goods and services: -36.2% (est.)

GDP - composition, by sector of origin:
agriculture: 22.3%
industry: 37.6%
services: 40.1% (est.)

Agriculture - products:
coffee, cocoa, copra, palm kernels, tea, sugar, rubber, sweet potatoes, fruit, vegetables, vanilla; poultry, pork; shellfish
Industries:
copra crushing, palm oil processing, plywood production, wood chip production; mining (gold, silver, copper); crude oil and petroleum products; construction, tourism

Industrial production growth rate:
4.8% (est.)

country comparison to the world: 39

Labor force:
4.365 million (est.)
country comparison to the world: 90

Labor force - by occupation:
agriculture: 85%
industry: NA%
services: NA% (2005 est.)
Unemployment rate:
2.5% (2014 est.)
2.5% (2013 est.)
country comparison to the world: 17

Population below poverty line:
37% (est.)

Household income or consumption by percentage share:
lowest 10%: 1.7%
highest 10%: 40.5%

Distribution of family income - Gini index:
50.9 (1996)
country comparison to the world: 13

Budget:
revenues: $3.169 billion
expenditures: $4.295 billion (est.)

Taxes and other revenues:
15.9% of GDP (est.)
country comparison to the world: 179

Budget surplus (+) or deficit (-):
-5.7% of GDP (est.)
country comparison to the world: 171

Public debt:
39.4% of GDP (est.)
36.9% of GDP (2015 est.)
country comparison to the world: 124

Fiscal year:
calendar year

Inflation rate (consumer prices):
6.3% (est.)
6% (2015 est.)
country comparison to the world: 187

Central bank discount rate:
14% (31 December 2010)
6.92% (31 December 2009)

country comparison to the world: 13

Commercial bank prime lending rate:
8.3% (31 December est.)
8.73% (31 December 2015 est.)
country comparison to the world: 101
Stock of narrow money:
$5.282 billion (31 December est.)
$4.936 billion (31 December 2015 est.)
country comparison to the world: 97

Stock of broad money:
$8.085 billion (31 December 2014 est.)
$7.477 billion (31 December 2013 est.)
country comparison to the world: 115

Stock of domestic credit:
$6.36 billion (31 December est.)
$6.118 billion (31 December 2015 est.)
country comparison to the world: 117

Market value of publicly traded shares:
$10.71 billion (31 December 2012 est.)
$8.999 billion (31 December 2011 est.)
$9.742 billion (31 December 2010 est.)
country comparison to the world: 73

Current account balance:
$3.051 billion (est.)
$4.148 billion (2015 est.)
country comparison to the world: 28

Exports:
$7.886 billion (est.)
$8.377 billion (2015 est.)
country comparison to the world: 94

Exports - commodities:
oil, gold, copper ore, logs, palm oil, coffee, cocoa, crayfish, prawns

Exports - partners:
Japan 17.4%, Australia 15.9%, China 12.1%

Imports:
$1.83 billion (est.)
$2.267 billion (2015 est.)
country comparison to the world: 165

Imports - commodities:
machinery and transport equipment, manufactured goods, food, fuels, chemicals

Imports - partners:
Australia 25.9%, China 20%, Singapore 12.6%, Malaysia 7.2%, US 4.2%, Indonesia 4.1%, South Korea 4% (2015)

Reserves of foreign exchange and gold:
$1.629 billion (31 December est.)
$1.738 billion (31 December 2015 est.)
country comparison to the world: 121

Debt - external:
$22.04 billion (31 December est.)
$20.41 billion (31 December 2015 est.)
country comparison to the world: 85

Stock of direct foreign investment - at home:
$NA

Exchange rates:
kina (PGK) per US dollar -
3.156 (est.)
2.7684 (2015 est.)
2.7684 (2014 est.)
2.4614 (2013 est.)
2.08 (2012 est.)

ENERGY

Electricity access:
population without electricity: 5,568,879
electrification - total population: 18%
electrification - urban areas: 72%
electrification - rural areas: 10%

Electricity - production:
3.2 billion kWh (2014 est.)
country comparison to the world: 128

Electricity - consumption:
3 billion kWh (2014 est.)
country comparison to the world: 133

Electricity - exports:
0 kWh (2013 est.)
country comparison to the world: 186

Electricity - imports:
0 kWh (2013 est.)
country comparison to the world: 189

Electricity - installed generating capacity:
900,000 kW (2014 est.)
country comparison to the world: 130

Electricity - from fossil fuels:
61.1% of total installed capacity (2012 est.)
country comparison to the world: 128

Electricity - from nuclear fuels:

0% of total installed capacity (2012 est.)
country comparison to the world: 167

Electricity - from hydroelectric plants:
30.9% of total installed capacity (2012 est.)
country comparison to the world: 75

Electricity - from other renewable sources:
8% of total installed capacity (2012 est.)
country comparison to the world: 47

Crude oil - production:
52,600 bbl/day (2015 est.)
country comparison to the world: 55

Crude oil - exports:
25,400 bbl/day (2013 est.)
country comparison to the world: 54

Crude oil - imports:
14,880 bbl/day (2013 est.)
country comparison to the world: 70

Crude oil - proved reserves:
200 million bbl (1 January 2016 es)
country comparison to the world: 62

Refined petroleum products - production:
28,340 bbl/day (2013 est.)
country comparison to the world: 87

Refined petroleum products - consumption:
42,000 bbl/day (2014 est.)
country comparison to the world: 109
Refined petroleum products - exports:
8,062 bbl/day (2013 est.)
country comparison to the world: 86

Refined petroleum products - imports:
21,180 bbl/day (2013 est.)
country comparison to the world: 115

Natural gas - production:
4.75 billion cu m (2014 est.)
country comparison to the world: 53

Natural gas - consumption:
100 million cu m (2014 est.)
country comparison to the world: 109

Natural gas - exports:
4.65 billion cu m (2014 est.)
country comparison to the world: 33

Natural gas - imports:
0 cu m (2013 est.)
country comparison to the world: 118

Natural gas - proved reserves:
151.3 billion cu m (1 January 2016 es)
country comparison to the world: 47

Carbon dioxide emissions from consumption of energy:
3.7 million Mt (2013 est.)
country comparison to the world: 137

COMMUNICATIONS

Telephones - fixed lines:
total subscriptions: 150,000
subscriptions per 100 inhabitants: 2 (July 2015 est.)
country comparison to the world: 137

Telephones - mobile cellular:
total: 3.56 million
subscriptions per 100 inhabitants: 53 (July 2015 est.)
country comparison to the world: 132

Telephone system:

general assessment: services are minimal; facilities provide radiotelephone and telegraph, coastal radio, aeronautical radio, and international radio communication services

domestic: access to telephone services is not widely available although combined fixed-line and mobile-cellular teledensity has increased to roughly 55 per 100 persons

international: country code - 675; submarine cables to Australia and Guam; satellite earth station - 1 Intelsat (Pacific Ocean); international radio communication service (2015)

Broadcast media:

2 TV stations, 1 commercial station operating since the late 1980s, and 1 state-run station launched in 2008; satellite and cable TV services are available; state-run National Broadcasting Corporation operates 3 radio networks with multiple repeaters and about 20 provincial stations; several commercial radio stations with multiple transmission points as well as several community stations; transmissions of several international broadcasters are accessible

Internet country code:

.pg

Internet users:
total: 527,000
percent of population: 7.9% (July 2015 est.)
country comparison to the world: 162

TRANSPORTATION

National air transport system:
number of registered air carriers: 6
inventory of registered aircraft operated by air carriers: 47
annual passenger traffic on registered air carriers: 2,062,584

annual freight traffic on registered air carriers: 34,827,034 mt-km

Civil aircraft registration country code prefix:
P2 (2016)

Airports:
561 (2013)
country comparison to the world: 12

Airports - with paved runways:
total: 21
over 3,047 m: 1
2,438 to 3,047 m: 2
1,524 to 2,437 m: 12
914 to 1,523 m: 5
under 914 m: 1

Airports - with unpaved runways:
total: 540
1,524 to 2,437 m: 11
914 to 1,523 m: 53
under 914 m: 476

Heliports:
2

Pipelines:
oil 264 km

Roadways:
total: 9,349 km
paved: 3,000 km
unpaved: 6,349 km
country comparison to the world: 139

Waterways:
11,000 km (2011)
country comparison to the world: 11

Merchant marine:
total: 31
by type: bulk carrier 7, cargo 22, petroleum tanker 2
foreign-owned: 8 (Germany 1, Malaysia 1, UAE 6)
country comparison to the world: 83

Ports and terminals:
major seaport(s): Kimbe, Lae, Madang, Rabaul, Wewak
LNG terminal(s) (export): Port Moresby

MILITARY

Military expenditures:
0.66% of GDP (2014)
0.68% of GDP (2013)
0.72% of GDP (2012)
0.5% of GDP (2011)
country comparison to the world: 127

Military branches:
Papua New Guinea Defense Force (PNGDF, includes Maritime Operations Element, Air Operations Element) (2013)

Military service age and obligation:
16 years of age for voluntary military service (with parental consent); no conscription; graduation from grade 12 required (2013)

TRANSNATIONAL ISSUES

Disputes - international:
relies on assistance from Australia to keep out illegal cross-border activities from primarily Indonesia, including goods smuggling, illegal narcotics trafficking, and squatters and secessionists

Refugees and internally displaced persons:
refugees (country of origin): 9,368 (Indonesia) (2015)
IDPs: 8,400 (natural disasters, tribal conflict, inter-communal violence, development projects)

Trafficking in persons:

current situation: Papua New Guinea is a source and destination country for men, women, and children subjected to sex trafficking and forced labor; foreign and Papua New Guinean women and children are subjected to sex trafficking, domestic servitude, forced begging, and street vending; parents may sell girls into forced marriages to settle debts or as peace offerings or trade them to another tribe to forge a political alliance, leaving them vulnerable to forced domestic service, or, in urban areas, they may prostitute their children for income or to pay school fees; Chinese, Malaysian, and local men are forced to labor in logging and mining camps through debt bondage schemes; migrant women from Indonesia, Malaysia, Thailand, China, and the Philippines are subjected to sex trafficking and domestic servitude at logging and mining camps, fisheries, and entertainment sites

tier rating: Tier 2 Watch List - Papua New Guinea does not fully comply with the minimum standards for the elimination of trafficking; however, it is making significant efforts to do so; the Criminal Code Amendment of 2013, which prohibits all forms of trafficking was brought into force in 2014; the government also formed an anti-trafficking committee, which drafted a national action plan; despite corruption problems, trafficking-related crimes were prosecuted in village courts rather than criminal courts, resulting in restitution to the victim but no prison time for offenders; the government did not investigate, prosecute, or convict any officials or law enforcement personnel complicit in trafficking offenses; the government made no efforts to proactively identify trafficking victims, has no formal victim identification and referral mechanism, and does not provide care facilities to victims or funding to shelters run by NGOs or international organizations (2015)

Illicit drugs:

major consumer of cannabis

IMPORTANT INFORMATION FOR UNDERSTANDING THE COUNTRY

Official Name: Independent State of Papua New Guinea

PROFILE

Geography
Land area: 462,860 sq. km.; about the size of California.
Cities: *Capital*--Port Moresby (254,158). *Other cities*--Lae (78,038), Mt. Hagen (27,789).
Terrain: Mostly mountains with coastal lowlands and rolling foothills. The largest portion of the population lives in fertile highlands valleys that were unknown to the outside world until the 1930s, but that supported agriculture some 10,000 years ago, possibly before agriculture was developed elsewhere.
Climate: Tropical. NW monsoon, Dec.-Mar.; SE monsoon, May-Oct.

People
Population: 5.8 million.
Annual growth rate: 3.1%.
Languages: Three official: English, Tok Pisin, and Motu. There are approximately 860 other languages.
Education: *Years compulsory*--0. *Literacy*--57.3%
Health: *Infant mortality rate*--68.4/1,000. *Life expectancy*--56.0 yrs.

Government
Type: Constitutional monarchy with parliamentary democracy.
Constitution: September 16, 1975.
Branches: *Executive*--British monarch (chief of state), represented by governor general; prime minister (head of government). *Legislative*--unicameral parliament. *Judicial*--independent; highest is Supreme Court.
Administrative subdivisions: 19 provinces and the national capital district (Port Moresby).
Major political parties: National Alliance (NA), People's Progress Party (PPP), Pangu Pati, People's Democratic Movement (PDM), and Melanesian Alliance (MA).
Suffrage: Universal over 18 years of age.

Economy
Natural resources: Gold, copper ore, oil, natural gas, timber, fish.
Agriculture (38% of GDP): *Major products*--coffee, cocoa, coconuts, palm oil, timber, tea, vanilla.
Industry (25% of GDP): *Major sectors*--copra crushing; palm oil processing; plywood production; wood chip production; mining of gold, silver, and copper; construction; tourism; crude oil production.
Trade: *Exports*--66% of GDP: gold, copper ore, oil, timber, palm oil, coffee. *Major markets*--Australia, Japan, China, Germany, U.K., Indonesia. *Imports*--31% of GDP: machinery and transport equipment, manufactured goods, food, fuels, chemicals. *Major suppliers*--Australia, Singapore, New Zealand, China, Japan, Malaysia.

Papua New Guinea is a young, vibrant nation with a great deal to offer foreign investors. Some of the key reasons for taking a closer look at Papua New Guinea include:

Political stability: The country is politically stable with a well-entrenched democratic system of government and institutions;

Positive attitude to foreign investment: The Government of Papua New Guinea recognises the importance of the private sector to the country's development and guarantees the security of foreign investment;

Investment incentives: Generous incentives are available to approved ventures. Impediments to the development of new, worthwhile businesses are being removed;

Joint venture flexibility: The government does not dictate the level of foreign ownership in joint ventures. This is left to mutual agreement between the investor and the local counterpart;

Preferential market access for certain goods: Many products originating in Papua New Guinea are allowed duty-free or preferential entry into a number of important markets;

No language barriers: English is widely spoken and understood, despite the country boasting more than 800 other languages;

Boundless opportunities: The business environment is relatively uncrowded and there are many opportunities for profitable investments;

Resource-driven potential: The country is on the verge of substantial development as large-scale mining and petroleum projects create flow-on activities to many sectors of the economy;

Abundance of natural, renewable resources: The country has an abundance of forest and marine resources; and,

Agricultural opportunities: The climatic conditions of the country are highly-favourable for agricultural activities.

Papua New Guinea genuinely welcomes foreign investment that contributes to the economic development and prosperity of the country.

Investing in Papua New Guinea can be a profitable exercise, irrespective of the size of the project. Some of the world's leading corporate entities already know that Papua New Guinea can be a good place to do business.

PEOPLE

The indigenous population of Papua New Guinea is one of the most heterogeneous in the world. Papua New Guinea has several thousand separate communities, most with only a few hundred people. Divided by language, customs, and tradition, some of these communities have engaged in low-scale tribal conflict with their neighbors for millennia. The advent of modern weapons and modern migration into urban areas has greatly magnified the impact of this lawlessness.

The isolation created by the mountainous terrain is so great that some groups, until recently, were unaware of the existence of neighboring groups only a few kilometers away. The diversity, reflected in a folk saying, "For each village, a different culture," is perhaps best shown in the local languages. Spoken mainly on the island of New Guinea--composed of Papua New Guinea and the Indonesian province of West Papua--some 800 of these languages have been identified; of these, only 350-450 are related. The remainder seem to be totally unrelated either to each other or to the other major groupings. Most native languages are spoken by a few hundred to a few thousand, although Enga, used in part of the highlands, is spoken by some 130,000 people.

However, the Enga people are subdivided into clans that regularly conflict with each other. Many native languages are extremely complex grammatically.

Melanesian Pidgin serves as the lingua franca. English is spoken by educated people and in Milne Bay Province. The overall population density is low, although pockets of overpopulation exist. Papua New Guinea's Western Province averages one person per square kilometer (3 per sq. mi.). The Chimbu Province in the New Guinea highlands averages 20 persons per square kilometer (60 per sq. mi.) and has areas containing up to 200 people farming a square kilometer of land. The highlands are home to 40% of the population.

A considerable urban drift toward Port Moresby and other major centers has occurred in recent years. The trend toward urbanization accelerated in the 1990s, bringing in its wake squatter settlements, ethnic disputes, unemployment, and attendant social problems, especially violent crime.

Approximately 96% of the population is Christian. The churches with the largest number of members are the Roman Catholic Church, the Evangelical Lutheran Church, the United Church, and the Seventh Day Adventist church. Although the major churches are under indigenous leadership, a large number of missionaries remain in the country. The bulk of the estimated 2,000 Americans resident in Papua New Guinea are missionaries and their families. The non-Christian portion of the indigenous population, as well as a portion of the nominal Christians, practices a wide variety of religions that are an integral part of traditional culture, mainly animism (spirit worship) and ancestor cults.

Foreign residents comprise about 1% of the population. More than half are Australian; others are from the United Kingdom, New Zealand, the Philippines, and the United States, most of whom are missionaries. Since independence, about 900 foreigners have become naturalized citizens.

Though cultures vary widely, traditional Papua New Guinea social structures generally include the following characteristics:

- The practice of subsistence economy;
- Recognition of bonds of kinship with obligations extending beyond the immediate family group;
- Generally egalitarian relationships with an emphasis on acquired, rather than inherited, status; and
- A strong attachment of the people to land, which is held communally. Traditional communities do not recognize a permanent transfer of ownership when land is sold.
- Though land and other possessions may be inherited through the female line in some cultures, women generally are considered and treated as inferiors. Gender violence is endemic.
- Patterns and frequency of sexual activity, though never publicly discussed, contribute to the current rapid spread of HIV.

Most Papua New Guineans still adhere strongly to this traditional social structure, which has its roots in village life.

HISTORY

Archeological evidence indicates that humans arrived on New Guinea at least 60,000 years ago, probably by sea from Southeast Asia during an Ice Age period when the sea was lower and distances between islands shorter. Although the first arrivals were hunters and gatherers, early evidence shows that people managed the forest environment to provide food. There also are indications of gardening having been practiced at the same time that agriculture was developing in Mesopotamia and Egypt. Early garden crops--many of which are indigenous--included sugarcane, Pacific bananas, yams, and taros, while sago and pandanus were two commonly exploited native forest crops. Today's staples--sweet potatoes and pigs--were later arrivals, but shellfish and fish have long been mainstays of coastal dwellers' diets.

When Europeans first arrived, inhabitants of New Guinea and nearby islands--while still relying on bone, wood, and stone tools--had a productive agricultural system. They traded along the coast, where products mainly were pottery, shell ornaments, and foodstuffs, and in the interior, where forest products were exchanged for shells and other sea products.

The first Europeans to sight New Guinea were probably the Portuguese and Spanish navigators sailing in the South Pacific in the early part of the 16th century. In 1526-27, Don Jorge de Meneses accidentally came upon the principal island and is credited with naming it "Papua," a Malay word for the frizzled quality of Melanesian hair. The term "New Guinea" was applied to the island in 1545 by a Spaniard, Íñigo Ortiz de Retes, because of a fancied resemblance between the islands' inhabitants and those found on the African Guinea coast. Although European navigators visited the islands and explored their coastlines for the next 170 years, little was known of the inhabitants until the late 19th century.

New Guinea

With Europe's growing need for coconut oil, Godeffroy's of Hamburg, the largest trading firm in the Pacific, began trading for copra in the New Guinea Islands. In 1884, Germany formally took possession of the northeast quarter of the island and put its administration in the hands of a chartered company. In 1899, the German imperial government assumed direct control of the territory, thereafter known as German New Guinea. In 1914, Australian troops occupied German New Guinea, and it remained under Australian military control until 1921. The British Government, on behalf of the Commonwealth of Australia, assumed a mandate from the League of Nations for governing the Territory of New Guinea in 1920. That mandate was administered by the Australian Government until the Japanese invasion in December 1941 brought about its suspension. Following the surrender of the Japanese in 1945, civil administration of Papua as well as New Guinea was restored, and under the Papua New Guinea Provisional Administration Act, 1945-46, Papua and New Guinea were combined in an administrative union.

Papua

On November 6, 1884, a British protectorate was proclaimed over the southern coast of New Guinea (the area called Papua) and its adjacent islands. The protectorate, called British New Guinea, was annexed outright on September 4, 1888. The possession was placed under the authority of the Commonwealth of Australia in 1902. Following the passage of the Papua Act of 1905, British New Guinea became the Territory of Papua, and formal Australian administration began in 1906. Papua was administered under the Papua Act until the Japanese invaded the northern parts of the islands in 1941 and began to advance on Port Moresby and civil administration was suspended. During the war, Papua was governed by a military administration from Port Moresby, where Gen. Douglas MacArthur occasionally made his headquarters. As noted, it was later joined in an administrative union with New Guinea during 1945-46 following the surrender of Japan.

Postwar Developments

The Papua and New Guinea Act of 1949 formally approved the placing of New Guinea under the international trusteeship system and confirmed the administrative union of New Guinea and Papua under the title of "The Territory of Papua and New Guinea." The act provided for a Legislative Council (established in 1951), a judicial organization, a public service, and a system of local government. A House of Assembly replaced the Legislative Council in 1963, and the first House of Assembly opened on June 8, 1964. In 1972, the name of the territory was changed to Papua New Guinea.

Elections in 1972 resulted in the formation of a ministry headed by Chief Minister Michael Somare, who pledged to lead the country to self-government and then to independence. Papua New Guinea became self-governing in December 1973 and achieved independence on September 16, 1975. The 1977 national elections confirmed Michael Somare as Prime Minister at the head of a coalition led by the Pangu Party. However, his government lost a vote of confidence in 1980 and was replaced by a new cabinet headed by Sir Julius Chan as Prime Minister. The 1982 elections increased Pangu's plurality, and parliament again chose Somare as Prime Minister. In November 1985, the Somare government lost a vote of no confidence, and the parliamentary majority elected Paias Wingti, at the head of a five-party coalition, as Prime Minister. A coalition, headed by Wingti, was victorious in very close elections in July 1987. In July 1988, a no-confidence vote toppled Wingti and brought to power Rabbie Namaliu, who a few weeks earlier had replaced Somare as leader of the Pangu Party.

Such reversals of fortune and a revolving-door succession of prime ministers have characterized Papua New Guinea's national politics. From 1988 to 2002, the country had numerous prime ministers. A plethora of political parties, coalition governments, shifting party loyalties, and motions of no confidence in the leadership all lent an air of instability to political proceedings. For the first 27 years of independence, a "first past the post" electoral system resulted in many parliamentarians elected with less than 15% of their constituency. Fractious politics and a 75% loss rate for incumbents precluded the development of strong political parties or a stable national leadership. Many hope that limited preferential voting, introduced in 2003, and an organic law on political parties will stabilize national politics.

In the 2002 elections, virtually the entire previous cabinet lost their seats. The government was formed by a coalition of several parties, and Sir Michael Somare, the leader of the National Alliance (and the nation's first Prime Minister in 1975), was elected Prime Minister. The 2007 elections returned Somare as Prime Minister. His government was the first to complete a 5-year term since independence.

GOVERNMENT AND POLITICAL CONDITIONS

Papua New Guinea, a constitutional monarchy, recognizes the Queen of England as head of state. She is represented by a Governor General who is elected by parliament and who performs mainly ceremonial functions. Papua New Guinea has three levels of government--national, provincial, and local. There is a 109-member unicameral parliament, whose members are elected every 5 years. The parliament in turn elects the prime minister, who appoints his cabinet from members of his party or coalition.

Members of parliament are elected from 19 provinces and the national capital district of Port Moresby. Parliament introduced reforms in June 1995 to change the provincial government system, with regional (at-large) members of parliament becoming provincial governors, while retaining their national seats in parliament.

Papua New Guinea's judiciary is independent of the government. It protects constitutional rights and interprets the laws. There are several levels, culminating in the Supreme Court.
Papua New Guinea's politics are highly competitive with most members elected on a personal and ethnic basis within their constituencies rather than as a result of party affiliation. Members of parliament are now elected in a limited preferential voting (LPV) system. There are several parties, but party allegiances are not strong. Winning candidates are usually courted in efforts to forge the majority needed to form a government, and allegiances are fluid. No single party has yet won enough seats to form a government in its own right.

Papua New Guinea has a history of changes in government coalitions and leadership from within parliament during the 5-year intervals between national elections. New governments are protected by law from votes of no confidence for the first 18 months of their incumbency, and no votes of no confidence may be moved in the 12 months preceding a national election. In an effort to create greater stability by reducing incessant votes of no confidence, the Integrity of Political Parties Act was passed in 1999, forbidding members of each party in parliament from shifting loyalty to another party.

In 2003, the electoral system was changed to limited preferential voting, which many hope will encourage politicians to strike alliances and to be responsive to constituent concerns once elected. The new system was first used in a 2004 by-election with modest, but positive results. On Bougainville Island, a 10-year rebellion was halted by a truce in 1997 and a permanent cease-fire was signed in April 1998. A peace agreement between the Government and ex-combatants was signed in August 2001. Under the eyes of a regional peace-monitoring force and a UN observer mission, the government and provincial leaders established an interim administration and made significant progress toward complete surrender/destruction of weapons. A constitution was drafted in 2004 and provincial government elections were held in May 2005. The elections were deemed to be free and fair by international observers, and Joseph Kabui was elected to serve as the first president of the Autonomous Bougainville Government.

GOVERNMENT OFFICIALS

The **Cabinet of Papua New Guinea** functions as the policy and decision-making body of the executive branch within the government system of Papua New Guinea. The Prime Minister and Ministers serve as members of the Cabinet.

With Prime Minister Sir Michael Somare having been hospitalised for a serious heart condition, leadership of the nation was vested in Deputy Prime Minister Sam Abal in April 2011. In August, following a Cabinet reshuffle which had led three ministers to join the Opposition, the latter brought a successful motion of no confidence in Abal's government. Parliament chose Peter O'Neill to serve as Prime Minister.

On 27 February 2012, O'Neill removed the Finance portfolio from Don Polye, taking it on himself. He cited "the continuing lack of ability by the department and ministry of finance to contain expenditure overruns outside of the budget appropriations". Polye retained the Treasury portfolio, and gained that of Border Development. O'Neill hinted that the Finance ministry would eventually be returned to him, and also hinted at an imminent major Cabinet reshuffle.

On 9 August 2012, following a general election, O'Neill announced the following cabinet for the 2012-2017 term:

Portfolio	Minister	Minister's province	Minister's party	Parliamentary secretary	Opposition shadow minister
Prime Minister	Peter O'Neill	Southern Highlands Province	People's National Congress Party		
• Deputy Prime Minister • Minister for Inter-	Leo Dion	East New Britain Province	Triumph Heritage Empowerment Party		

Portfolio	Minister	Minister's province	Minister's party	Parliamentary secretary	Opposition shadow minister
Government Relations					
Minister for Agriculture & Livestock	Tommy Tomscoll	Madang Province	People's Democratic Movement Party		
Minister for Bougainville Affairs	Steven Kamma	Autonomous Region of Bougainville	United Resources Party		
Minister for Civil Aviation	Davis Steven	Milne Bay Province	People's Party		
Minister for Communication & Information Technology	Jimmy Miringtoro	Autonomous Region of Bougainville	People's National Congress Party		
Minister for Community Development, Religion & Youth	Loujaya Toni	Morobe Province	Indigenous People's Party		
Minister for Correctional Services	Jim Simatab	East Sepik Province	National Alliance Party		
Minister for Defence	Fabian Pok	Jiwaka Province	United Resources Party		
Minister for Education	Paru Aihi	Central Province	People's National Congress Party		
Minister for Environment & Conservation	John Pundari	Enga Province	People's Party		
Minister for Finance	James Marape	Hela Province	People's National Congress Party		
Minister for Fisheries & Marine Resources	Mao Zeming	Morobe Province	People's National Congress Party		
Minister for Foreign Affairs & Immigration	Rimbink Pato	Enga Province	United Party		
Minister for Forests & Climate Change	Patrick Pruaitch	West Sepik Province	National Alliance Party		
Minister for Health & HIV/AIDS	Michael Malabag	National Capital District	People's National Congress Party		
Minister for Higher Education, Research, Science, & Technology	[Francis Marus]]				

Portfolio	Minister	Minister's province	Minister's party	Parliamentary secretary	Opposition shadow minister
Minister for Housing & Urban Development	Paul Isikiel	Morobe Province	People's National Congress Party		
Minister for Justice & Attorney-General	Kerenga Kua	Chimbu Province	National Alliance Party		
Minister for Labour & Industrial Relations	Mark Maipakai	Gulf Province	Triumph Heritage Empowerment Party		
Minister for Lands & Physical Planning	Benny Allan	Eastern Highlands Province	People's National Congress Party		
Minister for Mining	Byron Chan	New Ireland Province	People's Progress Party		
Minister for National Planning	Charles Abel	Milne Bay Province	People's National Congress Party		
Minister for Petroleum & Energy	William Duma	Western Highlands Province	United Resources Party		
Minister for Police	Nixon Duban	Madang Province	People's National Congress Party		
Minister for Public Enterprises & State Investment	Ben Micah	New Ireland Province	People's Progress Party		
Minister for Public Service	Sir Puka Temu	Central Province	Our Development Party		
Minister for Sports & Pacific Games	Justin Tkatchenko	National Capital District	Social Democratic Party		
Minister for Tourism, Art & Culture	Boka Kondra	Western Province	People's National Congress Party		
Minister for Trade, Commerce & Industry	Richard Maru	East Sepik Province	Independent		
Minister for Transport & Works	Ano Pala	Central Province	People's National Congress Party		
Minister for Treasury	Don Polye	Enga Province	Triumph Heritage Empowerment Party		
Minister for Works & Implementation	Francis Awesa	Southern Highlands Province	People's National Congress Party		

In February 2014, the following reshuffle took place. Police Minister Nixon Duban (MP for Madang, National Congress Party) was reshuffled to the position of Minister of Petroleum and Energy, replacing William Duma (MP for Mount Hagen, United Resources Party), who was dropped from the Cabinet; O'Neill suggested that Duma had not adhered to the principle of Cabinet solidarity. Robert Atiyafa (MP for Henganofi) was appointed as Minister for Police. David Arore (MP for the Northern Province, T.H.E. Party) was replaced as Minister for Higher Education by Delilah Gore (MP for Sohe, T.H.E. Party), while Nick Kuman (MP for Gumine) was appointed Minister for Education. It was the first time ever that the country's Cabinet included two women: Delilah Gore, and Community Development Minister Loujaya Kouza (MP for Lae)

Papua New Guinea maintains an embassy at 1779 Massachusetts Ave. NW, Washington, DC 20036 (tel. 202-745-3680; fax 202-745-3679). The Papua New Guinea mission to the United Nations is at 801 Second Avenue, New York, NY 10017 (tel. 212-682-6447).

ECONOMY

Currency	kina (PGK)
Fiscal year	calendar year
Trade organisations	WTO, APEC
	Statistics
GDP	$16.93 billion (2014 World Bank est.)
GDP rank	115th (nominal) / 130th (PPP)
GDP growth	8.5% (2014 World Bank est.)
GDP per capita	$2,800 (2015 CIA World Factbook est.)
GDP by sector	Agriculture: 29.9%, industry: 37.6%, services: 32.4% (2011 est.)
Inflation (CPI)	5.2% (2014 World Bank est.)
Population below poverty line	39.9% (2009 World Bank est.)
Labour force	3.896 million (2011 est.)
Labour force by occupation	agriculture: 85%, industry: NA%, services: NA% (2005 est.)
Unemployment	1.9% (2008)
Main industries	copra crushing, palm oil processing, plywood production, wood chip production; mining (gold, silver, and copper); crude oil production, petroleum refining; construction, tourism
Ease-of-doing-business rank	119th (2017)
	External
Exports	$6.748 billion (est.)
Export goods	oil, gold, copper ore, logs, palm oil, coffee, cocoa, crayfish, prawns
Main export partners	Australia 29.0% Japan 9.6% China 4.8% (est.)
Imports	$6.106 billion (est.)
Import goods	Machinery and transport equipment, manufactured goods, food, fuels, chemicals
Main import partners	Australia 36.3% Singapore 13.8% Malaysia 8.4% China 7.9% Japan 5.8% United States 4.8%

	Public finances
Public debt	$5.296 billion
Revenues	$4.168 billion
Expenses	$4.194 billion
Economic aid	no data
Credit rating	Standard & Poor's: BB- (Domestic) B+ (Foreign) BB (T&C Assessment) Outlook: Stable Moody's: B2 Outlook: Stable

Papua New Guinea's economy is dominated by two sectors: the agricultural, forestry, and fishing sector, where most of the labour force of the country is engaged, and the minerals and energy extraction sector from which most of the export earnings are made. PNG's GDP growth is driven by the extraction industries and real GDP growth per capita has averaged 4% since mid-2000. The country has made significant progress investing proceeds from oil and gas in infrastructure building. As a result, its major cities like Port Moresby and Lae have received increased international investor attention, giving rise to unprecedented building boom to exploit the opportunities presented by the country's rise as a regional economic leader in the South Pacific region. This is well supported by its strategic location as a Pacific's gateway to Asia as well as its comparatively huge landmass and demographic profile (almost 7 times that the rest of smaller Pacific Island nations). International Monetary Fund. Despite this poverty it is richly endowed with natural resources, but exploitation has been hampered by the rugged terrain and the high cost of developing infrastructure.

Agriculture provides a subsistence livelihood for the bulk of the population. Mineral deposits, including oil, copper, and gold, account for 72% of export earnings. Budgetary support from Australia and development aid under World Bank auspices have helped sustain the economy. In 1995, Port Moresby reached an agreement with the International Monetary Fund (IMF) and World Bank on a structural adjustment program, of which the first phase was successfully completed in 1996. In 1997, droughts caused by the El Niño weather pattern wreaked havoc on Papua New Guinea's coffee, cocoa, and coconut production, the mainstays of the agricultural-based economy and major sources of export earnings. The coffee crop was slashed by up to 50% in 1997. Despite problems with drought, the year 1998 saw a small recovery in GDP. Growth increased to 3.6% in 1999 and may be even higher in 2000, say 4.3%.

MINERAL RESOURCES

Papua New Guinea is richly endowed with gold, copper, oil, natural gas, and other minerals. In 2005 mineral export receipts accounted for 49.7% of GDP. Government revenues and foreign exchange earnings depend heavily on mineral exports. Indigenous landowners in areas affected by minerals projects also receive royalties from those operations. Copper and gold mines are currently in production at Porgera, Ok Tedi, Misima, and Lihir. A consortium led by Exxon/Mobil hopes to begin the commercialization of the country's estimated 22.5 trillion cubic feet of natural gas reserves through the construction of a liquefied natural gas (LNG) production facility. Interoil, an American-owned firm, opened Papua New Guinea's first oil refinery in 2004. It has the capacity to produce 30,000 barrels of product a day.

Agriculture, Timber, and Fish

Papua New Guinea also produces and exports valuable agricultural, timber, and marine products.

Agriculture currently accounts for 30.4% of GDP and supports more than 85% of the population. Cash crops ranked by value are coffee, oil, cocoa, copra, tea, rubber, and sugar. About 40% of the country is covered with exploitable trees, but a domestic woodworking industry has been slow to develop. A number of Southeast Asian companies are active in the timber industry, but World Bank and other donors have withdrawn support from the sector over concern for unregulated deforestation and environmental damage. Recently enacted forestry legislation has exacerbated those concerns. Papua New Guinea has an active tuna industry, but much of the catch is made by boats of other nations fishing in Papua New Guinea waters under license. Papua New Guinea is a signatory to the South Pacific Tuna Treaty (SPTT), under which U.S. purse seiners fish for tuna in the exclusive economic zones (EEZs) of the Pacific Island parties. Locally produced fish exports are confined primarily to shrimp.

Industry
In general, the Papua New Guinea economy is highly dependent on imports for manufactured goods. Its industrial sector--exclusive of mining--accounts for only 9% of GDP and contributes little to exports. Small-scale industries produce beer, soap, concrete products, clothing, paper products, matches, ice cream, canned meat, fruit juices, furniture, plywood, and paint. The small domestic market, relatively high wages, and high transport costs are constraints to industrial development.

Trade and Investment
Australia, Singapore, and Japan are the principal exporters to Papua New Guinea. Petroleum and mining machinery and aircraft have been the strongest U.S. exports to Papua New Guinea. Australia is Papua New Guinea's most important export market, followed by Japan and the European Union. The U.S. imports modest amounts of gold, copper ore, cocoa, coffee, and other agricultural products from Papua New Guinea. Most of those exports take place through third countries.

With the 2003 withdrawal of Chevron/Texaco, Australian companies are the most active in developing Papua New Guinea's mining and petroleum sectors. Exxon/Mobil retains a major share of natural gas reserves and is currently exploring the feasibility of building a liquefied natural gas processing facility. Interoil, an American-owned firm backed by an Overseas Private Investment Corporation (OPIC) loan, operates an oil refinery in Port Moresby. China is increasing its investment in Papua New Guinea, including development of the $1 billion Ramu nickel mine. Papua New Guinea became a participating economy in the Asia-Pacific Economic Cooperation (APEC) Forum in 1993. It joined the World Trade Organization (WTO) in 1996. It is an observer at ASEAN and a member of the ASEAN Regional Forum.

Development Programs and Aid
Australia is by far the largest bilateral aid donor to Papua New Guinea, offering about $300 million a year in assistance. Budgetary support, which has been provided in decreasing amounts since independence, was phased out in 2000, with aid concentrated on project development. In 2004, Australia and Papua New Guinea embarked on the Enhanced Cooperation Program (ECP), under which Australia agreed to provide direct assistance, including 210 line police officers, to the Papua New Guinea constabulary. The ECP met with initial success, but was abruptly ended when Papua New Guinea's Supreme Court stripped Australian police officers of immunity in May 2005. Virtually all ECP personnel left Papua New Guinea following the court's decision. The governments of Papua New Guinea and Australia are now involved in protracted negotiations on a scaled-down version of the ECP.
Other major sources of aid to Papua New Guinea are Japan, the European Union, the People's Republic of China, Taiwan, the United Nations, the Asian Development Bank, the International Monetary Fund, and the World Bank. Volunteers from a number of countries and mission church workers also provide education, health, and development assistance throughout the country.

Foreign assistance to Papua New Guinea is approximately $46 per capita. The U.S. funds a $1.5 million-per-year HIV/AIDS project in Papua New Guinea.

Current Economic Conditions
After years of decline and government deficit, Papua New Guinea was bolstered in recent years by a general rise in commodity prices and by government steps toward spending control. The economy continues to grow modestly and the government recorded a modest surplus in 2006. However, the economic improvements are based almost entirely on high commodity prices and the nation continues to have serious problems of corruption, a lack of law and order, land tenure concerns stifling investment, political interference in business, and a lack of political will to adopt needed sweeping reforms.

FOREIGN RELATIONS

Papua New Guinea's foreign policy reflects close ties with Australia and other traditional allies. Papua New Guinea is by far the largest Pacific Island nation and has traditionally viewed itself as part of the Pacific. However, in recent years it has also been cultivating relations with Asian nations. Its views on international political and economic issues are generally moderate. Papua New Guinea has diplomatic relations with 56 countries.

U.S.-PAPUA NEW GUINEA RELATIONS

The United States and Papua New Guinea established diplomatic relations upon the latter's independence on September 16, 1975. The two nations belong to a variety of regional organizations, including the Asia-Pacific Economic Cooperation (APEC) forum; the ASEAN Regional Forum (ARF); the Secretariat of the Pacific Community (SPC); and the South Pacific Regional Environmental Program (SPREP).

The United States established diplomatic relations with Papua New Guinea in 1975, following its independence from a United Nations trusteeship administered by Australia. As the most populous Pacific Island state (7.8 million: 2013 estimate), Papua New Guinea is important to peace and security in the Asia-Pacific region. The country has experienced recent economic progress and has abundant energy, agricultural, and mineral resources. But it faces challenges including weak governance, corruption, limited capacity to deliver basic services, a deterioration of its health system, and a serious concentrated HIV/AIDS epidemic among key populations and in the Highland provinces.

The United States and Papua New Guinea have enjoyed a close friendship, and the U.S. Government seeks to enhance Papua New Guinea's stability as a U.S. partner. The two countries work together on many issues from improving transparency and good governance, to combating trafficking in persons, curbing the effects of climate change, protecting fisheries, improving public health, and promoting gender equality. Their militaries have had a cooperative security assistance relationship that has focused primarily on joint humanitarian exercises and the training of Papua New Guinean military personnel.

U.S. ASSISTANCE TO PAPUA NEW GUINEA

U.S. bilateral and multilateral assistance funds public health programs in Papua New Guinea including the President's Emergency Plan For AIDS Relief (PEPFAR), TB, and Malaria and Neglected Tropical Diseases and aims to advance the country's public health system. The U.S. Agency for International Development's Pacific Islands Regional Office and the U.S. Centers for Disease Control and Prevention Country Office are both located in Papua New Guinea. The United States builds the capacity and resilience of Papua New Guinea to adapt to climate change through regional assistance that covers 12 Pacific Island countries. United States assistance supports Papua New Guinea's efforts to protect biodiversity; it contributes to the Coral Triangle Initiative to preserve coral reefs, fisheries, and food security in six countries including Papua New Guinea. The United States also supports efforts to improve the country's disaster preparedness and response. In 2015 and 2016 the United States provided funding for relief efforts in a number of Papua New Guinea's provinces that had suffered from natural disasters caused by continuous heavy rain. U.S. military forces, through Pacific Command in Honolulu, Hawaii, provide training to the Papua New Guinea Defense Force and have held small-scale joint training and engineering exercises. The United States provides police and other education and training courses to national security officials. U.S. companies based in Papua New Guinea have also funded a range of health and development projects.

BILATERAL ECONOMIC RELATIONS

Petroleum and mining machinery and aircraft have been the strongest U.S. exports to Papua New Guinea. The United States imports modest amounts of gold, copper ore, cocoa, coffee, and other agricultural products from Papua New Guinea. The ExxonMobil-led liquefied natural gas project has been a success for Papua New Guinea, hailed for its timely and close-to-budget construction and smooth operation. Papua New Guinea is a party to the U.S.-Pacific Islands Multilateral Tuna Fisheries Treaty, which provides access for U.S. fishing vessels in exchange for a license fee from the U.S. industry. Under a separate Economic Assistance Agreement (EAA) associated with the Treaty, the United States Government currently provides $21 million per year to Pacific Island parties. According to U.S. Census Bureau data, in 2016 the United States exported $126.8 million worth of goods to Papua New Guinea and imported $91.8 million worth.

PAPUA NEW GUINEA'S MEMBERSHIP IN INTERNATIONAL ORGANIZATIONS

Papua New Guinea and the United States belong to a number of the same international organizations, including the United Nations, International Monetary Fund, World Bank, World Trade Organization, Asia-Pacific Economic Cooperation (APEC) forum, ASEAN Regional Forum, the Pacific Community, and Secretariat of the Pacific Regional Environment Programme. Papua New Guinea also belongs to the Pacific Islands Forum, of which the United States is a Dialogue Partner. Papua New Guinea will host APEC in 2018, culminating in a leaders' summit in November 2018.

BILATERAL REPRESENTATION

Papua New Guinea maintains an **embassy** in the United States at 1779 Massachusetts Ave. NW., Washington, DC 20036 (tel. 202-745-3680).

One of the most successful cooperative multilateral efforts linking the U.S. and Papua New Guinea is the U.S.-Pacific Islands Multilateral Tuna Fisheries Treaty, under which the U.S. grants $18 million per year to Pacific Island parties and the latter provide access for U.S. fishing vessels. The United States has provided significant humanitarian assistance to Papua New Guinea and contributed to the rehabilitation of Bougainville. USAID funds a $1.5 million-per-year HIV/AIDS project in Papua New Guinea.

The U.S. also supports Papua New Guinea's efforts to protect biodiversity. The U.S. Government supports the International Coral Reef Initiative aimed at protecting reefs in tropical nations such as Papua New Guinea. U.S. military forces, through Pacific Command (PACOM) in Honolulu, Hawaii, provide training to the Papua New Guinea Defense Force (PNGDF) and have held small-scale joint training exercises. The U.S. provides police and other education and training courses to national security officials. The U.S. also annually sponsors a handful of PNG officials and private citizens to meet and confer with their professional counterparts and to experience the U.S. first-hand through the International Visitor Leadership Program (IVLP).

The U.S. Peace Corps ceased operations in Papua New Guinea in 2001 due to security concerns. About 2,000 U.S. citizens live in Papua New Guinea, with major concentrations at the headquarters of New Tribes Mission and the Summer Institute of Linguistics, both located in the Eastern Highlands Province.

Principal U.S. Embassy Officials
Ambassador (vacant); Charge D'Affaires Elias Rahuromo WOHENGU (since 30 September 2017)Deputy Chief of Mission--Thomas Weinz
Consular Officer--Leslie Livingood

The U.S. Embassy in Papua New Guinea is located on Douglas Street, Port Moresby (tel. 675-321-1455; fax 675-321-3423). The mailing address is 4240 Port Moresby Pl., U.S. Department of State, Washington, DC 20521-4240.

TRAVEL AND BUSINESS INFORMATION

The U.S. Department of State's Consular Information Program advises Americans traveling and residing abroad through Country Specific Information, Travel Alerts, and Travel Warnings. **Country Specific Information** exists for all countries and includes information on entry and exit requirements, currency regulations, health conditions, safety and security, crime, political disturbances, and the addresses of the U.S. embassies and consulates abroad. **Travel Alerts** are issued to disseminate information quickly about terrorist threats and other relatively short-term conditions overseas that pose significant risks to the security of American travelers. **Travel Warnings** are issued when the State Department recommends that Americans avoid travel to a certain country because the situation is dangerous or unstable.

For the latest security information, Americans living and traveling abroad should regularly monitor the Department's Bureau of Consular Affairs Internet web site at http://www.travel.state.gov, where the current Worldwide Caution, Travel Alerts, and Travel Warnings can be found. Consular Affairs Publications, which contain information on obtaining passports and planning a safe trip abroad, are also available at http://www.travel.state.gov. For additional information on international travel, see http://www.usa.gov/Citizen/Topics/Travel/International.shtml.
The Department of State encourages all U.S citizens traveling or residing abroad to register via the State Department's travel registration website or at the nearest U.S. embassy or consulate abroad. Registration will make your presence and whereabouts known in case it is necessary to contact you in an emergency and will enable you to receive up-to-date information on security conditions.

Emergency information concerning Americans traveling abroad may be obtained by calling 1-888-407-4747 toll free in the U.S. and Canada or the regular toll line 1-202-501-4444 for callers outside the U.S. and Canada.

The National Passport Information Center (NPIC) is the U.S. Department of State's single, centralized public contact center for U.S. passport information. Telephone: 1-877-4USA-PPT (1-877-487-2778). Customer service representatives and operators for TDD/TTY are available Monday-Friday, 7:00 a.m. to 12:00 midnight, Eastern Time, excluding federal holidays.
Travelers can check the latest health information with the U.S. Centers for Disease Control and Prevention in Atlanta, Georgia. A hotline at 877-FYI-TRIP (877-394-8747) and a web site at http://wwwn.cdc.gov/travel/default.aspx give the most recent health advisories, immunization recommendations or requirements, and advice on food and drinking water safety for regions and countries. A booklet entitled "Health Information for International Travel" (HHS publication number

CDC-95-8280) is available from the U.S. Government Printing Office, Washington, DC 20402, tel. (202) 512-1800.

PRINCIPAL U.S. EMBASSY OFFICIALS

U.S. Ambassador to Papua New Guinea, Solomon Islands and Vanuatu, Catherine Ebert-Gray

Ambassador Catherine Ebert-Gray is a Minister-Counselor in the Senior Foreign Service. She was sworn in as the U.S. Ambassador to Papua New Guinea, Solomon Islands and Vanuatu on January 22, 2016.
Between 2011 and 2015 she served as the Deputy Assistant Secretary for Logistics Management and Co-Chair of the Defense – State Executive Steering Group supporting the transitions in Iraq and Afghanistan. Her global division annually managed $7 billion in State Department acquisition in addition to oversight of the Department's global supply chain.

Deputy Chief of Mission--Thomas Weinz
Consular Officer--Leslie Livingood

The U.S. Embassy in Papua New Guinea is located on Douglas Street, Port Moresby (tel. 675-321-1455; fax 675-321-3423). The mailing address is 4240 Port Moresby Pl., U.S. Department of State, Washington, DC 20521-4240.

PRACTICAL AND LEGAL INFORMATION FOR CONDUCTING BUSINESS[1]

LEGAL SYSTEM

The legal system in Papua New Guinea is based largely on the Australian system which, in turn, has its roots in the English system. Court hearings are held in English and the law is applied fairly. The final court of appeal is the Supreme Court of Papua New Guinea. There are, however, areas where the traditional or "customary" law applies. Under the Constitution, courts are required to have regard to both the common law and the customary law. This "underlying" law is determined by the courts and can be particularly important when dealing with cases about land tenure and the use of natural resources.

Legal System and Judicial Independence

The legal system is based on English common law. Contract law in Papua New Guinea is very similar to and applies in much the same way as in other common law countries such as Great Britain, Australia, Canada, and New Zealand. There is, however, considerably less statutory regulation of the application and operation of contracts in Papua New Guinea than in those other countries.

The Supreme Court is the nation's highest judicial authority and final court of appeal. Other courts are the National Court; district courts, which deal with summary and non-indictable offenses; and local courts, established to deal with minor offenses, including matters regulated by local customs.

In addition to the courts mentioned above, there is also a system of Village Courts established under the Constitution and the Village Courts Act. Matters involving customary law claims are likely to arise at the Village Court level. There is no jury system in Papua New Guinea. Lawyers operating in Papua New Guinea are governed by the Papua New Guinea Law Society, and only lawyers registered with the Society should be used.

While often painstakingly slow, the judiciary system is widely viewed as independent from government interference. The Supreme Court is the ultimate appeal court in Papua New Guinea. It has original jurisdiction in matters of constitutional interpretation and enforcement and has appellate jurisdiction in appeals from the National Court, certain decisions of the Land Titles Commission, and those of other regulatory entities as prescribed in their own Acts. The National Court also has original jurisdiction for certain constitutional matters and has unlimited original jurisdiction for criminal and civil matters. The National Court has jurisdiction under the Land Act in proceedings involving land in Papua New Guinea other than customary land.

[1] This section based in part on the materials of the US Department of Commerce

INVESTMENT AND BUSINESS CLIMATE - STRATEGIC INFORMATION AND CONTACTS FOR STARTING BUSINESS

Papua New Guinea (PNG) remains open to foreign direct investment (FDI) and stepped up initiatives to increase business and investment opportunities, to counter declining economic, social, and private sector development over the years. PNG is focused on bolstering small and medium enterprises (SMEs) to make economic growth as inclusive as possible. In the past, even when PNG's economy grew above 12 per cent, that growth did not translate into increased incomes for most Papua New Guineans.

As an economy heavily reliant on commodity exports, PNG has been hit hard by the falling global commodity prices. Its export volumes in the agricultural commodity sectors have also seen a steady decline due to a lack of capital investment and research. These export difficulties have combined to drive a significant shortage of foreign currency flowing into the PNG economy.

Outside of extractive industries, most private sector investment has been in the wholesale and retail sector.

The public service, while critical to PNG's future, is ineffective and lacks capacity to deliver on its mandated roles and responsibilities. The full and effective implementation of policies and the enforcement of laws and regulations remain the biggest challenges for the public service. Proper intragovernmental coordination in the public service suffers from a lack of institutional governance and compliance.

These challenging trends in the country also present enormous opportunities for public private partnerships. The government is keen to use public private partnerships to fill capacity shortfalls in the country's priority growth areas: agriculture, manufacturing, mining and petroleum industries, energy, health, and wholesale and retail.

Table 1

Measure	Year	Index/Rank	Website Address
TI Corruption Perceptions Index	2017	135 of 175	http://www.transparency.org/research/cpi/overview
World Bank's Doing Business Report "Ease of Doing Business"	2017	109 of 190	http://www.doingbusiness.org/rankings
Global Innovation Index	2017	N/A of 128	https://www.globalinnovationindex.org/analysis indicator
U.S. FDI in Partner Country (M USD, stock positions)	2016	USD 239	http://www.bea.gov/international/factsheet/
World Bank GNI per capita	2016	USD 2,680	http://data.worldbank.org/indicator/NY.GNP.PCAP.CD

1. OPENNESS TO, AND RESTRICTIONS UPON, FOREIGN INVESTMENT

Policies Toward Foreign Direct Investment

The PNG Government frequently and publicly commits to fostering an environment for businesses to grow and to attracting foreign direct investment.

PNG aims to increase FDI in mining and petroleum/gas sector from USD 40 million in 2016 to USD 100 million by 2022. FDI stock reached USD 4.2 billion in 2016. The mining, oil, and gas sectors attract the vast majority of PNG's FDI. The government has set an FDI stock target of USD 10 billion by 2022. A new government focus for FDI has been in the renewable sector.

This goal was reiterated in PNG's first-ever national trade policy, *PNG National Trade Policy for 2017-2032*, which was launched in August 2017. The policy set a goal to maximize trade and investment by increasing exports, reducing imports of goods that could be produced in PNG, and increasing Foreign Direct Investment (FDI).

The trade policy also sets very ambitious economic targets, including the creation of more than 100,000 new jobs, USD 10 billion in new foreign investment, increased foreign exchange reserves, reduced government debt to GDP ratio, and a more diversified economy in the next five years.

The success of this plan will be mostly determined by the dedication of the PNG Government to carrying it out, something that many prior policies and strategies have suffered from

There are no laws or practices that discriminate against foreign investors by prohibiting, limiting or conditioning foreign investment in a sector of the economy.

Papua New Guinea has the Investment Promotion Authority (IPA), which was established by an Act of Parliament in 1992. Its primary mandate is to promote and facilitate investment in Papua New Guinea and also to regulate the business industry in the country. The services provided by IPA include: business registration, regulation and certification (under the Business Registration and Certification or Office of the Registrar of Companies), investor servicing and export promotion (under the Investor Services and Promotion Division), protection of intellectual property rights (under the Intellectual Property Office of PNG), and regulation of capital markets (under the Securities Commission of PNG).

PNG regularly engages with investors through multiple high-level summits and conferences. Extractive industries dominate PNG's formal economy, so most engagement is directed towards them. In the last year, the government, through the state-owned enterprise, Kumul Petroleum Holdings Limited (KPHL), helped host two forums: the annual PNG Mining and Petroleum Investment Conference, the inaugural PNG Petroleum and Energy Summit.

Limits on Foreign Control and Right to Private Ownership and Establishment

Foreign investment in Papua New Guinea is facilitated, regulated and monitored by the Investment Promotion Act.

Section 37 of the Act guarantees that the property of a foreign investor shall not be nationalized or expropriated except in accordance with law, for a public purpose defined by law and in payment of compensation as defined by law.

Foreigners are not allowed to own land in PNG. Most foreign businesses use long-term leases for land instead of direct purchases. There are no other specific requirements. PNG recently changed its citizenship laws to allow dual citizenship which had previously been a limiting factor for Papua New Guineans returning from overseas having naturalized elsewhere. Additionally, it allows long-term residents to naturalize as PNG citizens with full legal rights and responsibilities.

There are no specific sectors with restrictions, limitations, or requirements applied to foreign ownership and control.

The GOPNG screens foreign direct investment. When reviewing an FDI proposal, the Investment Promotion Authority (IPA) may consider a number of factors, including the:

- Potential for positive development of human and natural resources;
- Investor's past record in Papua New Guinea and elsewhere;
- Creation of additional employment and income-earning opportunities;
- Likelihood the proposal will generate additional government revenue and contribute to economic growth;
- Transfer of technologies and skills and the contribution to training citizens of Papua New Guinea; and

There is no specific investment level. The IPA may, however, pursuant to Section 28(7) of the Investment Promotion Act require an applicant for Certification to deposit the prescribed amount prior to a Certificate being issued. The prescribed amounts are per Section 6B of the Investment Promotion Regulation:

- Individual – PGK 50,000 (USD 15,340);
- Partnership – PGK 50,000 (USD 15,340) per partner; and
- Corporate Body – PGK 100,000 (USD 30,680).

The purpose of the screening mechanism is to assess the net economic benefit and consistency with national interest. The possible outcomes of a review are prohibition, divestiture, and imposition of additional requirements. The IPA and other regulatory bodies in particular sectors make the decision on the outcome.

Appeal processes differ among the sectors. For IPA related matters, a company must submit its appeal to the Ministry of Commerce and Industry. An accompanying fee of PGK 200 (USD 61) is required. Appeals may be lodged in response to any decision made by the IPA, including rejection of an application or the cancellation of a registration.

The Bank of Papua New Guinea, PNG's Central Bank, approves all foreign investment proposals. Such proposals include the issue of equity capital to a non-resident, the borrowing of funds from a non-resident investor or financial intermediary, and the supply of goods and services on extended terms by a non-resident. In its review, the Bank is mostly concerned that the terms of the investment funds are reasonable in the context of prevailing commercial conditions and that full subscription of loan funds are promptly brought to Papua New Guinea. A debt/equity ratio of 5:1 is generally imposed with respect to overseas borrowings and a ratio of 3:1 with respect to local borrowings.

U.S. investors are generally welcomed by the PNG government, and are not especially disadvantaged or singled out by any of the ownership or control mechanisms, sector restrictions, or investment screening mechanisms, relative to other foreign investors.

Other Investment Policy Reviews

The government has not undergone any third-party investment policy reviews (IPRs) through a multilateral organization within the past three years.

Business Facilitation

PNG has made efforts to make doing business easier. IPA has a website and is open and responsive. Despite these efforts, the IPA does not control all aspects of new business registration and operation of existing businesses. As such, government agencies that are less responsive can cause significant delays for businesses in need of government services.

The Investment Promotion Authority (IPA) is the lead agency for GPNG's business facilitation efforts. It can be reached online at http://www.ipa.gov.pg/. The new Do It Online section allows both overseas and domestic business registration. Previously, the processing times were substantial, but the current processing time for IPA is seven (7) days. A foreign company must first register under the Companies Act of 1997. Foreign companies have two options for registration in PNG: to incorporate a new company in PNG or to register an overseas company under the Companies Act of 1997. In practice, most foreign companies incorporate a new PNG subsidiary when entering the PNG market.

Once incorporated and registered with the IPA, a newly incorporated PNG company or overseas company should also register with the Internal Revenue Commission for tax and employment purposes. Typically, this process takes nine (9) days.

PNG's government has made efforts to include women in the formal economy with forums, micro-lending, and training. These efforts have met with limited success.

Outward Investment

There are no incentives for outward investment from PNG, and there are no explicit legal restrictions on outward investment. The most likely barrier for this type of investment would be sufficient access to foreign currency. There have been no recent large-scale outward investments originating from PNG.

2. BILATERAL INVESTMENT AGREEMENTS AND TAXATION TREATIES

PNG has Bilateral Investment Treaties (BITs) with Australia, China, Germany, Japan, Malaysia, and the United Kingdom. PNG has a free trade agreement (FTA) with the countries of the Melanesian Spearhead Group: Solomon Islands, Vanuatu, and Fiji.

PNG does not have a bilateral taxation treaty with the U.S. It currently has "double tax treaties" with the following countries: Australia, Canada, China, Fiji, Germany, Indonesia, South Korea, Malaysia, New Zealand, Singapore, and the United Kingdom. PNG also has a tax information exchange agreement with Australia.

PNG has long struggled to collect all taxes owed to the government. There have been recent efforts to step up tax collection due to a growing government budget deficit. In response to efforts to collect more from large companies, these large companies (including many nationwide retailers) have accused smaller companies, often owned by Chinese businesspeople, of evading taxes through incorrect accounting or bribery.

3. LEGAL REGIME

Transparency of the Regulatory System

The ICCC (Independent Consumer and Competition Commission) is charged with fostering competition. While there are transparent policies in place, the competition regime works more towards the regulation of existing monopolies and does little to foster competition. Tax, labor, environment, health, and safety and other laws do not distort or impede investment. However, the lack of implementation of existing laws by some government entities frustrates some investors. For example there are long bureaucratic delays in the processing of work permits and frequent complaints about corruption and bribery in government departments.

The IPA and the Government are moving, with the assistance of the International Finance Corporation, towards more investment promotion and a more streamlined regulatory framework to encourage foreign investment. The IPA's move to an online registration process for businesses is evidence of this.

Proposed laws and regulations are made available for public comment, but comments are not always taken into consideration or acted on by lawmakers or regulators.

There are informal regulatory processes managed by nongovernmental organizations and private sector associations. There are impediments to the licensing of skilled foreign labor that are imposed by local professional associations, such as the Papua New Guinea Institute of Engineers and the Law Society(both of which have their own regulatory processes), that foreigners must go through before they can work/practice in the country.

There are no private sector and/or government efforts to restrict foreign participation in industry standards-setting consortia or organizations.

Legal, regulatory, and accounting systems are transparent and consistent with international norms, but there are delays in the dispute resolution system due to a lack of human resources in the judiciary.

When possible, proposed laws are made available for public comment, but comments are not always taken into consideration or acted on by lawmakers. Frequently, important Parliamentary decisions, such as the annual budget, are taken with no hearings and little or no debate before voting. Many PNG government functions and documents are available online, but not all and they are not centralized.

Regulatory decisions can sometimes be capricious and opaque, but they do not specifically target foreign-owned businesses. Most regulatory decisions can be appealed to courts with jurisdiction. There are no regulatory reforms currently planned.

International Regulatory Considerations

PNG is a party to the Melanesian Free Trade Agreement. The agreement came into effect in 2017 and does address the need for competent regulatory authorities in each country (PNG, Solomon Islands, Vanuatu, and Fiji). However, the regulatory chapter is small and is designed to be strengthened and improved going forward. When international standards are used in PNG, they are most often Australian due to PNG's colonial past and continuing close economic ties with Australia.

The government has notified the WTO Committee on Technical Barriers to Trade only once. That notification covered food safety issues and was issued in 2006.

Papua New Guinea accepted the Trade Facilitation Agreement (TFA) on March 7, 2018. As the acceptance has happened only recently, there have been no government efforts of note on implementing TFA requisites.

Laws and Regulations on Foreign Direct Investment

Foreign investors can either be incorporated in PNG as a subsidiary of an overseas company or incorporated under the laws of another country and therefore registered as an overseas company under the Companies Act 1997.

The 1997 Companies Act and 1998 Companies Regulation oversee matters regarding private and public companies, both foreign and domestic. All foreign business entities must have IPA approval and must be certified and registered with the government before commencing operations in PNG. While government departments have their own procedures for approving foreign investment in their respective economic sectors, the IPA provides investors with the relevant information and contacts. The regulations governing foreign investments in PNG include:

- Free Trade Zone Act 2000;
- Investment Promotion Act 1992;
- Papua New Guinea Companies Act 1997;
- Forestry Act 1991;
- Mining Act 1992;
- Fisheries Act 1994; and
- Oil and Gas Act 1998.

In 2014, the government amended the 1997 Companies Act to improve corporate governance and ease regulatory burdens. This amendment allowed IPA to begin using its online company registry. The main changes to the act are as follows:

1. Increased protection and benefits for shareholders;
2. Clarification of duties imposed upon directors;
3. A more transparent and streamlined process of issuing shares;
4. Increased protection of creditors, including a more disciplined liquidation process;
5. A clearer process for filing annual returns; and
6. Streamlined filing requirements in anticipation of implementing an online registration.

A summary of the changes to the Act can be found on the IPA website: http://www.ipa.gov.pg/wp-content/uploads/Changes-to-the-company-Act.pdf.

In 2013, the government amended the Takeovers Code to include a test for foreign companies wishing to buy into the ownership of local companies. The new regulation states that the Securities Commission of Papua New Guinea (SCPNG) shall issue an order preventing a party from acquiring any shares, whether partial or otherwise, if the commission views that such acquisition or takeover is not in the national interest of PNG. This applies to any company, domestic or foreign, registered under the PNG Companies Act, publicly traded, with more than 5 million PGK (USD 1.53 million) in assets, with a minimum of 25 shareholders, and more than 100 employees.

In recent years, this law has not been used to prevent ExxonMobil's acquisition of InterOil or Chinese company Zijin Mining's purchase of 50 percent of the Porgera Joint Venture gold mine.

Competition and Anti-Trust Laws

The 2002 Independent Consumer and Competition Commission Act, is the law that governs competition. It also established the Independent Consumer & Competition Commission (ICCC), the country's premier economic regulatory body and consumer watchdog; introduced a new regime for the regulation of utilities, in particular in relation to prices and service standards; and allowed the ICCC to take over the price control tasks previously undertaken by the Prices Controller as well as the consumer protection tasks previously undertaken by the Consumer Affairs Council.

The Act's competition laws, contained in Part VI of the Act, prohibit:

- Entering into, or giving effect to contracts, arrangements or understandings having the purpose, effect or likely effect of substantially lessening competition (Section 50);
- Arrangements between competitors that contain exclusionary provisions, which have the purpose of preventing, restricting or limiting dealings with any particular person or class of persons who are in competition with one or more of the parties to the arrangement;
- Price fixing agreements between competitors (but fixing prices of joint venture products, recommended prices and joint buying and promotion arrangements, are not absolutely prohibited, although they may still be subject to the prohibition on contracts, arrangements, and understandings that substantially lessen competition) (Sections 53-56);
- A person with a substantial degree of market power from taking advantage of that power for the purpose of restricting the entry of a new competitor into a market, preventing or deterring a competitor from engaging in competitive conduct, or eliminating a competitor from that market (Section 58);
- The practice of resale price maintenance, which occurs where a supplier tries to specify a price below which a reseller may not sell the supplier's product. This prohibition also applies to third parties seeking to insist that products not be resold below a specified price (Sections 59-64); and
- Mergers or acquisitions that would have the effect or likely effect of substantially lessening competition in a market (Section 69).

The ICCC's website is http://www.iccc.gov.pg.

There have been no significant actions taken by ICCC in the last 12 months that have affected international investors.

Expropriation and Compensation

The judicial system upholds the sanctity of contracts, and the Investment Promotion Act of 1992 expressly prohibits expropriation of foreign assets.

After years of environmental issues, in September 2013, the Government of Papua New Guinea nationalized the country's largest taxpaying company, Ok Tedi Mining Limited. The nationalization raised concerns about the government's policy. Some observers saw this event as a special case, given that much of the company's profits are held in trust for the people of PNG, and its effective ownership by a company – the PNG Sustainable Development Program's (PNGSDP) – would transfer benefits from the mine back to the people. By a unanimous vote in Parliament, the government annulled PNGSDP's share in the mine and issued new shares to the state. This vote also removed BHP Billiton's immunity from environmental liability and gave the state the right to restructure PNGSDP. As there have been no other expropriating acts since late 2013, the Ok Tedi Mining Limited nationalization does appear to have been a one-off.

The OK Tedi nationalization was an Act of Parliament considered and voted on in the regular order of business. There was no recourse or due process beyond the Parliament.

Dispute Settlement

ICSID Convention and New York Convention

Since 1978, Papua New Guinea has been a member of the International Centre for Settlement of Investment Disputes (ICSID Convention). In agreements with foreign investors, GPNG traditionally adopts the Arbitration Rules of the United Nations Commission on International Trade Law (UNCITRAL model law). There is no specific legislation providing for enforcement of awards under the 1958 New York Convention or the ICSID Convention.

Investor-State Dispute Settlement

Investment disputes may be settled through diplomatic channels or through the use of local remedies before having such matters adjudicated at the International Centre for the Settlement of Investment Disputes or through another appropriate tribunal of which Papua New Guinea is a member. The Investment Promotion Act 1992 that is administered by the IPA also protects against expropriation, cancellation of contracts, and discrimination through the granting of most favored nation treatment to investors. PNG does not have a Bilateral Investment Treaty (BIT) with the United States, and no claims have been made under such an agreement. There is not a recent history of international judgments against GPNG nor is there a recent history of extrajudicial action against foreign investors.

There have been no investment disputes involving a U.S. person or other foreign investor within the last 10 years, and there is no history of extrajudicial action against foreign investors. Local courts have not recognized and enforced any arbitral awards issued against the government.

There are no alternative dispute resolution (ADR) mechanisms as means for settling disputes between private parties outside of the courts and contract enforcement. There is not a recognized domestic arbitration body/mechanism in PNG, and most recent arbitration has occurred in international jurisdictions. Local courts in PNG have previously recognized and enforced judgements of foreign courts, such as a 2015 international arbitration decision in favor of Interoil (which has since been acquired by ExxonMobil) and against Oil Search was respected in PNG.

Bankruptcy Regulations

Papua New Guinea's bankruptcy laws are included in chapter 253 of the Insolvency Act of 1951 and sections 254 through 362 of the Companies Act of 1997, which covers receivership and liquidation. Bankruptcy and litigation searches can only be conducted in person at the National Court in Port Moresby.

According to the World Bank's Doing Business Report, resolving insolvency in Papua New Guinea takes an average of three years, and typically costs 23 percent of the debtor's estate. The average recovery rate is 25.2 cents on the dollar. Globally, Papua New Guinea stands at 141 out of 189 economies on the Ease of Resolving Insolvency.

The Credit Data Bureau (CDB) is used by commercial banks for making creditworthiness decisions.

4. INDUSTRIAL POLICIES

Investment Incentives

Performance requirements/incentives are applied uniformly to both domestic and foreign investors. The investment incentives currently available are designed primarily to encourage the development of industries that are considered desirable for the long-term economic development of Papua New Guinea or specific underdeveloped regions within the country and are as follows.

The Investment Promotion Act contains guarantees that there will be no nationalization or expropriation of foreign investors' property except in accordance with law, for a public purposes defined by law or in payment of compensation as defined by law.

Accelerated depreciation rates are available for new manufacturing and agricultural plants, generous deductions are available for capital expenditure on land used for primary production, and accelerated deductions are available for mining and petroleum companies. For more details, see Price Waterhouse Cooper's Global Tax Solutions page (http://www.pwc.com/gx/en/tax/index.jhtml).

A 10-year exemption from tax is available where certain new businesses are established in specified rural development areas. Businesses, resident or non-resident, engaged in the following activities qualify for this exemption:

- Agricultural production of any kind;
- Manufacturing of any kind;
- Construction;
- Transport, storage and communications;
- Real estate;
- Business services; and
- Provision of accommodation, motels or hotels.

The following have been specified as rural development areas:

- Central province – Goilala;
- Enga province – Kandep, Lagalp, Wabag, Wapenamunda;
- Gulf province – Kaintiba, Kikori;
- Eastern Highlands province – Henganofi, Lufa, Okapa, Wonenave;
- Southern Highlands province – Jimi, Tambal;
- Madang province – Bogia, Rai Coast, Ramu;
- Milne Bay province – Losula, Rabaraba;
- Morobe province – Finschaffen, Kabwum, Kaiapit, Menyamya, Mumeng;
- East New Britain province – Pomio;
- West New Britain province – Kandrian;
- East Sepik province – Ambuti, Angoram, Lumi, Maprik;
- West Sepik province – Amanab, Nuku, Telefomin; and
- Simbu province – Gumine, Karimui.

The exemption does not apply to businesses in areas in which a special mining lease or a petroleum development license is granted.

Businesses that commence exporting qualifying goods manufactured by them in Papua New Guinea are exempt from income tax on the profits derived from those sales for the first three complete years. For the following four years, the profit derived from the excess of export sales over the average export sales of the three previous years is exempt from income tax. The list of qualifying goods include, among other items, motor vehicles, matches, paint, refined petroleum, soaps, wooden furniture, dairy products, flour, chopsticks, artifacts, clothing and manufactured textiles, and jewelry.

A wage subsidy is payable to new businesses that manufacture new manufactured products. The business will receive a prescribed percentage of the value of the minimum wage paid by the business, multiplied by the number of Papua New Guineans permanently employed by the business.

The relevant percentages are as follows:

- Year 1 – 40 percent
- Year 2 – 30 percent
- Year 3 – 20 percent
- Year 4 – 15 percent
- Year 5 – 10 percent

Eligible products are, broadly, all products listed under division D of the International Standard Classification of All Economic Activities (Third Revision), provided the products are not subject to quota pricing without import pricing or to tariff protection.

Registered foreign companies must file an annual certification with the Registrar of Companies accompanied by audited financial statements. A foreign company must apply for Certification under the Investment Promotion Act 1992 within 14 days of registering. Any foreign company automatically falls under this category and therefore must complete the same process.

However, a company may apply to be exempted from certain requirements. A company which chooses to conduct business through a branch registered in Papua New Guinea can repatriate its profits without being subject to withholding tax. On the other hand, the dividends of a Papua New Guinea incorporated subsidiary may attract dividend withholding tax. A higher rate of income tax is imposed on non-resident companies. If a foreign company merely wishes to have a representative office in Papua New Guinea, it may be exempt from lodging tax returns if it derives no income in Papua New Guinea. The Companies Act adopts similar principles and standards of corporate regulation to those in place in New Zealand. Companies registered in Papua New Guinea must lodge an annual return every year with the Registrar of Companies within six months of the end of its financial year. Currently, the Papua New Guinea government is reviewing its structure.

There are no discriminatory or preferential export and import policies affecting foreign investors, and there are low levels of import taxes.

Foreign Trade Zones/Free Ports/Trade Facilitation

Papua New Guinea has not established geographically defined duty-free export zones.

Performance and Data Localization Requirements

All non-citizens seeking employment in PNG must have a valid work permit before they can be hired. The work permit must be granted by the Secretary of the Department of Labor and Industrial Relations (DLIR) in accordance with the Employment of Non-Citizens Act of 2007. It can take weeks or even months to obtain both a work permit and visa for non-citizens to work in Papua New Guinea, and delays are common due to a lengthy bureaucratic clearance process. In the past, the government has used its immigration powers to block visas for personnel to come to

Papua New Guinea to fill positions that it believes can be filled by Papua New Guineans. There are no government imposed conditions on permission to invest in PNG.

Papua New Guinea does not follow forced localization.

Post is not aware of any requirements for foreign IT providers to turn over source code and/or provide access to surveillance. Likewise, Post is not aware of any rules on maintaining a certain amount of data storage within the country.

5. PROTECTION OF PROPERTY RIGHTS

Real Property

Property rights exist and are enforced. Mortgages and liens do exist. For non-customary land, the system is reliable. PNG's legal system does not allow direct foreign ownership of land. To get around this limitation, long-term government leases are used. The legal system protects and facilitates acquisition and disposition of all property rights, but there are substantial delays particularly within the Department of Lands.

The majority of land (over 80 percent) is customarily owned meaning that there is little legal documentation. The lack of documentation makes acquisition difficult as even after a transaction settles, it can be challenged by an individual that also claims customary ownership. The government has been working to standardize and document customary ownership, but the problem persists. If property that is legally purchased is unoccupied, property ownership cannot revert to other owners, such as squatters.

Intellectual Property Rights

The IPA through the Intellectual Property Office of PNG (IPOPNG) administers the Trade Marks Act, Chapter 385, Copyright and Neighbouring Rights Act (2000) and the Patents and Industrial Design Act (2000).

Protections for intellectual property rights relating to the reproduction and sale of counterfeit and pirated products, particularly music and movies, are insufficient. Such counterfeit products are openly sold on the streets and in shops. Sales persist despite sporadic law enforcement action. Other counterfeit products that infringe on copyrights, patents, and/or trademarks are often imported from Asian countries and sold in Papua New Guinea. Customs periodically seizes such shipments, but there are significant gaps in their enforcement regime. Adequate protection for trade secrets and semiconductor chip layout design exist in law, and minimal infringements appear to occur. For additional information about treaty obligations and points of contact at local IP offices, please see WIPO's country profiles at http://www.wipo.int/directory/en/. PNG does not track and report on seizures of counterfeit goods, nor does it prosecute IPR violations. PNG is not listed in USTR's Special 301 report, and it is not listed in the notorious market report.

6. FINANCIAL SECTOR

Capital Markets and Portfolio Investment

Portfolio investments are unregulated and limited to the availability of stocks.

PNG has one stock market in Port Moresby, POMSoX. It was founded in 1999. It is closely aligned with the Australian Stock Exchange (ASX), and its procedures are the same as ASX.

There is no factor market, and the free flow of remission of funds offshore is subject to approval by the Central Bank (Bank of Papua New Guinea) and the International Revenue Commission. Owing to a persistent shortage of foreign currency at the Bank of Papua New Guinea, companies have struggled to make international remissions. In its most recent Article IV consultation, the IMF found multiple restrictions on current international payments and two multiple currency practices (MCPs) that are inconsistent with Article VIII of the IMF's Articles of Agreement.

In its previous Article IV consultation in late 2017, the IMF found no restrictions on current international payments and no multiple currency practices (MCPs) that are inconsistent with Article VIII of the IMF's Articles of Agreement. Credit is allocated on market terms, and foreign investors are able to get credit on the local market, much more so than in previous years due to the liberalization of policies, provided that foreign investors have a good credit history. Credit instruments are limited to leasing and bank finance.

Money and Banking System

There are multiple nationwide banks in PNG. Most banks have branches in major and secondary cities. However, due to the very rural and remote nature of much of PNG's population, the majority of the population remains unbanked. GPNG is working on multiple fronts to increase financial inclusion amongst its population.

There are both domestic and international banks in PNG and all have reported profits in their most recent reporting. BSP Bank (formerly Bank South Pacific) is Papua New Guinea's largest domestic bank and is the largest in the country with total assets of PGK20.364 billion (USD 6.26 billion) at year's end in 2016. Branches/subsidiaries of two Australian banks represent the number two and number three largest financial institutions operating in the country. While the Australian banks do not provide reports of PNG-specific assets, the Australia and New Zealand (ANZ) Bank had total global assets of USD 889.9 billion at year's end 2015, and Westpac Bank had USD 812.2 billion in total global assets at the end of 2015. The banking system in Papua New Guinea is sound.

The Bank of Papua New Guinea is the central bank for Papua New Guinea. The Central Banking Act of 2000 outlines the powers, functions and objectives of the Bank.

Foreigners are required to show documentation either of their employment or their business along with proof of a valid visa in order to register for a bank account.

There have been experimental projects announced in PNG, both by GPNG and donor governments. However, the projects have been small pilot projects with no current plans to scale up.

There are no alternative financial services in PNG.

Foreign Exchange and Remittances

Foreign Exchange Policies

While there are no legal restrictions on such activities, a lack of available foreign exchange makes such conversions, transfers, and repatriations time consuming or impossible.

Bank of Papua New Guinea requires that all funds held in PNG be held in PNG kina (PGK). This rule was announced with little notice and caught many businesses off-guard in 2016. While there was an appeals process for businesses that wished to keep non-PGK accounts, none of the appeals were granted.

On June 4, 2014, the Central Bank introduced measures which have effectively pegged the kina at levels that led to foreign exchange shortages. While the kina does fluctuate somewhat in value, it only trades in a tight band as allowed by the central bank (Bank of Papua New Guinea). Recently, the central bank has allowed PGK to slowly depreciate against the USD and other currencies.

Remittance Policies

There have been no recent changes or plans to change remittance policies. Remittance is done only through direct bank transfers. All remittances overseas in excess of PGK 50,000 (USD 15,340) per year require a tax clearance certificate issued by the Internal Revenue Commission (IRC). In addition, approval of PNG's Central Bank – the Bank of Papua New Guinea – is required for annual remittances overseas in excess of PGK 500,000 (USD 153,420). Remittances related to the payment of trade-related goods are not taken into account. There are no specific restrictions on the repatriation of capital owned by or due to non-residents. The Central Bank's principal objectives in assessing applications for capital repayments are to ensure that the funds are due and payable to a non-resident and that Papua New Guinea assets are not sold at an artificial value.

While there are no legal time limitations on remittances, foreign companies have waited many months for large transfers or performed transfers in small increments over time due to a shortage of foreign exchange.

Sovereign Wealth Funds

A Sovereign Wealth Fund Bill was passed in Parliament on July 30, 2015. However, falling commodity prices have severely impacted government revenues. Plans for the SWF have been put on hold indefinitely.

7. STATE-OWNED ENTERPRISES

The SOEs operate and provide services in aviation, mobile and telecommunication, water and sewerage, motor vehicle insurance, development banking and finance, petroleum sector, data service, port services, electricity, and postal services. SOE's total state assets stand at K9.3 billion with 7,000 employees. There are eight SOEs down from eleven in 2017 due to recent mergers. Each SOE has an independent board that is appointed by the cabinet which then reports to the government minister.

SOE profitability has steadily declined since 2005.

In 2015, GPNG set up Kumul Consolidated Holdings (KCH) as the one organization to oversee all SOEs. Despite this supposedly separate holding company, politicians remain engaged in the running of SOEs. The law gives the cabinet the powers to appoint SOE directors and to grant approvals for corporate plans, remuneration levels, tenders, engagement of consultants, among others, thereby reducing the autonomy of SOEs.

The ability for government to have direct control over SOE boards has led many to question the independence of SOEs and to see political considerations involved in business decisions.

Most SOEs in PNG continue to fail to produce financial accounts in a timely manner to allow for more informed government and legislative decision-making. KCH itself has failed to publicly report its audited financial statements to date.

http://www.kch.com.pg/portfolio/ provides a list of SOEs in PNG.

Privatization Program

There is no privatization program in place and thus no guidelines or structure on when and how foreign investors are allowed to participate in privatization programs. The government has funding available for privatization and is currently using the Public Private Partnership (PPP) structure as a model for privatization. The trend has been towards growing SOEs. The cumulative asset value of SOEs grew from USD 1.58 billion in 2012 to USD 6.32 billion by the end of 2015.

8. RESPONSIBLE BUSINESS CONDUCT

PNG does not have a national action plan for responsible business conduct (RBC). However, most multinational companies in PNG do operate with a sense of standards. The concept of a social license to operate is pervasive in the extractive industries and guides interactions with all stakeholders.

Due to limited resources and capacity, many human rights, labor rights, consumer protection, environmental protections, and other such laws to protect individuals from adverse business impacts go largely unenforced. While there are occasional cases of government action in these situations, that action is the exception, not the norm.

There are no corporate governance, accounting, and executive compensation standards to protect shareholders in place.

There are currently no NGOs specifically monitoring RBC in PNG.

While PNG does not have specific RBC policies, most large, international companies use international best practices as standards.

PNG is a member of the Extractive Industries Transparency Initiative (EITI). PNG's EITI efforts have thus far been hampered by a lack of cooperation from relevant government ministries and a severe lack of data.

9. CORRUPTION

Corruption is widespread in Papua New Guinea, particularly the misappropriation of public funds, skimming of inflated contracts, and nepotism.

Giving or accepting a bribe is a criminal act. Penalties differ for Members of Parliament (MPs), public officials, and ordinary citizens. For MPs the penalty is imprisonment for no more than seven years; for public officials the penalty is imprisonment for no more than seven years and a fine at the discretion of the court; for ordinary citizens the penalty is a fine not exceeding PGK 400 (USD 123) or imprisonment of no more than one year. A bribe by a local company or individual to a foreign official is a criminal act. A local company cannot deduct a bribe to a foreign official from taxes. The Leadership Code extends to family members of officials.

The PNG economy currently has laws or regulations to counter conflict-of-interest in awarding contracts or government procurement, but enforcement is insufficient.

The government encourages companies to establish internal codes of conduct that, among other things, prohibit bribery of public officials.

Most of the larger domestic companies and international firms from Europe, North America, Japan, Australia, and New Zealand have effective internal controls, ethics, and compliance programs to detect and prevent bribery. Many firms from elsewhere in East and Southeast Asia, particularly those in the resource extraction sectors, lack such programs.

Papua New Guinea has signed and ratified the UN Convention against Corruption. Papua New Guinea is not a party to the UN Convention against Transnational Organized Crime or the OECD Convention on Combating Bribery of Foreign Public Officials in International Business Transactions.

No specific protections are provided to NGOs involved in investigating corruption.

U.S. firms routinely identify corruption as a challenge to foreign direct investment. Some critical areas in which corruption is pervasive include budget management, forestry, fisheries, and public procurement.

No local industry or non-profit groups offer services for vetting potential local investment partners.

Resources to Report Corruption

Contact at government agency or agencies are responsible for combating corruption:
Dickson Morehari
Director of Corporate Services
Ombudsman Commission
Tower Building
Douglas Street
+675 308 2618
Dickson.morehari@ombudsman.gov.pg

Contact at watchdog organization :
Jerry Bagita
Director of Operations
Transparency International
2nd Floor, IPA Haus, Konedobu, NCD
P.O. Box 591, Port Moresby, NCD
+675 320 2182
opmtipng@gmail.com

10. POLITICAL AND SECURITY ENVIRONMENT

Periodic tribal conflicts occur, particularly in the Highlands and Sepik regions of the country, and there was election-related violence following the 2017 national elections. While foreign investors/interests have not been the target of these often violent confrontations, project infrastructure can occasionally be inadvertently damaged or their operations disrupted due to the prevailing security situation.

Incidents of damage to projects and/or installations over the past few years have not been specifically politically motivated. The majority of disruption and damage caused to projects is due to disputes between landowners and the central government, which are fueled by a perception in certain cases that the central government has failed to uphold its financial commitments to landowners. Landowners in these disputes have taken out their frustration with the central government by damaging the infrastructure or disrupting the operations of foreign projects in their regions.

The central bureaucracy is increasingly politicized, which has eroded the capacity of government departments and allowed nepotism/political cronyism to thrive in parts the public service. Civil disturbances have been triggered by the government's failure to deliver financial and development commitments, particularly to landowners in the resource project areas. They have also occurred in major urban areas based on disputes between long-term residents and newly arrived migrants and/or between competing criminal networks.

11. LABOR POLICIES AND PRACTICES

Papua New Guinea has a severe skilled labor shortage, which presents a major constraint to business and investment, as investors are often forced to recruit from abroad. Such recruitment is expensive given the very high cost of living in Papua New Guinea. The country spends up to PGK 750 million (USD 230.1 million) a year to bring in foreign consultants to fill gaps in the workforce. The government generally adheres to the ILO conventions protecting worker rights, and labor unions are very active in the country. The majority of the population works in the informal economy where problem areas persist, including child labor and trafficking in persons, though neither occurs in large numbers.

Skilled labor is in short supply. Most expatriate laborers are occupied in "white collar" work.

There are no specific legal requirements to hire national staff, but most foreign companies hire nationals to maximum extent possible due to the expense and paperwork requirements of bringing expatriate staff to PNG.

There are no seasonal adjustment restrictions in PNG. While companies do provide severance packages as a practice when conducting layoffs, there is no specific legal requirement to do so. There is no social insurance or other safety net programs for unemployed workers.

Labor laws are not waived in order to attract or retain investment.

The majority of PNG's workers are not members of unions. The most active unions are at state-owned enterprises, not private businesses.

The Government through the Department of Labour and Industrial Relations does intervene in labor disputes. In fact, one of its main/core functions is to deal with industrial relations. Its main activities with labor disputes are:

1. Settling of minor complaints;
2. Conciliation and mediation; and
3. Arbitrary tribunals.

The Industrial Relations Division, the Industrial Registrar's Office, and the Office of the Industrial Arbitration Tribunal and Minimum Wages Board all work on labor disputes.

12. OPIC AND OTHER INVESTMENT INSURANCE PROGRAMS

The Overseas Private Investment Corporation (OPIC) had a project worth USD 10.2 million to expand cellular phone service in Papua New Guinea in 2012.

PNG currently has an OPIC agreement and the United States.

The Chinese Export Import Bank is very active in PNG and provides millions of dollars in financing for Chinese firms, mostly in infrastructure.

13. FOREIGN DIRECT INVESTMENT AND FOREIGN PORTFOLIO INVESTMENT STATISTICS

Table 2: Key Macroeconomic Data, U.S. FDI in Host Country/Economy

	Host Country Statistical Source*		USG or International Statistical Source		USG or International Source of Data: BEA; IMF; Eurostat; UNCTAD, Other
Economic Data	Year	Amount	Year	Amount	
Host Country Gross Domestic Product (GDP) (M USD)	2015	USD 17,550	2016	USD 20,213	www.worldbank.org/en/country
Foreign Direct Investment	Host Country Statistical Source*		USG or International Statistical Source		USG or International Source of Data: BEA; IMF; Eurostat; UNCTAD, Other
U.S. FDI in Partner Country (M USD , stock positions)	N/A	N/A	2016	USD 239	BEA data available at http://bea.gov/international/direct_investment_multinational_companies_comprehensive_data.htm
Host Country's FDI in the United States (M USD , stock positions)	N/A	N/A	2016	USD 2	BEA data available at http://bea.gov/international/direct_investment_multinational_companies_comprehensive_data.htm
Total Inbound Stock of FDI as % host GDP	N/A	N/A	2016	.12%	N/A

*Local: https://www.nso.gov.pg/

14. CONTACT FOR MORE INFORMATION

Beatrice Kapigeno
Economic Specialist
Douglas Street, P.O. Box 1492, NCD Port Moresby
+675 321-1455, ext. 2218
EconPortMoresby@state.gov

INVESTMENT AND PROMOTION AUTHORITY

The Investment Promotion Authority (IPA) was set up in 1992 to promote investment in Papua New Guinea IPA has regulatory functions but there is a great emphasis on promotion and assisting foreign investment. It has a Board with strong representation by the private sector to manage and direct its affairs. The main functions of IPA are:

- To provide information to investors in the country and overseas;
- To encourage and facilitate investment in the country by assisting investors to obtain an necessary licences, compliances and approvals;
- To facilitate the introduction of citizen and foreign investors to each other and to activities and investments of mutual benefit;
- To provide a system of certification of a foreign enterprise and to require that a foreign enterprise may only carry on business if so certified;
- To monitor the activities of foreign enterprises so as to determine whether or not a foreign enterprise is certified and complies with the terms and conditions of its certificate to carry on business in the country;
- To advise the Minister (for Commerce and Industry) on policy issues which relate to the Investment Promotion Act;
- To maintain a register of foreign investment opportunities;
- To facilitate citizen participation in investment and in the ownership of national and foreign enterprises;
- To carry out other functions as given the to Investment Promotion Authority; and
- To generally do whatever is necessary or convenient for the carrying out of its functions.

In addition, the IPA, through the Business Registration Office, administers the Companies Act, the Associations Incorporation Act, Business Names Act, Business Groups Incorporation Act and the Trademarks Act.

There are three main divisions within IPA:

1. INVESTOR AND PROMOTION SERVICES

When in doubt about where to go and what to do regarding any investment activity, this division win be able to assist. It is most often the first point of contact within IPA for investors new to Papua New Guinea Specifically, this division provides information about investment matters to investors, maintains an investor database for the purposes of facilitating business introductions, produces a monthly newsletter for investors, undertakes investment missions within the country and abroad, and other general activities which assist investors.

2. CERTIFICATION AND RESEARCH

This division is responsible for an matters relating to certification of foreign enterprises as contained in Part IV of the Investment Promotion Act (Sections 25 to 36). Its officers ensure foreign investors are certified to carry on business in activities other than reserved activities, and that only bona fide applications are considered.

When assessing an application by a foreign investor to carry on business in PNG, officers in this division will carry out checks on information supplied by the applicant. Investors should note that these procedures are routine and must be undertaken to comply with the requirements of the Act. Written notice of the grant or refusal of an application for certification must be given to the applicant within 35 working days of the IPA receiving the complete and correct application.

3. BUSINESS REGISTRATION

Incorporating the Offices of the Registrar of Companies and the Registrar of Trademarks, this division is responsible for all matters in relation to incorporation of companies, registration of trademarks, incorporation of business groups, incorporation of associations, registration of business names and offenses committed under the various legislation administered by the IPA.

CITIZEN, NATIONAL AND FOREIGN ENTERPRISES

The Investment Promotion Act categorizes business enterprises as follows:

Citizen Enterprise: An enterprise wholly owned by a PNG citizen, including the State.

National Enterprise: An enterprise which is more than 50% owned by PNG citizens unless the enterprise is controlled by noncitizens.

Foreign Enterprise: An enterprise which is 50% or more owned by noncitizens or which is controlled by noncitizens.

An enterprise may be an individual or a company, partnership or other legally recognised person or body. All forms of enterprise are subject to other relevant legislation, such as the Companies Act.

The categorization of enterprises is relevant for two important reasons:

1. All foreign enterprises must be certified by IPA prior to carrying on business in PNG, and

2. Certain business activities are restricted to citizen and national enterprises. A list of Reserved Activities for citizen enterprises can be obtained from IPA. To date, there are no such activities restricted solely for national enterprises.

INVESTMENT INCENTIVES

The security of investment in Papua New Guinea has always been granted the highest priority by the Government.

The Government is fully aware of the perception investors have about risks they take when investing in Papua New Guinea. It has made an undertaking to minimise the perceived risks (including expropriation, repudiation of contracts and discrimination) through the granting of the most favoured nation treatment to investors as if they were nationals of Papua New Guinea.

International agreements so far concluded include those with the Federal Republic of Germany, Malaysia, Australia, United States, United Kingdom. Peoples' Republic of China, Canada.. Negotiations are currently being conducted with the Philippines, Belgium, and the Republic of

Korea.

Papua New Guinea's membership of the World Bank's Multilateral Investment Guarantee Agency (MIGA) in 1990 also demonstrates the Government's commitment to ensuring that if nationalisation did occur for the national good, the investor concerned would be adequately compensated.

The issue of repudiating or cancelling contracts must be settled through diplomatic channels or through the use of other local remedies, before having any such matters adjudicated at the International Centre for the Settlement of Investment Disputes or through another appropriate tribunal of which Papua New Guinea is a member.

The establishment of the Investment Promotion Authority in 1992 through the Investment Promotion Act (the Act) was done so in recognition of the comfort that investors look for when considering Papua New Guinea as an investment destination. The Act has provided for such matters under Section 37 which protects against expropriation, cancellation of contracts and discrimination through the application of the most favoured nation treatment to investors.

The globalisation of trade and investment has advocated a lot of the above principles which Papua New Guinea has implemented in its domestic legislation as well as by adopting those principles when it became a member of MIGA. This international practice demonstrates Papua New Guinea's seriousness in fair play and in protecting investors and their investment in the country.

THE INVESTMENT PROMOTION AUTHORITY

The Government of Papua New Guinea welcomes legitimate, non-speculative foreign investment and offers assistance through the Investment Promotion Authority. Business people investigating the investment potential of Papua New Guinea are advised to contact the IPA in the first instance. The IPA was established by an Act of Parliament to promote and facilitate investment in the country.

While there are few limits on the types of investment possible by foreign investors, there may be specific laws in place which investors must follow.

Foreign investors in resource-based ventures are required, for example, to follow the laws of the government departments specifically responsible for the resource. These relate to investment in the mining and petroleum, agriculture, livestock, fisheries and forestry sectors.

There are other laws and regulations which will affect investors. These include laws of the National Government which cover areas such as foreign exchange, taxation and customs matters. Provincial governments and urban authorities may also require investors to follow certain laws and regulations. It is the responsibility of investors to comply with all relevant laws.

COMPANY REGISTRATION

Foreign companies may obtain registration by making an application in the correct form. Investors are advised to seek independent professional advice about forming legal structures which will best suit their needs. Investors should note that even though a foreign company registered in Papua New Guinea is incorporated in a foreign jurisdiction, it is still subject to the laws of Papua New Guinea as well as those of the jurisdiction of its own country.

A PNG-registered company has Papua New Guinea as its place of incorporation and is subject to the laws of Papua New Guinea.

A company incorporated in Papua New Guinea is required to have two directors, one of whom must be resident in the country. A foreign company registered in Papua New Guinea is required to appoint an agent who is a resident in the country.

All companies carrying on business in Papua New Guinea must register with the Registrar of Companies. It is an offence for a company to carry on business without registration with the Companies Office (within the Business Registration Division of the IPA).

The Trademarks Office exists to provide protection for property rights in respect of intellectual property held by persons both within and outside of Papua New Guinea who wish to carry on business in this country. Businesses are encouraged to register their trademarks in Papua New Guinea.

CERTIFICATION

Applications for certification should be lodged with the IPA using the prescribed form and accompanied by the prescribed fee.

Investors are encouraged to contact the IPA to receive the most up to date information on certification procedures as reforms may result in procedural changes.

Currently, however, the application form must be accompanied by supporting documentation, including the following, where appropriate:

- Either the Certificate of Incorporation or the Certificate of Registration as a foreign company;
- Statement of criminal record for natural persons and natural persons who are shareholders in a company which is applying for certification;
- Evidence of any change of names, if appropriate;
- Certificate of Registration of a Business Name, if applicable;
- A copy of the register of shareholders and directors if the applicant is a company;
- A copy of the register of directors if the applicant is a corporate body;
- Latest annual statement and the balance sheet of the applicant, if applicable;
- A copy of any agreement if a joint venture is proposed; and,
- Other documents that may be requested by the IPA.

Investors may wish to expand or diversify their business activities. In such cases, the terms of their certificate may be varied by lodging an application for variation on the prescribed form

TAXATION, CUSTOMS AND EXCISE

Ongoing comprehensive reforms of taxation and trade policies have resulted in Papua New Guinea having one of the lowest corporate income tax regimes in the region. Relative to neighbouring countries, it provides a very competitive footing.

All income tax returns are based on the income period 1 January to 31 December, unless approval is granted from the Internal Revenue Commission (IRC) to adopt a substituted tax year. Losses may be carried forward for up to seven years for normal businesses and indefinitely for primary industry businesses. They cannot be carried back.

When royalties are paid by a resident to an overseas recipient they are subject to a withholding tax of varying rates depending on how the royalty is paid. These rates may be modified by double tax treaties.

In its efforts to limit double taxation of incomes in Papua New Guinea, the Government has struck a number of agreements with key trading partners and continues to negotiate new agreements.

Companies engaged in business in Papua New Guinea must appoint a public officer who is the representative of the company in all its dealings with the IRC. The public officer need not be an employee or shareholder of the company but must be resident in Papua New Guinea.

Tax Clearances
Individuals leaving the country do not require tax clearance. However, amounts of money exceeding K50,000 per person, per year, can be remitted only after a tax clearance certificate has been obtained, certifying that no taxes are outstanding and all tax requirements to date have been met. In most cases, two weeks notice should be given. If money is being sent to a tax haven country, all amounts of money, irrespective of size, require tax clearance.

Adult residents of Papua New Guinea may remit up to the foreign currency equivalent of K500,000 each calendar year for any purpose, subject to taxation clearance. Certain categories of transactions do not count towards the remittance allowance. These include, for example, payments which are trade related involving the physical movement of goods.

Taxation of Companies
The world-wide income of resident companies and the Papua New Guinea-sourced income of non-residents is taxed.

Companies incorporated in Papua New Guinea or companies which carry on business in Papua New Guinea and whose management and control is located in Papua New Guinea are resident companies.

The tax laws define taxable income not as accounting profit, but as "assessable income, less all allowable deductions".

Since there are a number of items of both income and expense which require treatment for taxation purposes which are different from accounting practice and convention, taxable income frequently differs from accounting profit.

The main items of difference are depreciation, mining expenditure, valuation of inventories, provisions for such expenses as doubtful debts and deferred employee benefits, management fees, dividends and royalties and expenses for which there is a double deduction.

Specific time periods cover write-offs under the mining and petroleum provisions in the Income Tax Act, as well as a limit of 11 years in which exploration expenditure can be accumulated before a Special Mining Lease (SML) or Petroleum Development Licence (PDL) is granted.

Losses in primary production can be carried forward indefinitely. For a corporation to be able to carry forward losses, there must be continuity of either ownership or nature and conduct of business.

Income Tax Rates
The rates of company tax are:

- Resident companies not engaged in mining or petroleum operations - 25 per cent
- Non-resident companies, including those engaged in mining operations - 48 per cent
- Resident mining companies - 35 per cent
- Petroleum companies, resident and non-resident - 50 per cent

Dividend Withholding Tax
Whenever a Papua New Guinea resident company (other than a petroleum company), pays a dividend it must deduct 17 per cent dividend withholding tax (dwt) and remit it to the IRC. The dwt is legally a tax on the recipient of the dividend and its subsequent status therefore depends on the status of the recipient.

Sales Tax
Sales and services taxes, imposed on consumer goods and services, are levied by provincial governments. They provide a major source of revenue. The average tax is three per cent. Present tax reforms will see sales taxes replaced by a Value Added Tax (VAT) to be introduced in the near future. A formula on the collection of the provinces' share of the VAT is expected to be discussed with the provinces.

Note: Starting from July 2000, Sales tax has been replaced with the Value Added Tax (VAT).

Training Levy
All businesses whose annual payroll exceeds K100,000 are subject to a two per cent training levy. Internal expenditure on training is allowed as a deduction to reduce calculated payments.

Natural Resources Tax
Mining operations are required to pay a royalty of 1.25 per cent on the f.o.b. export sales value of mined products or net smelter returns. For petroleum products, it is based on the net wellhead value.

Export Duties
Export duties are imposed on exports of logs and fish, including shellfish, at varying rates.

Income Reporting System
Certain types of income must be reported to the IRC by 15 March in the following year. The system applies to certain business payments in a range of industries.

Management Fee (Withholding) Tax
All management and administration fees paid overseas for services performed outside Papua New Guinea are subject to a 17 per cent withholding tax. The tax does not apply to non-residents who are operating through a permanent branch in Papua New Guinea. In certain cases the tax does not apply where a double tax agreement is in force between Papua New Guinea and the recipient country.

Foreign Contractor (Withholding) Tax
When a person or company in Papua New Guinea engages a non-resident contractor to carry out building or construction work in Papua New Guinea they are required to pay withholding tax of 12 per cent.

Overseas Shipping
When freight is paid to an overseas ship carrying goods within or from Papua New Guinea, a withholding tax is deductible amounting to 2.4 per cent of the goods' freight charge.

Timber and Logging
Timber and logging companies are allowed to deduct the capital costs incurred in the building of access roads, the provision of housing and amenities for employees and the provision of structural improvements for the secondary processing of timber.

The total cost is deductible over either the term of the timber lease or 15 years, whichever is the lesser.

In addition, timber companies which reafforest logged areas qualify as primary producers and are allowed a deduction for the full cost of reafforestation, in the years in which the expenditure is incurred, as well as the indefinite carrying forward of losses.

Non-resident Insurers
Papua New Guinea businesses insured with non-resident insurers are required to pay tax on premiums paid to the insurer at the rate of 4.8 per cent of the gross premium.

TAXATION OF INDIVIDUALS

The Papua New Guinea-sourced income of non-resident individuals and the world-wide taxable income of resident individuals are taxed.

The Income Tax Act includes as a resident, anyone who has been in Papua New Guinea for more than six months during the year, whether continuously or intermittently, unless the person did not intend becoming a resident (the person did not enter Papua New Guinea with the intention of staying for more than six months).

Income Tax Rates
The top marginal tax rate is 35 per cent for those earning incomes above K20,000 per annum.

All remunerations paid by way of allowance to an employee for services rendered are fully-taxable in the hands of the employee, unless specifically exempted by the Income Tax Act.

Provisional Tax
Provisional tax is levied on non-salary or wages income to ensure that, as far as possible, all income is taxed in the year in which it is earned. Every taxpayer who earns in excess of K100 from non-salary or wages sources has a liability to pay provisional tax.

Land Tax
Land taxes are imposed by about 12 provincial governments plus the National Capital District Commission at fairly nominal levels.

Stamp Duties
The National Government imposes duties on documents evidencing certain transactions. The rates vary with the type of document.

CUSTOMS AND EXCISE

The Internal Revenue Commission uses the Harmonised Commodity Description and Coding System (H S Tariff).

Import Duties
All importers of goods are equally liable to import duty, irrespective of the country of origin. The same tariff is therefore applied to all countries.

All import and export duties are specified under the Customs Tariff Act 1990 but there are provisions to allow for exemptions or reductions to import and export duties after special consultants have investigated the warranting of such action.

The Government has been concerned at past excessive levels of protection for some domestic producers. Tariff reforms began with the 1996 National Budget. It was announced that the reforms will lead to significantly lower tariff bands for raw materials and inputs, intermediate products and final products, and a moderate protective tariff rate.

This tarrif reform exercise is allied with the introduction of the Value Added Tax.

The tariff reforms will take place over the next three years. The main policies include:

- Maintain general imports at 11% until the introduction of a VAT;
- Emphasise the duty drawback system for exporters;
- Phased reductions from 8% to 5% in 1997 for a range of business inputs;
- Maintain a 40% protective rate for viable infant industries;
- Move from non-tariff protection to the 40% protective rate;

Customs duties are imposed on most imports other than rice (part of the Papua New Guinea's staple diet), medical supplies and certain newspapers, magazines and children's books. Also exempt from import duties are certain specified goods, including:

- All aircraft, helicopters, spacecraft, air-cushion vehicles, hovercrafts, aircraft engines and all other parts specifically designed when purchased and imported by Papua New Guinea registered companies, holding PNG airline operator's licence.
- All cruise ships, excursion boats, ferry boats, tankers, refrigerated vessels, other vessels for the transport of goods, hovercrafts, fishing vessels, tugs, dredgers, floating or drilling platforms (except pleasure yachts and sports boats) when purchased and imported by Papua New Guinea registered shipping companies;
- Marine propulsion engines and outboard motors up to 100hp when purchased and imported by Papua New Guinea registered companies.

EXPORT PROMOTION

(1) Export Income

The export income incentive is available for firms producing new manufactured products and for firms producing certain other specified goods.

The Commissioner-General for Internal Revenue is responsible for declaring a product to be a new manufactured product and also for the issuance of a certificate to a company which intends to produce a new manufactured product. A company which manufactures a product which is subject to either tariff protection or quota protection without import parity pricing may not apply for a New Product Manufacturing Certificate.

Under the incentive, profits made from the export sale of qualifying goods are exempt from company income tax for the first three years of export and for the following four years, the profits on any increase in export sales over the average for the first three years are also exempt.

Goods which qualify for exemption include:

Activated carbon, electrical appliances, motor vehicles, artefacts, essential oils/oleoresins, paint, beverages ready for consumption, fabricated steel, paper products, fibreglass products, plastic products, biscuits, fishing nets, processed and canned meat products, flexible packaging materials, smoked fish, processed ginger, canned fruit and vegetables, flour, refined petroleum, foam products, rubber products, cement and concrete products, mouldings, plywood and laminated products, ceramics, chopsticks, glass products, ship and boat building and repairing products, cigarettes, hand tools, clothing and manufactured textiles, industrial and medical gases, soaps, treated and processed crocodile skins, confectionary, jewellery, dairy products, livestock feeds, wood pulp, dry cell batteries, matches and wooden furniture.

(2) Export Market Development

The market development cost exemption gives a deduction of income from taxable income equal to twice the amount of any expenditure on developing an export market (therefore it is a double deduction).
The incentive is available for the promotion of sales of goods manufactured totally in Papua New Guinea, or where the Papua New Guinea labour cost component exceeds 10 per cent of the sale price of the product. The double deduction is not absorbed by any exempt export sales income (see Export Income above).

It is not available for the sale of unprocessed primary commodities or for the marketing of services, so the tourism industry does not benefit from this incentive.

The types of expenditure to qualify include overseas publicity and advertising, market research, tender preparation, samples, trade fair expenses, overseas sales office expenses and certain travel costs.

NEW INDUSTRIES

(1) Pioneer Industries Scheme

The scheme provides a five year tax holiday for pioneer, or new, industries associated with the development of manufacturing-related activities, mainly downstream processing of Papua New Guinea's vast wealth of natural resources, in the country.

A pioneer industry refers to any industry producing a product or a service not yet established or in operation in Papua New Guinea or which manufactures goods solely for export. Pioneer status is granted to any industry, other than primary production or the primary processing of timber, or mining or quarrying. A product of any such industry is called a "pioneer product" and a service provided by any such industry is called a "pioneer service".

(2) Wage Subsidy

The wage subsidy promotes other objectives in addition to the pure development of new industries. The wage subsidy, by subsidising wages, promotes employment. However, the incentive is available only to those firms which possess a new manufactured products certificate.

A firm producing a manufactured product never before manufactured in Papua New Guinea or a product which is manufactured but where import substitution is incomplete may apply for a new products manufacturing certificate from the Commissioner-General for Internal Revenue.

This certificate enables the firm to gain both the wage subsidy and the export income exemption subject to the fulfilment of certain other criteria. To be eligible for the wage subsidy, a firm must not receive quota protection without import parity pricing or tariff protection such that the tariff on the final goods they produce exceeds the weighted average tariff on their imported inputs by more than 15%. The aim of these requirements is to prevent the establishment of inefficient industries which survive due to a combination of a high level of subsidy and protection.

Wage subsidy payments last for five years from the commencement of operations. For each full-time citizen employee, a subsidy is paid which is a proportion of the minimum wage relevant to that area. In the first year, the subsidy is equal to 40% of the prevailing minimum wage. This declines to 30%, 20%, 15% and 10% in subsequent years.

CAPITAL INVESTMENT

(1) Initial Year Accelerated Depreciation

The initial year accelerated depreciation allows the capital cost of certain new assets, converting existing oil-fired plant to non oil-fired plant, or improving the efficiency of fuel-using plant, to be written down at a faster rate than would otherwise be possible.

(2) Flexible Depreciation for Agriculture and Fishing

As with the accelerated depreciation provisions above, the flexible depreciation provisions allow the capital assets to be written down at a faster rate than would otherwise be possible. In the case of the flexible depreciation for agriculture and fisheries, expenditure on new plant or articles used in agricultural production or commercial fishing activities can be written off 100 per cent in the first year. Boats or ships exceeding seven metres in length are specifically excluded, together with ancillary equipment fitted to such vessels.

(3) Industrial Plant Depreciation

Industrial plant not previously used in Papua New Guinea is eligible for increased depreciation of up to 100 per cent of cost. The taxpayer may elect the amount to be claimed in any year, but not so as to create a loss.

To qualify, the plant must have a life exceeding five years and be used by the taxpayer or any other person (for example a lessee), in a manufacturing process. Expenditure on building housing for such plant, or for storing raw materials or finished products, also qualifies.

OTHER INCENTIVES

(1) Rural Development

The rural development incentive aims to spread development to the less-developed areas of the nation. Any new business activity started since 1 January, 1988, in a designated rural development area can gain a 10-year exemption from corporate income tax, provided it is engaged in one of the following industries:

- Agricultural production
- Manufacturing of any kind
- The restaurant or hotel trade
- Transport, storage or communication
- Real estate and business services (excluding financial institutions and insurance) or,
- Community, social and personal services.

Businesses involved in the exploitation of non-renewable resources (mainly mining and petroleum companies) are specifically excluded from the exemption. Losses arising from those exempt activities are deductible against taxable income from other activities.

(2) Rabaul Incentive

The Government has introduced a tax holiday for businesses in Rabaul. From 1 January 1996 until 31 December 2000, businesses operating in Rabaul will be able to enjoy a five year tax holiday. The tax holiday is aimed at restoring the town following the volcano eruptions in 1994.

(3) Primary Production Investment

Development expenditure by companies on land for primary production is deductible by the shareholders of those companies, if the company transfers the deduction to them. (Primary production development expenditure is defined to include the cost of assets used for agricultural production.)

The incentive is different from other incentives in that it allows the deduction by shareholders against their personal income tax liabilities. The amount surrendered to each shareholder is in proportion to the respective amounts of their paid up capital, (paid on or after 1 January 1987). The total deduction available to a shareholder may not exceed the total amount paid on their shares. Shareholders may waive their entitlement if they wish.

The rationale for this incentive is that some of the agricultural sector is not recording taxable profits so that a deduction against company income tax would be an irrelevance. Outright deductions are allowed for certain capital expenditure including clearing or preparing or conserving land for agriculture, the eradication of pests, labourers' accommodation and for the conservation and conveyance of water. Also, an initial accelerated depreciation deduction is allowed for new agricultural plant with a life exceeding five years.

Losses incurred in carrying on a primary production business can be carried forward indefinitely - they are not restricted to the seven year limit that applies generally to company tax losses.

(4) Staff Training Deductions

The double deduction for staff training allows a double deduction against company income tax for the payment of salary and wages to:

- Registered apprentices;
- Citizen employees attending a full-time training course at a government training institute or a prescribed place of tertiary education; and,
- Training officers engaged wholly in training or educational activities - not engaged directly in deriving the employer's income.

The tax saving from these deductions is limited to 75 per cent of actual expenditure incurred.

(5) Staff Training Levy

All businesses whose annual payroll exceeds K100,000 are subject to a two per cent training levy calculated on the taxable salary and wages, including benefits, of all personnel. The levy is assessed on an annual basis. The amount of the levy payable is reduced by qualifying training expenses incurred in the training of citizen employees. Qualifying training expenses are very widely defined.

(6) Solar Heating

This incentive promotes the use of natural resources instead of fossil fuels to provide energy sources. In Papua New Guinea, solar energy is extensively used especially for the heating of domestic water supplies. Expenditure on the acquisition and installation of solar heating plant for use in deriving income is allowable as an outright deduction.

(7) Exemption of Certain Interest Income

Interest income received by persons and corporations, including non-resident companies and individuals, from deposits lodged with licensed financial institutions within Papua New Guinea is exempt from income tax.

(8) Import Duty Drawback

Duty drawback is a rebate paid to exporting manufacturers, when they export goods, equal to the amount of duty already paid on the raw materials. It is offered so that locally-manufactured goods can compete effectively in overseas markets.

Requests for the consideration of duty drawback must include a detailed description of the manufacturing process involved, including the nature and volume of inputs used, accompanied by unit cost data based on import/export documents and commercial invoices.

(9) Assistance for Project Start-Up

Papua New Guinea offers other investment incentives such as the Feasibility Study Grant Scheme and start-up loans for Papua New Guinea entrepreneurs - which is of particular interest to foreign investors who wish to enter into joint ventures with Papua New Guinea companies. Investors interested in obtaining further information about these forms of assistance are encouraged to contact the Investment Promotion Authority for further information.

(10) Market Access Privileges

Papua New Guinea has preferential access to a number of overseas markets. Products of Papua New Guinea origin are allowed duty-free access to Australia, New Zealand and the European Community under the PNG - Australia Trade & Commercial Relations Agreement (PATCRA) and South Pacific Regional Trade & Economic Cooperation Agreement (SPARTECA) and the Lome Convention respectively. Local products also have preferential access to numerous other developed countries including Japan and the United States of America under the GSP system.

Further, Papua New Guinea qualifies as an underdeveloped country entitled to the benefits of the US General System of Preferences and enjoys similar privileges in Japan and Canada. Further information about Papua New Guinea's market access privileges should be directed, in the first instance, to the Investment Promotion Authority.

(11) Tariff Exemptions or Reductions

Proposals for the consideration of any exemption or reduction in duty are examined on the merit of each case depending upon the overall benefit to the country and revenue implications within the cash-flow estimate by the Government. Such matters are handled by the Internal Revenue Commission, within the Department of Finance, in consultation with other administrative departments when considered necessary.

To assist the IRC and the Department in its decision, any organisation or investor seeking any duty concessions should provide all the cost data with supportive evidence covering broad aspects such as quantum of investment, nature of project, types of materials, machinery, equipment, annual importation and corresponding value at c.i.f. level whether the manufacturing unit is exclusively export orientated by utilising national resources and to what extent locally-procured materials will be utilised.

(12) Imports of Specialised Capital Equipment

The Import of certain specialised capital equipment is exempt from duty. Such equipment must not be readily available in Papua New Guinea and can be imported only on a temporary basis for a specific purpose and a specific time. The importers must satisfy the Commissioner-General of Internal Revenue that the equipment will be used on an approved project and a security must be lodged for the period of temporary importation.

The importer must undertake to re-export the equipment at the end of the specified activity. This exemption is expected to be particularly welcome for the mining and petroleum industries, since equipment that they require for exploration is included.

Also eligible for duty exemption are imports of capital equipment which will be used in the establishment of new industries or the expansion of existing industries, provided that approval for importation has been given by the Commissioner General and that the equipment is not available in Papua New Guinea. It applies to manufacturing industry only.

(13) Tax-Free Bank Deposit Interest

All interest paid by registered financial institutions in Papua New Guinea is exempt from tax.

When interest is paid by a Papua New Guinea resident company to an overseas recipient it is generally free of tax but may, in some circumstances, be subject to a withholding tax (45% of the gross amount).

LEGAL NATURE OF THE PAPUA NEW GUINEA PETROLEUM ARRANGEMENT[2]

Petroleum exploration and development in Papua New Guinea (PNG) are carried out under a policy regime that fixes in advance, conditions under which rights to explore for and produce petroleum are granted. The legal regime is set out primarily in the legislation[1] and complemented by petroleum agreements that are entered into in respect of each exploration licence.[2]

Some countries do not use the legislation to set out the terms and conditions of petroleum development. If there is such a law, it is of a general nature. The government grants exploration and production titles on the basis of individually negotiated agreements.[3]

Other countries take the middle ground by using a hybrid system of fixing the terms of petroleum exploration and production, partly by legislation and partly by agreements. In such cases, certain fundamental terms of petroleum exploration and production are set out in the legislation while the specific terms and conditions are negotiated and settled by agreements.[4]

Petroleum agreements are used in many countries as the main policy instruments, to set the scope of, and govern petroleum exploration and production. These agreements are used exclusively or in association with petroleum legislation.

The public and private arrangements under which petroleum exploration and production are authorised and undertaken have gone through a variety of phases since the emergence of petroleum as an internationally traded commodity, from the earliest grants of concessions by various sovereigns in the Middle East to the modern concessions, joint venture agreements, service contracts, production sharing contracts or combination of one or more of these traditional forms of petroleum arrangements.

[2] Melvin Yalapan Law School, University of Papua New Guinea.

Petroleum arrangements of some countries have the characteristics of more than one formally recognised legal arrangements. This paper will endeavour to identify and consider the salient features of these legal arrangements and apply them to the Papua New Guinea's (PNG) petroleum arrangement. The object of this exercise will be, firstly, to highlight the fundamental features of PNG's petroleum arrangement and, secondly, to classify the PNG's petroleum arrangement under one or more of the recognised forms of petroleum arrangements that are in use in the petroleum industry, globally.

A. Different Petroleum Arrangements

Whilst various legal arrangements are used by different countries to secure and regulate petroleum exploration and production, they deal with common considerations that are essential for petroleum exploration and production. It is the treatment of these features that distinguish the different legal arrangements under which petroleum development is conducted.

(a) Concessions

The history of petroleum agreements begins with the granting of an oil concession by the Persian Government to William D'Arcy in 1901.[5] The original 1901 D'Arcy concession was granted over the whole of the Persian Empire with the exception of 5 provinces, covering 480,000 square miles. Concessions granted by the rulers of Abu Dhabi and Kuwait covered their entire countries.[6] The concessions were granted for very long periods[3] and on modest fiscal terms.[7] Professor Charles Lipton summarised the traditional concession arrangement as follows:

> "It was a long term agreement. 99 years was not untypical. It created enclave and give rise to exception to the general law application. Management 'prerogative' were left to the operating company. There was no government participation in the basic decisions such as the rate of operation or marketing. The investor provided all capital typically, and was entitled to all profits, originally paying the government a per ton royalty."*[8]*

Thus under the traditional concession, the concessionaire was granted, and had, the exclusive right to explore for, produce and deal with petroleum within the concession area. The oil companies therefore made decisions affecting all aspects of the petroleum operation. In terms of petroleum exploration, it meant that the oil companies decided exclusively how much or how little exploration they wished to undertake. Upon discovery, the oil companies decided the rate, extent and level of production.[9]

The companies also had, in a traditional concession, by the grant of the concession, title to the petroleum *in situ*. The host government, or ruler, normally received an initial consideration, roughly amounting to the modern day signature bonus and only the right to receive financial return from the petroleum operation. Originally, this was in the form of royalty payment, and later royalty and taxes.[10]

The scope of the traditional concession is startling when other aspects of a concession are considered. The 1901 Mexican petroleum law, for example, authorised, granting of liberal tax exemption, the right to import machinery, equipment and materials duty free and other special privileges, which included the right to expropriate land necessary to conduct petroleum operations.[11]

The situation existed until the late 1950's when governments with the aid of progress in technology, considerable discovery of new oil fields and worldwide dependence on oil, broke the shackle that underpinned the traditional concession arrangement. These enabled governments to demand and secure improved terms under which the petroleum resources located within their territories could be developed.

The post 1950's concessions provided significant new terms. The financial return to the host country increased significantly with provisions for equitable profit sharing. The petroleum acreages were reduced, and provisions for relinquishment of the concession areas or part of the concession areas, driven by work program and budget were introduced. It was during this period that governments began to take direct equity participation in petroleum projects. In addition, host governments also enacted legislation that dealt specifically with petroleum exploration and production, thus establishing uniformity the basic terms under which petroleum exploration and production were undertaken within the country.[12]

The increased concerns of governments with regard to ownership and control of the natural resources led to the assertion of permanent sovereignty over the natural resources within the states' territories. The 1962 *UN Resolution on the Permanent Sovereignty over Natural Resources[13]* is the reflection of the assertion of sovereignty, particularly by the newly independent third world governments, to natural resources within their territories.

The *UN Resolution on the Permanent Sovereignty over Natural Resources* also provided further impetus for the creation of alternative legal arrangements for petroleum development. These were structured not only to enable host states to retain ownership of the resources *in situ* in their national boundaries but at the same time, to allow oil companies to conduct petroleum operation in the country. Old concession arrangements were revised and new concession arrangements were established.[14]

The modern concessions differ in important respect from the traditional form of concession. Under the new concession arrangements:

> "...ownership of petroleum in the ground remains with the State, and at best provision is made for 'sharing' of petroleum at the well-head between governments and companies. Power of management and control over operations are vested in the government. Duration is shorter and the size of the area covered by the agreement considerably smaller than under the traditional concession".*[15]*

Provisions for relinquishment of, and reduction in, the concession areas were introduced. Minimum work and expenditure commitments were established. Requirements for training of national work force and procurement of local goods and services were also introduced. In some instances, provisions were made for crude oil to be made available for local consumption and host states also participated in the petroleum development either directly or through a state enterprise. Generally, greater powers of management and control of petroleum development shifted from the oil companies to the host states. One can say that the entire bundle of rights that governed petroleum development changed hands, from the oil companies to the host governments.

New legal arrangements for petroleum development were also developed and introduced. Such arrangements included joint venture agreements, service contracts and production sharing contracts.

(b) Joint Ventures

The oil companies traditionally prefer partnership with the host government in the petroleum exploration and production to be limited to *profit sharing.*[16] As host governments become conscious of the need to actively participate in petroleum development, they began pressing for greater control over the resources in their territories.

Under the traditional concessions, the near total control exercised by the companies was based on its ownership of the petroleum resources. However, the exclusive ownership of the petroleum resources by the concessionaire naturally militated against the desire by governments to own the petroleum resources located in their territory and to develop these resources to pursue national development objectives. The joint venture arrangement was therefore developed to realise these national goals and aspirations.

The joint venture agreement was pioneered as a new form of petroleum arrangement by Italian State Oil Company – ENI. The first of such agreement was entered into between ENI through its subsidiary Agip Mineraria and the National Iranian Oil Company (NIOC). The Agip-NIOC Joint Venture was established under a joint stock company, and a joint Board of Directors managed the company.[17]

Under the joint venture arrangement, the entire petroleum operation is a joint activity. A joint operation company is formed between the host country (more usually the host country's national oil company), and the company to develop the petroleum reserves. The acreage is jointly licensed and the petroleum operation is jointly conducted, consistent with the joint ownership of the venture. However, the entire exploration expenditure is financed solely by the oil company. In the event of a commercial discovery, the oil company is fully reimbursed either in kind or out of revenue earned either directly by the state or through the allocation of part of the state's share of the petroleum produced. *[18]* The joint venture arrangement is therefore a partnership arrangement between the state through its national oil company and the non-state oil company, under an arrangement of share equity, ownership rights and interest in the project. Martin Olisa summarised the arrangement as follows:
"The structure and content of various joint ventures vary considerably...(On) the national side you have private, or government controlled enterprises. The foreign enterprise supplies the risk capital for, and carries out, exploration. Explorations expenses in whole or in part are recoverable from production, if obtained. If commercial production is obtained, an equity joint venture company is established as an operating company. Participation may be on 50:50 basis or one 'partner' may be in a minority position, in which case, a management contract is entered into."*[19]*

The joint venture arrangement was therefore seen as a realisation of host governments' aspirations, not only to take greater management and control over the natural resources within their territories, but also as a realisation of joint ownership of the exploration and production titles.

(c) Production sharing Contract

The "Production Sharing Contract" was pioneered in Indonesia in 1967 and is still used there. Libya, Egypt, India, Ghana, Malaysia and Trinidad and Tobago are some of the countries that also use this contractual arrangement.[20] A. Zen Umar Purba summarised the main features of the Indonesian Production Sharing Contract as follows:

- management of the oil operations rest with PERTAMINA.[21]

- at the time the contract is signed, the contractor pays a bonus to PERTAMINA, which can be treated as a tax credit.

- exploration expenses are recoverable if oil is discovered by contractor.

- after the exploration cost and expenses are deducted from the oil extracted, the balance (after tax) is divided under a certain formula, mainly 85%:15% in favour of PERTAMINA.

- the contractor is required to spare 8.5% of its portion (based on the above formula) to supply the domestic market in Indonesia.

- after a certain period of time, the contractor has to relinquish areas of its operations, the

area must be re-surrendered if oil is not discovered, or if at the end of the exploration stage, the areas are considered not commercially viable.
- title to equipment used in the exploration rest with PERTAMINA as soon as the goods enter Indonesian customs."[22]

Under the production sharing contract arrangement, the exploration and production of petroleum can be undertaken only by the State, and is exclusively carried out by the State enterprises. The oil company has no proprietary interest in the petroleum exploration and production titles. The company is engaged as a contractor for the state enterprise to undertake services that cannot or yet to be undertaken by the state enterprise.[23]

Although, the oil companies are engaged as contractors to undertake petroleum operations, they however bear all the exploration risk so that if no commercial discovery of petroleum is made, the loss is borne by the contractor. In the event of a commercial discovery, the contractor is entitled to be reimbursed by a percentage of the oil produced. This is achieved by applying portions of petroleum produced as *"cost oil,"* to defray the pre-development expenditure. Once all the authorised expenses have been deducted up to the maximum percentage of "cost oil" set out in the agreement, the remaining oil, usually called the *"profit oil,"* (less *"cost oil,"*) is shared between the contractor and the national oil company in accordance with an agreed formula.[24]

Ownership of the petroleum, either in the ground or as produced, rest with the state until it reaches the point of export. This differs from the traditional concession arrangement where title in petroleum rest in the oil company, and under the new concession arrangement where the petroleum companies acquire title to the petroleum at the wellhead.

The legal rational for using the production sharing contract is that from the host government's standpoint, it does not involve surrender of the host country's sovereignty in the title to the resource. In entering into a production sharing contract, the company receives less than title or interest to the oil.[25]

(d) Service Contracts

The final form of petroleum exploration and production arrangement that require specific consideration for the purpose of this paper is the service contract. Under this contractual arrangement, the foreign oil company is engaged by the national oil company to conduct petroleum exploration for a fee or a share of production. The oil company also provides the host country and its national oil company with technical services and information relating to the development of the petroleum resources.

Upon discovery of petroleum in the area, the national oil company engages the foreign oil company as its agent to produce the oil, and if it so agrees, also to market the oil produced on behalf of the national oil company. The feature of a service contract is summarised as follows: "The national oil company is by law the sole titular holder of the area under the agreement. All petroleum deposit and oil and/or gas produced are the property of the national oil company at the wellhead. The foreign company either directly or through a subsidiary, acts as general contractor for the national oil company and as such carries out, in the name and on behalf the latter, all operations necessary for exploration and development of oil deposits. Thus the contractor is not a concession holder or partner, but merely a hired agent."*[26]*

In a pure service contract, the host country's national oil company would contract the oil company to perform a specified service for a flat fee. However, in view of the difficulties that countries face in obtaining capital to finance the payment of service fees, some agreements provide that the contractor may be paid in kind with a certain specified amount of production from the acreage, the subject of the service contract. Thus service contracts can be arranged as *Risk-Service Contract* or *Service Contract (Non-Risk)*. Under a Risk-Service Contract arrangement, the host government pays for the services of the oil companies in cash and not in kind. On the other hand, under the Service Contract (Non-Risk) arrangement, the oil company is paid a flat rate for its services usually by applying a percentage of the oil produced.[27]

Generally, the oil company provides all the risk capital. If oil is found, the amount spent in exploration is "deemed" as loan to the national oil company to be debited from the national oil company's accounts. The oil company may also sell for the national oil company, if agreed, the oil produced. From the revenue earned by the national oil company, a percentage is applied towards the repayment of the "deemed loan" until the loan is reduced to zero.[28]

The title in the petroleum *in situ* rests in the state and upon production is transferred at the wellhead to the national oil company. The oil company does not acquire exploration or production title nor does it acquire ownership to the petroleum produced at any stage of the production chain. It is engaged simply as an agent to the national oil company and is paid a fee either in cash or in kind from the oil produced, in consideration for the services rendered.

Service contracts are used in countries like Venezuela, Brazil and Iran as a form of legal arrangement for the development of petroleum located within the territories of these countries.[29]

(e) Petroleum Arrangements

Petroleum arrangements developed post 1950's also included contracts under names such as Operations Agreement[30] and Works and Technical Services Agreement.[31]

The post 1950's contractual arrangements have different *"labels"* but they have common objectives and hence share common features. For instance, the production sharing contract petroleum arrangement is similar in terms to the service contract arrangement. The arrangements differ from each other on the consideration as to who bears the exploration risk. In a service contract, the title to petroleum *in situ* rests with the host state through its national oil company and the oil company is engaged by the national oil company as a contractor to conduct petroleum operations for consideration either in cash or in kind from petroleum produced from the petroleum operations. The exploration and production risk rest with the national oil company or the host government. However, under the production sharing contract, the oil company undertakes the petroleum exploration and production at its risk. It then takes the share of production as *"cost oil."* The balance of the production, which is normally termed *"profit oil,"* is shared between the host government or its national oil company and the oil company. On the other hand, under the joint venture structure, title to the licence and the means of production are jointly held between the state and the oil companies, and petroleum is jointly produced and sold. The following features are common in the post-1950 petroleum arrangements.[32]

- (i) The risk of exploration is borne by the oil company and the cost of exploration is not recoverable unless a commercial discovery is made.
- (ii) The exploration phase is distinguished from the production phase. Accordingly, if no significant discovery of petroleum is made within the stipulated period, the company must surrender the acreage.
- (iii) The oil company is subjected to minimum work and expenditure program.
- (iv) The oil company is subject to obligations to provide information and data to the host government.
- (v) Provisions are made for division of revenue generated by the projects which feature increased financial take by governments in the form of income tax and revenue from equity in the projects.
- (vi) Provisions are made for procurement of local goods and services and for the training and employment of nationals.

There are variances in the treatment of different considerations under different petroleum arrangements. Notable among these is the treatment of title in the oil produced, whether title in the oil is acquired by the oil company either at the point of export or at the wellhead. The second consideration relates to exploration and production risk – whether the exploration and production risk is borne by the oil company or the host government. The third consideration relates to the fiscal arrangement under which governments take active participation in the management and control over the project; in essence, equity participation in the project.

The key features of the petroleum titular system, the arrangement for State equity participation under the petroleum arrangements and the fiscal regime applicable to petroleum exploration and development will be considered in some details with particular reference to the PNG's petroleum arrangement.

B. PNG's Petroleum Exploration and Production Licencing Regime

The PNG legal and fiscal regime that governs petroleum development could be described as that which is governed primarily by legislation. The terms for the granting of petroleum exploration and production licences are set out in the legislation[33] and these are supplemented by details set out in the petroleum licence.

The basic considerations in dealing with natural resources development is firstly, the question of who has the title to the resources and secondly, who has right to exclusive use, control or management of the resources. Generally, the owner of the resources would have the right to use, control and manage the exploitation of these resources. Ownership therefore underpins property rights and provides the basis to manage the exploitation of the resources.[34]

The English Common Law presumes that the owner of the land is entitled to all that is located above and below the land*; cujus est solum ejus est usque ad colum et usque ad inferos*. Under common law, minerals naturally occurring form part of the land on which they are situated unless these minerals are specifically severed from the crown land grant. The only exceptions are the royal metals; gold and silver, which remain subject to crown ownership, notwithstanding the crown grant of the land on which minerals are naturally occurring.[35]

PNG's natural resources laws adopted the practice of reserving title to mineral and petroleum *in situ* exclusively to the State.[36] Ownership in resources *in situ* therefore rests with the State. The vesting of ownership of mineral and petroleum resources *in situ* together with the vesting of the prerogative to licence the exploration and production of these resources, and the prerogative to manage the exploration and development of same, provides the foundation of resources law. It underpins the legal arrangement under which the resources are developed. The prerogative to manage the exploitation of these resources is a significant factor that one would need to examine in the quest to identify the contractual arrangement of the PNG's petroleum regime. This is underlined by the fact that despite State ownership of the petroleum naturally occurring, the resources will be developed by private enterprise and hence the petroleum policy regime is geared towards encouraging private sector investment in petroleum development.

The licensing system governing petroleum exploration and production is therefore the ultimate exercise of the host state's ownership of these resources and the exercise of the management prerogative is the ultimate exercise of sovereignty over the exploration and production of the resources that lay within its national boundaries.

(a) Exploration Licence

The PNG's petroleum exploration and development licensing system is primarily a two-tier system. A Petroleum Prospecting Licence (PPL) is an exploration licence issued to an oil company pursuant to which the oil company undertakes petroleum exploration.[37] The

Petroleum Development Licence (PDL) is a production licence[38] issued to the holder of a PPL upon commercial discovery of petroleum, to produce and deal with the petroleum produced within the acreage.

The process of granting a PPL commences on application for or upon invitation by the Minister, for a PPL.[39] For the purpose of granting an exploration or a production licence, the earth's surface is divided up into gratucular sections called-blocks, comprising five minutes longitudes and five minutes latitude.[40] An application for a PPL would be made in respect of not more than 60 blocks[41]and in special circumstances the minimum acreage could be increased to 200 blocks.[42]

The conditions under which petroleum exploration and production will be undertaken are prescribed by legislation.[43] A PPL is granted for a term not exceeding 6 years[44]and renewable for a further term of 5 years but for a reduced area,[45] and is also subject to work and expenditure requirements.[46]

A licence sets out the basic terms and conditions under which petroleum exploration will be undertaken.[47]

Where petroleum discovery is made in a exploration acreage, a declaration would be made of a location, within the exploration acreage, of a petroleum discovery. [48] Subsequent to the declaration of a location, the oil company may apply for and be granted a further extension of the exploration licence for a further period of not more than 3 years.[49]

A PPL confers on the licensee the exclusive right to explore for petroleum, to carry out appraisal work in respect of the petroleum discovery, and to undertake such task as are necessary to otherwise explore for, produce and sell or otherwise disposed of petroleum produced. The legislation provides the scope of a PPL as follows:

> "A petroleum prospecting licence, while it remains in force, confers on the licensee, subject to this Act, and to the conditions specified in the licence, the exclusive right to explore for petroleum, and to carry out appraisal of a petroleum discovery, and to carry on such operations and execute such works as are necessary for those purposes, in the licence area, including the construction and operations of water lines, tests for appraisal of a petroleum pool (including the construction in accordance with the authorization and disposal), and the recovery and sale or other disposal of all petroleum so produced."*[50]*

As noted, the legislation gives sufficient scope and rights, in exclusivity, to the holder of an exploration licence to explore for, produce and sell or dispose of petroleum produced within the exploration acreage. The scope of a PPL is therefore as wide as a PDL. The case on point is the Moran Petroleum Project.[51] In September 1996, oil was discovered in Moran IX sidetrack well in PDL 2.[52] In early 1997, the State approved the PDL 2 (Kutubu Joint Venture) to carry out an Extended Well Test Program (EWT)[53] within PDL 2 pursuant to which the PDL 2 licensee produced oil within the block under the EWT program.[54]

Moreover, the State proceeded to approve the licence holders of PPL 138[55] to conduct EWT program using Moran 4 well and the PPL 138 licensees produced oil within the exploration licence area from Moran 4 exploration well under a EWT program. Hence, oil was produced at PPL 138 under the EWT program prior to carving out the area and grant of PDL.[56] The production of petroleum at Moran 4 well within Moran PPL 138 is a case on point to demonstrate that the scope of a PPL - an exploration licence, includes exclusive rights not only to explore for, but also to produce and sell or dispose of, petroleum produced within the exploration acreage. A PPL could also contain incidental features as are necessary to undertake and facilitate production of oil within the PPL, including construction of flow-lines and gathering lines, roads and bridges, and other infrastructure.

Technical justifications can be advanced to justify oil production within the exploration acreage under an EWT program but consideration of the same is not within the scope of this paper. The fact that petroleum production is undertaken within the exploration acreage is, for the purposes of this paper, sufficient endorsement of the view that petroleum production can be undertaken under an exploration licence in the PNG's petroleum arrangement.
(b) Petroleum Retention Licence
An exploration licensee may also exclusively apply for a Petroleum Retention Licence (retention licence) in respect of blocks within the exploration acreage in which petroleum is located.[57] This may be done within 2 years from the date on which the blocks were declared as a location.[58]

A retention licence can be issued over *"... a gas field or, a part of the gas field or, for better administration of petroleum activities."* [59] The provision is designed primarily to allow holders of an exploration licence to retain and hold natural gas discoveries within the acreage pending commercial extraction of the same. However, provisions are also made for retention licence to be issued in respect of oil discoveries within the acreage "... *for better administration of petroleum activities."* The proviso creates scope for retention licences to be issued in respect of marginal oil fields where the reserves cannot be commercially produced.[60] That is, where a discovery is over a marginal field and it is not commercially viable to produce the petroleum discovered within the location, a retention licence may be issued over the respective blocks in the exploration acreage, which would allow the exploration licensee to retain the discovery pending further appraisal, further and additional discovery and commercial production of the petroleum discovered within the acreage.[61]

A retention licence may be granted for 5 years[62]and may be extended for further terms of 5 years at each extension.[63] Accordingly, a retention licence can be further extended over number of 5 years extension periods before commercial production can be realised. It therefore allows a holder of an exploration licence to hold onto the acreage pending commercial production of the discovery.[64]
(c) Petroleum Development Licence

If significant petroleum discovery is made that can sustain commercial production, a PDL, which is the production licence, will be issued to the holder of the PPL.[65] The basic requirement of a PDL is fixed by legislation.[66] A PDL is issued to the holder of an exploration or retention licence for a period not exceeding 25 years, renewable for a term not exceeding 20 years.[67]

A PDL confers on the licensee the exclusive rights to explore for petroleum within the licence area, to produce petroleum within the licence area, to sell or otherwise disposed of petroleum so produced and to carry out such other works in the licence area as are necessary to conduct petroleum operations in accordance with the terms of the licence.[68] The works necessary to carry out petroleum operations include construction of flow lines and gathering lines, roads, bridges and other civil works, airports, seaports and related facilities.[69]

In the case of the Kutubu project, the PDL 2 licensees also own and operate the only oil pipeline in PNG that transport oil from the oil fields to the offshore loading terminal.

The development licensee is therefore licensed not only to produce and sell or disposed of petroleum produced, but also the added right to *"...carry on such operations and execute such work as are necessary for or in connection..."* with carrying out petroleum operations.[70]

C. Charecteristics of Petroleum Agreements

The PNG petroleum agreements deal with matters, which include State equity participation, foreign currency management, local business development and procurement of local goods and services. For the purpose of this paper, particular consideration is given to those provisions dealing with State equity participation.

The State takes its share of the revenue from production and sale of petroleum, primarily from petroleum taxation computed and collected under the *Income Tax Act*,[71] petroleum royalty and from direct equity participation in the project. In computing the State's share of the petroleum produced or the revenue derived from sale of petroleum produced within the acreage, and the oil companies' share of the petroleum produced, the amount taken up by the State pursuant to the exercise of its rights to take equity participation in the petroleum project within a license area is regarded and treated by oil companies as the State's share of the oil or revenue. Accordingly, the State equity participation policy regime is an important element of the State's petroleum policy regime, and that which forms the core of the petroleum agreement.

The terms under which the State may take equity participation in the petroleum project are set out in the petroleum agreements entered into in respect of each PPL. The petroleum agreements are entered into pursuant to the petroleum legislation.[72] The respective petroleum agreements, as a matter of policy, are entered into prior to discovery of petroleum. Therefore the subsequent PDL incorporates provisions of both the negotiated agreement and legislation, which form the conditions of the PDL.[73] Both instruments are therefore needed to undertake petroleum development.

The detailed features of State equity participation in a petroleum project are not covered by the legislation[74] but are set out in the respective petroleum agreements. This is a major feature of the PNG's petroleum arrangement that can be termed as *the heart* of the petroleum agreement. It is therefore the fiscal arrangement and the arrangement for the State's equity participation in the projects that distinguish the PNG's petroleum agreement from other recognised forms of petroleum agreements.

The basis of the State's equity participation in petroleum projects is legislatively framed[75] and forms part and parcel of the State's petroleum policy regime. The genesis of the State equity participation policy can be traced backed to the 1976 petroleum policy white paper which provides that the government's *"total financial take"* from oil produced in any production licence area follows:

> "(I) 11/4 percent royalty on well-head value of production;
> (II) a percentage income tax at a rate of 50 per cent of taxable income;
> (III) an additional profits tax at rate 50 per cent of after tax cash flow after total investment has been recouped with a money returned of 25 per cent;
> (IV) State participation in development of commercial fields on 'carried interest' principles"[76] (My emphasis).

The State's equity participation in petroleum projects is, therefore, on the basis of *"carried interest principles."*

As a matter of practice, the holder of a PPL is advised to enter into a petroleum agreement with the State before any well is drilled in the exploration acreage. The agreement defines, *inter alia,* the State's equity participation in the subsequent petroleum discovery. [77] The agreements state that the State has an option to take equity participation in the project, up to the nominated

percentage.[78] It can also elect not to take equity participation in a particular project. For instance, the *PPL 100 (Kutubu) Petroleum Agreement*, provides that:
"...the State may acquire for a Nominee of the State from the Oil Companies constituting the Development Licensee in the Development License Area, an unencumbered ... interest in the venture interest attributable to the Development Licence Area... up to nominated percentage not exceeding twenty – two and one-half percent (22 ½%) and where the State has acquired such a Joint Venture Interest for a Nominee of the State, the Nominee of the State shall have the right to share... production from that Development Licence Area equal to the nominated percentage,..."*[79]*

The provisions of the petroleum agreement[80] set out the terms under which the State will take equity participation in the project.[81] The State upon electing to take equity participation in the project acquires equity through its Nominee,[82] to the value of the nominated percentage.[83] It also enters into joint venture arrangement with the oil companies that are holders of the PDL. In entering into a joint venture agreement with the oil companies, the State's Nominee becomes a joint participant under the joint venture arrangement,[84] effectively a tenant in common of the PDL under the joint venture structure with the other joint participants. In this respect it also subscribes to all licences, permits and authorisations necessary for the conduct of project development as a joint venturer and holds the petroleum titles jointly and severally with the oil companies in the joint venture as a tenant in common.

The State in taking up equity in the project, through its Nominee, also becomes a joint venturer and a joint licensee of the PDL. The non-State joint venturers finance the Nominee's *pro rata* percentage of exploration, development and other cost and expenditures under the *"carried interest"* arrangement. Under the arrangement, the amount owed to the oil companies by the Nominee is "deemed" as a loan from the oil companies to the Nominee at a commercial interest rate, to be debited from the Nominee's revenue from its proportionate share of the petroleum produced within that PDL.[85]

The production titleholders acquire title to the petroleum, upon production, at the wellhead. Similarly, the State, through the Nominee, as joint licensee and tenant in common, acquires title to petroleum produced at the wellhead. However, the Nominee does not lift the petroleum produced and deal with oil produced during the period it has outstanding liability to the oil companies under the *carried interest* arrangement. Instead, the oil companies lift the State's proportionate share of the petroleum produced, sell same and apply the revenue derived to defray the liability of the State under the *carried interest* arrangement. When the aggregate of the exploration, development and operation expenditures, proportionately owed to the respective oil companies, is reduced to zero, the *carried interest* arrangement is discharged and the State, through the Nominee, is able to take petroleum, unencumbered, at the well-head and sell or dispose of same as a joint licensee and a member of the joint venture.

The liability to the oil companies is computed, applying a pre-agreed formula.[86] This is ascertained, at any given time, by deducting from the State's proportionate share of the revenue earned, the *pro rata* share of exploration and capital expenditures, and amount spent by the oil companies attributable to the oil production. The arrangement remains in place for the duration of the period when income from the share of oil produced, attributable to the State's equity participation, is insufficient to discharge its liability to the oil companies.

The legal arrangement under which the State equity participation is accommodated and facilitated by the oil companies constituting the relevant licence is similar to the arrangement under the joint venture agreement.[87]
D. Income Tax Treatment of the "Carried Interest Arrangement"

The treatment of the petroleum exploration and production titles in the petroleum legislation and the petroleum agreements is followed through in the taxation regime.[88] Under the taxation regime, a petroleum project is *"re-fenced"* for taxation purposes and taxed on project basis.[89] That is, each oil company as a taxpayer (taxpayer) is assessed in relation to each project as if the assessable income of the taxpayer from petroleum operations attributable to the petroleum project was the only assessable income derived by that taxpayer, and conversely, all allowable deductions are deducted against future income from the petroleum project.[90]

For petroleum tax purposes, the pre-PDL exploration expenditures incurred by the taxpayer within the relevant exploration licence area in relation to a petroleum project are carried forward and accumulated for 20 years.[91] Upon commencement of petroleum production, the exploration expenditure is deducted from the income derived by the taxpayer from sale of petroleum produced from petroleum operations conducted within the PDL area. The exploration expenditure incurred in relation to the PDL is reduced; firstly in paying for the exploration expenditure incurred by the taxpayer in relation to the PDL in the relevant year of income; and secondly, any excess amount is applied to reduce the exploration expenditure incurred by the taxpayer in relation the PDL against the expenses earliest incurred within the 20 years period to the year of income, until the amount is fully recovered. [92] This has the effect of accelerating the recovery of exploration expenditures by applying all the available income derived from sale of petroleum produced from the petroleum project.

The *Income Tax Act's* treatment of allowable capital expenditures is similar to treatment of allowable exploration expenditure under income tax principles.[93] In substance, the capital expenditures are carried forward and depreciated against future income derived by the taxpayer from sale of petroleum produced from petroleum operations conducted within the PDL area until the amount is fully depreciated by applying the relevant rate of depreciation.[94]

As to the nature of the petroleum titles, the *Income Tax Act* recognises that interest in the petroleum title is proprietary in nature, which can be sold or transferred for valuable consideration by the titleholders. In such transaction, the vendor and the purchaser can agree to treat the exploration expenditures as exploration expenditure *per se*, or capital expenditures, or partly capital and partly exploration expenditures, at their discretion, with minimum requirement to inform the Commissioner General of the Internal Revenue Commission of the arrangement as between the parties.[95] The holder of a petroleum title can therefore deal with the petroleum titles as a property right.[96]

The State, through its Nominee, is also treated as a purchaser of petroleum title, from the oil companies constituting the relevant petroleum title, as a tenant in common. The interest in the petroleum title, acquired by the State through its Nominee, is treated by the *Income Tax Act* as a sale of petroleum interest between oil companies. The tax treatment of the State's equity in the petroleum projects also endorses the proprietary nature of the PDL. The *Income Tax Act* treatment of the petroleum title held by the State, through its Nominee, is also consistent with the treatment of the same under the petroleum legislation and the petroleum agreements.

Upon becoming a joint licensee and a member of the relevant joint venture, the Nominee, as a joint licensee, produces petroleum and acquires title to same at the well-head[97] together with other joint licensees, as tenant in common,[98] and pay royalty, for the petroleum produced, which is also computed and paid using the well head value. The Nominee, for the purpose of petroleum operations, is treated as a joint licensee of the PDL. This is the arrangement under which states or their nominee take an active participation in petroleum operations conducted within the country under the new concession arrangement.

In addition to the concession based tax regime, the petroleum agreements guarantee the holder of a production licence, the right to export petroleum free of export tax.[99] The oil company is also given a degree of comfort in relation to import duties in that the petroleum agreement guarantees non-discriminatory rates, taxes, duties, levies and other impost.[100] The concessions accorded in export duty exemptions for the petroleum exported and the degree of comfort given in relation to rate, taxes, import duties, levies and other impost are incidence of a concession based contract.

The PNG petroleum taxation regime is, without doubt, a concession based taxation regime.

E. Conclusion, The Nature of Petroleum Arrangement

The question to be considered at this juncture is; what is the legal nature of the PNG's petroleum arrangement if one has to classify the arrangement under one or more of the internationally recognised petroleum arrangements.

(a) The Legal Nature of the Licensing Regime

As observed in this paper, there is little doubt that the PNG's petroleum licensing regime is concession based. It can also be noted that the general emphasis in the petroleum licensing or titular system has always been to create and give certainty as to petroleum title. The petroleum titular regime therefore guarantees the holder of an exploration licence the exclusive right to be given a retention licence[101]where an application for such a licence can be sustained. An exploration licence also gives the holder of the licence exclusive right to explore for, produce petroleum and sell or dispose of the petroleum produced within the exploration acreage and to undertake works that are necessary to explore for and produce petroleum within the exploration acreage.[102] The exploration licence is also issued over a relatively large area. These are incidents of a concession-based licensing system.

The introduction of retention licence to the licensing regime underlines the concession nature of the licensing regime.[103] Upon petroleum discovery, the holder of the exploration licence is guaranteed a production licence. In addition, the exploration licensee is guaranteed the right to produce marginal fields in future by utilising the provisions for retention licences, which can be issued exclusively to the holder of a PPL, where the discovery is not sufficient to undertake commercial production of the discovery. Further, the scope of the production licence is such that it guarantees exclusive rights to produce and sell or disposed of petroleum.[104] Upon production of the petroleum, title to the petroleum produced transfers from the State to the holder of the production licence at the wellhead.[105] The holder of a production licence may also undertake such work as are necessary to produce petroleum.[106] These are features of the new concession arrangement.

The terms of the petroleum exploration, retention and production licences are relatively longer compared to petroleum titular regimes where petroleum exploration and production is conducted under the joint venture, service contract and the production sharing contract petroleum arrangements. The comparatively longer terms of the petroleum exploration licences, retention licences and production licences give the PNG petroleum titular regime the nature of a petroleum concession arrangement. Further, the tenants of the PNG's petroleum regime are closely related to the concession arrangement where the concessionaire has the exclusive right to explore for, produce and deal with petroleum produced within the concession for relative long title period.[107]

Title to petroleum *in situ* is vested in the State and passes to the production licensee at the wellhead.[108] This is an incident of the modern concession arrangement as opposed to the traditional oil concession arrangement where title to petroleum *in situ* is granted to and held by the concessionaire. The treatment of title to petroleum *in situ* is consistent with the new concession arrangement, where title to petroleum is owned by the State, but upon production, the title in the petroleum produced shifts from the State to production licensees.

The petroleum titular regime is without doubt a concession-based licensing regime.

(b) Legal Nature of the Petroleum Agreements

Several matters can be considered as distinguishing features of the PNG's petroleum agreements.

Firstly, petroleum title is acquired and exclusively held by the oil companies and not by the State enterprise. In this respect, the oil companies own the petroleum titles and operate the projects as opposed to the production sharing contract, and service contract arrangements where the host state holds the petroleum title, either directly or through its national oil company, and the oil company is engaged as a service provider. Further, under the PNG's petroleum arrangement, title to the petroleum produced passes from the State to the oil company at the wellhead. This is opposed to the production sharing contract and service contract arrangements where title to petroleum always rest with the host state.

Secondly, the State's share of revenue from the project is appropriated, primarily through petroleum taxation and by modest royalty rate of 2%, applied at the wellhead. [109] This can be contrasted with the production sharing contract arrangements where the petroleum produced is apportioned as cost oil and profit oil, and under the service contract arrangement where the oil company is engaged as a contractor and hence the issue of royalty payment for the oil produced is not a relevant consideration. These place the PNG's petroleum arrangement away from the production sharing contract and service contract petroleum arrangements and align the arrangement with the new concession arrangement and joint venture arrangement.

Thirdly, oil companies are granted exploration title, exclusively of the State, with the State retaining the right to participate in petroleum production. Upon successful petroleum exploration and discovery, the State may elect to take up an equity position in the ensuing petroleum project. In such case, the State, through its Nominee, is assigned a portion of the petroleum production licence and other titles, leases, licences, permits and authorisations proportionate to its participating interest. It also enters into a joint operating agreement with the oil companies, and hold the petroleum title and the project assets and liabilities, jointly and severally with the oil companies as a tenant in common. These are features of joint venture contractual arrangements.

Fourthly, the State's equity participation, as set out under the relevant petroleum agreements, is paid for under a carried interest arrangement. Under this arrangement, the *pro rata* amount on account of exploration, capital and operation expenditure is represented as a debt from the State to the oil companies. The debt is classified as a loan to the State from the oil companies, from the issuance of the production licence. The amount owed to the oil companies accrues interest at a commercial rate and the debt or the "deemed loan" is defrayed by the revenue earned from sale of "oil foregone" in favour of the oil companies during the period the liability remains outstanding. The financial arrangement under which the State pays for its participation in the project reflects features of a service contract and joint venture arrangement. However, the treatment of the title to petroleum produced under the PNG's petroleum arrangement is not analogous to the arrangements under the service contract arrangements[110] but is more aligned with the treatment of title to oil produced and owned under a joint venture agreement, where title to the petroleum passes at the wellhead upon production. The petroleum titles, under the PNG's petroleum arrangement rest with the oil companies, which are granted the same under the petroleum legislation. This is unlike the service contract arrangement or the production sharing contract where the petroleum title rest[5] with the state enterprise, and the oil company is engaged as a contractor and its services are paid for either in cash or from portion of the oil produced. Further, the State equity participation is carried by the oil companies and defrayed through the allocation of the State's share of petroleum produced. This incident is consistent with that of a joint venture petroleum arrangement.

Fifthly, title in the petroleum *in situ* rests with the State and is acquired upon production at the wellhead. Accordingly, it can be argued that the petroleum title is of proprietary nature.[111] This is confirmed by the taxation treatment of the titles, which gives the petroleum titles proprietary nature. The acquisition of title to petroleum by the companies from the State at the wellhead, upon production, is a feature of the concession arrangement.

In summation, the PNG's petroleum arrangement cannot be exclusively classified under one of the established petroleum arrangements. However, it contains basic features, primarily of the joint venture and the new concession arrangements. The bundle of legal incidences governing petroleum exploration and production and the fiscal regime is a concession-based regime. However, the State equity participation arrangement, established under the petroleum agreement, is primarily a joint venture agreement.

Generally, the PNG's petroleum arrangement is a *unique hybrid* with features of different established petroleum arrangements, fixed partly by legislation and partly by agreement. The salient features of the arrangement that distinguish it from other petroleum arrangement are the legal incidences of the petroleum titles set out under the legislation,[112] the arrangement for the State's equity participation in the projects as set out under the petroleum agreements[113] and the tax treatment of title to petroleum produced as set out under the *Income Tax Act*.[114]

The titular regime established by legislation and the income tax regime are concession based, and the petroleum agreement shows elements of arrangements under joint venture agreement. Consistently therefore, the PNG petroleum agreements can be *labeled* as a *Concession Based Joint Venture Agreement.*

AL=SVI (E+D+OC)+S-F-W-Z-R. Where-

AL= total amount owing to the PDL licensee at any time by the State Nominee.

SVI= State Nominee's interest expressed in percentage.

E= Pre-PDL exploration expenditures.

D= PDL Capital Expenditures

OC= Any amount spent by the oil companies in the PDL area attributable to the State's equity participation, during the period in which income from pro rata share of the oil production is insufficient to finance project cost that is not specifically included under E&D.

S= Amount spent on behalf of the State Nominee during the shortfall period when its pro rata share of the revenue from the petroleum produced an sold is insufficient to meet project costs.

F= Aggregate revenue from sale of oil attributable to the State Nominee's equity interest.

W= Amounts attributable to money spent by the State in funding any project facility or amount spent in connection with project development.

Z= Amount contributed by the Nominee of the State or the State in reduction of the AL.

R= Amounts foregone by the State Nominee (share of insurance proceeds, etc.) that is credited to the oil companies towards payment and discharge of the AL.

OIL AND GAS ACT 1998

Being an Act to enact comprehensive legislation governing the exploration for and production of petroleum (including oil and gas) in Papua New Guinea, including the offshore area, and the grant to traditional landowners and Provincial Governments and Local-level Governments of benefits arising from projects for the production of petroleum (including oil and gas), and the processing and transportation in Papua New Guinea of petroleum and petroleum products, and to repeal various Acts, and for related purposes.

PART I. – PRELIMINARY.

1. COMPLIANCE WITH CONSTITUTIONAL REQUIREMENTS, ETC.

(1) This Act, to the extent that it regulates or restricts a right or freedom referred to in Subdivision III.3.C (*qualified rights*) of the *Constitution*, namely–

(*a*) Section 44 (*the freedom from arbitrary search and entry*); and
(*b*) Section 48 (*the right to freedom of employment*); and
(*c*) Section 49 (*the right to privacy*); and
(*d*) Section 51 (*the right to freedom of information*),

is a law made for that purpose, taking into account the National Goals and Directive Principles and the Basic Social Obligations, in particular the National Goals and Directive Principles entitled–

(*e*) national sovereignty and self reliance; and
(*f*) natural resources and environment,

for the purpose of giving effect to the public interest in public order and public welfare.
(2) For the purposes of Section 53(1) (*protection from unjust deprivation of property*) of the *Constitution* and the *Land Act 1996*, and any other relevant law, the purpose and reason for which this Act permits possession to be compulsorily taken of any property and permits any interest in or rights over property to be compulsorily acquired are set out below and are declared and described to be a public purpose, whether pursued by a licensee, the State or any other person exercising rights under this Act, and to be a reason that is reasonably justified in a democratic society that has a proper regard for the rights and dignity of mankind–

(*a*) the conducting of geological surveys, seismic tests, test drilling and other prospecting operations for petroleum in a licence area; and
(*b*) the drilling for and the recovery of petroleum in a licence area; and
(*c*) the storage of petroleum or petroleum products in connection with the operations of a licensee; and
(*d*) the processing of petroleum or petroleum products by a licensee; and
(*e*) the conveyance of petroleum or petroleum products by a licensee, whether by pipeline, land transport, sea transport or air transport, including the pumping, loading, unloading and discharging of petroleum or petroleum products; and
(*f*) the accommodation of the officers, agents and employees of a licensee or any contractor or sub-contractor of a licensee in connection with the prospecting for, recovery or conveyance or processing of petroleum or petroleum products; and
(*g*) the disposal of waste material from operations for, or associated with prospecting for, recovery or conveyance or processing of petroleum or petroleum products; and
(*h*) the establishing of a town to service an industry for the recovery, conveyance or

processing of petroleum or petroleum products including civic, cultural and social facilities in the town; and
(*ha*)[1] the construction, maintenance or operation of facilities (including, without limitation, access roads, docks, ports, airports, marinas and accommodation) to be used by a licensee in connection with the prospecting for, recovery, conveyance or processing of petroleum or petroleum products; and
(*i*) the acquisition of land or other property for activities in connection with the above purposes; and
(*j*) the acquisition of a participating interest in a petroleum project in accordance with Part IV.

(3) For the purposes of Section 53(2) of the *Constitution*, this Act is expressed to be made and each of the activities described above in Subsection (2) is expressed to be in the national interest.
(4) For the purposes of–

(*a*) Section 29 of the *Organic Law on Provincial Government*; and
(*b*) Section 41 of the *Organic Law on Provincial Governments and Local-level Governments*,

it is declared that this Act relates to a matter of national interest.

2. APPLICATION OF PROVISIONS OF ORGANIC LAW ON PROVINCIAL GOVERNMENTS AND LOCAL-LEVEL GOVERNMENTS.

(1) For the purpose of Section 98 of the *Organic Law on Provincial Governments and Local-level Governments* it is hereby declared that this Act–

(*a*) establishes the benefits and levies which are payable pursuant to Subsection (2) of that section in respect of petroleum projects; and
(*b*) provides for the rates, management, sharing arrangement and application of such development levies; and
(*c*) establishes the trust funds referred to in Subsection (3) of that section for the controlling and distribution of development levies.

(2) For the purpose of Section 99 of the *Organic Law on Provincial Governments and Local-level Governments* it is hereby declared that this Act establishes the principles by which the National Government and its statutory agencies will share with applicable Provincial Governments and Local-level Governments the revenues of the National Government generated from petroleum projects.
(3) For the purpose of Section 116 of the *Organic Law on Provincial Governments and Local-level Governments* it is hereby declared that this Act establishes–

(*a*) the consultation process amongst stakeholders, including the establishment and procedures for development forums, for petroleum projects; and
(*b*) the extent to which the parties may participate in petroleum projects.

3. INTERPRETATION.

(1)[2] In this Act, unless the contrary intention appears–

"access arrangements" means the access arrangements applying to strategic pipelines which are referred to in Section 75, or the access arrangements applying to strategic petroleum processing facilities which are referred to in Section 89, as the case may be;
"affected Local-level Government" means, in relation to a petroleum project, a Local-level Government within whose geographic jurisdiction lies a dedicated project facility of that petroleum project or any part of a petroleum development licence the production of petroleum from which is part of that petroleum project;
"affected Provincial Government" means, in relation to a petroleum project, a Provincial Government within whose geographic jurisdiction lies a dedicated project facility of that petroleum project or any part of a petroleum development licence the production of petroleum from which is part of that petroleum project;
"annual fee" means a fee prescribed by Subsection 157(2);
"approved" means approved by the Minister;
"arbitration" means arbitration under the *Arbitration Act 1951* or, where the Minister or the State and a licensee have agreed to substitute some other form of arbitration for that Act, that other form of arbitration;
"authorized officer" in relation to–

(*a*) the doing of any act; or
(*b*) the exercise of any power or function; or
(*c*) the performance of any duty,

means the officer authorized in writing by the Minister for that purpose;
"block" means a block constituted as provided by Section 17;
"the Board" means the Petroleum Advisory Board established under Section 13;
[3][4]**"buffer zone"** means, in relation to a petroleum project, the area around the dedicated project facilities of that petroleum project determined by the Minister to be the buffer zone for that petroleum project, but does not include land within a petroleum development licence pursuant to which the petroleum project is conducted or any land not within five kilometres of a dedicated project facility;
"the Chief Inspector" means the Chief Inspector appointed under Section 151(1);
[5]**"the Chief Warden"** means the Chief Warden appointed under Section 119(1)(a);
"commence to construct" means any clearing of land, excavation, construction or other action at the site for the purpose of constructing any petroleum processing facility, but does not include temporary use of sites for less than 90 days, conducting tests, taking samples or borings, preparing plans and designs, contracting for the fabrication of equipment and improvements, or the legal occupation of land;
"commencement date" means the date of coming into operation of this Act;
"the Company" means Orogen Minerals Limited;
[6]**"Customary land"** means the land that is owned or posssed by an automatic citizen or community of automatic citizens by virtue of rights of proprietary or possessory kind that belonged to that citizen or community and arise from and are regulated by custom;
[7]**"customary land owner"** means a person who has an interest in customary land.
"dedicated project facility" means, in relation to a petroleum project–

(*a*) a pipeline; or
(*b*) a pipe or system of pipes referred to in Paragraphs (a) to (d) inclusive of the definition of "pipeline"; or
(*c*) a petroleum processing facility; or
(*d*) any other facility used exclusively by the

tenement holder or other person in carrying on that petroleum project,

the operations of which are part of the same "petroleum project" or "designated gas project" as those terms are defined in the *Income Tax Act 1959*, but does not include a facility which is excluded as a dedicated project facility by an instrument signed by the Minister;
[8]**"Department"** means the Department responsible for petroleum matters;
"development agreement" means, in relation to a petroleum project, a written agreement between–

(*a*) the State; and
(*b*) the project area landowners, affected Local-level Governments or affected Provincial Governments of the petroleum project, or any of them, as the case may be;

[9]**"development forum"** means, in relation to a petroleum project or a proposed petroleum project, a meeting or combination of meetings convened in accordance with Section 48;
"the Director" means the Director appointed under Section 11;
"document" includes any map, book, record, or writing;
"domestic gas operator" means a person who connects, installs or repairs equipment and appliances for the purpose of the combustion of gas for domestic utilisation, other than a portable gas appliance that is designed to have within it, or attached to it, its own source of gas;
"domestic gas supplier" means a person who supplies in Papua New Guinea by pipeline or in cylinders or other containers natural gas or liquefied petroleum gas for domestic utilisation;
"domestic utilisation" means the consumption or distribution of petroleum or petroleum products as a fuel or feedstock within Papua New Guinea;
"drilling" means the perforation of the earth's surface whether the hole is vertical, inclined, or horizontal and includes–

(*a*) all operations for preventing the collapse of the sides of the hole or for preventing the hole from becoming filled by extraneous materials (including water); and
(*b*) the fitting of wellheads, coring, and logging;

"equity benefit" means, in relation to a petroleum project, a 2% participating interest in that petroleum project, free of encumbrances or liabilities as at the commencement of commercial production of petroleum from that petroleum project;
"Expenditure Implementation Committee" means a committee established in accordance with Subsection 178(2);
"flow lines or gathering lines" means pipes or a system of pipes for one of the uses referred to in Paragraphs (a), (b) and (c) of the definition of "pipeline";
"former Act" means the Acts repealed by Section 186;
"gas agreement" means an agreement referred to in Section 184;
[10]**"gas field"** means a petroleum pool consisting, in some part, of petroleum recoverable as natural gas at the surface where oil recovery is not, or is not expected to be, the primary object of petroleum recovery;
[11]**"gas operations"** means petroleum operations relating to the recovery from a gas field;
"gas project" means–

(*a*) where a gas agreement does not apply to a project–a petroleum project having the purpose

of recovering natural gas (other than recovery of natural gas which is incidental to the recovery of other petroleum); and
(*b*)[12] where a gas agreement applies to the project – a petroleum project, as and to the extent defined in such gas agreement, having the purpose of recovering: –

(i) natural gas; and
(ii) other petroleum which is incidental to the recovery of natural gas or which is otherwise dealt with in or the subject of that gas agreement;

"good oilfield practice" means practice which is generally accepted within the petroleum industry as good and safe–

(*a*) in the carrying on of exploration for petroleum; or
(*b*) in operations for the recovery of petroleum,

as the case may be;
"graticular section" means a section referred to in Section 17(1);
"improvements" means–

(*a*) any building or structure; or
(*b*) any yard, fence, wall or other erection, construction or appliance affixed to land–

(i) for the working or management of the land or of stock depastured on the land; or
(ii) for maintaining or increasing the natural capacity of the land to produce or to give shelter or enjoyment to humans or animals; or

(*c*) any planted crop or trees, whether planted for commercial or domestic purposes,

and includes–

(*d*) any well, bore, reservoir, spring, dam or other artificial water course or watering place; or
(*e*) any road, track, footpath, railway, tramway, culvert, bridge or crossing; or
(*f*) the site of any sports ground, recreation area, sing sing ground, village or community meeting place, burial place or sacred ground;

"incorporated land group" has the meaning given in the *Land Groups Incorporation Act 1974*;
"in-plant piping" means pipes or a system of pipes referred to in Paragraph (d) of the definition of "pipeline";
"inspector" means a person appointed under Section 151, and includes the Chief Inspector;
"land" includes the offshore area and the bed of any river, stream, estuary, lake or swamp;
"licence" means–

(*a*) a petroleum prospecting licence issued under Section 23; or
(*b*) a petroleum retention licence issued under Section 40; or
(*c*) a petroleum development licence issued under Section 57; or

(*d*) a pipeline licence issued under Section 74; or
(*e*) a petroleum processing facility licence issued under Section 88,

or any of them, as the context requires, and includes any extension of those licences;
"licence area" means the area constituted by the blocks that are the subject of a tenement;
"licensee" means the registered holder of a licence;
"location" means the blocks in respect of which a declaration under Section 34 is in force;
"low water line" means–

(*a*) the low water line on a coast of Papua New Guinea at mean low water springs; or
(*b*) any line declared by the Minister to be a low water line under Section 4;

"major modification" means, in relation to a petroleum processing facility–

(*a*) installation of new processing units or debottlenecking of existing processing units which results in an increase of the rated capacity of the petroleum processing facility to more than one hundred and twenty five percent of its original design capacity; or
(*b*) the installation of new facilities or modification of existing facilities costing in excess of 30% of the replacement cost of the petroleum processing facility; or
(*c*) any other modification to the petroleum processing facility involving a fundamental change to the process or the petroleum products produced by the petroleum processing facility;

"month" means the period from and including a day in one calendar month to and excluding the corresponding day in the next calendar month and including the last day in the next calendar month if there is no corresponding day;
"MRDC" means Mineral Resources Development Company Pty Limited;
"natural gas" means fluid obtained from a well which is a gas at standard temperature and pressure and which consists primarily of hydrocarbons;
"NGC" means a company called or to be called National Gas Corporation Limited to be incorporated in accordance with Section 179;
"offshore area" means the area that comprises–

(*a*) the seabed underlying the waters (if any) between the low water line and the baseline; and
(*b*) the seabed underlying the territorial sea; and
(*c*) the seabed adjacent to the coast of Papua New Guinea that underlies the offshore seas to a depth not exceeding 200 m or, beyond that limit, to a depth where the superjacent waters admit of the exploitation of the natural resources in the subsurface or on the seabed of that area;

[13]**"operator"** means, in relation to a license –

(*a*) where there is only one registered holder of that license –that registered holder; and
(*b*) in all other cases –the person, who shall be a licensee, for the time being designated by the operating agreement, in respect of that license as the operator of operations conducted in relation to that licence;

[14]**"operating agreement"** means, in respect of a license, the agreement executed between the holders of that license and provided to the Director pursuant to Section 123A in relation to that licence.
"option" has the meaning given to it in the option agreement;
"option agreement" has the meaning given to it in the *Mineral Resources Development Company Pty Limited (Privatisation) Act 1996*;

"Orogen option project" means a petroleum project which is also a Project as defined in the option agreement;
"participating interest" means, in relation to a petroleum project an undivided beneficial interest in all of the project assets of that petroleum project;
"petroleum" means–

(*a*) any naturally occurring hydrocarbons, whether in a gaseous, liquid, or solid state; or
(*b*) any naturally occurring mixture of hydrocarbons, whether in a gaseous, liquid, or solid state; or
(*c*) any naturally occurring mixture of one or more hydrocarbons, (whether in a gaseous, liquid, or solid state) and any other substance,

and includes any processed petroleum, and any petroleum as defined by Paragraph (a), (b) or (c) that has been returned to a natural reservoir, but does not include coal, shale, or any substance that may be extracted from coal, shale, or other rock;
"petroleum development licence" means a licence issued under Division III.7;
"petroleum development licensee" means the registered holder of a petroleum development licence;
"petroleum pool" means a naturally occurring discrete accumulation of petroleum;
"petroleum processing" means refining, separating, stabilising, liquefying, storing, reclaiming, treating, fractionation, cracking, polymerisation, reforming or re-refining of petroleum, or the conversion of petroleum to other petroleum derivates, and all related operations; and "processed", in relation to petroleum or petroleum products, has the corresponding meaning;
"petroleum processing facility" means a facility, whether onshore or offshore, for petroleum processing, and includes tanks for bulk storage of petroleum or petroleum products and in-plant piping;
"petroleum processing facility licence" means a licence granted under Division III.10;
"petroleum processing facility licensee" means the registered holder of a petroleum processing facility licence;
"petroleum product" means a distillate of petroleum or a reformate or derivate of petroleum;
"petroleum project" means a project in Papua New Guinea for the production of petroleum, and includes, if they are part of the same project or developed in conjunction with the petroleum production development, the construction and operation pursuant to a licence of facilities for the recovery, processing or transportation of petroleum, and a project which is the subject of a licence and over which the Company has the right to exercise an option under the option agreement;
"petroleum prospecting licence" means a licence issued under Division III.2;
"petroleum prospecting licensee" means the registered holder of a petroleum prospecting licence;
"petroleum retention licence" means a licence issued under Division III.4;
"petroleum retention licensee" means the registered holder of a petroleum retention licence;
"pipeline" means pipes and other interconnected facilities operated as an integrated system (including pumping stations, metering stations, valve stations, storage tanks and pig launching and receiving stations) for transporting petroleum or petroleum products from receipt points to delivery points either for petroleum processing within the country or for further processing or export, but does not include pipes and facilities for–

(*a*) returning petroleum to a reservoir for pressure maintenance or storage or conservation; or
(*b*) transporting petroleum that is to be flared or vented, or recovered for test purposes under a tenement (including drill stem or extended production tests) and transported to facilities for testing or measurement or disposal; or
(*c*) gathering petroleum for transportation to petroleum processing facilities within a licence area where all such pipes and transportation facilities are within a licence area; or
(*d*) transporting petroleum or petroleum products between receipt points and delivery points in a petroleum processing facility;

"pipeline licence" means a licence to construct and operate a pipeline issued under Division III.9;
"pipeline licensee" means the registered holder of a pipeline licence;
"private land" means land other than Government land as defined in Section 2 of the *Mining Act 1992*;
"processed petroleum" means stabilised crude oil, condensate, processed natural gas that conforms to a quality specification prescribed in a sales contract or elsewhere, liquefied petroleum gas, or liquefied natural gas, or any other petroleum which has been processed but which is not a petroleum product;
[15]**"project area landowners"** means, in relation to a petroleum project, the persons who are customary land owners or who have registered title to–

(*a*) any part of the licence area of a petroleum development licence the operations under which are part of that petroleum project; or
(*b*) any land within the buffer zone of that petroleum project;

"project assets" means, in relation to a petroleum project–

(*a*) the licence or licences pursuant to which the petroleum project or any part of it is conducted; and
(*b*) the property, real or personal, present or future, owned or acquired or held for use by or on behalf of the licensee or licensees or other persons affiliated with the licensee or licensees who are carrying out the petroleum project, which is held for the purposes of the petroleum project or any part of it, including all property in dedicated project facilities of the petroleum project; and
(*c*) the right to receive in kind and to dispose of all petroleum recovered in the course of the petroleum project,

in each case to the extent that such petroleum project is an entire or more than one entire "petroleum projects" or "designated gas projects" as defined in the *Income Tax Act 1959*;
"project pipeline" means a pipeline which is not a strategic pipeline;
"pumping station" means equipment for pumping petroleum or petroleum products or water and includes any structure associated with that equipment;
"Register" means a Register kept under Division III.11;
"registered holder", in relation to a licence, means the person whose name is for the time being shown in the Register as being the holder of the licence;
"royalty benefit" means, in relation to a petroleum project, a sum of money each month equal to the amount of royalty payable in the previous month pursuant to Section 159 by a licensee in respect of that petroleum project, less any tax or withholding payable to the State in respect of such royalty upon payment to third persons;
"royalty period", in relation to a tenement means–

(*a*) the period commencing on the date on which the tenement comes into effect to the end of that month; and
(*b*) each month afterwards;

"State equity entitlement" means the entitlement of the State, pursuant to Section 165, to acquire, directly or through a nominee, a participating interest in a petroleum project;
"storage" means the accumulation of petroleum or petroleum products pending transportation to a petroleum processing facility or loading for transportation or sale;
"strategic petroleum processing facility" means a petroleum processing facility directly connected to or directly integrated with a strategic pipeline, either upstream or downstream, but does not include a petroleum processing facility which is exempted under Section 89(7);
"strategic pipeline" means a pipeline referred to in Section 75(1);

"tank station" means a tank or system of tanks for holding or storing petroleum, and includes any structure associated with that tank or system of tanks;
"temporary operations" means any of the following operations:–

(*a*) geological, geochemical and geophysical surveying;
(*b*) taking samples by hand or hand held methods;
(*c*) aerial and land surveying;
(*d*) transportation of crews and equipment by haul roads, navigable waterways or aircraft;
(*e*) any activity prescribed by regulation as a preliminary survey,

and any lawful act incidental to any activity to which Paragraphs (a) to (e) relate to the extent that it does not involve any activity that results in surveys of greater than minimum scale and in no circumstances shall include activities involving–

(*f*) exploring for petroleum; or
(*g*) the cutting, destroying, removing or injury of any vegetation on greater than a minimum scale; or
(*h*) the use of explosives, other than for geophysical survey; or

(i) damage to improvements, stock or chattels on any land; or

(*j*) any breach of the provisions of this or any other Act, including provisions relating to protected native plants, water, noise and historic sites; or
(*k*) the use of more persons for any particular activity than is reasonably necessary; or
(*l*) any survey prescribed as a prohibited survey; or
(*m*) entry on land prescribed as prohibited land;

"tenement" means–

(*a*) a petroleum prospecting licence issued under Section 23; or
(*b*) a petroleum retention licence issued under Section 40; or
(*c*) a petroleum development licence issued under Section 57,

or any of them, as the context requires, and includes any extension of those licences;
"tenement holder" means the registered holder of a tenement;
"this Act" includes the regulations;
"transportation" means the act of delivering petroleum or petroleum products, whether by barge, pipeline, road tanker, ship, drums or other container or otherwise, from a receipt point to a destination point including back hauls, displacement, exchange and in-transit storage;
"valve station" means equipment for regulating the flow of petroleum, and includes any structure associated with that equipment;
"vessel" means a vessel used in navigation, other than air navigation, and includes a barge, lighter or other floating vessel;
[16]**"Warden"** means a Warden appointed under Section 119(1)(b);
"water line" means a pipe or system of pipes for conveying water to be used in connection with prospecting for, or the recovery of, petroleum;
"well" means a hole in land or the subsoil of land, made by drilling, boring or any other means–

(*a*) in connection with exploration for petroleum;
or
(*b*) in operations for the recovery of petroleum,

but does not include a seismic shot hole.

(2) In this Act, a reference–

(*a*) to the term of a licence, is a reference to the period during which the licence remains in force and includes the period of any extension of such licence; and
(*b*) to the date of expiration of a licence, is a reference to the day on which the licence ceases to have effect.

(3) In this Act, a reference to a year of the term of a licence is a reference to a period of one year commencing on the date from and including which the licence has effect or on any anniversary of that date.
(4) In this Act, a reference to a licence is a reference to the licence as varied from time to time under this Act.
(5) For the purposes of this Act, **"Papua New Guinea"** includes the offshore area.

4. DECLARATION OF LOW WATER LINE.

In any case where he considers there is doubt as to the location of a low water line, the Minister may, by notice in the National Gazette, declare the location of the line by whatever method appears to him to be appropriate, and the line so declared shall be the low water line.

5. APPLICATION.

This Act applies–

(*a*) to all natural persons, whether resident in the country or not; and
(*b*) to all corporations, whether incorporated or carrying on business in the country or not.

6. PETROLEUM THE PROPERTY OF THE STATE.

(1) Subject to this Act, but notwithstanding anything contained in any other law or in any grant, instrument of title or other document, all petroleum and helium at or below the surface of any land is, and shall be deemed at all times to have been, the property of the State.
(2) Nothing in Subsection (1) shall be construed as an additional acquisition of property in relation to Section 53 of the *Constitution* beyond that which prevailed under the former Act and all previous Acts.
(3) Petroleum and helium shall not be removed from the land from which it has been obtained, or disposed of in any manner, except–

(*a*) subject to Subsection (4), by a tenement holder, for the purpose of sampling or analysis; or
(*b*) by a tenement holder in accordance with the terms of his tenement or a written agreement with the State; or
(*c*) as otherwise permitted by this Act.

(4) A licensee shall not take or send out of the country any samples of petroleum or helium without the written consent of the Director.

7. THE DIRECTOR MAY CARRY ON OPERATIONS.

(1) The Director may, on behalf of the State, carry on prospecting for, and the recovery and conveyance of, petroleum and helium, and activities incidental to those operations.
(2) Where the Director carries on any operations under this section, he has the same rights, benefits, and privileges as a licensee.
(3) Where the Director carries on any operations under this section, he shall to the extent that they can be practicably applied to him, be subject to the same duties and obligations under this Act as apply to a licensee.

8. EXPLORATION FOR AND RECOVERY OF PETROLEUM.

A person who–

(*a*) explores for petroleum otherwise than under and in accordance with a tenement or an instrument of consent issued under this Act; or
(*b*) carries on operations for the recovery of petroleum otherwise than under and in accordance with a tenement,

is guilty of an offence.
Penalty: A fine not exceeding K50,000.00.
Default penalty: A fine not exceeding K50,000.00.

PART II. – APPLICATION OF LAWS AND ADMINISTRATION.

9. LAWS OF PAPUA NEW GUINEA TO APPLY.

(1) Subject to this Act, the provisions of all laws for the time being in force in Papua New Guinea, and the provisions of any instrument having effect under any of those laws, apply in the offshore area.
(2) The provisions referred to in Subsection (1) apply to and in relation to–

(*a*) all acts, omissions, matters, circumstances and things touching, concerning, arising out of, or connected with the exploration for petroleum of the sea, seabed or subsoil of the offshore area; and
(*b*) the exploitation of the natural resources, being petroleum, of the sea, seabed or subsoil of the offshore area.

(3) Without limiting the generality of Subsection (2), the provisions that apply in accordance with this section in the offshore area apply–

(*a*) to and in relation to–

(i) an act or omission that takes place in, on, above, below, or in the vicinity of the sea, seabed or subsoil of that area; and
(ii) a matter, circumstance, or thing that exists or arises with respect to or in connection with a vessel, aircraft, structure or installation or equipment or other property that is in that area

for any reason touching, concerning, arising out of or connected with–

(A) the exploration for petroleum; or
(B) the exploitation of the natural resources, being petroleum, of the sea, seabed or subsoil of that area; and

(*b*) to and in relation to a person who–

(i) is in that area; or
(ii) is in, on, above, below, or in the vicinity of a vessel, aircraft, structure or installation, or equipment or other property that is in that area,

for any reason of the kind referred to in Paragraph (a); and

(*c*) to and in relation to a person in respect of his carrying on any operation or doing any work in that area for any reason of the kind referred to in Paragraph (a).

(4) The regulations may provide that such of the provisions that apply in accordance with this section in the offshore area that are specified in the regulations do not apply, or apply with such modifications as are specified in the regulations.
(5) For the purposes of Subsection (4), **"modifications"** includes the omission or addition of a provision or the substitution of a provision for another provision.

10. JURISDICTION OF COURTS.

(1) The National Court of Papua New Guinea is vested with jurisdiction in all matters arising under this Act, including all matters arising under the provisions applied by Section 9, and shall have jurisdiction to hear and determine all actions, suits, claims, demands, disputes, prosecutions and questions which may arise under this Act or those provisions.
(2) Subject to this Act, the laws with respect to the arrest and custody of offenders or persons charged with offences, and the procedure for–

(*a*) their summary conviction; and
(*b*) their examination and committal for trial on indictment; and
(*c*) their trial and conviction on indictment; and
(*d*) the hearing and determination of appeals arising out of any such trial or conviction or out of any proceedings connected with t,

and for holding accused persons to bail apply, so far as they are applicable, to a person who is charged with an offence against any of the provisions applied by Section 9.

11. APPOINTMENT OF DIRECTOR.

The Minister may, by notice in the National Gazette, appoint a person to be the Director for the purposes of this Act.

12. DELEGATION.

The Director may, by notice in the National Gazette, delegate to an officer all or any of his powers and functions under this Act (except this power of delegation).

13. PETROLEUM ADVISORY BOARD.

(1) There shall be a Petroleum Advisory Board.
(2)[17] [18]Subject to Subsection (3), the Board shall consist of –

(*a*) the Director, who shall be the Chairman, or his delegate; and
(*b*) the Secretary of the Department responsible for national planning matters or his delegate appointment in writing and furnished to the Director; and
(*c*) the Secretary of the Department responsible for treasury matters or his delegate appointed in writing and furnished to the Director; and
(*d*) the Secretary of the Department responsible for provincial and Local government matters or his delegate appointed in writing and furnished to the Director; and
(*e*) the Director of Petroleum Division of the Department, who shall be the Deputy Chairman, or his delegate appointed in writing; and
(*f*) the Chief Inspector appointed pursuant to Section 151 or his delegate appointed in writing and furnished to the Director; and
(*g*) the Director of the Investment Promotion Authority or his delegate appointed in writing and furnished to the Director.

(3) If a member of the Board, other than the Chairman or Deputy Chairman is, for any reason, unable to perform his duties as a member, that member may, in writing, appoint a person to act as his substitute for the period of that member's inability, and a person so appointed shall, while so appointed, be a member of the Board.

(3A)[19] [20]In the absence of the Chairman, the Deputy Chairman appointed pursuant to Section 12(2)(e) shall act as Chairman and exercise all powers and responsibilities of the Chairman.
(4)[21] [22]For the purposes of this section, a delegate appointed under this section shall be a senior officer at the Assistant Secretary level or above.

14. MEETINGS OF THE BOARD.

(1) The Board shall meet as often as is necessary to carry out its functions and at such times and places as the Chairman, or in his absence the Deputy Chairman, directs.
(2) At a meeting of the Board–

(*a*)[23] the Chairman or in his absence the Deputy Chairman, and three other persons specified in Section 13(2) are a quorum.
(*b*) all matters shall be decided by a majority of votes and the Chairman, or in his absence the Deputy Chairman, has a deliberative, and, in the event of an equality of votes, also a casting vote.

15. POWERS AND DUTIES OF BOARD.

(1) The Minister may refer to the Board for advice any question or matter relating to the administration of this Act.
(2) The Board shall inquire into and advise the Minister on any question or matter referred to it under Subsection (1) or as required by this Act.
(3) The referral of a question or matter under Subsection (1) shall be deemed to be a Commission issued under the *Commissions of Inquiry Act 1951*, and the provisions of that Act, including the provisions relating to penalties, apply to and in respect of an inquiry under this section as if the Minister were the Head of State, acting on advice, and the members of the Board were Commissioners within the meaning of that Act.

16. NO PERSONAL LIABILITY FOR BOARD, MINISTER OR DIRECTOR.

A member of the Board, the Minister, the Director, or a servant or agent of the State acting under the direction of one of them or an authority delegated to him under this Act, or an inspector, shall not be personally liable to an action, suit or proceeding or claim for damages for or in respect of an act or matter done or omitted to be done in good faith in exercise or purported exercise of any power or authority conferred by this Act.

PART III. – PETROLEUM EXPLORATION AND DEVELOPMENT.

DIVISION 1. PRELIMINARY.

17. GRATICULATION OF EARTH'S SURFACE AND CONSTITUTION OF BLOCKS.

(1) For the purposes of this Act, the surface of the Earth shall be deemed to be divided into sections–

(*a*) by the meridian of Greenwich and by meridians that are at a distance from that meridian of five minutes, or a multiple of five minutes, of longitude; and
(*b*) by the equator and by parallels of latitude that are at a distance from the equator of five minutes, or a multiple of five minutes, of latitude,

each of which is bounded–

(*c*) by portions of two of those meridians that are at a distance from each other of five minutes of longitude; and
(*d*) by portions of two of those parallels of latitude that are at a distance from each other of five minutes of latitude.

(2) Subject to Subsection (3), all or so much of a graticular section that is contained in the area of the country and the offshore area constitutes a block.
(3) Where the area in respect of which a tenement is in force includes one or more portions of a block constituted as provided by Subsection (1)–

(*a*) the area of that portion or those portions constitutes a block; and
(*b*) the area of the remaining portion or portions of the first-mentioned block (but not including any part of that area in respect of which a tenement is in force) constitutes a block.

(4) Where a tenement ceases to be in force in respect of an area referred to in Subsection (3)(a), the Minister may, by instrument determine that the area shall be amalgamated with another block or blocks, being a block or blocks–

(*a*) constituted as provided by this section; and
(*b*) forming part of the graticular section of which the area forms part; and
(*c*) that is or are either–

(i) a block or blocks in respect of which a tenement is in force; or
(ii) a block or blocks constituted under Subsection (3)(b).

(5) Where a determination is made under Subsection (4)–

(*a*) the area and blocks both the subject of the determination, cease to constitute separate blocks and their areas together constitute a single block; and
(*b*) in respect of the area and a block in respect of which there is a tenement in force–the block constituted by the determination is a block for the remainder of the term of that tenement.

(6) In this Act–

(*a*) a reference to a block that is constituted by a graticular section includes a reference to a block that is constituted by the area of a part of a graticular section; and
(*b*) a reference to a graticular section that constitutes a block includes a reference to a graticular section part only of which constitutes a block.

18. PROSPECTING LICENCES UNDER TORRES STRAIT TREATY.

(1) This Part, other than this section and Divisions 3, 10, 13 and 14 does not apply to licences issued under this section.
(2) In Divisions 3, 10, 13 and 14 **"licence"** and **"tenement"** shall, where applicable, include a licence granted under this section.
(3) In this section **"the Treaty"** means the Treaty between the Independent State of Papua New Guinea and Australia concerning Sovereignty and Maritime Boundaries in the area between the two countries, including the area known as Torres Strait and related matters signed at Sydney 18 December 1978.
(4) Where, under Article 5 of the Treaty, a person entitled to apply for a petroleum prospecting licence, so applies, the Minister shall grant to him a petroleum prospecting licence.
(5) A licence granted under Subsection (4) shall be granted on terms that are not less favourable than a tenement granted under Division 2.

19. ISSUE OF LICENCES.

(1) Subject to this Act, a tenement may be issued to a person in respect of any block except a block that is–

(*a*) comprised in a tenement; or
(*b*) reserved by declaration under Section 20.

(2) A licence may be held by–

(*a*) a natural person; or
(*b*) a body corporate that is incorporated in Papua New Guinea or registered as an overseas company under the *Companies Act 1997*; or
(*c*) an unincorporated combination of–

(i) natural persons; or
(ii) corporations to which Paragraph (b) applies; or
(iii) a natural person or natural persons and a corporation or corporations to which Paragraph (b) applies.

(3) A notification of the issue of a licence shall be published in the National Gazette.

20. RESERVATION OF BLOCKS.

(1) The Minister may, by notice in the National Gazette, declare that a block or blocks specified in the notice (not being a block or blocks in respect of which a tenement is in force) shall not be the subject of a tenement, and may in the same manner revoke or vary such notice.
(2) While a declaration under Subsection (1) remains in force in respect of a block or blocks, a tenement shall not be granted in respect of that block or those blocks.

DIVISION 2. PETROLEUM PROSPECTING LICENCES.

21. APPLICATIONS FOR PETROLEUM PROSPECTING LICENCE.

(1) A person may make an application to the Director for the grant of a petroleum prospecting licence in respect of any block or blocks.
(2) The Minister may, by notice in the National Gazette–

(*a*) invite applications for the grant of a petroleum prospecting licence in respect of the block or blocks specified in the notice; and
(*b*) specify the period during which an application may be made.

22. FORM OF APPLICATION FOR PETROLEUM PROSPECTING LICENCE.

(1) An application made under, or as a result of an invitation under, Section 21–

(*a*) shall be in an approved form; and
(*b*) shall be made in an approved manner; and
(*c*) subject to Subsection (2)–shall be in respect of not more than 60 blocks; and
(*d*) shall be accompanied by particulars of–

(i) the detailed proposals of the applicant for work and expenditure in respect of the block or blocks specified in the application during the first two years of the term of the licence and an outline of proposals for work and expenditure during the remaining four years of the licence; and
(ii) the technical qualifications of the applicant and of his employees; and
(iii) the technical advice available to the applicant; and
(iv) the financial resources available to the applicant; and

(*e*) may set out any other matters that the applicant wishes the Minister to consider; and
(*f*) shall be accompanied by the fee prescribed by Section 157.

(2) The Minister may consider an application in respect of more than 60 but not more than 200 blocks where he is satisfied that special circumstances exist for his doing so.
(3) The blocks specified in the application referred to in Subsections (1) and (2) shall be constituted by graticular sections that–

(*a*) form a single area; and
(*b*) are such that each graticular section in that area has a side in common with at least one other graticular section in that area.

(4) The Director may, at any time, by instrument served on the applicant, require him to furnish, within the time specified in the instrument, such further written information in connection with his application as the Director considers necessary.
(5) Where an application is received under, or as a result of an invitation under, Section 21–

(*a*) notice of the application shall be published by the Director in the National Gazette; and
(*b*) any person who claims to be affected by the application may file notice of his objection to that application with the Director within one month after the date of publication of the notice of application and all objections shall be considered by the Board before the Board reports on the application.

(6) As soon as practicable after the granting of a licence in respect of any block or blocks specified in an application made under, or as a result of an invitation under, Section 21, the Minister shall cause to be published in the National Gazette, particulars of any licence so granted.

23. GRANT OR REFUSAL OF PETROLEUM PROSPECTING LICENCE.

(1) Where an application has been made under, or as a result of an invitation under, Section 21, the Minister may, after consideration of a report from the Board and after having regard to physical planning considerations–

(*a*) by instrument served on the applicant, inform the applicant–

(i) that he is prepared to grant to the applicant a petroleum prospecting licence in respect of any or all of the blocks specified in the instrument, being blocks to which the application relates; and
(ii) that the applicant will be required to lodge a security for compliance with the conditions to which the licence, if granted, will be subject, and with the provisions of this Act, and to pay the first annual fee; or

(*b*) refuse to grant a licence to the applicant.

(2) An instrument under Subsection (1)(a) shall contain–

(*a*) the conditions subject to which the licence is to be granted; and
(*b*) a statement to the effect that the application will lapse if the applicant does not make a request under Subsection (3) in respect of the grant of the licence and lodge with the Director the security specified in the instrument and the first annual fee.

(3) An applicant who has been served with an instrument under Subsection (1) may, within a period of one month after the date of service of the instrument on him, or within such further period, not exceeding three months, as the Minister may allow–

(*a*) by instrument served on the Minister request the Minister to grant him the licence; and
(*b*) lodge with the Director the security referred to in Subsection (1)(a) and the first annual fee referred to in that subsection.

(4) Where an applicant has complied with the requirements of Subsection (3), the Minister shall grant to him a petroleum prospecting licence in respect of the block or blocks specified in the instrument, subject to the conditions specified in the instrument or such other conditions as are agreed on by the Minister and the applicant, but in any other case the application lapses.

24. VARIATION OF PETROLEUM PROSPECTING LICENCE.

(1) The holder of a petroleum prospecting licence may, at any time, make an application to the Minister for a variation of the petroleum prospecting licence.
(2) An application under Subsection (1) shall–

(*a*) specify the reasons for proposed variation; and
(*b*) be made in an approved form and contain the information specified in Section 22.

(3) The Director may require the applicant to furnish such further information in connection with his application as the Director considers necessary.
(4) Following receipt of an application under Subsection (1) the Minister may, after considering a report of the Board and any matters submitted to him under this section–

(*a*) amend the terms of the petroleum prospecting licence to provide as stipulated in the application or as otherwise agreed with the petroleum prospecting licensee; or
(*b*) refuse the application, in which case the existing petroleum prospecting licence shall remain in full force and effect.

25. RIGHTS CONFERRED BY PETROLEUM PROSPECTING LICENCE.

A petroleum prospecting licence, while it remains in force, confers on the licensee, subject to this Act, and to the conditions specified in the licence, the exclusive right to explore for petroleum, and to carry out appraisal of a petroleum discovery, and to carry on such operations and execute such works as are necessary for those purposes, in the licence area, including the construction and operation of water lines, and, if authorized by the Director, the completion of wells, the conduct of drill stem or extended production tests for appraisal of a petroleum pool (including the construction in accordance with the authorization and the operation of pipes and facilities to gather and transport petroleum to a point of testing or treatment or disposal), and the recovery and sale or other disposal of all petroleum so produced.

26. TERM OF PETROLEUM PROSPECTING LICENCE.

Subject to this Act and to any condition in the licence, a petroleum prospecting licence remains in force–

(*a*) for a period of six years commencing on the day the licence takes effect; and
(*b*) where the licence is extended under Section 29–for a further period of five years; and
(*c*) where the licence is extended under Section 30–for the further period specified by the Minister on the grant of the extension.

27. APPLICATION FOR EXTENSION OF PETROLEUM PROSPECTING LICENCE.

(1) Subject to Section 28, the holder of a petroleum prospecting licence may make an application to the Director for the extension of the petroleum prospecting licence in respect of any block or blocks in the licence area.
(2) An application under this section may be made once only in respect of any petroleum prospecting licence.
(3) An application under this section–

(*a*) shall be in an approved form; and
(*b*) shall be made in an approved manner; and
(*c*) shall be made not less than three months before the day on which the licence is due to expire; and
(*d*) shall be accompanied by particulars of–

(i) the work carried out in, and the amounts expended in respect of, the licence area during the term of the licence up to and including the date of the application; and
(ii) the proposals of the applicant for work and

expenditure in respect of the blocks specified in the application; and

(*e*) may set out any other matters that the applicant requires the Minister to consider; and
(*f*) shall be accompanied by the fee prescribed by Section 157.

(4) The Minister may, after considering a report from the Board, accept an application for the extension of a petroleum prospecting licence less than three months before, but not in any case after, the date of expiry of the licence.

28. APPLICATION FOR EXTENSION TO BE IN RESPECT OF REDUCED AREA.

(1) The number of blocks in respect of which an application for the extension of a petroleum prospecting licence may be made shall not exceed the number that is the sum of–

(*a*) the number of blocks (if any) the subject of the petroleum prospecting licence that, at the date of expiration of the petroleum prospecting licence, were a location not subject to a petroleum retention licence or an application for a petroleum retention licence; and
(*b*) the number of blocks (if any) the subject of the petroleum prospecting licence that, at the date of expiration of the petroleum prospecting licence, are contained within a petroleum retention licence or the subject of an application for a petroleum retention licence; and
(*c*) half the number of blocks in respect of which the petroleum prospecting licence was issued.

(2) The blocks specified in an application for the extension of a petroleum prospecting licence shall be blocks that relate to graticular sections that–

(*a*) constitute a single area or not more than three discrete areas; and
(*b*) are such that each graticular section in each area has a side in common with at least one other graticular section in that area.

29. GRANT OR REFUSAL OF EXTENSION OF PETROLEUM PROSPECTING LICENCE.

(1) Where a licensee has made an application under Section 27 for an extension of a petroleum prospecting licence and has furnished any additional information in connection with the application required by the Director, the Minister–

(*a*) shall, if the licensee has complied with the conditions to which the licence is subject and the provisions of this Act; or
(*b*) may, if the licensee has not complied with the conditions to which the licence is subject or the provisions of this Act and the Minister after considering a report from the Board is satisfied that although the licensee has not so complied, special

circumstances exist that justify the granting of the extension of the licence,

inform the licensee, by instrument served on the licensee–

(*c*) that he is prepared to grant to the licensee the extension of the licence; and
(*d*) that the licensee will be required to lodge a security, or extend a security already lodged, for compliance with–

(i) the conditions to which the licence, if the extension is granted, will from time to time be subject; and
(ii) with the provisions of this Act; and

(*e*) of the amount of the next annual fee.

(2) If the licensee has not complied with the conditions to which the licence is subject or with the provisions of this Act, and if the Minister is not satisfied that special circumstances exist that justify the granting of the extension of the licence, the Minister shall, subject to Subsection (3), by instrument served on the licensee, refuse to grant the extension of the licence.
(3) The Minister shall not refuse to grant the extension of a petroleum prospecting licence under this section unless–

(*a*) he has, by instrument served on the licensee, given not less than one month's notice of his intention to refuse to grant the extension of the licence; and
(*b*) he has caused a copy of the instrument to be served on such other persons (if any) as he thinks fit; and
(*c*) he has, in the instrument–

(i) given particulars of the reasons for the intention; and
(ii) specified a date on or before which written submissions may be served on the Minister in connection with the proposed refusal; and

(*d*) after–

(i) taking into account any matters submitted to him under Paragraph (c)(ii) on or before the specified date; and
(ii) considering a report from the Board on those matters,

he is not satisfied that special conditions exist that justify the granting of the extension of the licence.
(4) An instrument under Subsection (1) shall–

(*a*) specify the conditions to which the licence, on the grant of the extension, is to be subject; and (*b*) contain a statement to the effect that the application will lapse if the applicant does not–

(i) make a request under Subsection (5) in respect of the grant of the extension of the licence; and
(ii) lodge with the Director the security specified in the instrument and the annual fee.

(5) A licensee who has been served with an instrument under Subsection (1) may, within a period of one month after the date of service of the instrument on him–

(*a*) by instrument served on the Minister request the Minister to grant to him the extension of the licence; and
(*b*) lodge with the Director the security specified in the instrument and pay the annual fee.

(6) Where a licensee who has been served with an instrument under Subsection (1) has, within the period specified in Subsection (5)–

(*a*) made a request under Subsection (5); and
(*b*) lodged with the Director the security specified in the instrument referred to in Subsection (1) and paid the next annual fee,

the Minister shall grant to the licensee the extension of the licence.
(7) Where a licensee who has been served with an instrument under Subsection (1) has not, within the period specified in Subsection (5)–

(*a*) made a request under Subsection (5); or
(*b*) lodged with the Director the security specified in the instrument and paid the annual fee,

the application lapses at the end of that period.
(8) Where–

(*a*) an application for the extension of a licence has been made; and
(*b*) the licence expires–

(i) before the Minister grants, or refuses to grant, the extension of the licence; or
(ii) before the application lapses under Subsection (7),

the licence shall be deemed to continue in force until the Minister grants or refuses to grant the extension of the licence, or the application lapses under Subsection (7), whichever first occurs.
(9) As soon as practicable after the grant or refusal of an extension of a licence under this section, the Minister shall cause to be published in the National Gazette particulars of any extension so granted or, in the case of a refusal, a statement to that effect.
(10) Where a petroleum prospecting licence is not extended on an application under this section, 90% of the fee referred to in Section 27(3)(f) shall be refunded to the applicant.

30. EXTENSION OF PETROLEUM PROSPECTING LICENCE IN RESPECT OF LOCATION.

(1) Where–

(*a*) petroleum is discovered in a petroleum prospecting licence area within the period of two years before the date of expiration of a petroleum prospecting licence that has been extended under Section 29; and
(*b*) the Minister has made a declaration of a location under Section 34, or the licensee has nominated a block or blocks under that section for the purpose of a declaration of a location,

the Minister may grant a further extension of the licence in respect of the block or blocks to which Paragraph (b) applies.
(2) A further extension granted under Subsection (1)–

(*a*) shall be for a period not exceeding three years; and
(*b*) shall be subject to any conditions that the Minister, after considering a report of the Board, thinks fit and specifies in the licence.

(3) Where, before the expiration of a petroleum prospecting licence that includes blocks that constitute a location, the licensee–

(*a*) makes written application to the Minister for an extension or a further extension of the licence in respect of some or all of those blocks; and
(*b*) satisfies the Minister that–

(iii) the blocks contain all or part of a petroleum pool or are otherwise properly included in a location; and
(iv) the construction, establishment and operation of facilities for the recovery of petroleum is not economically feasible,

the Minister may grant an extension or a further extension of the petroleum prospecting licence in respect of those blocks.
(4) An extension under Subsection (3) shall be for a period not exceeding one year.

31. CONDITIONS OF GRANT OF PETROLEUM PROSPECTING LICENCE.

(1) A petroleum prospecting licence may be granted subject to such conditions as the Minister, after considering the advice of the Board, thinks fit and specifies in the licence.
(2) In addition to conditions included in a petroleum prospecting licence under Subsection (1) or on an extension of that licence under Section 29, the licence is subject to the conditions–

(*a*) that acceptable proposals for work and expenditure in the third, fourth, fifth, and sixth years, if applicable, of the licence or that extension shall be submitted to the Minister for approval not later than two months before the expiration of the second and fourth years of the licence or that extension, as the case requires; and

(*b*) that in, or in relation to, the licence area, the licensee will, during the first two years of the licence, carry out the work and expend the amounts specified in the licence conditions for those years; and
(*c*) that at the end of the period of six months after the date of grant of the licence and at the end of every subsequent period of six months of the term of the licence, the licensee shall forward to the Director, in duplicate, a report showing the nature and results of prospecting operations conducted during the immediately preceding period of six months, with a plan of the area prospected, showing all available information together with a programme of his operations for the next succeeding six months; and
(*d*) that, at the end of the period of six months after the date of grant, and at the end of every subsequent period of six months, the licensee shall forward to the Director a statement, in duplicate, showing the amounts expended in relation to the licence during the immediately preceding period of six months; and
(*e*) that the licensee will provide to the Director reports on the activities of the licensee in respect of the licence containing such information and at such frequency as are specified in and will otherwise comply with any direction given under Section 148; and
(*f*) that the licensee will carry out social mapping and landowner identification studies in accordance with Section 47; and
(*g*) that, in addition to complying with Paragraph (f), at the end of each year of the licence, the licensee shall present to the Director a report on prospecting operations in the previous year and proposed operations for the following year.

(3) The conditions to which a licence or an extension of that licence under Section 29 is subject, including the conditions specified in Subsection (2), may be varied in the third, fourth, fifth and sixth years, if applicable, insofar as they relate to the work programme and in accordance with proposals submitted under Subsection (2)(a).

DIVISION 3. DISCOVERY OF PETROLEUM IN LICENCE AREA.

32. DISCOVERY OF PETROLEUM TO BE NOTIFIED.

(1) Where petroleum is discovered in a licence area, the tenement holder–

(*a*) shall immediately inform the Director of the discovery; and
(*b*) shall, within a period of three days after the date of the discovery, furnish to the Minister written particulars of the discovery.

(2) Where petroleum is discovered in a licence area, the Director may, from time to time, by instrument served on the tenement holder, direct the tenement holder to furnish to him, within the period specified in the instrument, written particulars of–

(*a*) the chemical composition and physical properties of the petroleum; and
(*b*) the nature of the subsoil in which the petroleum occurs; and
(*c*) any other matters relating to the discovery that are specified by the Director in the instrument.

(3) A person to whom a direction is given under Subsection (2) who fails or refuses to comply with the direction is guilty of an offence.
Penalty: A fine not exceeding K5,000.00.

33. DIRECTIONS BY MINISTER ON DISCOVERY OF PETROLEUM.

(1) Where petroleum is discovered in a licence area, the Minister may, by instrument served on the tenement holder, direct the tenement holder to do, within the period specified in the instrument, such things as the Minister thinks necessary and specifies in the instrument, including the completion of wells, the conduct of drill stem or extended production tests for appraisal of the petroleum pool to which the discovery relates (including the construction in accordance with the direction and the operation of pipes and facilities to gather and transport petroleum to a point of testing or treatment or disposal), and the recovery and sale or other disposal of all petroleum so produced, to determine–

(*a*) the chemical composition and physical properties of the petroleum; and
(*b*) the quantity of petroleum in the petroleum pool to which the discovery relates, or if part only of that petroleum pool is within the licence area, in the part of the petroleum pool that is within the licence area.

(2) A person to whom a direction is given under Subsection (1) who fails or refuses to comply with the direction is guilty of an offence.
Penalty: A fine not exceeding K5,000.00.

34. DECLARATION OF LOCATION.

(1) In this section, **"discovery block"** means a block in which petroleum has been discovered.
(2) Where petroleum has been discovered in a block within a tenement (not being a block that is or is included in a location) the Minister–

(*a*) shall, on receipt of a request from the licensee; and
(*b*) may in any case,

declare by notice in the National Gazette–

(*c*) in a case referred to in Paragraph (a)–the discovery block and not more than eight adjoining blocks within the licence area that are nominated by the licensee; or
(*d*) in any other case–the discovery block and such adjoining blocks as the Minister thinks proper,

to be a location for the purposes of this Act.
(3) At the request of the tenement holder or of his own volition the Minister may, by notice in the National Gazette–

(*a*) include in a location additional adjoining blocks; or
(*b*) revoke the declaration of a location in respect of one or more blocks,

but a location may not at any time include more than nine blocks.
(4) For the purposes of this section, a block adjoins a discovery block, if the graticular section that constitutes or includes the first-mentioned block has a side in common with, or touches–

(*a*) the discovery block; or
(*b*) any block that has a side in common with, or touches, the discovery block.

35. INVESTIGATION, ETC., OF LOCATION.

(1) Where a location has been declared under Section 34, the Minister may, by written notice served on the tenement holder, direct that the tenement holder carry out, within a period specified in the notice of not less than two years, such investigations and studies as the Minister thinks proper to assess the feasibility of the construction, establishment and operation of an industry for the recovery of petroleum from the location.
(2) The investigations and studies referred to in Subsection (1) may include–
(*a*) technical and economic feasibility studies relating to the recovery and transport of petroleum from the location and processing of the petroleum; and
(*b*) studies of proposed sites for facilities that would be required by the industry referred to in Subsection (1); and
(*c*) studies of port or berthing facilities, and roads, pipelines or other transportation facilities; and
(*d*) investigations into–

(i) suitable water facilities and reticulation systems for industrial and town purposes; and
(ii) the location and design of a suitable airstrip and associated landing and terminal facilities, if required; and
(iii) the generation and transmission of electricity as required; and

(*e*) investigations into the development, if required, of a suitable town for the industry referred to in Subsection (1), including the design of housing facilities and associated civic, cultural and social facilities; and
(*f*) investigations of any other works, services or facilities that may be required by that industry in relation to the location; and
(*g*) studies of future labour requirements for that industry; and
(*h*) physical impact studies into the possible effects of that industry on the environment.

(3) The tenement holder shall furnish to the Minister, within the period specified in the notice under Subsection (1), such reports, analyses and data resulting from the investigations and studies carried out under this section as the Minister, by written notice served on the tenement holder, may require.

36. REVOCATION OF DECLARATION OF LOCATION.

(1) Where, in respect of a block included in a location, the licensee does not within–

(*a*) a period of two years following the declaration of the location under Section 34(2); or
(*b*) any further period that the Minister allows under Section 53(1),

apply–

(*c*) in the case of a location declared in a petroleum prospecting licence, for a petroleum retention licence or petroleum development licence in respect of the blocks included in the

location; or
(*d*) in the case of a location declared in a petroleum retention licence, for a petroleum development licence in respect of the blocks included in the location or a variation of the petroleum retention licence to cover the specific petroleum pool in respect of which the location was declared; or
(*e*) in the case of a location declared in a petroleum development licence, for a variation of the petroleum development licence to provide for the development of the specific petroleum pool in respect of which the location was declared,

the Minister shall, by notice in the National Gazette, revoke the declaration of the location.
(2) Where all applications made under Section 53(1) for a petroleum development licence or Section 37(1) for a petroleum retention licence in respect of a block that is included in a location have lapsed, the petroleum prospecting licence or petroleum retention licence, as the case may be, is revoked in respect of that block.
(3) Where a petroleum prospecting licence is revoked in respect of a block under Subsection (2), the Minister shall, by notice in the National Gazette, revoke the declaration of the location so far as it includes that block.

DIVISION 4. PETROLEUM RETENTION LICENCES.

37. APPLICATION FOR PETROLEUM RETENTION LICENCE.

(1) A licensee whose petroleum prospecting licence is in force in respect of the blocks that constitute a location may, within two years after the date on which the blocks were declared to be a location, or such further period as the Minister allows, make application to the Director for the grant of a petroleum retention licence in respect of such of the blocks as the licensee satisfies the Minister contain a gas field or a part of a gas field or, for the better administration of petroleum activities, should be included in a petroleum retention licence.
(2) A licensee may, during the term of a petroleum prospecting licence, make application to the Director for a petroleum retention licence in respect of any block or blocks within the licence area–

(*a*) that he satisfies the Minister contains or contain a gas field or part of a gas field, or, for the better administration of petroleum activities, should be included in a petroleum retention licence; and
(*b*) that do not at the time of making the application constitute a location.

(3) A person who is not the holder of a tenement in respect of a block or blocks may make application to the Director for a petroleum retention licence in respect of that block or those blocks where–

(*a*) he satisfies the Minister that such block or blocks contains or contain a gas field or part of a gas field; and
(*b*) that block is not a block or those blocks are not blocks in respect of which a tenement is in force at the time of the application.

38. FORM OF APPLICATION FOR PETROLEUM RETENTION LICENCE.

(1) An application under Section 37–

(*a*) shall be in an approved form; and
(*b*) shall be made in an approved manner; and
(*c*) shall be accompanied by particulars of–

(i) the proposals of the applicant for work and expenditure in respect of the area comprised in the block or blocks specified in the application; and
(ii) the commercial viability of the recovery of petroleum from the area comprised in the block or blocks specified in the application at the time of the application, and of the possible future commercial viability of the recovery of petroleum from that area; and

(*d*) may set out any other matters that the applicant wishes the Minister to consider; and
(*e*) shall be accompanied by the fee prescribed by Section 157.

(2) The Director may, by instrument served on the applicant, require him to furnish, within a period specified in the instrument–

(*a*) such further written information in connection with his application as the Director specifies in the instrument; and
(*b*) such proposals, in addition to or by way of alteration to any proposals that have already been furnished under Subsection (1) as the Director specifies in the instrument, including proposals relating to any of the matters referred to in Section 35(2).

39. NOTIFICATION OF GRANT OF PETROLEUM RETENTION LICENCE.

(1) Where an application for the grant of a petroleum retention licence has been made–

(*a*) under Section 37(1) or (2); and
(*b*) the applicant has furnished proposals and any further information required by the Director under Section 38; and
(*c*) the Minister, after considering a report from the Board, is satisfied as to the matters set out in Section 37(1) or (2) and with the proposals and other information provided under Section 38 and that recovery of petroleum from the area comprised in the blocks specified in the application–

(i) is not at the time of application commercially viable; and
(ii) could become commercially viable within the period of time ending at the expiration of a petroleum retention licence if extended for the maximum permitted period,

the Minister shall, by instrument served on the applicant, inform the applicant–

(*d*) that–

(i) he is prepared to approve the proposals wholly or in part, and to grant to the applicant, on the basis of the approved proposals, a petroleum retention licence in respect of the blocks specified in the application; and
(ii)[24] the applicant will be required to lodge a security for compliance with the conditions to which the licence, if granted, will be subject, and with the provisions of this Act, and to pay the first annual fee; or

(*e*) that he will defer consideration of a decision on the licence application until the applicant furnishes such proposals, in addition to or by way of alteration to the proposals furnished under Section 38 as the Minister specifies in the instrument, including proposals relating to any of the matters referred to in Section 35(2); or
(*e*) that he is prepared to approve the proposals and to grant to the applicant a petroleum retention licence in respect of the blocks specified in the application, subject to the applicant–

(i) making such alterations to the proposals; or
(ii) complying with such conditions in relation to the proposals,

as the Minister thinks reasonable.
(2) Where an application is made under Section 37(3), the Minister may–

(*a*) refuse to grant the application and advise the applicant accordingly; or
(*b*) treat the application as an application made under Section 37(1) or (2).

(3) Where, under Subsection (2), the Minister elects to treat an application as an application made under Section 37(1) or (2), that application shall, for the purposes of this section and Section 40, be deemed to be an application so made.
(4) In the case of an Instrument to which Subsection (1)(f) applies, the Minister shall give to the applicant details of his reasons for requiring the alterations or imposing the conditions referred to in the instrument.
(5) An instrument under Subsection (1)(d), (e) or (f) shall contain a statement to the effect that the application will lapse if–

(*a*) the applicant does not furnish any further proposals that the Minister requires within such period as the Minister specifies in the instrument, being a period of not less than two months nor more than one year; or
(*b*) the applicant does not make a request under Section 40(1) in respect of the grant of the licence; or
(*c*)[25] the applicant does not lodge with the Director the security referred to in Subsection (1)(d)(ii), and does not pay the first annual fee referred to in that Subsection.

(6) In determining whether recovery of petroleum is commercially viable for the purposes of Subsection (1)(c) and Section 45(1)(b), the Minister shall invite and consider submissions from the applicant and shall take into account all relevant matters including technical assessment of the petroleum situated within the blocks constituting the area at the time and the estimated development costs and likelihood that a development would earn a reasonable rate consistent with international petroleum industry anticipated returns on gas projects.

40. GRANT OR REFUSAL OF PETROLEUM RETENTION LICENCE.

(1) An applicant who has been served with an instrument under Section 39(1) may, before the expiration of–

(*a*) the period of three months after the date of service of the instrument on him or such further period, not exceeding three months, as the Minister allows; or
(*b*) the period specified by the Minister under Section 39(5)(a),

whichever is the later,

(*c*) by instrument served on the Minister–

(i) request the Minister to grant to him the licence to which the first-mentioned instrument relates; or
(ii) furnish the Minister with any further particulars required under Section 39(1)(e); and
(iii) pay the first annual fee to the Director.

(*d*)[26] lodged with the Director the security and the first annual fee referred to in Section 39(1)(d)(ii).

(2) Where–

(*a*) an applicant has, within the period specified in Subsection (1)–

(i) made a request under Subsection (1)(c); and
(ii)[27] lodge with the Director the security and the first annual fee referred to in Section 39(1)(d)(ii); and
(iii) furnished the Minister with any further proposals required under Section 39(1)(e); and

(*b*) the Minister is satisfied that the applicant's proposals and further proposals adequately provide for such market and technical studies as may reasonably be expected to provide sufficient information to enable the gas field to be brought to timely economic development,

the Minister shall approve the proposals and grant to the applicant a petroleum retention licence in respect of the blocks referred to in Section 39(1)(c), but in any other case the Minister may, by instrument, refuse to grant the licence.

(3) The Minister shall not refuse under Subsection (2) to grant the licence unless–

(*a*) he has, by the instrument referred to in Subsection (2) served on the applicant, given not less than one month's notice of his intention to do so; and
(*b*) he has, in that instrument–

(i) given the reasons for his intention; and
(ii) specified a date on or before which the applicant may, by instrument served on the Minister, submit any matter that the applicant requires the Minister to consider including new proposals generally or in respect of some particular matter; and

(*c*) he has given to the applicant, and to any persons whom the applicant thinks fit to consult, a full opportunity to consult with the Minister concerning the Minister's intention to refuse the licence; and
(*d*) he has taken into account, after considering a report from the Board, any matters raised in the course of such consultations by the applicant or by any other person referred to in Paragraph (c).

(4) Where the holder of a petroleum prospecting licence applies for a petroleum retention licence in respect of all or part of the area of that petroleum prospecting licence, then notwithstanding the provisions of Division 2 as to expiry of the petroleum prospecting licence that petroleum prospecting licence shall not expire in respect of the area for which a petroleum retention licence is sought until the Minister has granted or refused to grant, as the case may be, a petroleum retention licence under Subsection (2).
(5) Where the holder of a petroleum prospecting licence applies for a petroleum retention licence in respect of all or part of the area of that petroleum prospecting licence and the Minister refuses to grant a petroleum retention licence on the ground that he is not satisfied as to the matter referred to in Section 39(1)(c)(i), then notwithstanding the provisions of Division 2 as to expiry of the petroleum prospecting licence that petroleum prospecting licence shall not expire in respect of the area for which a petroleum retention licence was sought until one year after the date of the instrument referred to in Subsection (2).

41. VARIATION OF PETROLEUM RETENTION LICENCE.

(1) The holder of a petroleum retention licence may make application to the Minister for a variation of the licence by the inclusion of an additional block or group of blocks–

(*a*) having a side or sides in common, or touching, a block the subject of the petroleum retention licence; and
(*b*) not being the subject of a tenement held by a person other than the applicant or the subject of a petroleum development licence held by the applicant.

(2) Where an application is made under Subsection (1), the Minister may, by instrument served on the licensee, vary the petroleum retention licence to include in the licence area the block or blocks to which the application relates.
(3) From and including the day on which a variation of a licence under this section takes effect–

(*a*) the blocks included in the licence area by reason of the variation are, subject to this Act, for the remainder of the term of the licence, blocks in respect of which the petroleum retention licence is in force; and
(*b*) any petroleum prospecting licence that is in force in respect of the blocks so included is revoked in respect of those blocks.

(4) The holder of a petroleum retention licence may, at any time, make an application to the Minister for any other variation of the petroleum retention licence.
(5) An application under Subsection (4) shall–

(*a*) specify the reasons for proposed variation; and
(*b*) be made in an approved form and contain the information specified in Section 38.

(6) The Director may require the applicant to furnish such further information in connection with his application as the Director considers necessary.
(7) Following receipt of an application under Subsection (4) the Minister may, after considering a report of the Board and any matters submitted to him under this section–

(*a*) amend the terms of the petroleum retention licence to provide as stipulated in the application or as otherwise agreed with the petroleum retention licensee; or
(*b*) refuse the application, in which case the existing petroleum retention licence shall remain in full force and effect.

42. RIGHTS CONFERRED BY PETROLEUM RETENTION LICENCE.

A petroleum retention licence, while it remains in force, confers on the licensee, subject to this Act and to the conditions specified in the licence, exclusive rights–

(*a*) to explore for petroleum in the petroleum retention licence area; and
(*b*) to carry on field studies to obtain information to ensure timely economic development of the gas field in the petroleum retention licence area; and
(*c*)[28] to carry on such operations and execute such works in the petroleum retention licence area as are necessary for or in connection with the purposes specified in Paragraphs (a) and (b), including the construction and operation of water lines; and.
(*d*)[29] if authorized by the Director, to complete wells, carry out drill stem tests or extended production tests for appraisal of a petroleum pool (including the construction and the operation of pipes and facilities to gather and transport petroleum to a point of testing or treatment or disposal), and to recover ans sell or otherwise dispose of all petroleum do produced.

43. TERM OF PETROLEUM RETENTION LICENCE.

Subject to this Act and to any condition in the licence, a petroleum retention licence remains in force–

(*a*) for a period of five years commencing on the day on which the licence takes effect; and
(*b*) where the licence is extended under Section 45–for a further period of five years at each extension.

44. APPLICATION FOR EXTENSION OF PETROLEUM RETENTION LICENCE.

(1) The holder of a petroleum retention licence may make application to the Minister for an extension of the licence.
(2) An application under this section may be made twice only in respect of a licence.
(3) An application for an extension of a petroleum retention licence–

(*a*) shall be in an approved form; and
(*b*) subject to Subsection (4), shall be made in an approved manner not later than six months before the day on which the licence is due to expire; and
(*c*) shall be accompanied by particulars of–

(i) the blocks in respect of which the extension is sought; and
(ii) the work carried out and the amounts expended in respect of the licence area up to and including a date not earlier than one month immediately preceding the date of application; and
(iii) the proposals of the licensee for work and expenditure in respect of the area; and

(*d*) shall be accompanied by the applicant's submissions in respect of the matters set out in Paragraphs 45(1)(a), (b) and (c); and
(*e*) shall be accompanied by the fee prescribed by Section 157.

(4) The Minister may, after considering a report from the Board, accept an application for the extension of a petroleum retention licence later than six months before the licence is due to expire, but in any case not after the licence has expired.

45. GRANT OR REFUSAL OF EXTENSION OF PETROLEUM RETENTION LICENCE.

(1) Where a petroleum retention licensee who has complied with the conditions specified in the petroleum retention licence and with the provisions of this Act, makes an application under Section 44 for the extension of the licence, the Minister shall, if he is satisfied–

(*a*) that–

(i) the blocks in respect of which the extension is sought contain a gas field or part thereof; or
(ii) it is appropriate for the proper administration of petroleum activities that the blocks in respect

of which the extension is sought are included in the licence; and

(*b*) that the recovery of petroleum from the area comprised in the blocks specified in the application–

(i) is not at the time of application commercially viable; and
(ii) could become commercially viable within the period of time ending at the expiration of the petroleum retention licence if extended for the maximum permitted time; and

(*c*) that the applicant's proposals provide adequately for such market and technical studies and other work as may reasonably be expected to provide sufficient information to enable the gas field to be brought to timely economic development,

inform the licensee, by instrument served on the licensee, that he is prepared to grant to the licensee the extension of the licence.
(2) Where a petroleum retention licensee who has not complied with the conditions specified in the licence or with the provisions of this Act, makes an application under Section 44 for the extension of the licence, the Minister may, if, after considering a report from the Board, he is satisfied as to the matters set out in Subsection (1) and further satisfied that, although the licensee has not so complied, special circumstances exists that justify the granting of the extension of the licence, inform the licensee, by instrument served on the licensee, that he is prepared to grant to him an extension of the licence.
(3) Where a petroleum retention licensee has not complied with the conditions specified in the licence or with the provisions of this Act, and the Minister is not satisfied that special circumstances exist that justify the granting of the extension of the licence, the Minister shall, subject to Subsection (5), by instrument served on the licensee, refuse to grant the extension of the licence.
(4) Where the Minister is not satisfied as to the matters set out in Subsection (1), the Minister shall, subject to Subsection (5), by instrument served on the licensee, refuse to grant the extension of the licence.
(5) The Minister shall not refuse to grant the extension of a petroleum retention licence unless–

(*a*) he has, by instrument served on the licensee, given not less than one month's notice of his intention to refuse to grant the extension of the licence; and
(*b*) he has served a copy of the instrument on such other persons (if any) as he thinks fit; and
(*c*) he has, in the instrument–

(i) given the reasons for his intention to refuse; and
(ii) specified a date on or before which the licensee or a person on whom a copy of the instrument is served may, by instrument served on the Minister, submit any matters that he requires the Minister to consider; and

(*d*) he has taken into account, after considering a report from the Board, any matters so submitted to him, on or before the specified date, by the licensee or a person on whom a copy of the instrument has been served.

(6) An instrument under Subsection (1) or (2) shall contain–

(*a*) a summary of the conditions to which the grant of the extension is to be subject; and
(*b*) a statement to the effect that the application will lapse if the licensee–

(i) does not make a request under Subsection (7); or
(ii) does not pay the annual fee.

(7) A licensee who has been served with an instrument under Subsection (1) or (2) may, within a period of one month after the date of service of the instrument on him–

(*a*) by instrument served on the Minister, request the Minister to grant to him the extension of the licence; and
(*b*) pay the next annual fee.

(8) Where a licensee who has been served with an instrument under Subsection (1) or (2) has, within the period specified in Subsection (7)–

(*a*) made a request under Subsection (7); and
(*b*) paid the next annual fee,

the Minister shall approve the proposals and grant to the licensee the extension of the licence.
(9) Where a licensee who has been served with an instrument under Subsection (1) or (2) has not, within the period specified in Subsection (7)–

(*a*) made a request under Subsection (7); or
(*b*) paid the next annual fee,

the application lapses at the end of that period.
(10) Subject to Subsection (11), where–

(*a*) an application for the extension of a licence is made under Section 44; and
(*b*) the licence expires–

(i) before the Minister grants, or refuses to grant, the extension of the licence; or
(ii) before the application lapses under Subsection (9),

the licence shall be deemed to continue in force in all respects–

(*c*) until the Minister refuses to grant the extension of the licence; or

(*d*) until the application lapses under Subsection (9),

whichever first occurs.

(11) Where the Minister refuses to grant an extension under this section on the ground that he is not satisfied as to the matter referred to in Subsection (1)(b)(i), then notwithstanding the provisions of this Division as to expiry of the petroleum retention licence that petroleum retention licence shall not expire until one year after the date of service of the instrument referred to in Subsection (4).

46. CONDITIONS OF PETROLEUM RETENTION LICENCE.

A petroleum retention licence and any extension of a petroleum retention licence–

(*a*) is subject to conditions that–

(i) the licensee will carry out the proposals approved under Section 40(2) or 45(8); and

(ii) the licensee will provide to the Director reports on the activities of the licensee in respect of the licence containing such information and at such frequency as are specified in and will otherwise comply with any direction given under Section 148; and

(iii) the licensee will carry out social mapping and landowner identification studies in accordance with Section 47; and

(*b*) may be made subject to such other conditions not inconsistent with this Act–

(i) as the Minister thinks proper and as are specified in the licence or extension of the licence; or

(ii) in respect of any matter or matters arising out of the applicant's proposals referred to in Section 38(1)(c) that are not administered under this Act, as the Minister, after consultation with the Minister responsible for administering that matter or those matters, thinks proper and specifies in the licence or extension of the licence; and

(*c*) may require the licensee to enter into a gas agreement.

DIVISION 5. SOCIAL MAPPING AND LANDOWNER IDENTIFICATION STUDIES.

47. SOCIAL MAPPING AND LANDOWNER IDENTIFICATION STUDIES.

(1) It shall be a condition of every petroleum prospecting licence that the licensee undertake social mapping studies and landowner identification studies in accordance with this section.

(2) It shall be a condition of every petroleum retention licence that the licensee undertake social mapping studies and landowner identification studies in accordance with this section, to the extent that such studies have not been undertaken pursuant to a petroleum prospecting licence out of which the petroleum retention licence was granted.
(3) It shall be a condition of every petroleum development licence that the licensee undertake social mapping studies and landowner identification studies in accordance with this section, to the extent that such studies have not been undertaken pursuant to a petroleum prospecting licence or petroleum retention licence out of which the petroleum development licence was granted.
(4)[30] [31]Prior to first entry on to the licence area for the purposes of exploration pursuant to a petroleum prospecting licence or a petroleum retention licence, the licensee shall undertake–

(*a*) a preliminary social mapping study; and
(*b*) a preliminary landowner identification study,

of the customary land owners comprised in the licence area, with particular reference to that part of the licence area where the licensee's exploration activities are to be concentrated.
(5)[32] [33]If a licensee or a person makes an application for a petroleum development licence under Section 53, the licensee shall submit with that application a full-scale social mapping study and landowner identification study of customary land owners in –

(*a*) the licence area of that petroleum development licence; and
(*b*) other licence areas, including pipeline areas, which pertain to that petroleum development licence; and
(*c*) the land within five kilometres of any facility which would be a dedicated project facility (other than a facility which would be situated on such a petroleum development licence) of the petroleum project; and
(*d*) other areas which would be affected by the petroleum project if developed.

(5A)[34] [35]If a licensee makes an application for a variation of the licence under Section 85(1), to include an additional block or blocks in a petroleum development licence, the licensee shall submit with that application a full-scale social mapping study and landowner identification study os customary land owners in –

(*a*) the additional block or blocks that will form part of that petroleum development licence; and
(*b*) other licence areas, including pipeline easements, which are associated with the petroleum development licence upon variation of such licence; and
(*c*) the land within five kilometres of any facility which would be a dedicated project facility (other than a facility which would bc situated on such a petroleum development licence) of the petroleum project; and
(*d*) other areas which would be affected by the development of the additional block or blocks.

(6) The Minister may by regulation prescribe the scope and method of a social mapping study or landowner identification study conducted in accordance with this section, and requirements as to reports of such studies.
(7) Copies of any social mapping or landowner identification studies undertaken in accordance with this section (excluding any information which is confidential to the licensee or to the local groups of landowners) shall be provided to the Director.

DIVISION 6. PROJECT CONSULTATION.

48. DEVELOPMENT FORUM.

[36](1) Subject to Section 169(8), prior to the first grant of a licence or licences in respect of a petroleum project, the Minister shall convene a development forum at a place close to the proposed licence area to provide ease of access, being a meeting to which are invited persons who, in the view of the Minister, will be affected by that petroleum project, including –

(*a*) the applicant or intending applicant for the licence or licences; and
(*b*) the project area landowners determined under Section 169(2) or their duly appointed or elected respresentatives; and
(*c*) the Local-level Government or Governments who would be affected Local-level Governments of the project if the application is granted; and
(*d*) the Provincial Government or Governments who would be affected Provincial Governments of the project if the application is granted; and
(*e*) the State.

(2) If subsequent to the first grant of a licence or licences in respect of a petroleum project there is an application for a further licence or licences or the variation under Section 58(1) of a petroleum development licence in respect of that petroleum project, the Minister shall convene a further development forum in respect of that petroleum project to which are invited persons who, as a result of social mapping and landowner identification studies, in the view of the Minister, fairly represent those parties defined in Section 48(1)(a) to (e) inclusive.
(3) The purpose of a development forum is to endeavour to reach agreement on matters on which agreement among those present is desirable, including the matters referred to in Part IV.

49. MATTERS REQUIRED BEFORE DEVELOPMENT FORUM.

A development forum shall not be convened in respect of a proposed petroleum project until–

(*a*) the applicant or intending applicant for a licence or licences has completed and presented to the Minister full-scale social mapping and landowner identification studies in accordance with Subsection 47(5); and
(*b*) the Minister is satisfied, on the basis of the results of those studies, that the people who would be project area landowners of the petroleum project are truly represented by the persons who are to be invited to the development forum as their representatives; and
(*c*) the applicant or intending applicant has submitted to the Minister, and to the Minister responsible for environmental matters, a socio-economic impact study as part of the environmental plan required under the *Environmental Planning Act 1978*; and
(*d*) the Director has prepared a proposal, after giving due consideration to the results of the full-scale social mapping and landowner identification studies and the socio-economic impact study and the principle set out in Section 170(3), for the equitable sharing of the equity benefit and the royalty benefit

amongst project area landowners, and has provided that proposal to representatives of those future project area landowners.

50. DEVELOPMENT AGREEMENT.

(1) An agreement between the State and any of the project area landowners, the affected Local-level Governments and the affected Provincial Government of a petroleum project governing the matters subject to agreement which are referred to in Part IV shall be contained in a development agreement.
(2) In addition to the matters referred to in Subsection (1), a development agreement may contain any other matter agreed between the parties.

50A. COORDINATION OF BENEFITS FOR GAS PROJECTS.

[37](1) Where –

(*a*) licensees enter into aunit development under Section 64 or co-ordinated petroleum development under Section 65; or
(*b*) a gas agreement defines the extend of a particular gas project to include more than one licence,

the State and the project area landowners, the affected Local level-Governments and affected Provincial Governments may enter into a co-ordinated development agreement which may vary or replace an agreement or agreements in relation to petroleum projects under the former Act or a development agreement or agreements under this Act.
(2) A co-ordinated development agreement shall govern the matters subject to agreement referred to in Part IV of this Act and any other matter agreed to between parties.

51. POWER TO SIGN DEVELOPMENT AGREEMENT.

[38]The Minister, acting with the approval of the National Executive Council, has the power to execute on behalf of the State a development agreement or a co-ordinated development agreement and any amendment of such agreements.

52. CONSULTATION WITH AFFECTED LOCAL-LEVEL GOVERNMENTS AND AFFECTED PROVINCIAL GOVERNMENTS.

(1)[39] [40]The Minister shall, following notification to tenement holder under Section 35(1), notify each Local-level Government and Provincial Government which would likely be an affected Local-level Government or affected Provincial Government of the petroleum project if developed, of the details of the notice served on the tenement holder.
(2) The Minister shall, in relation to any proposed petroleum project, consult with each Local-level Government and Provincial Government which would likely be an affected Local-level Government or affected Provincial Government of the petroleum project if developed, on the terms of–

(*a*) any written agreement to be entered into by the State in relation to the proposed petroleum project; and
(*b*) any licence to be granted in respect of the proposed petroleum project.

52A. COORDINATION OF DEVELOPMENT FORUM.

[41](1) Where a licensee makes application under Section 53, or applies to vary a licence by the inclusion of additional blocks under Section 58, or where the State enters into a gas agreement under Section 184 with a licensee which defines the extent of the gas project to include all or part of the licence areas of a petroleum prospecting licence, a petroleum development licence or a petroleum retention licence, the licensee of any licence of any licence affected by such application, variation or gas agreement and the State shall upon a plan to coordinate convening a development forum pursuant to the provisions of Section 48.
(2) An applicant shall pay a prescribed amount, not exceeding K250,000.00, as its contribution towards the cost of the development forum, if a development forum is required under Section 48.
(3) Where a coordinated development pursuant to a gas agreement requires the grant of additional licences or the variation of licences, then that coordinated development will require only a development forum to be held in respect of that gas agreement as part of the coordinated development represented in that gas agreement unless the Minister considers that those factors mentioned in Section 48(2) requires more than one development forum to be held in respect of that coordinated development.

DIVISION 7. PETROLEUM DEVELOPMENT LICENCES.

53. APPLICATION FOR PETROLEUM DEVELOPMENT LICENCE.

(1) A licensee whose petroleum prospecting licence or petroleum retention licence is in force in respect of the blocks that constitute a location may, within two years after the date on which the blocks were declared to be a location, or such further period as the Minister allows, make application to the Director for the grant of a petroleum development licence in respect of such of the blocks as the licensee satisfies the Minister contain a petroleum pool or a part of a petroleum pool.
(2) A licensee may, during the term of a petroleum prospecting licence or petroleum retention licence, make application to the Director for a petroleum development licence in respect of any block or blocks within the licence area–

(*a*) that he satisfies the Minister contains or contain a petroleum pool or part of a petroleum pool; and
(*b*) that do not at the time of making the application constitute a location.

(3) A person who is not the holder of a tenement in respect of that block or those blocks may make application to the Director for a petroleum development licence in respect of a block or blocks–

(*a*) that he satisfies the Minister contains or contain a petroleum pool or part of a petroleum pool; and
(*b*) that is not a block or are not blocks in respect of which a tenement is in force at the time of the application.

54. FORM OF APPLICATION FOR PETROLEUM DEVELOPMENT LICENCE.

(1) An application under Section 53–

(*a*) shall be in an approved form; and
(*b*) shall be made in an approved manner; and

(*c*) shall be accompanied by detailed proposals by the applicant for the construction, establishment and operation of all facilities and services for and incidental to the recovery, processing, storage and transportation of petroleum from the licence area; and
(*d*) may set out any other matters that the applicant wishes the Minister to consider; and
(*e*) shall be accompanied by the fee prescribed by Section 157.

(2) The Director may, by instrument served on the applicant, require him to furnish, within a period specified in the instrument–

(*a*) such further written information in connection with his application as the Director specifies in the instrument; and
(*b*) such proposals, in addition to or by way of alteration to any proposals that have already been furnished under Subsection (1) as the Director specifies in the instrument, including proposals relating to any of the matters referred to in Section 35(2); and
(*c*) such information and proposals, or information and proposals in addition to or by way of alteration to information and proposals already supplied, relating to–

(i) the acquisition by the State or its nominee of a participating interest in the petroleum project in respect of which the application is made; and
(ii) the transfer of some or all of the participating interest in an Orogen option project to the Company in accordance with the option agreement and other matters and transactions contemplated by the option agreement.

55. NOTICE OF APPLICATION TO BE PROVIDED TO THE COMPANY, ETC.

(1)[42] [43]On receipt of an application under Section 53 or 73 or 86 in relation to an Orogen option project, the Director or the Minister, as the case may be, shall give written notice to the Company of the receipt of the application.
(2) At any time after receipt of a notice under Subsection (1), the Company may request the applicant to provide to the Company, or to allow the Company access to, such information concerning the application and the applicant's proposals as the Company may reasonably require for the purpose of determining whether it will exercise its option under the option agreement in respect of the Orogen option project.
(3) On receipt of a request under Subsection (2), the applicant shall provide to the Company or allow the Company access to the information requested within such reasonable period as the Company may specify in its request on the condition that the Company–

(*a*) pays the reasonable costs of the applicant incurred in providing or allowing the Company access to the information requested; and
(*b*) subject to Subsection (4), keeps the information confidential on such terms and conditions as the applicant may reasonably require.

(4) The Company shall be permitted to disclose the information referred to in Subsection (2) to–

(*a*) such of its employees, officers or agents whose duties in connection with the exercise of the option require the disclosure of the information; and

(*b*) any adviser or other expert retained in connection with a proposal by the Company to exercise the option,

who undertakes to keep the information confidential on such terms and conditions as the applicant may reasonably require.

(5) A person who discloses the information referred to in Subsection (2) in contravention of the terms and conditions required by the applicant in accordance with Subsections (3)(b) or (4) is guilty of an offence.

Penalty: A fine not exceeding K10,000.00 or imprisonment for a term not exceeding four years or both.

56. NOTIFICATION OF GRANT OF PETROLEUM DEVELOPMENT LICENCE.

(1) Where an application for the grant of a petroleum development licence has been made under Section 53(1) or (2) and the applicant has furnished proposals and any further information required by the Director under Section 54, the Minister, after having regard to physical planning considerations shall, by instrument served on the applicant, inform the applicant–

(*a*) that–

(i) he is prepared to approve the proposals wholly or in part, and to grant to the applicant on the basis of the approved proposals, a petroleum development licence in respect of the blocks specified in the application; and

(ii) the applicant will be required to lodge a security deposit for compliance with–

(A) the conditions relating to the protection and restoration of the environment; and

(B) the provisions of this Act; and

(C) any requirement in any law relating to the protection and restoration of the environment, or any condition imposed on the licensee under any such law; and

(D) any condition relating to the physical planning of the area; and

(iii) the applicant will be required to pay the first annual fee as a condition of the grant of the licence; or

(*b*) that he will defer consideration of a decision on the proposals until the applicant furnishes such proposals, in addition to or by way of alteration to the proposals furnished under Section 54 as the Minister specifies in the instrument, including proposals relating to any of the matters referred to in Section 35(2) or 54(2)(c); or

(*c*) that he is prepared to approve the proposals and to grant to the applicant a petroleum development licence in respect of the blocks specified in the application, subject to the applicant–

(i) making such alterations to the proposals; or
(ii) complying with such conditions in relation to the proposals,

as the Minister thinks reasonable.
(2) Where an application is made under Section 53(3), the Minister may–

(*a*) refuse to grant the application and advise the applicant accordingly; or
(*b*) treat the application as an application made under Section 53(1) or (2).

(3) Where, under Subsection (2), the Minister elects to treat an application as an application made under Section 53(1) or (2), that application shall, for the purposes of this section and Section 57, be deemed to be an application so made.
(4) In the case of an instrument to which Subsection (1)(c) applies, the Minister shall give to the applicant details of his reasons for requiring the alterations or imposing the conditions referred to in the instrument.
(5) An instrument under Subsection (1)(a), (b) or (c) shall contain a statement to the effect that the application will lapse if–

(*a*) the applicant does not furnish any further proposals that the Minister requires within such period as the Minister specifies in the instrument, being a period of not less than two months nor more than one year; or
(*b*) the applicant does not make a request under Section 57(1) in respect of the grant of the licence; or
(*c*) the applicant does not pay to the Director the first annual fee; or
(*d*) the applicant does not lodge with the Director the security specified in the instrument.

57. GRANT OR REFUSAL OF PETROLEUM DEVELOPMENT LICENCE.

(1) An applicant who has been served with an instrument under Section 56(1) may, before the expiration of–

(*a*) the period of three months after the date of service of the instrument on him or such further period or periods as the Minister allows; or
(*b*) the period specified by the Minister under Section 56(5)(a),

whichever is the later, by instrument served on the Minister–

(*c*) request the Minister to grant to him the licence to which the first-mentioned instrument relates; and
(*d*) furnish the Minister with any further proposals required under Section 56(1)(b); and
(*e*) pay the first annual fee to the Director; and
(*f*) lodge with the Director the security deposit referred to in the instrument issued under Section 56(1)(a).

(2) Where–

(*a*) an applicant has, within the period specified in Subsection (1)–

(i) made a request under Subsection (1)(c); and
(ii) paid the first annual fee to the Director; and
(iii) furnished the Minister with any further proposals required under Section 56(1)(b); and
(iv) lodged with the Director the security deposit referred to in the instrument issued under Section 56(1)(a); and

(*b*) the Minister is satisfied, having considered the applicant's proposals and any further submissions of information, and a report from the Board and where it is available the relevant cost-benefit analysis carried out and made available to the National Executive Council by the National Economic and Fiscal Commission under Section 117(8)(a)(v) of the *Organic Law on Provincial Governments and Local-level Governments*, that the proposals for development–

(i) will achieve maximum efficient recovery and prevention of resource waste by applying good oilfield practice; and
(ii) do not interfere with the rights of licensees of adjacent tenements covering common petroleum pools; and
(iii) comply with the State's policy on non-discriminatory access for other persons to any strategic pipelines or strategic petroleum processing facilities involved in the proposals; and
(iv) provide adequately for the protection of the environment and the welfare of the people of the area; and
(v)[44] demonstrate that the applicant has adequately identified the persons who are customary land owners in areas specified under Section 47(5); and
(vi) have duly considered co-ordinated development of any adjacent petroleum discoveries which studies and investigations conducted pursuant to a direction given under Section 65 reveal to be in the interest of the State; and
(vii) promote viable domestic utilisation of petroleum and petroleum products to the extent reasonably possible; and
(viii) will otherwise be in the best interests of the Independent State of Papua New Guinea,

the Minister shall approve the proposals and grant to the applicant a petroleum development licence in respect of the blocks referred to in Section 56(1)(c), but in any other case the Minister may, by instrument, refuse to grant the licence.
(3) The Minister shall not refuse under Subsection (2) to grant a petroleum development licence unless–

(*a*) he has, by the instrument referred to in Subsection (2) served on the applicant, given not less than one month's notice of his intention to do so; and
(*b*) he has, in that instrument–

(i) given particulars of the reasons for his intention; and
(ii) specified a date on or before which the applicant may, by instrument served on the Minister, submit any matters that the applicant requires the Minister to consider, including new proposals generally or in respect of some particular matter; and

(*c*) he has given to the applicant, and to any persons whom the applicant thinks fit to consult, a full opportunity to consult with the Minister concerning the Minister's intention to refuse to grant the licence; and
(*d*) he has taken into account, after considering a report from the Board, any matters raised in the course of such consultations by the applicant or by any other person referred to in Paragraph (c).

(4) Where the grounds for the Minister's refusal, under this section, of an application is that the applicant's proposals or further proposals do not satisfy the requirements of Subsection (2)(b), the applicant may, by written notice to the Minister before the date referred to in Subsection (3)(b)(ii), require that the question be referred to arbitration.
(5) The method of arbitration for the purpose of Subsection (4) may be the subject of a written agreement between the State and the applicant, and the method so agreed will be binding on the Minister.
(6) Where the method of arbitration is not the subject of an agreement referred to in Subsection (5), the matter stands referred to arbitration in accordance with the *Arbitration Act 1951* on receipt by the Minister of the requirement.
(7) Where a matter is referred to arbitration under this section, the application does not lapse until the arbitrator has made his award and, where the award is made in the applicant's favour, the Minister has granted the petroleum development licence.
(8) Subject to Subsection (7), where an applicant has been served with an instrument under Subsection (2) refusing to grant an application, the application lapses at the end of the period referred to in Subsection (3)(b)(ii) unless the Minister withdraws his refusal.
(9) Where a licensee makes application under Section 53(1) or (2) for a petroleum development licence and the petroleum prospecting licence or petroleum retention licence would but for this subsection expire before the application has been dealt with in accordance with this section, the petroleum prospecting licence or petroleum retention licence, as the case may be, shall, notwithstanding the provisions of Division 2 or 4 as to the expiry thereof, continue in force in respect of the block or blocks until the first-mentioned application has been dealt with.
(10) The Minister shall not grant a petroleum development licence under this section in relation to an Orogen option project unless the Minister has first given to the Company written notice.

58. VARIATION OF PETROLEUM DEVELOPMENT LICENCE.

[45](1) The holder of a petroleum development licence may make application to the Minister for a variation of the licence by the inclusion of an additional block or group of blocks –

(*a*) having a side or sides in common, or touching, block the subject of the petroleum development licence; and
(*b*) subject to Subsection (2), not being the subject of a tenement held by a person other than the applicant.

(2) The holder of a petroleum development licence may make an application under Subsection (1) for the inclusion of an additional block or group of blocks even they are the subject of a tenement held by a person other than the applicant if –

(*a*) the holder of the tenement in respect of the additional block or groups of blocks has entered into an agreement in writing with the holder of the petroleum development licence consenting to the variation; and
(*b*) the State or Company pursuant to Section 165 and 166 and the applicable petroleum agreement have an entitlement to acquire a participating interest in the additional blocks or group of blocks, and all of the affected tenement holders including the holder of the petroleum development licence, have entered into an agreement concerning the terms of the State or Company participation in the enlarged petroleum licence; and
(*c*) a copy of any such agreement is provided to the Minister with the application for the variation; and
(*d*) any such agreement provided to the Minister shall have been lodged and registered in accordance with Section 100.

(3) The Minister shall not approve an application under Subsection (1) unless he is satisfied, after considering a report of the Board, that the additional block or group of blocks proposed to be included in the licence contain a petroleum pool or part of a petroleum pool.
(4) Where an application is made under Subsection (1), the Minister shall, after considering a report of the Board and having used all reasonable efforts, by instrument served on the applicant within one month from having received the application either –

(*a*) inform the applicant that the variation of the licence by the inclusion of the additional block or group of blocks as the case may be will be approved; or
(*b*) refuse the application in which case the existing licences remain in full force and effect.

(5) An applicant who has been served with an instrument under Subsection (4)(a) may, within one month after the date of service of the instrument on him or such further period as the Minister allows, by instrument served on the Director accept the variation and upon service of such instrument or the Director, the petroleum development licence shall be varied to include in the licence area the block or group of blocks to which the application relates.
(6) From and including the day on which the variation of a licence takes effect under Subsection (5), the blocks included in the licence area by reason of the variation are –

(*a*) subject to this Act, for the remainder of the term of the licence, blocks in respect of which an applicant's petroleum

development licence is in force; and
(*b*) any other licence that is in force in respect of the blocks so included is revoked in respect of those blocks.

(7) The holders of a petroleum development licence may, at any time, make an application to the Minister for any other variation of the petroleum development licence.
(8) An application under Subsection (7) shall –

(*a*) specify the reason for the proposed variation; and
(*b*) be made in an approved form and contain the information specified in Section 54.

(9) The Director may require the applicant to furnish such information in connection with his application as the Director considers necessary.
(10) Following receipt of an application under Subsection (7) the Minister shall, after considering a report of the Board and any matters submitted to him under this section and having used all reasonable efforts, by instrument served on the applicant within two months from the date of receiving the application –

(*a*) inform the applicant that he is prepared to approve the variation of the licence as stipulated in the application or as otherwise agreed with the applicant; or
(*b*) refuse the application, in which case the existing petroleum development licence will remain in full force and effect.

(11) An applicant who has been served with an instrument under Subsection (10)(a) may, within one month after the date of service of the instrument on him or such further periods as the Minister allows, by instrument served on the Director accept the variation and upon service of such instrument on the Director the petroleum development licence shall be varied as stipulated in the application or as otherwise agreed with the applicant.

59. RIGHTS CONFERRED BY PETROLEUM DEVELOPMENT LICENCE.

A petroleum development licence, while it remains in force confers on the licensee, subject to this Act and to the conditions specified in the licence, exclusive rights–

(*a*) to explore for petroleum in the licence area; and
(*b*) to carry on operations for the recovery of petroleum in the licence area; and
(*c*) to sell or otherwise dispose of the petroleum so recovered; and
(*d*) to carry on such operations and execute such works in the licence area as are necessary for or in connection with the purposes specified in Paragraphs (a), (b), and (c) including the construction and operation of flow lines or gathering lines and water lines.

60. TERM OF PETROLEUM DEVELOPMENT LICENCE.

[46]Subject to this Act and to any condition in the licence, a petroleum development licence remains in force –

(*a*) for a period of 25 years commencing on the day on which the licence takes effect; and
(*b*)[47] where the licence has been extended under Section 62–for such further period or periods not exceeding 20 years as the Minister determines is reasonably required to recover from the licence area the maximum amount of petroleum the recovery of which is consistent with good oil field practice.

61. APPLICATION FOR EXTENSION OF PETROLEUM DEVELOPMENT LICENCE.

(1) The holder of a petroleum development licence may make an application to the Minister for an extension of the licence.
(2)[48] [49]Unless otherwise provided in a written agreement entered into between the holder of the petroleum development licence and the State, an application under this section may be made once only in respect of a licence.
(3) An application for an extension of a petroleum development licence–

(*a*) shall be in an approved form; and
(*b*) subject to Subsection (4), shall be made in an approved manner not later than six months before the day on which the licence is due to expire; and
(*c*) shall be accompanied by–

(i) a detailed assessment of the field life and the economically recoverable and economically unrecoverable petroleum within the pool or pools which are the subject of the licence, providing a justification for the assessment of petroleum as economically recoverable or unrecoverable, as the case may be; and
(ii) a detailed statement of anticipated future operations under the licence; and
(iii) the fee prescribed by Section 157.

(4)[50] [51]The Minister may, after considering a report of the Board, accept an application at any time prior to the last year of the current term of the licence where that application also relates to a variation of a petroleum development licence pursuant to Section 58(7) and the applicant can demonstrate that the remaining period of current term of licence is insufficient to permit the maximum recovery of the petroleum from the licence area.

62. GRANT OR REFUSAL OF EXTENSION OF PETROLEUM DEVELOPMENT LICENCE.

(1) Where a licensee who has complied with the conditions specified in the licence and with the provisions of this Act, makes an application under Section 61 for the extension of a licence, the Minister shall inform the licensee, by instrument served on the licensee, that he is prepared to grant to the licensee the extension of the licence.
(2) Where a licensee who has not complied with the conditions specified in the licence or with the provisions of this Act, makes an application under Section 61 for the extension of a licence, the Minister may, if after considering a report from the Board, he is satisfied that, although the licensee has not so complied, special circumstances exist that justify the granting of the extension

of the licence, inform the licensee, by instrument served on the licensee, that he is prepared to grant to him an extension of the licence.
(3) If a licensee has not complied with the conditions specified in the licence or with the provisions of this Act, and the Minister is not satisfied that special circumstances exist that justify the granting of the extension of the licence, the Minister shall, subject to Subsection (4), by instrument served on the licensee, refuse to grant the extension of the licence.
(4) The Minister shall not refuse to grant the extension of a licence under this section unless–

(*a*) he has, by instrument served on the licensee, given not less than one month's notice of his intention to refuse to grant the extension of the licence; and
(*b*) he has served a copy of the instrument on such other persons (if any) as he thinks fit; and
(*c*) he has, in the instrument–

(i) given particulars of the reasons for his intention to refuse; and
(ii) specified a date on or before which the licensee or a person on whom a copy of the instrument is served may, by instrument served on the Minister, submit any matters that he requires the Minister to consider; and

(*d*) he has taken into account, after considering a report from the Board, any matters so submitted to him, on or before the specified date, by the licensee or a person on whom a copy of the instrument has been served.

(5) An instrument under Subsection (1) or (2) shall contain–

(*a*) a summary of the conditions to which the grant of the extension is to be subject; and
(*b*) a statement to the effect that the application will lapse if the licensee

(i) does not make a request under Subsection (6); and
(ii) does not pay the annual fee.

(6) A licensee who has been served with an instrument under Subsection (1) or (2) may, within a period of one month after the date of service of the instrument on him–

(*a*) by instrument served on the Minister, request the Minister to grant to him the extension of the licence; and
(*b*) pay the next annual fee.

(7) Where a licensee who has been served with an instrument under Subsection (1) or (2) has, within the period specified in Subsection (6)–

(*a*) made a request under Subsection (6); and
(*b*) paid the next annual fee,

the Minister shall grant to him the extension of the licence.
(8) Where a licensee who has been served with an instrument under Subsection (1) or (2) has not, within the period specified in Subsection (6)–

(*a*) made a request under Subsection (6); or
(*b*) paid the next annual fee,

the application lapses at the end of that period.
(9) Where–

(*a*) an application for the extension of a licence is made under Section 61; and
(*b*) the licence expires–

(i) before the Minister grants, or refuses to grant, the extension of the licence; or
(ii) before the application lapses under Subsection (8),

the licence shall be deemed to continue in force in all respects–

(*c*) until the Minister refuses to grant the extension of the licence; or
(*d*) until the application lapses under Subsection (8),

whichever first occurs.

63. CONDITIONS OF PETROLEUM DEVELOPMENT LICENCE.

[52]A petroleum development licence and any extension or variation of a petroleum development licence–

(*a*) is subject to conditions that–

(i) the licensee will carry out the proposals approved under Section 57(2); and
(i) the licensee will provide to the Director reports on the activities of the licensee in respect of the licence containing such information and at such frequency as are specified in and will otherwise comply with any direction given under Section 148; and
(iii)[53] the licensee will carry out social mapping and landowner identification studies as directed by the Minister in accordance with Section 47; and

(*b*) may be made subject to such other conditions not inconsistent with this Act–

(i) as the Minister thinks proper and specifies in the licence or extension of the licence; or

(ii) in respect of any matter or matters arising out of the applicant's proposals referred to in Section 54(1)(c) that are not administered under this Act, as the Minister, after consultation with the Minister responsible for administering that matter or those matters, thinks proper and specifies in the licence or extension of the licence.

64. UNIT DEVELOPMENT.

(1) In this section, **"unit development"** means, in relation to a petroleum pool, the co-ordination of operations for the recovery of petroleum being carried on or to be carried on in a licence area in which there is part of the pool, with other operations for the recovery of petroleum being carried on or to be carried on in any other licence area in which there is part of the same pool.
(2) The Minister may of his own motion or on written application made to him by a licensee in whose licence area there is a part of a particular petroleum pool, after receiving the advice of the Board, for the purpose of securing the more effective recovery of petroleum from that petroleum pool, direct any licensee whose licence area includes part of that petroleum pool to enter into a written agreement within the period specified by the Minister for or in relation to the unit development of the petroleum pool, and to lodge the agreement with the Minister immediately for approval and registration in accordance with Section 100.
(3) Where–

(*a*) a licensee who is directed under Subsection (2) to enter into an agreement for or in relation to the unit development of a petroleum pool does not enter into such an agreement within the specified period; or
(*b*) a licensee enters into such an agreement but the agreement is not lodged with the Minister in accordance with Subsection (2), or if so lodged is not approved under Section 100,

the Minister may, by instrument served on the licensee, direct the licensee to submit to him, within the period specified in the instrument, a scheme for or in relation to the unit development of the petroleum pool.
(4) An agreement under this section is an instrument to which Section 100 applies.

65. CO-ORDINATED PETROLEUM DEVELOPMENTS.

(1) Where the Director considers that, in order to prevent waste, avoid unnecessary competitive drilling, protect the correlative rights of licensees of adjacent tenements, secure the maximum ultimate recovery of petroleum or achieve the optimum economic development of petroleum resources, the interests of the State might best be furthered through two or more licensees developing a co-ordinated petroleum development with each other, the Director may give a licensee a direction under this section.
(2) A licensee given a direction under this section shall, within the period, if any, and in accordance with any other directions specified in the instrument, conduct such studies and investigations into the possibilities and merits of a co-ordinated petroleum development as are specified in the direction.

66. DIRECTIONS AS TO RECOVERY OF PETROLEUM.

(1) Where petroleum is not being recovered in a licence area and the Minister, with the advice of the Board, is satisfied that there is recoverable petroleum in that licence area, he may, by instrument served on the licensee, direct the licensee to take all necessary and practicable steps to recover that petroleum.
(2) Where the Director is not satisfied with the steps taken or being taken by a licensee to whom a direction has been given under Subsection (1), the Director may, by instrument served on the licensee, give to the licensee such directions as the Director thinks necessary for or in relation to the recovery of petroleum in the licence area.
(3) Where petroleum is being recovered in a licence area, the Minister may, with the advice of the Board, by instrument served on the licensee, direct the licensee to take all necessary and practical steps to increase or reduce the rate at which the petroleum is being recovered to such rate, not exceeding the capacity of existing production facilities, as the Minister specifies in the instrument.
(4) Where the Director is not satisfied with the steps taken or being taken by a licensee to whom a direction has been given under Subsection (3), the Director may, by instrument served on the licensee, give to the licensee such directions as the Director thinks necessary for or in relation to the increase or reduction of the rate at which petroleum is being recovered in the licence area.

67. DOMESTIC MARKET OBLIGATION.

(1)[54] [55]A person shall, in disposing of processed petroleum produced in Papua New Guinea which is owned by him, comply with this section.
(2) A person referred to in Subsection (1) shall–

(*a*) if approached by a *bona fide* prospective purchaser wishing to purchase processed petroleum from that person, negotiate in good faith with that *bona fide* purchaser for the sale and supply of such processed petroleum; and
(*b*) if offered by a *bona fide* prospective purchaser equivalent export terms for a quantity of his processed petroleum, sell and supply that quantity of processed petroleum to that *bona fide* prospective purchaser on those equivalent export terms.

(3) In this section, **"equivalent export terms"** means a purchase price and terms which are no less favourable to the seller than the price and terms which he could obtain at that same time as such offer by selling and exporting that processed petroleum, adjusted for such differences as quality, quantity, delivery, transportation, and other terms, but excluding government-to-government sales, barter, swaps, sales between related corporations, and similar non-arms-length transactions.
(4) A person referred to in Subsection (1) shall, if offered equivalent export terms, accommodate the reasonable requirements of the offer or for adjustments from the normal practices of that person in selling and delivering processed petroleum in relation to quantities sold, delivery arrangements and transportation requirements.
(5) The obligations of a person under this section are subject to–

(*a*) the purchaser within a reasonable time offering to enter into an agreement containing commercial sale and purchase terms which are standard in the international petroleum industry, including payment in a currency appropriate for that processed petroleum having regard to normal international industry standards at a place acceptable to the seller within a reasonable time after delivery; and
(*b*) prior *bona fide* contractual commitments of the seller in

respect of the sale or consumption of such processed petroleum; and
(*c*) the reasonable requirements of the seller as to the timing of the disposal of his processed petroleum and the creditworthiness of the purchaser; and
(*d*) the seller being at liberty to sell his processed petroleum in Papua New Guinea for a higher price or on terms which objectively are preferable, and for that purpose to retain in Papua New Guinea that quantity of processed petroleum; and
(*e*) the seller being at liberty to use any processed petroleum required for his own operations; and
(*f*) the provisions of any written agreement between the State and that person; and
(*g*) the requirements of all laws for the time being in force in Papua New Guinea.

(6) A *bona fide* prospective purchaser aggrieved at the failure of another person to comply with his obligations under this section shall have standing to seek injunctive relief and damages from a person who has failed to comply with his obligations under this section.

DIVISION 8. PROCESSING AND EXPORT OF NATURAL GAS.

68. PROCESSING OF NATURAL GAS.

(1) This section applies to all natural gas recovered in a petroleum project, other than natural gas which is–

(*a*) reinjected; or
(*b*) flared in accordance with this Act; or
(*c*) consumed in Papua New Guinea in operations under a licence.

(2) All natural gas produced in a petroleum project shall be processed in a petroleum processing facility in Papua New Guinea.

69. EXPORT OF NATURAL GAS.

(1) Natural gas shall only be exported from Papua New Guinea if permitted by–

(*a*) the terms of a written agreement to which the State is a party; or
(*b*) a licence; or
(*c*) the Minister, by instrument.

(2) Subject to Subsection (3), any natural gas which is exported from Papua New Guinea shall conform with quality specifications prescribed by the Minister, by instrument.
(3) In the event of an emergency affecting the operation of a petroleum processing facility which processes natural gas which is permitted to be exported in accordance with Subsection (1), natural gas which does not conform with the quality specifications stipulated by Subsection (2) may be exported, but–

(*a*) within 24 hours of the emergency occurring, the exporter shall file a report with the Director setting out the details of the emergency, the steps being taken to deal with it and the reason why natural gas conforming with the quality specifications stipulated by Subsection (2) is not being produced; and
(*b*) the exporter shall not continue to export natural gas not conforming with the specifications for more than 72 hours after first doing so, without written permission from the Director or the Minister.

(4) An exporter relying upon a written permission granted under Subsection (3) shall, whilst the emergency continues, only export natural gas in accordance with the terms of the written permission.
(5) A written permission granted under Subsection (3) may be varied or revoked by the author.

DIVISION 9. PIPELINE LICENCES.

70. PIPELINE LICENCE REQUIRED.

(1) No person shall commence to construct or continue the construction of or operate or alter or reconstruct a pipeline except under and in accordance with a pipeline licence.
(2) A person who commences to construct or continues the construction of or operates or alters or reconstructs a pipeline otherwise than pursuant to a pipeline licence is guilty of an offence.
Penalty: A fine not exceeding K10,000.00 for each day of the offence.

71. ACTS DONE IN AN EMERGENCY.

It is not an offence against Section 70–

(*a*) if, in an emergency, a person does an act to avoid loss or injury or to maintain the pipeline in good order and repair and notifies an inspector as soon as practicable of the act done; or
(*b*) if a person does an act in compliance with a direction given under this Act.

72. REMOVAL OF PIPELINE.

(1) Where the construction of a pipeline is commenced, continued, completed, altered or reconstructed in contravention of this Act, the Director may, by instrument served on the appropriate person, direct him–

(*a*) to make such alterations to the pipeline as are specified in the instrument; or
(*b*) to move the pipeline to a specified area or to remove it entirely,

within the period specified in the instrument.
(2) For the purpose of Subsection (1), the appropriate person is–

(*a*) where construction of the pipeline has been completed–its owner; or (*b*) where the construction of the pipeline has not been completed–the persons for whom it is being constructed.

(3) Where a person who has been served with an instrument under Subsection (1) does not, within the period specified in the instrument, comply with the direction, the Director may do all or any of the things required by the direction to be done.
(4) Any costs and expenses incurred by the Director under Subsection (3) are a debt due from the person referred to in that subsection to the State.

73. APPLICATION FOR PIPELINE LICENCE.

(1)[56] [57]A person may make an application to the Minister for the grant of a pipeline licence and the Minister shall cause a notice for an application for a pipeline licence and the Minister shall cause a notice for an application for a pipeline licence under this section to be published in the National Gazette.
(2) An application for a pipeline licence–

(*a*) shall be in an approved form; and
(*b*) shall be made in an approved manner; and
(*c*) shall be accompanied by particulars of–

(i) the proposed design and construction of the pipeline; and
(ii) the proposed size and capacity of the pipeline; and
(iii) the proposals of the applicant for work and expenditure in respect of the construction of the pipeline; and
(iv) the technical qualifications of the applicant and his employees; and
(v) the technical advice available to the applicant; and
(vi) the financial resources available to the applicant; and
(vii) any agreement entered into, or proposed to be entered into, by the applicant for or in relation to the supply or conveyance of petroleum by means of the pipeline; and

(*d*) shall be accompanied by a plan, drawn to an approved scale, showing–

(i) the route to be followed by the pipeline; and
(ii) the sites of pumping stations, tank stations, and valve stations to be part of or used in connection with the pipeline, and

(*e*) may set out any matter that the applicant wishes the Minister to consider; and
(*f*) shall be accompanied by the fee prescribed by Section 157.

(3) Where a proposed pipeline is in any part of a physical planning area under the *Physical Planning Act 1989*, the applicant for the pipeline licence shall–

(*a*) notify the National Physical Planning Board; and
(*b*) notify any Physical Planning Board under the *Physical Planning Act 1989* within whose jurisdiction the proposed pipeline lies; and
(*c*) provide these Physical Planning Boards with a copy of the plan referred to in Subsection (2)(d),

and these Physical Planning Boards may, within 28 days of the receipt of such notification, give their views on the application to the Minister.
(4) Where a notice under Subsection (1) of an application by a person for a pipeline licence in respect of the construction of a project pipeline for the conveyance of petroleum recovered or to be recovered from a petroleum development licence is published in the National Gazette, the registered holder of that petroleum development licence may, within a period of two months after the date of publication, make an application to the Minister for such a pipeline licence and, in the application, request that the application referred to in the notice be rejected.
(5) Where a pipeline licence is granted to a registered holder of a petroleum development licence on an application under Subsection (4), the Minister shall, by instrument served on the original applicant, reject the application referred to in the notice under Subsection (1).
(6) The Director may, at any time, by instrument served on a person who has made an application under this section, require him to furnish such written information in connection with his application as the Minister considers necessary.
(7) An application for a pipeline licence in respect of a strategic pipeline shall, in addition to the matters set out in Subsection (2), be accompanied by–

(*a*) draft access arrangements which the applicant proposes should be the access arrangements applying to that strategic pipeline; and
(*b*) pro forma accounts for the pipeline and the other petroleum processing facilities referred to in Section 75(7), and an explanation of how the financial records for the pipeline will be maintained separately from other operations of the pipeline licensee.

(8) Prior to submitting an application for a pipeline licence in respect of a strategic pipeline, the applicant shall make all reasonable efforts to consult with existing and potential third party users of the pipeline, and shall furnish to the Minister a report on the possible third party users and their possible requirements in using the pipeline and their views on the contents of the access arrangements to apply to the pipeline.
(9)[58] [59]Where an application for a pipeline licence relates to a strategic pipeline, the notice referred to in Subsection (1) shall invite potential third party users of the pipeline to make submissions to the Minister within the period stipulated in the notice as to their potential requirements in using the pipeline and the contents of the access arrangements to apply to the pipeline.
(10) The draft access arrangements submitted by the applicant shall be a public document, and any person may inspect that document or those documents at the office of the Director.
(11) The Minister shall notify the applicant of any submissions received in response to invitations made in accordance with Subsection (9) and provide the applicant with a copy of all such submissions if requested.

74. GRANT OR REFUSAL OF PIPELINE LICENCE.

(1) Where a person makes an application in accordance with Section 73 for a pipeline licence in respect of the construction of a project pipeline for the conveyance of petroleum recovered or to be recovered from a petroleum development licence, the Minister, after having regard to physical planning considerations–

(*a*) shall, if that person–

(i) is the registered holder of that petroleum development licence; and
(ii)[60] has complied with the conditions specified in the licence and with the provisions of this Act; or

(*b*) may, if that person is not the registered holder of that petroleum development licence and the application has not been rejected under Section 73(5),

inform that person, by instrument served on him, that the Minister is prepared to grant a pipeline licence to him.
(2) Where–

(*a*) an application is made in accordance with Section 73 for a pipeline licence in respect of the construction of a project pipeline for the conveyance of petroleum recovered or to be recovered from a petroleum development licence, by a person who is the registered holder of that petroleum development licence; and
(*b*) that person has not complied with the conditions specified in that licence or with the provisions of this Act,

the Minister may inform that person, by instrument served on him, that–

(*c*) he is prepared to grant a pipeline licence to that person; or
(*d*) he has refused to grant a pipeline licence to that person.

(3) The Minister shall not, under Subsection (2), refuse to grant a pipeline licence unless–

(*a*) he has, by instrument served on the person who made the application, given to that person not less than one month's notice of his intention to refuse to grant the pipeline licence; and
(*b*) he has served a copy of the instrument on such other persons as he thinks fit; and
(*c*) he has, in the instrument–

(i) given particulars of the reasons for his intention; or
(ii) specified a date on or before which the person who made the application or a person on whom a copy of the instrument is served may, by instrument served on the Director, submit any matters that he wishes the Minister to consider; and

(*d*) he has taken into account any matters so submitted to him on or before the specified date by the person who made the application, or by a person on whom a copy of the instrument has been served.

(4) Where an application is made in accordance with Section 73 for a pipeline licence in respect of the construction of a pipeline for the conveyance of petroleum recovered or to be recovered from a petroleum development licence by a person other than the registered holder of that petroleum development licence, the Minister may, by instrument served on the applicant, refuse to grant a pipeline licence.

(5) Where the Minister is required, or proposes, to serve on a person an instrument under Subsection (1) or (2)(c), he shall, by the instrument, inform that person that he will be required to lodge a security for compliance with the conditions to which the pipeline licence, if granted, will from time to time be subject, and with the provisions of this Act.

(6) An instrument under Subsection (1) or (2)(c)–

(*a*) shall specify the route to be followed by the pipeline; and
(*b*) shall contain a summary of the conditions to be specified in the pipeline licence to be granted; and
(*c*) shall contain a statement to the effect that the application will lapse if the applicant does not–

(i) make a request under Subsection (8); and
(ii) lodge with the Director the security referred to in the instrument.

(7) The route to be specified in an instrument under Subsection (1) or (2)(c) shall be–

(*a*) the route shown in the plan accompanying the application; or
(*b*) if the Minister is of the opinion that, for any reason, that route is not appropriate–a route that, in the opinion of the Minister, is appropriate.

(8) A person who has been served with an instrument under Subsection (1) or (2)(c) may, within a period of three months after the date of service of the instrument on him or such further period or periods as the Minister allows–

(*a*) by instrument served on the Director, request the Minister to grant to him the pipeline licence; and
(*b*) lodge with the Director the security referred to in the instrument served on him under that subsection.

(9) Where a person who has been served with an instrument under Subsection (1) or (2)(c) has, within the period specified in Subsection (8)–

(*a*) made a request under Subsection (8); and
(*b*) lodged with the Director the security referred to in the instrument,

the Minister shall grant to that person a licence to construct and operate a pipeline specified in the instrument.

(10) Where a person who has been served with an instrument under Subsection (1) or (2)(c) has not, within the period specified in Subsection (8)–

(*a*) made a request under Subsection (8); or
(*b*) lodged with the Director the security referred to in the instrument,

the application lapses at the end of that period.
(11) Where a pipeline licence is not granted on an application, 90% of the fee under Section 157 shall be refunded to the applicant.
(12) Where a person makes application in accordance with Section 73 for a pipeline licence in respect of a strategic pipeline, the Minister, after having regard to physical planning considerations, may inform that person, by instrument served on him, that–

(*a*) the Minister is prepared to grant a pipeline licence to that person; or
(*b*) the Minister has refused to grant a pipeline licence to that person.

(13) The Minister shall only refuse under Subsection (12) to grant a pipeline licence after considering the advice of the Board.
(14) Where the Minister proposes to serve an instrument under Subsection (12)(a), he shall, by the instrument, inform that person that he will be required to lodge a security for compliance with the conditions to which the pipeline licence, if granted, will from time to time be subject, and with the provisions of this Act.
(15) An instrument under Subsection (12)(a)–

(*a*) shall specify the route to be followed by the pipeline; and
(*b*) shall contain the conditions to be specified in the pipeline licence to be granted; and
(*c*) shall specify the terms of the access arrangements, complying with Section 75, that will be approved by the Minister and apply to the pipeline in accordance with Section 75; and
(*d*) shall contain a statement to the effect that the application will lapse if the applicant does not–

(i) make a request under Subsection (17); and
(ii) lodge with the Director the security referred to in the instrument.

(16) The route to be specified in the instrument under Subsection (12)(a) shall be–

(*a*) the route shown in the plan accompanying the application; or
(*b*) if the Minister, in accordance with the advice of the Board, considers for any reason that that route is not appropriate–a route that the Minister, in accordance with the advice of the Board, considers appropriate.

(17) A person who has been served with an instrument under Subsection (12)(a) may, within a period of three months after the date of service of the instrument on him, or such longer period as may be specified in the instrument–

(*a*) by instrument served on the Director, request the Minister to grant to him the pipeline licence; and
(*b*) lodge with the Director the security referred to in the instrument served on him under Subsection (12)(a).

(18) Where a person who has been served with an instrument under Subsection (12)(a) has, within the period specified in Subsection (17) or such longer period or periods as the Minister allows–

(*a*) made a request under Subsection (17); and
(*b*) lodged with the Director the security referred to in the instrument,

the Minister shall approve the access arrangements specified in the instrument and grant to that person a pipeline licence conforming with the instrument.
(19) Where a person who has been served with an instrument under Subsection (12)(a) has not, within the period specified in Subsection (17)–

(*a*) made a request under Subsection (17); and
(*b*) lodged with the Director the security referred to in the instrument,

the application lapses at the end of that period.
(20) A pipeline licence shall not be granted under this section in respect of a strategic pipeline unless the Minister has approved access arrangements complying with Section 75 and the applicant has accepted those access arrangements in accordance with Subsection(17).

75. STRATEGIC PIPELINES.

(1) Pipeline licences in respect of the following pipelines shall contain a licence condition designating the pipeline to be a strategic pipeline:–

(*a*) pipelines constructed for the transportation of petroleum from two or more petroleum projects, or for the transportation of petroleum products from two or more petroleum processing facilities; and
(*b*) pipelines constructed for the transport of petroleum or petroleum products across an international boundary; and
(*c*) pipelines constructed for the transportation of petroleum or petroleum products from a strategic petroleum processing facility; and
(*d*) pipelines in respect of which the applicant for a pipeline licence elects that this section will apply; and
(*e*) pipelines which become strategic pipelines in accordance with Subsections 81(10) or 82(12).

(2) The pipeline licensee under a pipeline licence applying to a strategic pipeline shall adopt and comply with access arrangements approved by the Minister, whereby third parties may have petroleum or petroleum products transported by the pipeline licensee through that strategic pipeline.

(3) The access arrangements applying to a strategic pipeline shall be registered and the pipeline licensee shall make copies available to all prospective third party users requesting a copy of them.
(4) Subject to any written agreement between the State and the pipeline licensee, access arrangements applying to strategic pipelines–

(*a*) shall comply with the requirements of regulations on the operation of strategic pipelines; and
(*b*) shall comply with the following principles:–

(i) the arrangements should encourage third party use of the pipeline, without requiring reduced tariffs for marginally economic petroleum fields or petroleum processing facilities;
(ii) the arrangements should achieve the lowest sustainable tariffs for users which provide a reasonable return on investment for the pipeline licensee, having regard to the circumstances of the investment, including due consideration of risk;
(iii) the arrangements should provide commercial incentives for investors and foundation shippers in respect of risks assumed, improved efficiency and increased throughputs;
(iv) the arrangements should provide certainty of tariff methodology for the term of the transportation contract;
(v) the arrangements should constitute an open dissemination of information regarding the pipeline and the service available, so as to enable prospective third party users to evaluate the technical and economic feasibility of transporting petroleum or petroleum products using any spare capacity or developable capacity;
(vi) the arrangements should recognise the entitlement of the pipeline licensee to be assured as to the creditworthiness of third party users of the pipeline prior to entering into contracts for service;
(vii) the arrangements should recognise the legitimate business interests of the pipeline licensee and existing and potential third party users; and

(*c*) shall include–

(i) the route of the pipeline and the location and ownership of receipt and delivery facilities; and
(ii) reasonable definitions of total capacity, excess capacity, and developable capacity of the pipeline; and
(iii) a process for identifying the need for, and implementing, expansion to take up the pipeline's developable capacity; and
(iv) reasonable processes that may lead to the extension or expansion of the pipeline if demonstrated to be commercially, technically, and operationally viable; and
(v) a procedure for requesting service and concluding transportation arrangements within a reasonable period of time; and
(vi) the classes of transportation service offered to third parties by the pipeline licensee, separating the charges and tariffs to be charged in respect of each class of service; and
(vii) the terms and conditions of the agreement to be offered by the pipeline licensee and third-party users for the transportation of petroleum or petroleum products; and
(viii) tariff methodology, with sample calculations; and
(ix) billing and payment arrangements; and
(x) processes for the inclusion of additional receipt and delivery points on the system; and
(xi) procedures for nominations for deliveries under a transportation agreement; and
(xii) a queuing policy in respect of competing proposals for use of the pipeline; and
(xiii) a mechanism for inter-shipper trading of service entitlements under transportation agreements, without derogating from the safety or integrity of pipeline operations; and
(xiv) a policy for allocation of pipeline capacity in the event of capacity restrictions from time to time; and
(xv) a dispute resolution procedure; and
(xvi) reasonable pipeline entry quality specifications which are not unfairly discriminatory to third

party users, and where necessary intended procedures for system balancing and adjustments for differences in quality of petroleum or petroleum products entering the pipeline; and
(xvii) the expected pipeline operating pressure regime; and

(*d*) may include–

(i) different terms and conditions for foundation users of the pipeline which are commensurate with the different obligations undertaken and risks assumed by those users; and
(ii) any other provisions consistent with the normal international practice for open access pipelines which are approved by the Minister.

(5) Access arrangements approved by the Minister under Subsections 74(18), 81(8), 82(8) or 82(11) shall, for as long as the pipeline licence remains in force, be binding on the pipeline licensee and compliance with those access arrangements shall be a condition of the pipeline licence.
(6) The access arrangements referred to in Subsection (5) shall have legal effect and shall be enforceable according to their terms in a court of law by any person having a *bona fide* interest in the terms of the access arrangements.
(7) The pipeline licensee of a strategic pipeline shall maintain separate financial records and accounts for the operation of the pipeline, together with such other petroleum processing facilities as are agreed in writing between the Director and the pipeline licensee, and shall if requested by the Director lodge with the Director by the end of April in each calendar year a set of audited accounts for the strategic pipeline operations which accord with international generally accepted accounting practice setting out the financial results of the strategic pipeline and those other petroleum processing facilities.
(8) Nothing in this section limits the terms and conditions which a pipeline licensee may agree with a third party user as the terms of an access arrangement.
(9)[61] [62]Where a strategic pipeline is constructed as part of a petroleum project or a gas project and is linked to a strategic petroleum processing facility, which is also processing facility licensee may submit to the Minister for approval one access arrangement for such strategic pipeline and strategic petroleum processing facility, which may include a single published tariff for integrated processing and transportation.

76. RIGHTS CONFERRED BY PIPELINE LICENCE.

A pipeline licence, while it remains in force, authorizes the licensee, subject to this Act and in accordance with the conditions specified in the pipeline licence–

(*a*) to construct and operate a pipeline (including the pumping stations, tank stations and valve stations specified in the licence) of the design, construction, size and capacity specified in the licence, along the route specified in the licence; and
(*b*) to carry on all operations, to execute all works and to do all other things that are necessary for or incidental to the construction and operation of the pipeline.

77. TERM OF PIPELINE LICENCE.

(1) Subject to this Act and to any condition in the licence, a pipeline licence remains in force–

(*a*) for a period of 25 years commencing on the day on which the licence takes effect; and (*b*)[63] where the licence is extended under Section 79–for consecutive period or periods, not exceeding 20 years, as the pipeline licensee requires.

(2) Where the Minister is of the opinion that, having regard to the dates of expiration of the petroleum development licences that relate to the licence area from which the petroleum is, or is to be, conveyed by means of the pipeline it is not necessary for the pipeline licence to remain in force for the relevant period referred to in Subsection (1), the Minister may specify in the licence such lesser period as he thinks fit, and the pipeline licence shall remain in force for that lesser period so specified.

78. APPLICATION FOR EXTENSION OF PIPELINE LICENCE.

(1)[64] [65]A pipeline licensee may make an application to the Minister for extension of that licence on the following number of occassions –

(*a*) in the case of a pipeline licence for a project pipeline where no written agreement has been entered into between the holder of the pipeline licence and the State allowing for multiple extensions – once only; and
(*b*) in the case of a pipeline licence for a project pipeline where a written agreement has been entered into between the holder of the pipeline licence and the State allowing for multiple extensions – that number of times provided for in that agreement; and
(*c*) in the case of a pipeline licence for a strategic pipeline – unlimited number of occasions.

(2) An application for the extension of a pipeline licence–

(*a*) shall be in an approved form; and
(*b*) shall be made in an approved manner not later than six months before the day on which the pipeline licence is due to expire; and
(*c*) shall be accompanied by the fee prescribed by Section 157; and
(*d*) shall specify the period, not exceeding 20 years, for which the extension is sought.

(3)[66] [67]The Minister may, after considering a report of the Board, accept an application at any time prior to the last year of the current term of the licence where that application also relates to a variation of a pipeline licence pursuant to Section 58(7) or an application for a new pipeline licence and the applicant can demonstrate that the remaining period of the current term of the licence is insufficient to permit the transportation of petroleum from the one or more petroleum development licence areas.

79. GRANT OR REFUSAL OF EXTENSION OF PIPELINE LICENCE.

(1) Where a pipeline licensee makes an application for the extension of the pipeline licence under Section 78, the Minister–

(*a*) shall, if the pipeline licensee has complied with the conditions specified in the pipeline licence and with the provisions of this Act; or
(*b*) may, if the pipeline licensee has not complied with the conditions specified in the licence and with the provisions of this Act, and the Minister is satisfied that, although the pipeline licensee has not so complied, special circumstances exist that justify the granting of the extension of the pipeline licence,

inform the licensee, by instrument served on the licensee–

(*c*) that he is prepared to grant to the licensee the extension of the pipeline licence; and
(*d*) that the licensee will be required to lodge a security for compliance with the conditions to be specified in the pipeline licence, if the extension is granted, and with the provisions of this Act.

(2) The Minister shall not, under Subsection (1), refuse to grant a pipeline licence to a licensee unless–

(*a*) he has, by instrument served on the licensee, given not less than one month's notice of his intention to refuse to grant the pipeline licence; and
(*b*) he has served a copy of the instrument on such other persons as he thinks fit; and
(*c*) he has, in the instrument–

(i) given particulars of the reasons for his intention to refuse; and
(ii) specified a date on or before which the licensee or a person on whom a copy of the instrument has been served may, by instrument served on the Minister, submit any matters that he wishes the Minister to consider; and

(*d*) he has taken into account any matters so submitted to him, on or before the specified date, by the licensee, or by a person on whom a copy of the instrument has been served.

(3) Where an application for the extension of a pipeline licence is made under Section 78 and the pipeline licence otherwise expires before the Minister grants or refuses to grant the extension of the pipeline licence, the pipeline licence shall be deemed to continue in force in all respects until the Minister refuses to grant the extension of the pipeline licence.

80. CONDITIONS OF PIPELINE LICENCE.

A pipeline licence may be granted subject to such conditions as the Minister thinks fit and specifies in the licence.

81. VARIATION OF PIPELINE LICENCE ON APPLICATION BY LICENSEE.

(1) The holder of a pipeline licence may at any time make an application to the Minister for a variation of the pipeline licence to–

(*a*) extend the specified route of the pipeline; or
(*b*) include additional receipt and delivery points; or
(*c*) construct additional pipelines using the same route specified in the pipeline licence; or
(*d*) install pumping stations, compressors, valve stations, measurement stations, storage tanks or other improvements for the safety and operation of the pipeline or to increase its capacity; or
(*e*) convert a pipeline to transport a different form of petroleum or petroleum product from the petroleum or petroleum products described in the initial licence application; or
(*f*) make any other change which would improve the operating efficiency of the pipeline; or
(*g*) in the case of a project pipeline, change its designation to a strategic pipeline; or
(*h*) in the case of a strategic pipeline, vary the access arrangements applicable thereto.

(2) An application under this section shall–

(*a*) be in an approved form; and
(*b*) be made in an approved manner; and
(*c*) be accompanied by particulars of the proposed variation; and
(*d*) specify the reason for the proposed variation; and
(*e*) in the case of an application to convert a project pipeline to a strategic pipeline, be accompanied by–

(i) draft access arrangements which the applicant proposes should be the access arrangements applying to that pipeline; and
(ii) pro forma accounts for the pipeline and the other petroleum processing facilities referred to in Subsection 75(7), and an explanation of how the financial records for the pipeline will be maintained separately from other operations of the pipeline licensee; and

(*f*) in the case of an application to vary the access arrangements applicable to a strategic pipeline, be accompanied by draft modified access arrangements.

(3) The Minister may require the pipeline licensee to furnish such further information in connection with the application as the Minister considers necessary.
(4) In the case of an application to convert a project pipeline to a strategic pipeline or an application to vary the access arrangements applying to a strategic pipeline–

(*a*) the applicant shall, prior to submitting its application, consult with existing and potential third party users of the pipeline, and shall furnish to the Minister a report on the possible third party users and their possible requirements in using the pipeline and

their views on the contents of the access arrangements to apply to the pipeline; and
(*b*) upon receipt of the application the Minister shall cause a notice to be published in the National Gazette advising of the application and particulars of the pipeline, and inviting existing and potential third party users of the pipeline to make submissions to the Minister within the period specified in the notice as to their potential requirements in using the pipeline and the contents of the access arrangements to apply to the pipeline; and
(*c*) the draft access arrangements submitted by the applicant shall be a public document, and any person may inspect that document or those documents at the office of the Director; and
(*d*) the Minister shall notify the applicant of any submissions received in accordance with Subsection (4)(b) and provide the applicant with a copy of all such submissions if requested.

(5) In the case of any application under this section other than an application to convert a project pipeline to a strategic pipeline or an application to vary the access arrangements applying to a strategic pipeline, the Minister may, after considering a report from the Board and any matter submitted to him under this section–

(*a*) vary the pipeline licence in accordance with the application or otherwise as he may agree with the pipeline licensee; or
(*b*) reject the application.

(6) In the case of an application to convert a project pipeline to a strategic pipeline or an application to vary the access arrangements applying to a strategic pipeline, the Minister may, after considering a report from the Board and any matter submitted to him under this section–

(*a*) serve on the pipeline licensee an instrument–

(i) advising the pipeline licensee that the Minister is prepared to vary the pipeline licence to convert the pipeline to a strategic pipeline or vary the access arrangements, as the case may be; and
(ii) specifying the terms of the access arrangements or varied access arrangements, complying with Section 75, to be approved by the Minister and apply to the pipeline in accordance with Section 75; or

(*b*) reject the application.

(7) A pipeline licensee who has been served with an instrument under Subsection (6)(a) may, within a period of three months after the date of service of the instrument on him, by instrument served on the Director, request the Minister to vary the pipeline licence in accordance with the instrument referred to in that subsection.
(8) Where a pipeline licensee who has been served with an instrument under Subsection (6)(a) has, within the period specified in Subsection (7), made a request under Subsection (7), the Minister shall approve the access arrangements or varied access arrangements specified in the instrument and vary the pipeline licence in accordance with the instrument.

(9) A pipeline licence shall not be varied under this section to convert the pipeline to a strategic pipeline or to vary the access arrangements applying to a strategic pipeline unless the Minister has approved access arrangements or varied access arrangements complying with Section 75 and the applicant has accepted those access arrangements or varied access arrangements in accordance with Subsection (7).
(10) Where the Minister varies a pipeline licence under this section, he shall cause to be published in the National Gazette a notice of the variation.
(11) A project pipeline which is converted to a strategic pipeline under this section shall be a strategic pipeline with effect from the date the variation of the licence for that purpose takes effect, and thereafter those approved access arrangements shall apply to that pipeline in accordance with Section 75.
(12) Where the access arrangements applying to a strategic pipeline are varied under this section, the varied access arrangements shall apply to that pipeline in accordance with Section 75 with effect from the date the variation of the licence for that purpose takes effect.
(13) Notwithstanding Subsections (11) and (12), the establishment or variation under this section of the access arrangements applying to a strategic pipeline shall not affect the validity of agreements previously entered into by the pipeline licensee for transportation of petroleum.

82. VARIATION OF PIPELINE LICENCE BY MINISTER.

(1) The Minister may, if in his opinion it is necessary–

(*a*) for the protection of health and safety; or
(*b*) to avoid obstruction of, or interference with, the rights of other persons,

by instrument served on a pipeline licensee, direct the licensee to make such changes in the design, construction and route or position of the pipeline (including pumping stations, tank stations or valve stations) to which the pipeline licence relates as are specified in the instrument, within the period specified in the instrument.
(2) A person to whom a direction is given under Subsection (1) who fails or refuses to comply with the direction is guilty of an offence.
Penalty: A fine not exceeding K25,000.00.
Default penalty: A fine not exceeding K25,000.00.
(3) Where the Minister gives a direction under Subsection (1) and the person to whom the direction is given complies with the direction, the Minister may grant to that person such sum as he considers reasonable in the circumstances.
(4) Where the Minister gives a direction under Subsection (1), any pipeline licence affected by the direction shall be deemed to be varied to the extent reasonably necessary to enable the direction to be complied with.
(5) If, in the opinion of the Minister, acting in accordance with the advice of the Board–

(*a*) it is desirable that a project pipeline be used by third parties for transportation of their petroleum or petroleum products, and that such third parties will have petroleum or petroleum products to be transported in that pipeline, he may by instrument served on the pipeline licensee direct that a project pipeline be converted to a strategic pipeline; or
(*b*) it is desirable that the terms of access arrangements applying to a strategic pipeline be varied, he may by instrument served on the pipeline licensee direct that the access arrangements applying to that strategic pipeline be varied.

(6) If the Minister gives a direction under Subsection (5), he shall publish in the National Gazette notice advising of that direction and particulars of the pipeline, and inviting existing and potential third party users of the pipeline to make submissions to the Minister as to their potential requirements in using the pipeline and the contents of the access arrangements to apply to the pipeline.
(7) Within three months of receipt of a direction under Subsection (5), a pipeline licensee shall lodge with the Minister–

(*a*) draft access arrangements complying with Section 75, which the applicant proposes should be the access arrangements or varied access arrangements applying to that pipeline; and
(*b*) in the case of a direction to convert from a project pipeline to a strategic pipeline, pro forma accounts for the pipeline and the other petroleum processing facilities referred to in Subsection 75(7), and an explanation of how the financial records for the pipeline will be maintained separately from other operations of the pipeline licensee.

(8) Prior to submitting draft access arrangements, the applicant shall make all reasonable efforts to consult with existing and potential third party users of the pipeline, and shall furnish to the Minister a report on the possible third party users and their possible requirements in using the pipeline and their views on the contents of the access arrangements to apply to the pipeline.
(9) A notice referred to in Subsection (6) shall invite existing and potential third party users of the pipeline to make submissions to the Minister within the period stipulated in the notice as to their potential requirements in using the pipeline and the contents of the access arrangements to apply to the pipeline.
(10) The draft access arrangements submitted by the pipeline licensee shall be a public document, and any person may inspect that document or those documents at the office of the Director.
(11) The Minister shall notify the applicant of any submissions received in response to invitations made in accordance with Subsection (6) and provide the applicant with a copy of all such submissions if requested.
(12) If the draft access arrangements or varied access arrangements proposed by the pipeline licensee, as they may be amended by agreement between the Minister and the pipeline licensee, are acceptable to the Minister, the Minister shall approve those access arrangements, and vary the pipeline licence to convert the project pipeline to be a strategic pipeline or adopt the new access arrangements, as the case may be.
(13) If the draft access arrangements or varied access arrangements proposed by the pipeline licensee are not acceptable to the Minister and the pipeline licensee and the Minister are not able to reach agreement on amendments to the draft, the Minister may refer the question of the terms of the access arrangements or varied access arrangements to apply to the pipeline for expert determination in accordance with Subsection (14).
(14) If the Minister makes a reference under Subsection (13), then the terms of the access arrangements or varied access arrangements shall be determined by an expert appointed by the Minister for that purpose and paid for by the State, who shall–

(*a*) be independent of the State and the pipeline licensee; and
(*b*) be qualified by experience in dealing with open access arrangements for pipelines; and
(*c*) prior to making his decision, consult with the Minister and the pipeline licensee and any person who has made a submission under Subsection (6); and
(*d*) in making his decision have regard to the reasonable requirements of those persons making such submissions; and

(*e*) determine terms of access arrangements which comply with Section 75.

(15) When the access arrangements are determined by expert determination under Subsection (14), the Minister may–

(*a*) approve the access arrangements or varied access arrangements so determined; and
(*b*) vary the pipeline licence to convert the project pipeline to be a strategic pipeline or adopt the varied access arrangements, as the case may be.

(16) Where the Minister varies a pipeline licence under this section, he shall cause to be published in the National Gazette a notice of the variation.
(17) A project pipeline which is converted to a strategic pipeline under this section shall be a strategic pipeline with effect from the date the variation of the licence for that purpose takes effect, and thereafter those approved access arrangements shall apply to that pipeline in accordance with Section 75.
(18) Where the access arrangements applying to a strategic pipeline are varied under this section, the varied access arrangements shall apply to that pipeline in accordance with Section 75 with effect from the date the variation of the licence for that purpose takes effect.
(19) Notwithstanding Subsections (17) and (18), the establishment or variation under this section of the access arrangements applying to a strategic pipeline shall not affect the validity of agreements previously entered into by the pipeline licensee for transportation of petroleum.

83. COMMON CARRIER.

(1) Subject to the terms of a written agreement between the State and the pipeline licensee, the Minister, acting in accordance with a report of the Board, may by instrument served on the pipeline licensee of a project pipeline direct the pipeline licensee to be a common carrier in respect of that project pipeline.
(2) Where a pipeline licensee is given a direction under this section, that pipeline licensee shall thereafter be a common carrier in respect of that pipeline, and the provisions of this section and of any regulations prescribed under Subsection (3) shall apply to the pipeline operations conducted under that pipeline licence.
(3) Subject to Subsection (4), regulations may prescribe the manner of the operation of a pipeline in respect of which a direction has been given under this section.
(4) Any regulation made under Subsection (3) shall give priority to–

(*a*) *bona fide* prior contractual commitments of the pipeline licensee with unrelated parties; and
(*b*) the *bona fide* requirements of the pipeline licensee to transport petroleum or petroleum products produced from a petroleum project in respect of which the pipeline licensee holds a petroleum development licence.

(5) A pipeline licensee which has been given a direction under this section in respect of a pipeline may, notwithstanding that direction, make an application under Subsection 81(1)(g) in respect of that pipeline.
(6) If, on an application under Subsection 81(1)(g) in relation to a pipeline by a pipeline licensee which has been given a direction under this section in respect of that pipeline, the Minister grants a variation to that pipeline licence to convert the pipeline to a strategic pipeline, the provisions of

this section and the regulations in relation to common carriage shall cease to apply to that pipeline.

84. CEASING TO OPERATE PIPELINE.

(1) Except with the written consent of the Minister, and subject to compliance with such conditions (if any) as are specified in the instrument of consent, a pipeline licensee who ceases to operate the pipeline is guilty of an offence.
Penalty: A fine not exceeding K50,000.00.
(2) It is not an offence against Subsection (1) if the failure to operate the pipeline–

(*a*) was in the ordinary course of the operation of the pipeline; or
(*b*) was for the purpose of repairing or maintaining the pipeline; or
(*c*) was in an emergency in which there was a likelihood of loss or injury; or
(*d*) was as a result of an industrial strike or picket.

DIVISION 10. PETROLEUM PROCESSING FACILITY LICENCES.

85. PETROLEUM PROCESSING FACILITY LICENCE REQUIRED.

(1) Subject to this section, no person shall commence to construct or continue the construction of or make major modifications to or operate a petroleum processing facility without a petroleum processing facility licence in respect of that petroleum processing facility.
(2) The provisions of Subsection (1) shall not apply to the holder of a petroleum development licence in respect of a petroleum processing facility which is part of the proposals for development approved for that petroleum development licence by the Minister under Section 57(2) as varied from time to time, but the licensee thereof shall comply with all regulations prescribed for securing, regulating, controlling or restricting petroleum processing facilities and the facilities shall be subject to inspection under Section 152.
(3) The provisions of Subsection (1) shall not apply in relation to–

(*a*) storage and transportation facilities for domestic utilisation that are designated by regulation to be exempt; or
(*b*) pipelines in respect of which a pipeline licence is in force,

but the operator thereof shall comply with all regulations prescribed for securing, regulating, controlling or restricting petroleum processing facilities and the facilities shall be subject to inspection under Section 152.

86. APPLICATION FOR PETROLEUM PROCESSING FACILITY LICENCE.

(1) A person may make an application to the Minister for the grant of a petroleum processing facility licence.
(2) The Minister may, by notice in the National Gazette–

(*a*) invite application for the grant of a petroleum processing facility licence; and
(*b*) specify the period during which such an application should be made.

87. FORM OF APPLICATION FOR PETROLEUM PROCESSING FACILITY LICENCE.

(1) An application made under Section 86 shall–

(*a*) be made in an approved form; and
(*b*) be made in an approved manner; and
(*c*) be accompanied by particulars of–

(i) the names and address of the persons who will construct, operate and own the petroleum processing facility; and
(ii) the proposed site for the petroleum processing facility and arrangements for the legal occupation of the site; and
(iii) the design of the petroleum processing facility; and
(iv) the technical qualifications of the applicant and his contractors; and
(v) the financial capacity of the applicant to construct and operate the petroleum processing facility; and
(vi) environmental monitoring systems, waste disposal procedures and the results of environmental studies; and
(vii) the intended date for commencement of construction and estimated dates for commissioning and full operation; and
(viii) the intended output of petroleum or petroleum products; and

(*d*) be accompanied by payment of the application fee prescribed by Section 157.

(2) Where an application is received under Subsection (1)–

(*a*) notice of the application shall be published in the National Gazette; and
(*b*) any person who claims to be affected by the application may file notice of his objection to that application with the Director within one month after the date of publication of the notice of application and all objections shall be considered by the Board before it reports to the Minister on the application.

(3) An application for a petroleum processing facility licence in respect of a strategic petroleum processing facility shall, in addition to the matters set out in Subsection (1), be accompanied by draft access arrangements which the applicant proposes should be access arrangements applying to that strategic petroleum processing facility.
(4) Prior to submitting an application for a petroleum processing facility licence in respect of a strategic petroleum processing facility, the applicant shall make all reasonable efforts to consult with existing and potential third party users of the petroleum processing facility, and shall furnish to the Minister a report on the possible third party users and their possible requirements in using

the petroleum processing facility and their views on the contents of the access arrangements to apply to the petroleum processing facility.
(5) Where an application for a petroleum processing facility licence relates to a strategic petroleum processing facility, the notice referred to in Subsection (2) shall invite potential third party users of the petroleum processing facility to make submissions to the Minister as to their potential requirements in using the petroleum processing facility and the contents of the access arrangements to apply to the petroleum processing facility.
(6) The draft access arrangements submitted by the applicant shall be a public document, and any person may inspect that document or those documents at the office of the Director.
(7) The Minister shall notify the applicant of any submissions received in accordance with Subsection (5), and provide the applicant with a copy of all such submissions if requested.

88. GRANT OR REFUSAL OF PETROLEUM PROCESSING FACILITY LICENCE.

(1) Where an application has been made under Section 86 in respect of a petroleum processing facility which is not a strategic petroleum processing facility, the Minister may, after considering a report of the Board–

(*a*) by instrument served on the applicant, inform the applicant–

(i) that he is prepared to grant to the applicant a petroleum processing facility licence in respect of the site and for construction of the petroleum processing facility specified in the application; and
(ii) that the applicant will be required to lodge a security for compliance with the conditions to which the petroleum processing facility licence, if granted, will be subject and the provisions of this Act, and to pay the annual fee; or

(*b*) refuse to grant a petroleum processing facility licence to the applicant.

(2) An instrument under Subsection (1)(a) shall contain–

(*a*) the conditions subject to which the petroleum processing facility licence is to be granted; and
(*b*) a statement to the effect that the application will lapse if the applicant does not make a request under Subsection (3) in respect of the grant of the petroleum processing facility licence and lodge with the Director the security specified in the instrument and the first annual fee as prescribed by Section 157.

(3) An applicant who has been served with an instrument under Subsection (1) may, within a period of one month after the date of service of the instrument, or within such further period or periods as the Minister may allow–

(*a*) by instrument served on the Minister request the Minister to grant him the petroleum processing facility licence; and (*b*) lodge with the Director the security referred to in Subsection (1)(a) and the first annual fee referred to in that subsection.

(4) Where an applicant has complied with the requirements of Subsection (3), the Minister shall grant a petroleum processing facility licence for the site and the petroleum processing facility specified in the instrument, subject to the conditions specified in the instrument or such other conditions as are agreed by the Minister and the applicant, but in any other case the application lapses.

(5) Where an application has been made under Section 86 in respect of a strategic petroleum processing facility, the Minister may, after considering a report of the Board–

(*a*) by instrument served on the applicant, inform the applicant–

(i) that he is prepared to grant to the applicant a petroleum processing facility licence in respect of the site and for construction and operation of the petroleum processing facility specified in the application; and

(ii) that the applicant will be required to lodge a security for compliance with the conditions to which the petroleum processing facility licence, if granted, will be subject and the provisions of this Act, and to pay the annual fee; or

(*b*) refuse to grant a petroleum processing facility licence to the applicant.

(6) The Minister shall not refuse under Subsections (1) or (5) to grant a petroleum processing facility licence unless–

(*a*) he has, by the instrument referred to in those subsections served on the applicant, given not less than one month's notice of his intention to do so; and

(*b*) he has, in that instrument–

(i) given particulars of the reason for his intention; and

(ii) specified a date on or before which the applicant may, by instrument served on the Minister, submit any matters that the applicant requires the Minister to consider, including new proposals generally or in respect of some particular matter; and

(*c*) he has given to the applicant, and to any persons whom the applicant thinks fit to consult, a full opportunity to consult with the Minister concerning the Minister's intention to refuse to grant a petroleum processing facility licence; and

(*d*) he has taken into account, after considering a report from the Board, any matters raised in the course of such consultations by the applicant or by any other person referred to in Paragraph (c).

(7) An instrument under Subsection (5)(a) shall contain–

(*a*) the conditions subject to which the petroleum processing facility licence is to be granted; and
(*b*) the terms of the access arrangements, complying with Section 89, to be approved by the Minister and apply to the petroleum processing facility in accordance with Section 89; and
(*c*) a statement to the effect that the application will lapse if the applicant does not make a request under Subsection (8) in respect of the grant of the petroleum processing facility licence and lodge with the Director the security specified in the instrument and the first annual fee as prescribed by Section 157.

(8) An applicant who has been served with an instrument under Subsection (5)(a) may, within a period of one month after the date of service of the instrument, or within such further period or periods as the Minister may allow–

(*a*) by instrument served on the Minister request the Minister to grant him the petroleum processing facility licence; and
(*b*) lodge with the Director the security referred to in Subsection (5)(a) and the first annual fee as prescribed by Section 157.

(9) Where an applicant has complied with the requirements of Subsection (8), the Minister shall approve the access arrangements specified in the instrument and grant a petroleum processing facility licence for the site and the petroleum processing facility specified in the instrument, subject to the conditions specified in the instrument or such other conditions as are agreed by the Minister and the applicant, but in any other case the application lapses.
(10) A petroleum processing facility licence shall not be granted under this section in respect of a strategic petroleum processing facility unless the Minister has approved access arrangements complying with Section 89 and the applicant has accepted those access arrangements in accordance with Subsection (8).

89. STRATEGIC PETROLEUM PROCESSING FACILITIES.

(1) A petroleum processing facility licence in respect of a strategic petroleum processing facility shall contain a licence condition designating the petroleum processing facility to be a strategic petroleum processing facility.
(2) A petroleum processing facility licensee in respect of a strategic petroleum processing facility shall adopt and comply with access arrangements approved by the Minister, whereby third parties may have petroleum or petroleum products processed by the petroleum processing facility licensee through that strategic petroleum processing facility.
(3) The access arrangements applying to a strategic petroleum processing facility shall be registered and the petroleum processing facility licensee shall make copies available to all prospective third party users requesting a copy of them.
(4) Subject to any written agreement between the State and the petroleum processing facility licensee, access arrangements applying to strategic petroleum processing facilities–

(*a*) shall comply with the requirements of regulations on the operation of strategic petroleum processing facilities; and
(*b*) shall comply with the following principles:–

(i) the arrangements should encourage third party use of the facility, without requiring reduced tariffs for otherwise marginally economic use of the petroleum processing facilities;

(ii) the arrangements should achieve the lowest sustainable tariffs for users which provide a reasonable return on investment for the petroleum processing facility licensee, having regard to the circumstances of the investment, including due consideration of risk;
(iii) the arrangements should provide commercial incentives for investors in respect of risks assumed, improved efficiency and increased throughputs;
(iv) the arrangements should provide certainty of tariff methodology for the term of the processing contract;
(v) the arrangements should constitute an open dissemination of information regarding the facility and the service available, so as to enable prospective third party users to evaluate the technical and economic feasibility of processing petroleum or petroleum products using any spare capacity or developable capacity;
(vi) the arrangements should recognise the entitlement of the petroleum processing facility licensee to be assured as to the creditworthiness of third party users of the petroleum processing facility prior to entering into contracts for processing;
(vii) the arrangements should recognise the legitimate business interests of the petroleum processing facility licensee and existing and potential third party users; and

(*c*) shall include–

(i) the location and ownership of receipt and delivery facilities; and
(ii) reasonable definitions of total capacity, excess capacity, and developable capacity of the petroleum processing facility for specified conditions; and
(iii) a process for identifying the need for, and implementing, expansion to take up the petroleum processing facility's capacity or other modification of the petroleum processing facility; and
(iv) reasonable processes that may lead to the extension or expansion or modification of the petroleum processing facility if demonstrated to be commercially, technically, and operationally viable; and
(v) a procedure for requesting service and concluding processing arrangements within a reasonable period of time; and
(vi) the classes of processing service offered to third parties by the petroleum processing facility licensee, separating the charges and tariffs to be charged in respect of each class of service; and
(vii) the terms and conditions of the agreement to be offered by the petroleum processing facility licensee to third-party users for the processing of petroleum or petroleum products; and
(viii) tariff methodology, with sample calculations; and
(ix) billing and payment arrangements; and
(x) a queuing policy in respect of competing proposals for processing; and
(xi) a policy for allocation of petroleum processing facility capacity in the event of capacity restrictions from time to time; and
(xii) a dispute resolution procedure; and
(xiii) acceptable quality specifications for petroleum or petroleum products which are not unfairly discriminatory to third party users, measurement requirements, and balancing and adjustments for differences in quality of petroleum or petroleum products entering the petroleum processing facility; and

(*d*) may include–

(i) different terms and conditions for foundation users of the petroleum processing facility which are commensurate with the different obligations undertaken and risks assumed by those users; and
(ii) any other provisions consistent with the normal international practice for open access petroleum processing facilities which are approved by the Minister.

(5) Access arrangements approved by the Minister under Sections 88(9), 92(8), 93(9) or 93(12) shall, for as long as the petroleum processing facility licence remains in force, be binding on the petroleum processing facility licensee and compliance with those access arrangements shall be a condition of the petroleum processing facility licence.
(6) The access arrangements referred to in Subsection (5) shall have legal effect and shall be enforceable according to their terms in a court of law by any person having a *bona fide* interest in the terms of the access arrangements.
(7) A petroleum processing facility shall not be a strategic petroleum processing facility if it is exempted by a written agreement between the State and the holder of the petroleum processing facility licence or by a condition of the petroleum processing facility licence or by an instrument signed by the Minister.
(8) Where by an instrument the Minister exempts a petroleum processing facility under Subsection (7), that exemption may be revoked by the Minister by instrument.
(9) Nothing in this section limits the terms and conditions which a petroleum processing facility licensee may agree with a third party user as the terms of an access arrangement.
(10)[68] [69]Where a strategic petroleum processing facility is constructed as part of a petroleum project or a gas project and is linked to a strategic pipeline, which is also part of such a petroleum project or gas project, the petroleum processing facility licensee and the pipeline licensee may submit to the Minister for approval one access arrangement for such strategic petroleum processing facility and strategic pipeline, which may include a single published tariff for integrated processing and transportation.

90. RIGHTS CONFERRED BY PETROLEUM PROCESSING FACILITY LICENCE.

(1) Subject to Subsection (2), a petroleum processing facility licence, while it remains in force, confers on the petroleum processing facility licensee, subject to this Act and to the conditions specified in the petroleum processing facility licence, exclusive rights to–

(*a*) construct the petroleum processing facility at the site for which the petroleum processing facility licence was granted; and
(*b*) conduct operations for petroleum processing through the petroleum processing facility; and
(*c*) carry on such operations and execute such works at the site of the petroleum processing facility, other than a major modification, as are necessary and reasonable for or in connection with the purposes specified in Paragraphs (a) and (b).

(2) A petroleum processing facility licensee shall not make a major modification to his petroleum processing facility except pursuant to a variation of the petroleum processing facility licence under Section 92 or 93.
(3) Nothing in this section shall affect the rights conferred on the holder of a petroleum development licence under Section 59 or on a pipeline licensee under Section 76.

91. TERM OF PETROLEUM PROCESSING FACILITY LICENCE.

Subject to this Division, and to any condition in the petroleum processing facility licence, a petroleum processing facility licence remains in force until cancelled by the Minister under Section 138 or surrendered by the petroleum processing facility licensee under Section 137.

92. VARIATION OF PETROLEUM PROCESSING FACILITY LICENCE ON APPLICATION BY LICENSEE.

(1) The holder of a petroleum processing facility licence may, at any time, make an application to the Minister for a variation of the petroleum processing facility licence.
(2) An application under this section shall–

(*a*) specify the reasons for proposed variation; and
(*b*) be made in an approved form and contain the information specified in Section 87; and
(*c*) in the case of an application to vary a petroleum processing facility licence to vary the access arrangements applying to a strategic petroleum processing facility, be accompanied by draft access arrangements which the applicant proposes should be the access arrangements applying to the strategic petroleum processing facility.

(3) The Minister may require the applicant to furnish such further information in connection with his application as the Minister considers necessary.
(4) In the case of an application to vary a petroleum processing facility licence other than to vary the access arrangements applying to a strategic petroleum processing facility, the Minister may, after considering a report of the Board and any matters submitted to him under this section–

(*a*) amend the terms of the petroleum processing facility licence to provide as stipulated in the application or as otherwise agreed with the petroleum processing facility licensee; or
(*b*) refuse the application, in which case the existing petroleum processing facility licence shall remain in full force and effect.

(5) In the case of an application to vary a petroleum processing facility licence to vary the access arrangements applying to a strategic petroleum processing facility–

(*a*) the applicant shall, prior to submitting his application, make all reasonable efforts to consult with existing and potential third party users of the petroleum processing facility, and shall furnish to the Minister a report on the possible third party users and their possible requirements in using the petroleum processing facility and their views on the contents of the access arrangements to apply to the petroleum processing facility; and
(*b*) upon receipt of the application the Minister shall cause a notice to be published in the National Gazette advising of the application and particulars of the petroleum processing facility, and inviting existing and potential third party users of the petroleum processing facility to make submissions to the Minister as to their potential requirements in using the petroleum processing facility and the contents of the access arrangements to apply to the petroleum processing facility; and
(*c*) the draft access arrangements submitted by the applicant shall be a public document, and any person may inspect that document or those documents at the office of the Director; and
(*d*) the Minister shall notify the applicant of any submissions received in accordance with Subsection (5)(b) and provide the applicant with a copy of all such submissions if requested.

(6) In the case of an application to vary a petroleum processing facility licence to vary the access arrangements applying to a strategic petroleum processing facility, the Minister may, after considering a report from the Board and any matter submitted to him under this section–

(*a*) serve on the petroleum processing facility licensee an instrument–

(i) advising the petroleum processing facility licensee that the Minister is prepared to vary the petroleum processing facility licence to vary the access arrangements; and
(ii) specifying the terms of the varied access arrangements, complying with Section 89, to be approved by the Minister and apply to the petroleum processing facility in accordance with Section 89; or

(*b*) reject the application.

(7) A petroleum processing facility licensee who has been served with an instrument under Subsection (6)(a) may, within a period of three months after the date of service of the instrument on him, by instrument served on the Director, request the Minister to vary the petroleum processing facility licence in accordance with the instrument referred to in that Subsection.
(8) Where a petroleum processing facility licensee who has been served with an instrument under Subsection (6)(a) has, within the period specified in Subsection (7), made a request under Subsection (7), the Minister shall approve the varied access arrangements specified in the instrument and vary the petroleum processing facility licence in accordance with the instrument.
(9) A petroleum processing facility licence shall not be varied under this section to vary the access arrangements unless the Minister has approved varied access arrangements complying with Section 89 and the applicant has accepted those varied access arrangements in accordance with Subsection (7).
(10) Where the Minister varies a petroleum processing facility licence under this section, he shall cause to be published in the National Gazette a notice of the variation.
(11) Where access arrangements are established or varied under this section, the varied access arrangements shall apply to that petroleum processing facility in accordance with Section 89 with effect from the date the variation of the licence for that purpose takes effect.
(13) Notwithstanding Subsection (11), the establishment or variation under this section of the access arrangements applying to a strategic petroleum processing facility shall not affect the validity of agreements previously entered into by the petroleum processing facility licensee for processing of petroleum.

93. VARIATION OF PETROLEUM PROCESSING FACILITY LICENCE BY MINISTER.

(1) If the Minister gives to a pipeline licensee a direction under Section 82(5)(a) and as a consequence of the pipeline to which that direction relates becoming a strategic pipeline a petroleum processing facility would become a strategic petroleum processing facility, the Minister shall give to the petroleum processing facility licensee in respect of that petroleum processing facility a direction under this Section.
(2) If the Minister, acting in accordance with the advice of the Board, considers that it is desirable that the terms of access arrangements applying to a strategic petroleum processing facility be varied, the Minister may by instrument served on the petroleum processing facility licensee direct that the access arrangements applying to that strategic petroleum processing facility be varied.

(3) If the Minister gives a direction under Subsections (1) or (2) he shall publish in the National Gazette a notice advising of that direction and particulars of the petroleum processing facility, and inviting existing and potential third party users of the petroleum processing facility to make submissions to the Minister as to their potential requirements in using the petroleum processing facility and the contents of the access arrangements to apply to the petroleum processing facility.
(4) Within three months of receipt of a direction under Subsections (1) or (2), a petroleum processing facility licensee shall lodge with the Minister draft access arrangements complying with Section 89, which the applicant proposes should be the access arrangements or varied access arrangements applying to that petroleum processing facility.
(5) Prior to submitting draft access arrangements, the petroleum processing facility licensee shall make all reasonable efforts to consult with existing and potential third party users of the petroleum processing facility, and shall furnish to the Minister a report on the possible third party users and their possible requirements in using the petroleum processing facility and their views on the contents of the access arrangements to apply to the petroleum processing facility.
(6) A notice referred to in Subsection (3) shall invite existing and potential third party users of the petroleum processing facility to make submissions to the Minister within the period stipulated in the notice as to their potential requirements in using the petroleum processing facility and the contents of the access arrangements to apply to the petroleum processing facility.
(7) The draft access arrangements submitted by the petroleum processing facility licensee shall be a public document, and any person may inspect that document or those documents at the office of the Director.
(8) The Minister shall notify the petroleum processing facility licensee of any submissions received in response to invitations made in accordance with Subsection (3) and provide the petroleum processing facility licensee with a copy of all such submissions if requested.
(9) If the draft access arrangements or varied access arrangements proposed by the petroleum processing facility licensee, as they may be amended by agreement between the Minister and the petroleum processing facility licensee, are acceptable to the Minister, the Minister shall approve those access arrangements, and vary the petroleum processing facility licence to convert the petroleum processing facility to be a strategic petroleum processing facility or adopt the new access arrangements, as the case may be.
(10) If the draft access arrangements or varied access arrangements proposed by the petroleum processing facility licensee is not acceptable to the Minister and the petroleum processing facility licensee and the Minister are not able to reach agreement on amendments to the draft, the Minister may refer the question of the terms of the access arrangements or varied access arrangements to apply to the petroleum processing facility for expert determination in accordance with Subsection (11).
(11) If the Minister makes a reference under Subsection (10), then the terms of the access arrangements or varied access arrangements shall be determined by an expert appointed by the Minister for that purpose and paid for by the State, who shall–

> (*a*) be independent of the State and the petroleum processing facility licensee; and
> (*b*) be qualified by experience in dealing with open access arrangements for petroleum processing facilities; and
> (*c*) prior to making his decision, consult with the Minister and the petroleum processing facility licensee and any person who has made a submission under Subsection (3); and
> (*d*) in making his decision have regard to the reasonable requirements of those persons making such submissions; and
> (*e*) determine terms of access arrangements which comply with Section 89.

(12) When the access arrangements are determined by expert determination under Subsection (11), the Minister may–

(*a*) approve the access arrangements or varied access arrangements so determined; and
(*b*) vary the petroleum processing facility licence to convert the petroleum processing facility to be a strategic petroleum processing facility or adopt the varied access arrangements, as the case may be.

(13) Where the Minister varies a petroleum processing facility licence under this section, he shall cause to be published in the National Gazette a notice of the variation.
(14) A petroleum processing facility which is converted to a strategic petroleum processing facility under this section shall be a strategic petroleum processing facility with effect from the date upon which the variation of the licence for that purpose takes effect, and thereafter those approved access arrangements shall apply to that petroleum processing facility in accordance with Section 89.
(15)[70] [71]Where the access arrangements applying to a strategic petroleum processing facility are varied under this section, the varied access arrangements shall apply to that petroleum processing facilty in accordance with Section 89 with effect from the date the variation of the licence for that purpose takes effect.
(16) Notwithstanding Subsection (15), the establishment or variation under this section of the access arrangements applying to a strategic petroleum processing facility shall not affect the validity of agreements previously entered into by the petroleum processing facility licensee for processing of petroleum or petroleum products.

94. CONDITIONS OF PETROLEUM PROCESSING FACILITY LICENCE.

A petroleum processing facility licence may be granted, or an application for a variation approved, subject to such conditions as the Minister, after considering a report of the Board, thinks fit and specifies in his grant or approval and which may include, but are not limited to, conditions for–

(*a*) the construction, conduct, control, management and operation of the petroleum processing facility; and
(*b*) furnishing reports and information to the Director concerning in-put, out-put and sales volumes; and
(*c*) the removal of the petroleum processing facility and restoration of the site upon termination of the petroleum processing facility licence.

95. REGULATIONS FOR DOMESTIC UTILISATION BUSINESS.

(1) The Head of State, acting on advice, may make regulations prescribing the activities of–

(*a*) a domestic gas supplier; or
(*b*) a domestic gas operator; or
(*c*) the owner of a facility for the storage or transportation of cylinders containing compressed natural gas or liquefied petroleum gas.

(2) Nothing contained in regulations under Subsection (1) applies in respect of petroleum processing facilities licensed under this Act, or the activities of a petroleum development licensee, pipeline licensee or petroleum processing facility licensee in respect of the subject matter of his licence.

DIVISION 11. REGISTRATION OF INSTRUMENTS.

96. REGISTER TO BE KEPT.

(1) The Minister shall cause to be kept a Register of applications, grants, extensions, transfers and dealings in licences.
(2) The Register shall contain such details as are prescribed or as the Minister directs.
(3) A copy of any entry in the Register may be obtained on payment of the prescribed fee.

97. APPROVAL AND REGISTRATION OF TRANSFERS.

(1) Subject to this section, the Minister may approve the transfer of a licence from one person to another and such approval may be subject to such conditions (if any) as the Minister thinks fit.
(2) In addition to any other condition that the Minister may impose under Subsection (1), the Minister may require the transferee to lodge with him such security as the Minister thinks fit for the transferee's compliance with the conditions to which the licence is from time to time subject.
(3) The transfer of a licence shall have no effect until it is approved and registered in accordance with this section.
(4) Where the Minister approves the transfer of a licence from a company to a company that is a related corporation within the meaning of the *Companies Act 1997*, he shall impose no new conditions on the licence as a condition of that approval.
(5) A licensee who desires to transfer his licence to another person, or to himself and another person jointly, may lodge with the Director an application for approval of the transfer of the licence.
(6) The application shall be accompanied by an instrument of transfer of the licence duly executed by the transferor and transferee, together with a copy of that instrument of transfer.
(7) If the Minister approves the application, the Director shall–

(*a*) immediately endorse on the instrument of transfer and on the copy a memorandum of approval; and
(*b*) on payment of the prescribed fee enter in the Register a memorandum of the transfer and the name of the transferee.

(8) The transfer shall be deemed to be registered as soon as a memorandum of the transfer and the name of the transferee has been entered in the Register and, on that memorandum being so entered, the transferee becomes the registered holder of the licence to which the instrument of transfer relates.
(9) The copy of the instrument of transfer endorsed with the memorandum of approval shall be retained by the Director and is subject to inspection in accordance with this Division.
(10) The instrument of transfer endorsed with the memorandum of approval shall be returned to the person who lodged the application.
(11) The Minister shall not approve a transfer of a licence unless it is an absolute transfer of the whole of the transferor's interest in the licence.

98. ENTRIES IN REGISTER OF DEVOLUTION OF TITLE.

(1) A person on whom the rights of a licensee have devolved by operation of law may apply in writing to the Director to have his name entered in the Register as the registered holder of the licence.
(2) The Director shall, if he is satisfied that the rights of the holder have devolved on the applicant by operation of law, and on payment of the prescribed fee, enter the name of the applicant in the Register as the holder of the licence and, on that entry being so made, the applicant becomes the registered holder of the licence.

99. INTERESTS NOT TO BE CREATED, ETC., EXCEPT BY INSTRUMENT.

A legal or equitable interest in or affecting an existing or future licence is not capable of being created, assigned, affected or dealt with, whether directly or indirectly, except by an instrument.

100. APPROVAL OF INSTRUMENTS CREATING, ETC., INTERESTS.

(1) This section applies to an instrument by which a legal or equitable interest in, or affecting, an existing or future licence is or may be created, assigned, affected or dealt with, whether directly or indirectly, not being an instrument of transfer to which Section 97 applies.
(2) An instrument to which this section applies is of no force or effect until–

> (*a*) the instrument has been approved by the Minister either unconditionally or subject to such conditions as he thinks fit; and
> (*b*) an entry has been made in the Register by the Director in accordance with Subsection (5).

(3) A party to an instrument to which this section applies, or a person having an interest in or in relation to a licence by reason of such an instrument, may lodge with the Director an application for approval of the instrument.
(4) An application under Subsection (3) shall be accompanied by the instrument and by a copy of the instrument.
(5) If the Minister approves the instrument, the Director shall, on payment of the prescribed fee, immediately endorse on the original instrument and the copy of the instrument a memorandum of approval.
(6) The copy of the instrument endorsed with the memorandum of approval shall be retained in the Register by the Director and is subject to inspection in accordance with this Division.
(7) The original instrument endorsed with the memorandum of approval shall be returned to the person who lodged the application for approval.
(8) If the Minister refuses the application, the Director shall cause a notation of the refusal to be made in the Register.

101. TRUE CONSIDERATION TO BE SHOWN.

A party to a transfer referred to in Section 97 or to an instrument to which Section 100 applies who, with intent to defraud, executes the transfer or instrument if the transfer or instrument does not fully and truly set forth the true consideration for the transfer or instrument is guilty of an offence.
Penalty: A fine not exceeding K5,000.00.

102. MINISTER NOT CONCERNED WITH CERTAIN MATTERS.

The Minister or a person acting under his direction or authority shall not be concerned with the effect in law of any instrument lodged in accordance with this Division, nor does the approval of such an instrument give to it any force, effect or validity that it would not have had if this Division had not been enacted.

103. POWER OF MINISTER TO REQUIRE INFORMATION AS TO PROPOSED DEALINGS.

(1) The Minister or Director may require the person lodging an instrument for approval under this Division to furnish to him such written information concerning the instrument, or the transaction to which the instrument relates, as the Minister or Director thinks fit.

(2) A person who, when required under Subsection (1) to furnish information, furnishes information that is false or misleading in a material particular is guilty of an offence.
Penalty: A fine not exceeding K2,000.00.

104. PRODUCTION AND INSPECTION OF DOCUMENTS.

(1) The Minister or Director may require any person to produce to him, or to make available for inspection by him, any document in the possession or under the control of that person and relating–

(*a*) to an instrument lodged for approval under this Division; or
(*b*) to the transaction to which such an instrument relates.

(2) A person who refuses or fails within a reasonable time to comply with a requirement under Subsection (1) is guilty of an offence.
Penalty: A fine not exceeding K2,000.00.

105. INSPECTION OF REGISTER AND DOCUMENTS.

(1) The Register shall, at all reasonable times, be open for inspection by any person on payment of the prescribed fee.
(2) Any person may take copies of any licence or entry in the Register on payment of the prescribed fee.

106. EVIDENTIARY PROVISIONS.

(1) The Register shall be received by all courts as evidence of all matters required or authorized by this Division to be entered in the Register.
(2) The Director may, on payment of the prescribed fee, supply copies of or extracts from the Register certified by writing under his hand, and a document purporting to be a copy or extract so certified is admissible in evidence in all courts and proceedings without further proof or production of the original.
(3) The Director may, on payment of the prescribed fee, by instrument under his hand, certify that an entry, matter or thing required or permitted by or under this Division to be made or done or not to be made or done has or has not, as the case may be, been made or done and a document purporting to be such a certificate is evidence in all courts and proceedings of the statements contained in the certificate.

107. REGISTER MAY BE RECTIFIED.

Where the Minister is satisfied that there has been a mistake made in, or that some matter has been incorrectly entered in, the Register, he shall rectify the Register by correcting that mistake or incorrect entry.

108. MINISTER OR DIRECTOR NOT LIABLE FOR CERTAIN ACTIONS.

The Minister, the Director, or a person acting under the direction or authority of the Minister or the Director shall not be liable to an action, suit or proceeding for or in respect of an act or matter done or omitted to be done in good faith in the exercise or purported exercise of any power or authority conferred by this Division.

109. OFFENCES.

A person who wilfully–

(*a*) makes, causes to be made or concurs in making, a false entry in the Register; or
(*b*) produces or tenders in evidence a document falsely purporting to be a copy of or extract from an entry in the Register of or from an instrument lodged with the Minister under this Division,

is guilty of an offence.
Penalty: Imprisonment for a term not exceeding two years.

DIVISION 12. RIGHTS IN RESPECT OF LAND AND PROPERTY.

110. RIGHTS OF TENEMENT HOLDERS IN RESPECT OF LAND AND PROPERTY.

(1) Subject to this Division, the rights conferred on a tenement holder by Section 25, 42 or 59 are, by virtue of this Act, exercisable on any land within the licence area and, for the purpose of exercising those rights, a tenement holder, by himself or his agents or workmen, may to the extent reasonably necessary for the tenement holder's operations or proposed operations in the licence area–

(*a*) enter on any land in the licence area; and
(*b*) subject to Sections 117 and 118, occupy any land in the licence area that is from time to time required for–

(i) effectively carrying on the operations he is entitled under the tenement to carry on; and
(ii) adequately protecting those operations and the improvements and equipment on or under the land; and

(*c*) erect buildings on land occupied under Paragraph (b) and at any time remove any building so erected and, subject to Section 118, remove any other building from land so occupied; and
(*d*) bring any machinery or other equipment into the licence area and erect or install it on land occupied under Paragraph (b) or in any building erected under Paragraph (c), and at any time remove any such machinery or equipment; and
(*e*) request the Minister to acquire any land required by the tenement holder for a purpose specified in Section 120; and
(*f*) subject to the *Water Resources Act 1982*, take and divert water from any lake, stream or watercourse in the licence area; and
(*g*) construct in the licence area roads, airstrips or helicopter pads; and
(*h*) cut and use the timber in the licence area (other than timber forming part of any improvements) for building or construction work within the licence area; and
(*i*) remove any stone, clay or gravel in the licence area (other than that forming part of any improvements) for or in connection with building or construction work within the licence area.

(2) For the purposes of Section 20 of the *Water Resources Act 1982*, the rights conferred under this Act on a tenement holder shall be deemed to be rights in land to which that section applies.

111. RIGHTS OF PIPELINE LICENSEES IN RESPECT OF LAND AND PROPERTY.

Subject to this Division, the rights conferred on a pipeline licensee by Section 76 are, by virtue of this Act, exercisable on any land–

(*a*) that is occupied or to be occupied by the pipeline and other improvements required for safety of operations; or
(*b*) that is at a distance not exceeding 10m on either side of the pipeline,

and within that area of land and for the purpose of exercising those rights, the pipeline licensee, by himself or his agents or workmen, may to the extent reasonably necessary for the pipeline licensee's operations or proposed operations in that area–

(*c*) enter on any land; and
(*d*) subject to Sections 117 and 118, occupy with his pipeline land substantially along the route and on the sites specified in the pipeline licence; and
(*e*) erect buildings on land occupied under Paragraph (d) and at any time remove any building so erected and, subject to Section 118 remove any other building from any land so occupied; and
(*f*) bring any machinery or equipment on land occupied under Paragraph (d) and erect or install it on such land or in any building erected under Paragraph (e), and at any time remove any such machinery or equipment; and
(*g*) request the Minister to acquire any land required by the pipeline licensee for a purpose specified in Section 120; and
(*h*) construct roads to give adequate access to the pipeline; and
(*i*) cut and use the timber (other than timber forming part of any improvements) for building or construction work related to the pipeline; and
(*j*) remove any stone, clay or gravel (other than that forming part of any improvements) for or in connection with building or construction work related to the pipeline.

112. RIGHTS OF PETROLEUM PROCESSING FACILITY LICENSEES IN RESPECT OF LAND AND PROPERTY.

Subject to this Division, the rights conferred on a petroleum processing facility licensee by Section 90 are, by virtue of this Act, exercisable on any land–

(*a*) that is occupied or to be occupied by the petroleum processing facility and other improvements required for safety of operations; or
(*b*) that is at a distance not exceeding 100m of such petroleum processing facility and other improvements,

and within that area of land and for the purpose of exercising those rights, the petroleum processing facility licensee, by himself or his agents or workmen, may to the extent reasonably necessary for the petroleum processing facility licensee's operations or proposed operations in that area–

(*c*) enter on any land; and
(*d*) subject to Sections 117 and 118, occupy with his petroleum processing facility land at the sites specified in the petroleum processing facility licence; and
(*e*) erect buildings on land occupied under Paragraph (d) and at any time remove any building so erected and, subject to Section 118 remove any other building from any land so occupied; and
(*f*) bring any machinery or equipment on land occupied under Paragraph (d) and erect or install it on such land or in any building erected under Paragraph (e), and at any time remove any such machinery or equipment; and
(*g*) request the Minister to acquire any land required by the petroleum processing facility licensee for a purpose specified in Section 120; and
(*h*) construct roads to give adequate access to the petroleum processing facility; and
(*i*) cut and use the timber (other than timber forming part of any improvements) for building or construction work related to the petroleum processing facility; and
(*j*) remove any stone, clay or gravel (other than that forming part of any improvements) for or in connection with building or construction work related to the petroleum processing facility.

113. RIGHTS OF LANDOWNERS.

(1) The owner, occupier or other person having an interest in any private land in a licence area or occupied or to be occupied by a pipeline or petroleum processing facility or any part thereof may continue to use, occupy and enjoy the land, with the exception of any part of that land reasonably required from time to time by the licensee for the exercise of his rights under his licence.
(2) Where a dispute arises as to interests in customary land or the position of boundaries of customary land, such dispute shall not affect–

(*a*) the right of a person to make application for and be granted a licence under this Act; or
(*b*) the validity of a licence granted under this Act.

(3) A dispute referred to in Subsection (2) shall be settled as provided for in the *Land Disputes Settlement Act 1975.*

114. INTERFERENCE WITH OTHER RIGHTS.

(1) A person carrying on operations under a licence or instrument of consent under Section 150 shall carry on those operations in a manner that does not interfere with the existing use of the land to any greater extent than is reasonably necessary for the exercise of the rights, and performance of the duties, of that person.
(2) Without limiting the generality of Subsection (1), a person carrying on operations under a licence or instrument of consent under Section 150 shall not take any action that in any way interferes with–

(*a*) fishing; or
(*b*) navigation; or
(*c*) any other operation being lawfully carried on by way of–

(i) prospecting for, recovery of or conveyance or processing of petroleum, petroleum products, helium, minerals or gold; or
(ii) construction of a pipeline or petroleum processing facility,

unless he gives prior written notice to the Director of the expected nature and duration of such interference.
(3) A person who fails to comply with the provisions of this section is guilty of an offence.
Penalty: A fine not exceeding K5,000.00.

115. RESPONSIBILITY TO REPAIR DAMAGE.

(1) Subject to Sections 110 and 111, a licensee shall, as soon as and to the extent practicable having regard to his operations, repair any damage–

(*a*) to any improvements; or
(*b*) to any land capable of being used for any agricultural purposes; or
(*c*) to the water supply to such improvements or land,

resulting from his operations or from the flow of petroleum, petroleum products, water or waste from any of those operations.
(2) Where a licensee fails to comply with Subsection (1), the Minister may repair the damage, and any costs or expenses incurred are a debt due from the licensee to the State.

116. ADDITIONAL RIGHTS OF ENTRY.

(1) Where, in the opinion of the Minister, it is necessary for an applicant or intending applicant for a licence–

(*a*) to enter on to land to survey the proposed route of a pipeline or the proposed site of an exploration or appraisal or development activity or facility or a pipeline or petroleum processing facility; or
(*b*) to conduct tests or to obtain information in relation to any such route or site; or
(*c*) to conduct temporary operations,

the Minister may, on the application of that person and subject to Section 118, by instrument authorize that person to enter on the land for that purpose.
(1A)[72] [73]Where, in the opinion of the Minister, it is necessary or expedient for an applicant or an intending applicant for a licence to conduct activities in relation to or in preparation for construction works which are or will be proposed in the licence application of the applicant or intending applicant, the Minister may, on the application of that person and subject to Section 118, by instrument, authorize that person to enter or any land for that purpose for such period as may be reasonably required for the conduct of those activities as are specified in the instrument.

(2) Where, in the opinion of the Minister, it is necessary for the effective exercise of a licensee's rights or the performance of his duties under this Act for the licensee to enter on any land not held by him under a tenement in order to obtain geological information for use in relation to his licence area, the Minister may, on application by the licensee and subject to Section 118, authorize that licensee to enter on that land and there carry out such acts as are necessary to obtain that information.
(3) An authorization under Subsection (2) shall not entitle a licensee to prospect for petroleum by the drilling of wells on the land.
(4) Where, in the opinion of the Minister, it is necessary for the effective exercise of the rights or the performance of obligations under a licence or under this Act, or to enable the licensee to carry out other activities in the course of a project including business development activities, the provision of community services and incurring expenditure in accordance with Section 219C of the *Income Tax Act 1959*, for a licensee to enter on any land not held by him under a tenement, the Minister may by instrument authorize the licensee to enter on such other lands–

(*a*) in order to obtain access to any part of his tenement or to the site or proposed site of the pipeline or petroleum processing facility or any part thereof; or
(*b*) for the transport of personnel, equipment or materials for operational and construction activities approved under the licence; or
(*c*) in order to carry out specified activities or expenditure on such other lands.

(5) Where an applicant for a licence, a person intending to apply for a licence or a licensee is granted rights of entry under this section, he shall before entering the land serve a copy of the authorization on the licensee of any licence covering or pertaining to any land to which entry is so granted.
(6) If in the *bona fide* opinion of a licensee an emergency exists in his operations which threatens–

(*a*) the safety, health or welfare of persons engaged in those operations or in the licence area or the vicinity of the pipeline or petroleum processing facility; or
(*b*) the environment; or
(*c*) the State's petroleum resource in the licence area,

the licensee may, without first obtaining an authorization under this section, enter onto lands not held by him under a licence in order to obtain access to any part of the licence area or the site or proposed site of the pipeline or petroleum processing facility or to transport personnel, equipment or materials to deal with the emergency, but–

(*d*) within 24 hours of first entering onto that land, the licensee shall file a report with the Director setting out the details of the emergency, the steps being taken to deal with it and the reason why such access was needed; and
(*e*) the licensee shall not without obtaining a further authorization under this section continue to enter onto or occupy such land for more than 72 hours after first entering that land.

117. LAND OCCUPIED TO BE SURVEYED.

The licensee shall cause to be surveyed and, if so required by the Director, securely fenced, any part of the land in a licence area which the licensee requires in order effectively to carry on drilling operations.

118. COMPENSATION.

(1)[74] [75]A licensee shall be liable to pay compensation in accordance with this section to the lawful owners and rightful occupiers of, and any persons interested in, any private land in relation to their several interests, in respect of the entry on or occupation of the land by the licensee under this Division.
(2) Subject to this section, compensation shall be paid for–

(*a*) the deprivation of the use and enjoyment of the surface of the land or any part of it or of any rights customarily associated with it, except where there has been a reservation in favour of the State of the right to such use and enjoyment; and
(*b*) damage–

(i) to the surface of the land or any part of it, or any improvements on it; or
(ii) to any trees, fish or animals,

caused by the carrying on of operations by the licensee; and

(*c*) severance of the land from other land of any owner, occupier or person interested in the land; and
(*b*) rights of way and easements; and
(*c*) any other damage consequential on the licensee's use or occupation of the land.

(3) If any private land adjoining or in the vicinity of land comprised in any licence area or occupied under any pipeline licence or petroleum processing facility licence or any improvements on the land is or are damaged or depreciated in value–

(*a*) by any operations carried on by or on behalf of a licensee; or
(*b*) by reason of any right of way acquired by the licensee,

the owners and occupiers of, and any persons interested in, that private land or those improvements shall be entitled in respect of their several interests to compensation for all loss and damage sustained under Paragraph (a) or (b) and the amount of compensation shall be ascertained in accordance with this section.
(4) A licensee may agree with any person entitled to compensation under this section as to the amount of compensation.
(5) An agreement under Subsection (4) shall not be valid unless it is in writing and signed by the parties to it, or their agents, and is lodged with the Director.
(6) Where applicable, compensation payable under this section shall be determined with reference to the values for economic trees published by the Valuer-General, and any other values published by the Valuer-General.
(7) No compensation shall be payable and no claim for compensation shall lie, whether under this Act or otherwise, and compensation under this Section shall not be determined, by reference to any petroleum, helium or minerals known or supposed to be in, on or under the land.

(8) If the licensee and a person claiming compensation under this section are unable to agree on the compensation payable, either may, by notice to the Chief Warden, request that the Chief Warden or a Warden determine the amount payable.
(9) On receipt of a notice under Subsection (8), the Chief Warden shall–

(*a*) fix a place and date for conducting a determination of the amount of compensation to be paid; and
(*b*) notify the licensee and the person claiming compensation of the place and date so fixed; and
(*c*) at that place and on that date conduct a determination of the amount of compensation to be paid.

(10) In conducting a determination under this section the Warden shall allow the parties to present their evidence and arguments to him in such manner as he thinks fit, but shall at all times have regard to the principles of natural justice.
(11) The Warden shall–

(*a*) make a determination on the basis of the evidence presented to him and arguments submitted to him and in accordance with the principles of compensation contained in this section; and
(*b*) record his decision in writing; and
(*c*) give a copy of his decision to each of the parties.

(12) Where the Warden considers it impractical or inexpedient to assess the full amount of compensation to be paid in satisfaction of the loss or damage, he may make a determination of the amount of compensation payable in respect of a particular period or item of loss or damage and defer his determination of the remainder of the claim until a later time.
(13) The Warden may, at any stage of the determination process, make an order against the person from whom compensation is sought, restricting that person from commencing or continuing any operations under this Act until he has given such security as the Warden thinks fit for payment of any compensation for which he is or may become liable.
(14) If, after a Warden has determined any amount of compensation under this section, it is proved that further loss or damage, not being loss or damage in respect of which compensation has already been determined, has been sustained, the Warden may determine compensation for the further loss or damage and order that further compensation be paid by the licensee to the person entitled to that further compensation.
(15) Where a Warden has made an order for compensation or further compensation under this section, the amount of compensation stated in that order is an amount payable by the licensee for the purposes of Section 138(1)(d).
(16) In determining the amount of compensation payable under this section the Warden shall–

(*a*) take into consideration the amount of any compensation which the owners or occupiers of, or the persons interested in, the land or any of them or their predecessors in title have or has already received for the damage or loss for which compensation is being determined; and
(*b*) deduct that amount from the amount to which they or any of them respectively would otherwise be entitled.

(17) A party to a determination of a Warden under this section who is aggrieved as to the amount of compensation to which he is entitled or which he is obliged to pay, may appeal to the National Court.

(18) Where a dispute, as defined in the *Land Disputes Settlement Act 1975*, concerning the land the subject of a licence or petroleum processing facility licence or crossed by a pipeline licence makes agreement on compensation impracticable, the amount of compensation to be paid shall be determined by a Warden under this section, and the amount of such compensation shall be payable into a trust account established for that purpose by the Director to be held therein until the dispute has been finally resolved.
(19) Following final resolution of a dispute as provided in Subsection (18), compensation shall be paid out of the trust account in accordance with a compensation agreement or a further determination by a Warden under this section, and in making such a further determination the Warden shall be empowered, if he considers on the basis of the evidence and arguments then presented to him that the amount of compensation payable should be greater than the amount in the trust account, to order payment of amounts in addition to the amount in the trust account.

119. WARDENS.

[76](1) The Director shall appoint –

(*a*) a senior officer of the Department or the public service to be Chief Warden; and
(*b*) such other number of officers as considered necessary to be appointed as Warden,

for the purposes of the Act.
(2) The functions, powers and duties of a Warden are as specified in this Act or regulations.
(3) The Chief Warden shall undertake –

(*a*) the duties of a Warden; and
(*b*) such additional functions as are specifically allocated under this Act or regulations or as the Director may confer.

(4) The Chief Warden may, by instrument in writing, delegate all or any powers (except this power of delegation) to a Warden.

120. ACQUISITION OF LAND.

(1)[77] [78]Notwithstanding any provision of the *Land Act 1996* in determining the compensation payable for land compulsorily acquired for a purpose specified in Section 1(2)–

(*a*) no allowance shall be made for any petroleum, helium, minerals or gold known or supposed to be in, on or under the land acquired; and
(*b*) no compensation shall be payable in respect of improvements made to the land by a licensee.

(2) Whenever it is proved, to the satisfaction of a court of competent jurisdiction, under the *Land Act 1996* that damage has been sustained by a claimant by reason of the severance of the land acquired from other adjoining land of the claimant, or land in which he is interested, the court may order that such adjoining land or some portion of it shall also be acquired.
(3)[79] [80]Where land has been acquired for a purpose specified in Section 1(2) and has been made available to a licensee for the purposes of his operations under his licence, the amount of any compensation that the State has paid in respect of that land is a debt due and payable by the licensee to the State.

(4) An amount payable under Subsection (3), on written demand being served on the licensee, is an amount payable by him under this Act for the purposes of Section 138(1)(d).

121. DETERMINATION OF CUSTOMARY LAND.

(1) Where for the purposes of this Act it is necessary to determine the rightful owners or occupiers of, or persons having an interest in, any customary land, or any improvements on it other than in circumstances where Section 9 of the *Land Act 1996* applies, the determination may be made under the provisions of the *Land Disputes Settlement Act 1975* and for the purposes, and within the meaning, of that Act, there shall be deemed to be a dispute between such persons or groups as the court, within the meaning of that Act, may direct.
(2) Where the Director considers that a dispute of the type referred to in Subsection (1) exists, he may–

(*a*) refer that dispute to the Provincial Land Disputes Committee for the Province in question as a dispute under the *Land Disputes Settlement Act 1975*; or
(*b*) make an application in respect of the dispute to the applicable Local Land Court under Section 27 of that Act.

(3) Where the Director makes a referral or application under Subsection (2)–

(*a*) the dispute shall be deemed for the purpose of the *Land Disputes Settlement Act 1975* to be a dispute relating to land; and
(*b*) the Director shall be deemed to be a party to the dispute for all procedural matters under that Act, and he or his representative shall be entitled to participate in any mediation or court hearing in relation to the dispute.

(4) Where the Director makes a referral under Subsection (2)(a)–

(*a*) the reference to the Provincial Land Disputes Committee shall be deemed to be a request by a Local-level Government under Section 9(1) of the *Land Disputes Settlement Act 1975*; and
(*b*) the Committee shall declare the area which is the subject of the dispute to be a Land Mediation Area and a single Land Mediation Division, and forthwith appoint a Land Mediator for that Land Mediation Division.

(5) Where the Director makes an application under Subsection (2)(b), the dispute shall be deemed to have been the subject of a certificate given by a Land Mediator under Section 27(1) of the *Land Disputes Settlement Act 1975* and a certificate given by a Magistrate under Subsection 27(2) of that Act.

122. TRESPASS ON LAND HELD UNDER A LICENCE.

(1) A person (including the owner or occupier of, or any person interested in, private land) shall not enter on, occupy or interfere with–

(*a*) any land in a licence area which is being used by the licensee for or in connection with prospecting operations or operations for the recovery of petroleum, including land required to be kept vacant for the purpose of compliance with the licensee's obligations under this Act or any other law; or
(*b*) any pipeline or any land permanently occupied by a pipeline licensee under his pipeline licence or being lawfully used by the pipeline licensee for or in connection with pipeline operations or the construction of the pipeline or required to be kept vacant for the purpose of compliance with the licensee's obligations under this Act or any other law; or
(*c*) any petroleum processing facility or any land permanently occupied by the petroleum processing facility licensee under his petroleum processing facility licence or being lawfully used by the petroleum processing facility licensee for or in connection with petroleum processing facility operations or the construction of the petroleum processing facility, or required to be kept vacant for the purpose of compliance with the licensee's obligations under this Act or any other law,

unless authorized or permitted by or under this Act or any other law of the State, or by the licensee.
(2) Every entry, occupation or interference in contravention of Subsection (1) shall, in addition to constituting an offence under this Act, be deemed to be a trespass.
(3) A licensee may proceed in the National Court for trespass under this section and for damages in respect of the trespass.
(4) This section shall not be construed as depriving a licensee of any other right he might have under a law in force in the country in respect of his occupation and use of the land.

DIVISION 13. GENERAL.

123. DATE OF EFFECT OF LICENCES, ETC.

(1) A licence takes effect from and including the day specified for the purpose in the licence.
(2) A variation of a licence takes effect from and including the day on which notice of the variation is published in the National Gazette.

123A. DESIGNATION OF OPERATOR AND OPERATING AGREEMENT.

[81](1) Subject to Subsection (3), where there is more than one holder of a licence, the holders shall, as soon as reasonably practicable after the date of grant of the licence, provide to the Director a copy of an agreement between holders, relating to designation of operator and the conduct of operations in relation to that licence.
(2) Where an agreement has been provided to the Director under Subsection (1), the holders shall, within one month after any amendment, variation or replacement of that agreement, provide to the Director a copy of the agreement (if any) effecting the amendment, variation or replacement.
(3) The holders shall, upon providing a copy of an agreement to the Director under Subsections (1) or (2), and upon any change to the identity of the operator under the provisions of the agreement, give notice in writing to the Director of the name and address of the new operator appointed under the agreement.
(4) An agreement lodged for registration under Division 11 or previously registered under that Division in respect of a licence shall be deemed to have been provided under Subsection (1).

124. WORK PRACTICES FOR TENEMENT HOLDER.

(1) A tenement holder must–

(*a*) carry out all petroleum exploration operations and operations for the recovery of petroleum in the licence area in a proper and workman like manner and in accordance with good oilfield practice; and
(*b*) secure the safety, health and welfare of persons engaged in those operations in or about the licence area; and
(*c*) act in accordance with–

(i) this Act, including the regulations, and any direction given under this Act; and
(ii) any restriction imposed or requirement made by an inspector under this Act.

(2) In particular, and without limiting the generality of Subsection (1), a tenement holder must–

(*a*) control the flow and prevent the escape in the licence area of petroleum or water, except in accordance with a permit or licence issued under a law regulating the discharge or release of petroleum, petroleum products or water; and
(*b*) prevent the escape in the licence area of any mixture of water or drilling fluid and petroleum or any other matter; and
(*c*) prevent damage to petroleum-bearing strata in an area in respect of which the tenement is not in force; and
(*d*) keep separate–

(i) each petroleum pool discovered in the licence area; and
(ii) such of the sources of water (if any) discovered in that area,

as the Minister, by instrument served on the licensee, directs; and

(*e*) prevent water or any other matter entering any petroleum pool through wells in the licence area except when required by, and in accordance with, good oilfield practice; and
(*f*) prevent the pollution of any water-well, spring, stream, river, lake, reservoir, estuary, harbour or area of sea by the escape of petroleum, salt water, drilling fluid, chemical additive or any other waste product or effluent; and
(*g*) furnish to the Director, prior to the drilling of any well, a detailed report on the technique to be employed, the material to be used and the safety measures to be employed, in the drilling of the well.

(3) This section shall not prevent a tenement holder from flaring natural gas–

(*a*) where the written consent of the Director has been obtained; or
(*b*) where, in an emergency, flaring is required–

(i) to safeguard the health and safety of persons in the licence area; or
(ii) to prevent damage to the property of any person in the licence area.

125. WORK PRACTICES FOR PIPELINE LICENSEE.

(1) A pipeline licensee must operate the pipeline in a proper and workmanlike manner and must secure the safety, health and welfare of persons engaged in operations in connection with the pipeline.
(2) In particular and without limiting the generality of Subsection (1), a pipeline licensee must prevent the escape of petroleum or petroleum products or water from the pipeline, except in accordance with a permit or licence issued under a law regulating the discharge or release of petroleum, petroleum products or water.

126. WORK PRACTICES FOR PETROLEUM PROCESSING FACILITY LICENSEE.

(1) A petroleum processing facility licensee shall operate the petroleum processing facility in a proper and workmanlike manner and shall secure the safety, health and welfare of persons engaged in operations in connection with the petroleum processing facility.
(2) In particular and without limiting the generality of Subsection (1), a petroleum processing facility licensee shall prevent the escape of petroleum or petroleum products or water from the petroleum processing facility, except in accordance with a permit or licence issued under a law regulating the discharge or release of petroleum, petroleum products or water.
(3) The Head of State, acting on advice, may make regulations prescribing the conduct of petroleum processing facility operations, including the qualifications of persons in charge of those operations.

127. WORK PRACTICES FOR HOLDERS OF INSTRUMENTS OF CONSENT.

A person who is the holder of an instrument of consent under Section 150 must–

(*a*) carry out all petroleum exploration operations in the area in respect of which the instrument of consent is in force in a proper and workmanlike manner and in accordance with good oilfield practice; and
(*b*) secure the safety, health and welfare of persons engaged in those operations in or about that area.

128. PENALTY FOR BREACH OF SECTION 124, 125, 126 OR 127.

(1) A licensee or holder of an instrument of consent who contravenes or fails to comply with a requirement of Section 124, 125, 126 or 127, as the case may be, is guilty of an offence.
Penalty: A fine not exceeding K5,000.00.
(2) It is a defence to a charge for an offence under this section, if the person charged proves that he took all reasonable steps to comply with the requirements of the relevant section applicable to him.

129. LOCAL PURCHASE OBLIGATION.

(1) Subject to the provisions of this section, a licensee shall, in its operations in Papua New Guinea and in the construction and development of a project–

(*a*) use and purchase goods and services supplied, produced or manufactured in Papua New Guinea whenever the same can be obtained at equivalent terms, including prices, conditions and delivery or performance dates and are in all respects of a quality comparable with those available from outside Papua New Guinea; and
(*b*) encourage and assist citizens of Papua New Guinea who are desirous of establishing businesses providing goods and services for the operations or the project and for any town constructed primarily for the purposes of the project and the residents thereof; and
(*c*) make maximum use of Papua New Guinea contractors and subcontractors where services of a standard comparable with those which the licensee would obtain but for the operation of this section are available from such Papua New Guinea contractors or subcontractors at equivalent prices, and on equivalent terms, conditions and delivery or performance dates.

(2) A licensee which, for the purpose of its operations in Papua New Guinea or the construction and development of its project, requires imported vehicles, machinery, plant or equipment, and does not purchase such items direct from the manufacturer, shall effect the purchase of such items through traders based in Papua New Guinea or the Papua New Guinea operations of traders based elsewhere but having operations in Papua New Guinea.
(3) Subsection (2) does not apply to a licensee in respect of a particular purchase if–

(*a*) such items are not available through such traders or trading operations at an equivalent price, and on equivalent terms, conditions and delivery dates; or
(*b*) compliance would adversely affect the financing of the licensee's operations or the development of the licensee's project.

(4) Nothing contained in this section obliges a licensee to grant or lend money to any person or any local enterprise.
(5) Where a licensee seeks to grant to persons who are landowners in the area of the licensee's operations a contract for the supply of labour or services and a dispute which delays the grant of such a contract arises amongst persons claiming to be such landowners, the licensee may refer the dispute to the Director who may determine the dispute.

130. MEASUREMENT AND METERING.

(1) At such intervals as the Director determines, licensees shall measure and report to the Director the following, as applicable:–

(*a*) the continuous volume of petroleum produced (including separate recording of associated natural gas which is either flared or injected) where–

(i) the volume of oil shall be calculated on the basis of acceptable meter readings or tank measurements with such accuracy as is required by the Director; and
(ii) the volume of natural gas shall be measured by a meter approved for the purposes of Section 161; and
(iii) unless otherwise authorized by the Director, with all volumes produced, sold, injected or flared adjusted to a standard temperature and pressure base as determined by the Director;

(*b*) the continuous volume of petroleum or petroleum products transported by pipeline as measured at the meters for sale or transfer of custody;
(*c*) the continuous volume of the output of petroleum or petroleum products at a petroleum processing facility in units and in a manner acceptable to the Director,

in each case in accordance with internationally accepted measurement standards.
(2) Except as prescribed by regulation, a person shall not install in any facility or use any measuring device to measure the volume of petroleum or petroleum products unless such measuring device is approved by the Minister.

131. MAINTENANCE, ETC., OF PROPERTY.

(1) A tenement holder shall–

(*a*) maintain in good condition and keep in good repair all structures, equipment and other property in the licence area which are used by him in connection with the operations in which he is engaged; and
(*b*) remove from the licence area all structures, equipment and other property owned by him which is not being, or intended to be, so used.

(2) A pipeline licensee or petroleum processing facility licensee shall–

(*a*) maintain in good condition and repair all structures, equipment and other property in the area in which the pipeline or petroleum processing facility is constructed and which are used by him in connection with the operations in which he is engaged; and
(*b*) subject to Section 139, remove from the area all structures, equipment and other property owned by him which is not being, or intended to be, so used.

132. DRILLING NEAR BOUNDARIES.

(1) A tenement holder shall not make a well any part of which is less than 300 m from a boundary of a licence area, except with the written consent of the Director and in accordance with such conditions (if any) as are specified in the instrument of consent.

(2) Where a tenement holder fails to comply with Subsection (1), the Director may, by instrument served on the tenement holder, direct him–

(*a*) to plug the well; or
(*b*) to close off the well; or
(*c*) to comply with the directions relating to the making or maintenance of the well specified in the instrument,

within the period specified in the instrument and the tenement holder shall comply with the direction within that period.

133. DIRECTIONS.

(1) The Minister, the Director or an inspector may, by instrument served on a person, give to that person such directions as are prescribed.
(2) A direction under Subsection (1) has effect and shall be complied with notwithstanding anything in the regulations and, to the extent to which the regulations are inconsistent with the directions, the person to whom the direction is given is not obliged to comply with the regulations.
(3) A person who refuses or fails to comply with a direction given under Subsection (1) is guilty of an offence.
Penalty: A fine not exceeding K2,000.00.

134. COMPLIANCE WITH DIRECTIONS.

(1) Where a person fails to comply with a direction given to him under this Act or under the regulations, the Minister may do all or any of the things required by the directions to be done.
(2) Any costs or expenses incurred by the Minister under Subsection (1) in relation to a direction are a debt due by the person to whom the direction was given to the State.
(3) It is a defence to a charge of failing to comply with a direction given under this Act or under the regulations if the person charged proves that he took all reasonable steps to comply with the direction.

135. EXEMPTIONS, VARIATIONS, ETC.

(1) Where–

(*a*) under this Part, a licence is deemed to continue in force; or
(*b*) a licence is varied under Section 24 or 41 or 58 or 81 or 82 or 92 or 93; or
(*c*) a licensee enters into an agreement under Section 66 or a direction is given to the licensee under that section; or
(*d*) a tenement is partly cancelled, partly determined or surrendered as to one or more, but not all of the blocks in respect of which it is in force; or
(*e*) the term of a petroleum prospecting licence is extended under Section 29 or 30; or
(*f*) the term of a petroleum retention licence is extended under Section 45; or
(*g*) a licensee, by instrument served on the Director, applies–

(i) for a variation or suspension of the licence; or
(ii) for exemption from compliance with any of the conditions specified in the licence; or

(*h*) under this Act or the regulations the Minister gives a direction or consent to a licensee; or
(*i*) a direction is given to the pipeline licensee under Section 83,

the Minister may, at any time, by instrument served on the licensee–

(*j*) vary or suspend; or
(*k*) exempt the licensee from compliance with,

any of the conditions specified in the licence, on such conditions (if any) as the Minister determines and specifies in the instrument.
(2) Subsection (1) does not authorize the making of an instrument to the extent–

(*a*) that it would affect the term of a licence; or
(*b*) that it would be inconsistent with the terms of a petroleum agreement or gas agreement applying to the licence in question; or
(*c*) in the case of an instrument relating to an application referred to in Subsection (1)(f)–that it would not be in accordance with the application, or the application as varied by agreement, before the making of the instrument.

136. PREVENTION FROM CARRYING ON PROSPECTING OPERATIONS.

(1) A petroleum prospecting licensee or petroleum retention licensee who has been, or is being, prevented from carrying on in the licence area any operations authorized by the licence, may make an application to the Minister for a direction under this section.
(2) An application under Subsection (1)–

(*a*) shall be made not more than one month after the date of commencement of the circumstances causing the prevention, or such longer period as the Minister may allow, but in any event before the licence concerned ceases to have effect; and
(*b*) shall specify the operations that the licensee has been or is being prevented from carrying on; and
(*c*) shall set out the circumstances by reason of which the licensee has been or is being prevented from carrying on those operations; and
(*d*) may set out any other matters that the licensee wishes the Minister to consider.

(3) Where a licensee has made an application under Subsection (1), the Minister shall, after considering a report from the Board, by instrument served on the licensee–

(*a*) if he is satisfied that the licensee has been by reason of circumstances beyond the control of the licensee, prevented from carrying on in the licence area, during any period during which the licence was in force, any of the operations specified in

the application–direct that the term of the licence be extended for the period specified in the instrument being a period not greater than the period for which the licensee was prevented from carrying on operations, subject to such conditions (if any) as the Minister determines and specifies in the instrument; or
(*b*) in any other case–refuse the application.

(4) Where the Minister makes a direction under Subsection (3)(a), the licence continues in force for the period directed.
(5) Where a licensee has made an application under Subsection (1) and an instrument under Subsection (3) has not been served on the licensee before the licence would, but for this subsection, cease to have effect–

(*a*) any application under Section 27, 30 or 44 for the extension of the licence lapses; and
(*b*) the licensee may, notwithstanding anything contained in that section, make an application or further application under that section for the extension of the licence–

(i) if the Minister, by instrument under Subsection (3) directs that the term of the licence be extended for a specified period–within a period of one month after the expiration of the specified period; or
(ii) if the Minister, by instrument under Subsection (3), refuses the application under Subsection (1)–within a period of one month after the day on which the instrument is served on the licensee; and

(*c*) the licence continues in force by reason of this subsection until the expiration of that period of one month, or until an application is made under Section 27, 30 or 44 for the extension of the licence, whichever first occurs.

137. SURRENDER OF LICENCES.

(1) In this section, **"the area to which the surrender relates"** means–

(*a*) in relation to a surrender of a tenement–the area constituted by the blocks in relation to which the tenement is proposed to be surrendered; and
(*b*) in relation to a surrender of a pipeline licence or petroleum processing facility licence–the area in which the pipeline or petroleum processing facility or part thereof, in relation to which the licence is proposed to be surrendered, is constructed.

(2) A licensee may, at any time, by written notice served on the Director, apply to the Minister for consent to surrender the licence–

(*a*) in the case of a tenement–as to all or any of the blocks in respect of which it is in force; and (*b*) in the case of a pipeline licence or petroleum processing facility licence–as to the whole or part of the pipeline or petroleum processing facility in respect of which it is in force.

(2A)[82] [83]A licensee may state in its application under Subsection (2) that the surrender is, if consented to by the Minister, to take effect on a date or upon the occurrence of a particular event specified in the application in which case the surrender shall, if so consented to and if implemented by the applicant in accordance with Subsection (6), take effect on that date or upon the occurrence of that event, as the case maybe.
(3) Subject to Subsection (5), the Minister shall not give his consent to a surrender of a licence under Subsection (2) unless the licensee–

(*a*) has paid all fees and amounts payable by him under this Act or has made arrangements that are satisfactory to the Minister for the payment of those fees and amounts; and
(*b*) has, subject to Subsection (4), complied with the conditions specified in the licence and with the provisions of this Act; and
(*c*) has, to the satisfaction of the Minister, plugged or closed off all wells made in that area by any person engaged or concerned in the operations authorized by the licence or made arrangements with respect to the termination of operations of the pipeline or petroleum processing facility to which the surrender relates; and
(*d*) has to the satisfaction of the Minister–

(i) removed or caused to be removed from the area to which the surrender relates all property brought into that area by any person and any wastes deposited in that area by the licensee or any person on his behalf; or
(ii) made arrangements with respect to that property or waste; and

(*e*) has made provision, to the satisfaction of the Minister, for the reclamation of the site of the pipeline or petroleum processing facility in the area to which the surrender relates and the conservation and protection of the natural resources in that area.

(4) For the purpose of Subsection (3)(b), the holder of a petroleum prospecting licence or a petroleum retention licence who has otherwise complied with the conditions referred to in Section 31(2) or 46, as the case may be, shall not be taken to have failed to comply with the conditions specified in the licence for the reason only that he has failed to complete any work or expend any amount referred to, or specified, in the licence so far as it relates to any period subsequent to the date on which an application under this section, to which the Minister subsequently consents, is made.
(5) Where a licensee has not complied with the conditions specified in the licence, or with the provisions of this Act, the Minister may give his consent to a surrender of the licence under Subsection (2) if he is satisfied that, although the licensee has not so complied, special circumstances exist that justify the giving of consent to the surrender.
(6) Where the Minister consents to an application under Subsection (2), the applicant may, by instrument served on the Director, surrender the licence.
(7) The surrender of a licence under this section shall not release the licensee from any liability in respect of–

(*a*) the licence up to the date of surrender; or
(*b*) any act or omission under the licence up to the date of surrender giving rise to cause of action; or
(*c*) compliance with other obligations under the laws of Papua New Guinea.

(8) A licensee who permanently ceases operations under his licence shall–

(*a*) do all of the things specified in Subsection (3), unless the Minister, after considering a report of the Board, approves otherwise; and
(*b*) apply to the Minister under Subsection (2) to surrender the licence.

138. SUSPENSION AND CANCELLATION OF LICENCES.

(1) Where a licensee has not–

(*a*) in the opinion of the Minister, complied with a condition specified in the licence; or
(*b*) in the opinion of the Minister, complied with a direction given to him under this Act by the Minister, the Director or an inspector; or
(*c*) complied with a provision of this Act; or
(*d*) paid any amount payable by him under this Act within a period of three months after the date on which the amount became payable,

the Minister may, by instrument served on the licensee–

(*e*) in the case of a tenement–suspend for such period as the Minister thinks fit or cancel the licence as to all or any of the blocks in respect of which it is in force; or
(*f*) in the case of a pipeline licence or petroleum processing facility licence–suspend for such period as the Minister thinks fit or cancel the licence as to the whole or a part of the pipeline or petroleum processing facility in respect of which it is in force.

(2) The Minister shall not, under Subsection (1), suspend or cancel a licence as to all or any of the blocks, or as to the whole or part of the pipeline or petroleum processing facility, unless–

(*a*) he has, by instrument served on the licensee, given not less than one month's notice of his intention to suspend or cancel the licence, specifying the grounds upon which the suspension or cancellation is based; and
(*b*) he has caused a copy of the instrument to be served on such other persons (if any) as he thinks fit; and
(*c*) he has, in the instrument, specified a date, being not less than 14 days prior to the end of the period specified in the instrument referred to in Paragraph (a), on or before which written submissions may be served on the Minister in connection

with the proposed suspension or cancellation; and
(*d*) after taking into account–

(i) any action taken by the licensee to remove that ground or to prevent the recurrence of similar grounds; and
(ii) any matters so submitted to him on or before the specified date; and
(iii) a report on those matters from the Board,

he considers that special circumstances exist that justify a decision to suspend or cancel the licence.
(3) The suspension or cancellation of a licence by the Minister pursuant to this section shall not release the licensee from any liability in respect of the licence incurred before the date of cancellation or before or during the period of suspension.

139. REMOVAL OF PROPERTY, ETC., BY LICENSEE, ETC.

(1) Prior to abandonment of a well a tenement holder shall–

(*a*) furnish the Director with notice of his intention to abandon the well together with a request for the Director to approve a program for abandonment which includes removal of equipment, plugging the well bore, and reclaiming the well site; and
(*b*) complete logging and testing and submission of such information and relevant evaluations which have not previously been submitted to the Director with the tenement holder's notice under Paragraph (a); and
(*c*) conduct abandonment operations according to the manner prescribed by regulations.

(2) Where any licence has been wholly determined, partly determined, wholly cancelled or partly cancelled or has expired, the Minister may by instrument served on the person who was, or is, the licensee, direct that person to–

(*a*) make arrangements, to the satisfaction of the Minister, with respect to the complete or partial abandonment of any pipeline or petroleum processing facility or other plant and equipment which is or was the subject of the licence; and
(*b*) remove or cause to be removed from the area in respect of which the tenement has been determined or cancelled or has expired or the area in which the pipeline or petroleum processing facility or part thereof, in relation to which the licence is determined or cancelled or has expired, is constructed, all property brought into that area by any person engaged or concerned in the operations authorized by the licence, or to make arrangements that are satisfactory to the Minister with respect to that property; and
(*c*) plug or close off, to the satisfaction of the Minister, all wells made in that area by any person engaged or concerned in those operations; and
(*d*) make provision, to the satisfaction of the Minister, for the conservation and protection of the natural resources in that area.

(3) Notwithstanding Subsection (2), if agreed by the Minister by instrument or as a condition of a licence or by the State in a written agreement, buried pipelines, or pipes or facilities referred to in Paragraphs (a) to (d) inclusive of the definition of "pipeline", may be abandoned in place, subject to the terms of the licence condition or instrument or written agreement.
(4) The holder of any licence shall–

(*a*) at the time of surrender of the licence or cancellation by the Minister; and
(*b*) five years prior to the expiration of the term of the licence or in the case of a petroleum processing facility licence five years prior to the expected date of abandonment of the petroleum processing facility,

demonstrate to the satisfaction of the Minister that it is able to meet has or will have sufficient financial resources to meet its obligations under this section upon surrender, cancellation or expiry of the licence.
(5) The licensee shall demonstrate such financial resources–

(*a*) by establishing a reserve account for abandonment costs in accordance with the report of a certified independent auditor; or
(*b*) by providing, in a form acceptable to the Minister, a financial undertaking (or in the case of a licensee which is a joint venture, several undertakings) in the form of a bond, letter of credit or guarantee or other instrument acceptable to the Minister; or
(*c*) by granting the Minister a charge or similar security over its assets and income.

(6) A person to whom a direction under Subsection (2) is given who refuses, or fails, to comply with the direction within the period specified in the instrument by which the direction was given is guilty of an offence.
Penalty: A fine not exceeding K25,000.00.

140. REMOVAL AND SALE OF PROPERTY.

(1) Where a direction under Section 139 has not been complied with, the Minister may–

(*a*) do or cause to be done all or any of the things required by the direction to be done; and
(*b*) remove or cause to be removed, in such manner as he thinks fit, all or any of the property from the relinquished area concerned; and
(*c*) dispose of, in such manner as he thinks fit, all or any of the property referred to in Paragraph (b); and
(*d*) if he has served a copy of the instrument by which the direction was given on a person who he believed to be an owner of the property or part of the property–sell or cause to be sold by public auction or otherwise as he thinks fit, all or any of the property referred to in Paragraph (b) that belongs, or that he believes to belong, to that person.

(2) The Minister may deduct from the proceeds of a sale of property under Subsection (1) that belongs, or that he believes to belong, to a particular person–

(*a*) all or any part of any costs and expenses incurred by him under that subsection in relation to that property; and
(*b*) all or any part of any costs and expenses incurred by him in relation to the doing of anything required by a direction under Section 139 to be done by the person; and
(*c*) all or any part of any fees or amounts due and payable under this Act by the person.

(3) The costs and expenses incurred by the Minister under Subsection (1)–

(*a*) if incurred in relation to the removal, disposal or sale of property–are a debt due by the owner of the property to the State; or
(*b*) if incurred in relation to the doing of anything required by a direction under Section 139 to be done by a person who is or was a licensee–are a debt due by that person to the State,

and to the extent to which they are not recovered under Subsection (2) are recoverable by the State as a debt.
(4) Subject to Subsection (3), no action lies in respect of the removal, disposal or sale of property under this section.

141. PENALTY FOR LATE PAYMENTS.

(1) Where the liability of a person under this Act to pay an amount is not discharged on or before the time when the amount is payable, there is payable by that person an additional amount calculated at the rate of % per day on so much of that amount as from time to time remains unpaid, to be computed from the time that the amount became payable until it is paid.
(2) The Minister may, in a particular case, for reasons that in his opinion are sufficient, remit the whole or part of an amount payable under this section.

142. SECURITIES.

(1)[84] [85]A security referred to in Division 2, 4, 7, 9 or 10–

(*a*) shall be in such amount not exceeding K1,000,000.00 as the Minister thinks reasonable; and
(*b*) shall be by way of a bond to pay the amount, executed by the licensee, in an approved form, and be supported by–

(i) a cash deposit from the licensee; or
(ii) a guarantee of a bank acceptable to the Minister and in an approved form; or
(ii) some other approved form of security,

or any combination of the alternatives specified in sub-paragraph (i), (ii) or (iii).
(2) A bond, guarantee or other security document given in an approved form, although it is not sealed, shall bind the person subscribing to it as if it were sealed.
(3) Whenever a security under this Act is the subject of legal proceedings, the production of the security, without further proof, entitles the Minister to judgement against the person appearing to have executed the security, for the amount of his stated liability or for such lesser amount as is claimed, unless that person proves–

(*a*) compliance with the conditions of the security; or
(*b*) that the security was not executed by him; or
(*c*) release or satisfaction.

(4) For the purposes of Subsection (3)(a), the holder of a petroleum prospecting licence who has complied with a condition referred to in Section 31(2) shall not be taken to have failed to comply with the conditions of the security for the reason only that he has failed to complete any work referred to, or expend any amount specified, in the licence so far as it relates to any period subsequent to the date on which an application under Section 137(2), to which the Minister subsequently consents, is made.
(5) If it appears to the court that a condition of a security under this Act has not been complied with, the security shall not be deemed to have been discharged or invalidated, and the subscriber shall not be deemed to have been released or discharged from liability by reason of–

(*a*) any extension of time or other concession; or
(*b*) any consent to, or acquiescence in, a previous non-compliance with a condition; or
(*c*) any failure to bring legal proceedings against the subscriber on the occurrence of a previous non-compliance with the condition.

(6) If there is more than one subscriber to the security, each is bound, unless the security otherwise provides, jointly and severally and for the full amount.

143. FURTHER INFORMATION TO BE FURNISHED, ETC.

(1) Where the Minister, the Director or an inspector has reason to believe that a person is capable of giving information or producing documents relating to petroleum exploration operations, or operations for the recovery of petroleum, he may, by instrument served on that person, require that person–

(*a*) to furnish that information to him in writing within the period and in the manner specified in the instrument; or
(*b*) to attend before him or a person specified in the instrument, at such time and place as is so specified, and there to answer questions relating to those operations and to produce such documents relating to those operations as are specified in the instrument.

(2) A person is not excused from furnishing information, answering a question or producing a document when required to do so under this section, on the grounds that the information so furnished, the answer to the question or the production of the document might tend to incriminate him or make him liable to a penalty, but the information so furnished or his answer to the question is not admissible in evidence against him in proceedings other than proceedings for an offence against Section 144.

144. FAILING TO FURNISH INFORMATION, ETC.

A person who–

(*a*) refuses or fails to comply with a requirement in an instrument under Section 143 to the extent to which he is capable of

complying with it; or
(*b*) in purported compliance with a requirement referred to in Paragraph (a)–knowingly furnishes information that is false or misleading in a material particular; or
(*c*) when attending before the Minister, the Director or an inspector under a requirement referred to in Paragraph (a)–knowingly makes a statement or produces a document that is false or misleading in a material particular,

is guilty of an offence.
Penalty: A fine not exceeding K5,000.00.

145. DRILLING FOR AND DISCOVERY OF WATER.

A person shall not, except in accordance with such conditions as are determined by the Minister, or in accordance with the provisions of the *Water Resources Act 1982*, drill for water in any licence area.

146. SURVEY OF WELLS, ETC.

(1) The Minister or the Director may, at any time, by instrument served on a tenement holder, direct the tenement holder–

(*a*) to carry out a survey of the position of the well, structure or equipment specified in the instrument; and
(*b*) to furnish to the Minister or Director, as the case may be, a written report of the survey.

(2) Where the Minister or the Director is not satisfied with a report of a survey furnished to him under Subsection (1) by a tenement holder, he may, by instrument served on the tenement holder, direct the tenement holder to furnish further written information in connection with the survey.
(3) A person to whom a direction is given under Subsection (1) or (2) who fails to comply with the direction is guilty of an offence.
Penalty: A fine not exceeding K5,000.00.

147. RECORDS, ETC., TO BE KEPT.

The Minister or the Director may, by instrument served on a person carrying on operations under a licence or an instrument of consent under Section 150, direct that person–

(*a*) to keep such accounts, records and other documents in connection with those operations as are specified in the instrument; and
(*b*) to collect and retain such cores, cuttings and samples in connection with those operations as are specified in the instrument; and
(*c*) to furnish to the Minister in the manner specified in the instrument such reports, returns, other documents, cores, cuttings and samples in connection with those operations,

as are specified in the instrument.

148. REPORTING BY LICENSEES.

(1) The Minister or the Director may give directions to a licensee as to reports to be provided to the Director by the licensee on the activities of the licensee in respect of the licence, and as to the frequency of and information to be contained in such reports, and such other matters by way of reports in respect of the licence, including the production, sale, processing or transportation of petroleum or petroleum products, as the Minister or Director sees fit.
(2) A licensee to whom a direction is given under Subsection (1) shall provide such reports containing such information and at such frequency as is specified in the direction, and shall otherwise comply with the direction given.
(3) A person to whom a direction is given under Subsection (2) who fails or refuses to comply with the direction is guilty of an offence.
Penalty: A fine not exceeding K5,000.00.

149. CONFIDENTIALITY, ETC., OF INFORMATION.

(1) All information supplied to the Minister, the Director or an inspector under this Act shall, if the Minister so directs, be verified by statutory declaration in a prescribed form.
(2) The following information furnished to the Board, the Minister, the Director or an inspector under this or the former Acts, or to any other representative of the State, shall be treated as confidential:–

> (*a*) all geological and geophysical information (including information concerning cores or cuttings from, or samples of, the land surface, sea bed or subsoil in a block);
> (*b*) all intellectual property including, without limitation, industrial processes;
> (*c*) all information related to the business of the licensee to which the information relates including sales forecasts, market projections or marketing information;
> (*d*) all applications for licences, commercial and economic evaluations, marketing information, and other information which the person furnishing the information may designate as being commercially sensitive,

except where the licensee or person furnishing the information has given his consent for disclosure or the information is otherwise available in the public domain or is disclosed in accordance with Subsection (3).
(3) Information referred to in Subsection (2)(a) may be disclosed, and cores, cuttings or samples made available–

> (*a*) to an officer or other representative of the State expressly authorized by the Minister or Director to receive that information or to examine those cores, cuttings or samples; and
> (*b*) in respect of a block or part of a block that was previously the subject of a licence under this Act or a licence under the former Act and is not the subject of a current licence under this Act–to the public; and
> (*c*) in respect of a block the subject of a current petroleum prospecting licence or petroleum retention licence that is not, or is not included in, a location–to the public not earlier than two years after that information was, or those cores, cuttings or samples were, required to be supplied to the Minister, the

Director, or an inspector, as the case may be; and
(*d*) in respect of a block the subject of a current petroleum development licence–to the public not earlier than one year after that information was, or those cores, cuttings or samples were, required to be supplied to the Minister, the Director, or an inspector, as the case may be.

(4) Information referred to in Subsection (2)(a) to (d) inclusive may be disclosed to an officer or other representative of the State expressly authorized by the Minister or Director to receive that information.
(5) The Minister may at any time make use of any information or matter supplied by a licensee for the purpose of preparing and publishing aggregate returns and general reports with respect to operations under this Act.
(6) A person who acts in the execution of any duty under this Act shall not, except in the performance of that duty, divulge any information supplied to the Minister or to the Director in pursuance of this Act.
(7) A person who has been an officer or who has performed a duty under this Act shall not communicate any information acquired by him in the performance of that duty to any person other than a person authorized by law or by the Minister or the Director to receive that information.

150. SCIENTIFIC INVESTIGATIONS: INSTRUMENTS OF CONSENT.

(1) The Minister may, by instrument, consent to the carrying on by any person of petroleum exploration operations in the course of a scientific investigation.
(2) An instrument of consent shall be subject to such conditions (if any) as are specified in the instrument.
(3) An instrument of consent under this section authorizes the person to whom it is issued to carry out the petroleum exploration operation specified in the instrument–

(*a*) in the area; and
(*b*) subject to the conditions (if any),

specified in the instrument, in the course of scientific investigation.

151. INSPECTORS.

(1) The Minister may, by notice in the National Gazette, appoint–

(*a*) a person to be the Chief Inspector; and
(*b*) such other persons to be inspectors as he thinks necessary,

for the purposes of this Act.
(2) The Minister shall issue to the Chief Inspector and to each inspector a certificate stating that he is an inspector.
(3) Where the appointment of a person under this section expires or is revoked, that person shall immediately surrender to the Minister the certificate issued to him under this section.

152. POWERS OF INSPECTORS.

(1) For the purposes of this Act, an inspector, at all reasonable times may–

(*a*) enter any area, structure, vehicle, vessel, aircraft or building that, in his opinion, has been, is being or is to be, used in connection with–

(i) petroleum exploration operations; or
(ii) operations for the recovery of petroleum; or
(iii) operations connected with the construction or operation of a pipeline or a petroleum processing facility; and

(*b*) inspect and test any machinery or equipment that, in his opinion, has been, is being or is to be, used in connection with any of the operations referred to in Paragraph (a); and
(*c*) take or remove for the purpose of analysis or testing, or for use in evidence in connection with an offence against this Act, samples of petroleum, water or other substances from a well or samples of petroleum or petroleum products or other substances from a pipeline or a petroleum processing facility; and
(*d*) inspect, take extracts from, and make copies of, any document relating to any of the operations referred to in Paragraph (a); and
(*e*) with respect to the health and safety of persons employed by a licensee in or in connection with any of the operations referred to in Paragraph (a)–by instrument, issue directions to and impose restrictions on the licensee, or any person so employed; and
(*f*) order, by instrument–

(i) the cessation of operations on or in, and the withdrawal of all persons from, any structure or building that is being used in connection with any of the operations referred to in Paragraph (a); or
(ii) the discontinuance of the use of any machinery or equipment,

which he considers unsafe after taking into account the following matters:–

(iii) good oilfield practice or generally accepted petroleum processing operations practice, as the case may be;
(iv) consultation with the person referred to in Subsection (2);
(v) consultation with the Chief Inspector or the Director,

unless and until such action as is necessary for safety and specified in the instrument is taken and completed; and

(*g*) make such examinations and inquiries as are necessary to ensure that the provisions of this Act, and any directions issued, restrictions imposed or orders made under this Act, are being complied with; and (*h*) obtain and record statements from witnesses, and appear at or conduct inquiries held regarding accidents occurring in the course of any of the operations referred to in Paragraph (a), and appear at inquests, and call and examine witnesses, and cross-examine witnesses, and conduct or assist in conducting a prosecution for any offence against this Act.

(2) Before exercising any of his powers under Subsection (1), if there is any person present who is or appears to be in charge of the area, structure, vehicle, vessel, aircraft, building, machinery, equipment or matter or thing in respect of which the power is about to be exercised, the inspector shall produce his certificate referred to in Section 151(2) to that person and to any person to whom he is about to give an order or a direction.

(3) Any person who is aggrieved by a decision, direction or order of an inspector made under this section may appeal in writing to the Chief Inspector who shall, as soon as practicable, hear and dispose of the appeal, but the bringing of the appeal does not affect the operation of the decision, direction or order appealed from pending disposition of the appeal.

(4) On appeal under Subsection (3), the Chief Inspector may–

(*a*) rescind or affirm the decision, direction or order appealed from; or
(*b*) substitute a new decision, direction or order.

(5) In exercising his powers under Subsection (1), an inspector may be accompanied by any person who the inspector believes has special or expert knowledge of any matter being inspected, tested or examined.

(6) A person who is an occupier or person in charge of any building, structure or place, or the person in charge of any vehicle, vessel, aircraft, machinery or equipment referred to in Subsection (1), must provide an inspector with all reasonable facilities and assistance for the effective exercise of the inspector's powers under this section.

Penalty: A fine not exceeding K5,000.00.

(7) A person who–

(*a*) without reasonable excuse, obstructs, molests or hinders an inspector in the exercise of his powers under this section; or
(*b*) knowingly makes a statement or produces a document that is false or misleading in a material particular to an inspector engaged in carrying out his duties and functions under this Act,

is guilty of an offence.

Penalty: A fine not exceeding K5,000.00.

153. GENERAL PENALTY.

A person who contravenes or fails to comply with–

(*a*) a provision of this Act applicable to him and for which no other penalty is provided; or
(*b*) a requirement, direction, order or instruction lawfully given or made under this Act, other than a direction under Section 133,

is guilty of an offence.

Penalty: A fine not exceeding K1,000.00.

154. CONTINUING OFFENCES.

(1) Where an offence is committed by a person by reason of his failure to comply, within the period specified in a direction given to him under this Act, with the requirements specified in the direction, the offence, for the purposes of Subsection (3), shall be deemed to continue so long as any requirement specified in the direction remains undone, notwithstanding that the period has elapsed.
(2) Where an offence is committed by a person by reason of his failure to comply with a requirement made by this Act, the offence, for the purposes of Subsection (3), shall be deemed to continue so long as that failure continues, notwithstanding that any period within which the requirement was to be complied with has elapsed.
(3) Where, under Subsection (1) or (2), an offence is deemed to continue, the person who committed the offence commits an additional offence against this Act on each day during which the offence is deemed to continue and is liable, on conviction for such an additional offence, to a fine not exceeding K5,000.00.

155. ORDERS FOR FORFEITURE IN RESPECT OF CERTAIN OFFENCES.

(1) Where a person is convicted of an offence against this Act a court may, in addition to imposing a fine, make–

(*a*) an order for the forfeiture of any vehicle, aircraft, vessel or equipment used in the commission of the offence; and
(*b*) an order–

(i) for the forfeiture of petroleum recovered, or conveyed through a pipeline, as the case may be, in the course of the commission of the offence; or
(ii) for the payment by that person to the State of an amount equal to the proceeds of the sale of petroleum so recovered or conveyed; or
(iii) for the payment by that person to the State of the value at the wellhead, assessed by the court in respect of the quantity so assessed, of petroleum so recovered or conveyed or for the payment of such a part of that amount as the court, having regard to all the circumstances, thinks fit.

(2) Where the court is satisfied that an order made under Subsection (1)(b)(i) cannot for any reason be enforced, the court may, on the application of the person by whom the proceedings were brought, set aside the order and make an order referred to in Subsection (1)(b)(ii) or (iii).
(3) The court may, before making an order under this section require notice to be given to, and hear, such persons as the court thinks fit.

156. SERVICE.

(1) A document required or permitted by this Act to be served on a person, other than the Minister or the Director, shall be deemed to be duly served if sent by registered post addressed to the usual postal address last known to the Director of that person.
(2) A document required or permitted by this Act to be served on the Minister or the Director may be served by registered post addressed to the Director.

(3) Where a document to be served is served by post in accordance with this section, service shall be deemed to have been effected at the time at which the letter would have been delivered in the ordinary course of post.

156A. PRE-SUBMISSION OF INFORMATION.

[86]In this Act, where a section provides for information, particulars, proposals, studies, investigations, reports, accounts, documents or other like material to be furnished or provided to an inspector, the Director or the Minister for consideration in connection with that section, such information, particulars, proposals, studies, investigations, reports, accounts, documents or other like material may be submitted in a complete draft form for discussion purposes without prejudice to the rights of the submitting party or the State arising under the relevant section, to assist in the preparation and submission of a complete formal submission of that information, particulars, proposals, studies, investigations, reports, accounts, documents or other like material in due course and in accordance with the Act.

DIVISION 14. FEES AND ROYALTIES.

157. FEES.

(1) An applicant shall pay a fee of–

(*a*) K10,000.00 at the time of making application for a petroleum prospecting licence or an extension thereof; and
(*b*) K10,000.00 at the time of making application for a petroleum retention licence or an extension thereof; and
(*c*) K50,000.00 at the time of making application for a petroleum development licence or an extension thereof; and
(*d*) K50,000.00 at the time of making application for a pipeline licence or an extension thereof; and
(*e*) K50,000.00 at the time of making application for a petroleum processing facility licence.

(2) A licensee shall pay an annual fee on the anniversary of the licence at the rate of–

(*a*) in the case of a petroleum prospecting licence granted otherwise than by way of extension, K500.00 for each block in the licence area; and
(*b*) in the case of a petroleum prospecting licence granted by way of extension–for each block in the licence area–

(i) K1,000.00 in the first year of the term of extension; and
(ii) K1,500.00 in the second year of the term of the extension; and
(iii) K2,000.00 in the third year of the term of the extension; and
(iv) K3,000.00 in the fourth year of the term of the extension; and
(v) K4,000.00 in the fifth year of the term of the extension; and

(*c*) K30,000.00 in the case of a petroleum retention licence; and
(*d*) K100,000.00 in the case of a petroleum development licence; and
(*e*) in the case of a pipeline licence, the greater of–

(i) K10,000; and
(ii) the lesser of–

(A) K100,000; and
(B) K1,000 multiplied by the number of entire kilometres in the length of the pipeline; and

(*f*) K100,000.00 in the case of a petroleum processing facility licence.

(3) Subject to this Act, an annual fee referred to in Subsection (2) is payable–

(*a*) in the case of the first year of the term of a licence–before the licence is granted; and
(*b*) in the case of each subsequent year of the term of a licence–on the anniversary date of the day the licence took effect.

(4) Where a licence is surrendered or cancelled during a year of its term, no refund shall be made of any part of the annual fee paid for that year.
(5) A person who fails to pay the fees referred to in this section by the date they are payable is guilty of an offence.
Penalty: A fine not exceeding K10,000.00.

158. DETERMINATION OF VALUE OF PETROLEUM.

[87]Except as otherwise provided in the Schedule, the Minister shall, from time to time, after considering any information furnished by the tenement holder and any other information that the Minister thinks relevant, determine in accordance with Schedule 1 the value, for the purposes of this Act, of petroleum produced from a licence area–

(*a*) in the case of petroleum intended for export–as at the point of export; or
(*b*) in the case of petroleum not intended for export–as at the point of delivery to a refinery or processing facility in Papua New Guinea; or
(*c*) where a gas agreement applies, at the point specified in the gas agreement.

159. ROYALTY.

(1) Subject to Subsection (2), a tenement holder shall pay to the State royalty at a rate of 2.00% of the wellhead value of all petroleum produced from the licence area.
(2)[88] [89]For the purposes of Subsection (1), the wellhead value of any petroleum is the value of the petroleum determined in accordance with Section 158 less any deductions prescribed in the regulations to the extent and in the manner prescribed.
(3)[90] [*Repealed.*]
(4)[91] [92]Notwithstanding the provisions of the *Income Tax Act 1959*, where, in a financial year, in relation to the same licence area, a person has paid–

(*a*) royalty under this section; and
(*b*) development levy under Section 160,

the royalty paid by that person under this section shall be deemed to be income tax paid by that person in respect of its liability to income tax under the *Income Tax Act 1959* on its assessable income from petroleum operations derived from the petroleum project to which the royalty relates.

160. DEVELOPMENT LEVIES.

(1)[93] [94]Subject to this section, a petroleum development licensee shall pay in accordance with Section 98 of the *Organic Law on Provincial Governments and Local-level Governments* to the affected Provincial or Local-level Governments of a petroleum project development levies at a rate of 2.00% of the wellhead value of all petroleum product from the licence area, calculated in the same manner as provided for in Section 159.
(2) Subject to Subsection (3), this section shall not apply to production of petroleum from a petroleum development licence where the petroleum development licence was granted prior to the commencement date.
(3) Subsection (2) does not apply to production of petroleum from a petroleum project where a petroleum development licence granted prior to the commencement date is varied after the commencement date to permit the construction and operation of that petroleum project.
(4)[95] [96]Development levies payable under this section shall be payable directly by a petroleum development licensee to a trust fund in accordance with the *Public Finances (Management) Act 1995*, annually in arrears on or before 31 January in the year following the year of production to which the development levy relates.
(5) No other development levies pursuant to Section 98 of the *Organic Law on Provincial Governments and Local-level Governments* shall be applied to petroleum projects.
(6)[97] [98]Development levies which has been paid in accordance with this section shall be disbursed from the trust account only in accordance with an appropriation approved by Parliament.

161. ASCERTAINING QUANTITY OF PETROLEUM RECOVERED.

For the purposes of this Act, the quantity of petroleum recovered by a licensee during a period is–

(*a*) the quantity measured during that period by an approved measuring device installed at the wellhead or some other approved place; or
(*b*) where no such measuring device is installed, or the Minister is not satisfied that the quantity of petroleum recovered by the licensee has been properly or accurately measured by such a device–the quantity determined by the Minister as being the quantity so recovered during that period.

162. PAYMENT OF ROYALTY AND PENALTY FOR LATE PAYMENT.

(1)[99] [100]Royalty under this Act in respect of petroleum recovered during a royalty period is payable not later than the last day of the next succeeding royalty period except where a gas agreement applies, royalty is payable no later than one month after the last day of the next succeeding royalty period.
(2) Where the amount of royalty under this Act is not paid as provided by Subsection (1), there is payable to the Director by the licensee an additional amount calculated at the rate of % per day on the amount of royalty from time to time remaining unpaid, to be computed from the time when the royalty became payable until it is paid.

(3) An additional amount is not payable under Subsection (2) in respect of any period before the expiration of seven days after the value of the petroleum was determined under Section 158.

163. REGISTRATION FEES.

There is payable to the Director in respect of all instruments required to be registered under this Act such fees as are prescribed.

PART IV. – STATE EQUITY ENTITLEMENT AND PROJECT BENEFITS.

164. NO EFFECT ON COMPENSATION ENTITLEMENT.

Nothing contained in this Part affects the entitlement of a person to be compensated pursuant to Section 118.

165. STATE EQUITY ENTITLEMENT.

(1) The State has the right (but not the obligation) to acquire, directly or through a nominee, all or any part of a participating interest not exceeding 22.5% in each petroleum project.
(2)[101] [102]The right referred to in Subsection (1) may be exercised by the State–

(*a*) in the case of a petroleum project which is an Orogen option project–

(i) at the time of the grant of the licence or licences pursuant to which the petroleum project is conducted; or
(ii) if the Company has exercised its option under the option agreement in respect of that Orogen option project, at any time prior to the date upon which MRDC is required under the terms of the option agreement to complete the transfer to the Company of a participating interest in the Orogen option project; and

(*b*) in the case of any other petroleum project, at the time of the grant of the licence or licences pursuant to which the petroleum project is conducted.

(3) Subject to Subsection (4), the consideration payable by the State for an acquisition under Subsection (1) shall be a percentage of the unrecouped sunk costs of the vendor attributable to the vendor's interest in the petroleum project, equal to the percentage participating interest in the petroleum project being acquired by the State.
(4)[103] [104]Any interest acquired under Subsection (1) shall be acquired on and any consideration payable under Subsection (3) shall be calculated in accordance with specific terms and conditions contained in an agreement entered into in accordance with Section 183 or 184.
(5) The State shall exercise its right under Subsection (1) in respect of a petroleum project–

(*a*) if the Company has an option under the option agreement in respect of that petroleum project and has exercised that option, to the extent necessary to ensure that MRDC can complete the transfer of a participating interest in the petroleum project to the

Company under the option agreement; and
(*b*) to the extent necessary to ensure that any equity benefit required to be granted under Section 167 can be granted in accordance with that section.

(6) Subject to–

(*a*) Section 167; and
(*b*) the terms of the option agreement; and
(*c*) the terms of any written agreement between the State and the vendor of the participating interest in a petroleum project acquired by the State pursuant to the State equity entitlement,

the State or the nominee of the State which acquires a participating interest in a petroleum project in accordance with this section shall be free to deal with that participating interest as it sees fit.

166. ACQUISITION OF PARTICIPATING INTEREST BY THE COMPANY.

(1)[105] [106]Notwithstanding any other provision of this Act or the terms of any agreement made by the State,–

(*a*) the Company shall have the right to acquire, and the State or MRDC, as the case may be, shall have the right to transfer to the Company, out of the State equity entitlement, a participating interest in an Orogen option project in accordance with the option agreement; and
(*b*) without limitation–

(i) any petroleum prospecting licence or petroleum retention licence; and
(ii) the terms of any agreement made by the State in relation to a petroleum prospecting licence or petroleum retention licence; and
(iii) any petroleum development licence or pipeline licence or petroleum processing facility licence granted in relation to an Orogen option project or any part thereof,

granted or made after the coming into operation of Parts II and III of the *Mineral Resources Development Company Pty Limited (Privatisation) Act 1996* shall be subject to the exercise of those rights.
(2)[107] [108]The State shall, subject to and in accordance with the option agreement, nominate MRDC or the Company to acquire a participating interest referred to in Subsection (1).

167. EQUITY BENEFIT.

(1) Out of the State equity entitlement referred to in Section 165, there is reserved an equity benefit to be dealt with in accordance with this section.
(2) The cost of–

(*a*) acquiring the participating interest in the petroleum project for the purposes of the equity benefit; and (*b*) development attributable to that participating interest up until the commencement of commercial production of petroleum from that petroleum project,

shall be borne by the State.
(3) Subject to this section and Section 169, the State grants to the project area landowners and the affected Local-level Governments of a petroleum project, if any, an equity benefit in that petroleum project.
(4) The equity benefit granted under this section shall be shared between the project area landowners and affected Local-level Governments of the project in proportions agreed by them in a development agreement, but in default of such agreement in the proportions determined by the Minister, by instrument.
(5) The equity benefit granted under this section shall be held on trust for the grantees in accordance with Section 176.
(6) The participating interest in a petroleum project which comprises the equity benefit granted under this section shall be subject to the obligations applying thereto by law or by agreements to which the licensee is party, save that the State and not the grantee of the benefit shall be responsible for liabilities attributable to that participating interest until the commencement of commercial production of petroleum from that petroleum project.
(7) If in respect of a petroleum project there are no project area landowners or affected Local-level Governments, the State shall not be required to exercise its State equity entitlement to provide an equity benefit, but if it does so it shall be at liberty to grant that equity benefit to such organisations for such public purposes as it sees fit.
(8) This section shall only apply in respect of petroleum projects which commence development subsequent to the commencement date, and shall not affect arrangements in existence on the commencement date in relation to petroleum projects which on the commencement date are in production or have commenced development.

168. ROYALTY BENEFIT.

(1) Subject to this section and Section 169, the State grants to the project area landowners, the affected Local-level Governments and the affected Provincial Governments of a petroleum project, if any, a royalty benefit in respect of that petroleum project.
(2) The royalty benefit granted under this section shall be shared between the project area landowners the affected Local-level Governments and the affected Provincial Governments of the project in proportions agreed by them in a development agreement, but in default of such agreement in the proportions determined by the Minister, by instrument.
(3) The royalty benefit granted under this section shall be payable monthly, by the Minister, out of royalties payable to the Minister pursuant to Section 159.
(4) The royalty benefit granted under this section shall be paid to the trustee and held on trust for the grantees in accordance with Section 176.
(5) If in respect of a petroleum project there are no project area landowners or affected Local-level Governments or affected Provincial Governments, no royalty benefit shall be payable, and all royalties received pursuant to Section 159 shall be paid over to consolidated revenue.
(6) This section shall only apply in respect of petroleum projects which commence development pursuant to licences granted subsequent to the commencement date, and shall not affect arrangements in existence on the commencement date in relation to petroleum projects which on the commencement date are in production or have commenced development.

169. IDENTIFICATION OF LANDOWNER BENEFICIARIES.

(1) Notwithstanding any other provision of this Act, the persons (other than affected Local-level Governments or affected Provincial Governments) who shall receive the benefits granted by Sections 167 and 168 shall be identified in accordance with this section.
(2)[109] [110]Prior to convening or during a development forum under Section 48, the Minister shall determine, by instrument–

(*a*) the persons (other than affected Local-level Governments or affected Provincial Governments) who shall receive the benefits granted by Sections 167 and 168; and
(*b*) the incorporated land groups or, if permitted in accordance with Section 176(3)(f), any other persons or entities who shall represent and receive the benefit on behalf of the grantees of the benefit.

(3) An instrument under Subsection (2) shall only be valid if also signed by the Director and the Secretary of the Department of Treasury or other National Government Department responsible for financial matters.
(4)[111] [112]In making a determination under Subsection (2), the Minister shall consider any agreements by persons who are or claim to be project area landowners, the decisions of courts of Papua New Guinea as to ownership of land or rights in relation to land in the vicinity of the petroleum project in question, the results of social mapping and landowner identification studies carried out in accordance with this Act, and submissions from affected Local-level Governments or affected Provincial Governments of the petroleum project in question or from any other person claiming an interest or to be affected by the decision of the Minister.
(5) A petroleum development licensee or applicant for a petroleum development licence may, at any time after an application for the grant or variation of a petroleum development licence in respect of a petroleum project, apply to the Minister for a determination under Subsection (2).
(6) Where a licensee or an applicant for a licence applies to the Minister for a determination under Subsection (5), the Minister shall allow a period of 30 days, or such longer period as the Minister may allow, for persons referred to in Subsection (4) to make submissions or in the case of persons claiming to be project area landowners to advise him of agreements reached by them on the determination.
(7) Where a dispute exists as to which persons or incorporated land groups or other entities should be identified to receive benefits in accordance with this section, the Minister may make a determination under Subsection (2) or may direct that monies or other benefits which are the subject of the dispute shall be held in abeyance pending a resolution of that dispute by other means, and where such a direction is given by the Minister the trustee referred to in Section 176 shall hold such monies or other benefits in accordance with that direction.
(8)[113] [114]Where the minister directs that monies or other benefits are to be held in abeyance under Subsection (7) or where the Minister's determination under Subsection (2) is subject to judicial review, the Minister may grant the licence or licences in respect of the petroleum project.
(9)[115] [116]Where the Minister has granted the licence or licences under Subsection (8) and the dispute is resolved the Minister shall make a determination under Subsection (2) and convene a development forum under Section 48.
(10)[117] [118]A ministerial determination made pursuant to the section shall not be reviewable before any court unless an application for review is made within 28 days of the Ministerial determination.

169A. IDENTIFICATION OF LANDOWNERS BENEFICIARIES AND SHARING OF BENEFITS IN RELATION TO EXISTING PETROLEUM PROJECTS.

[119](1) If in respect of petroleum projects which on the commencement date are in production or have commenced development, persons, or incorporated land groups or other entities, who should be receiving benefits from such petroleum projects, have not been identified or where a

dispute exists as to which persons or incorporated land groups or other entities should be identified to receive such benefits, the Minister may make a determination as to the persons or incorporated land groups or other entities who should receive the benefits arising from such petroleum project.

(2) In making a determination under Subsection (1), the Minister shall consider any agreements by persons who are or claim to be project area landowners, the decisions of courts of Papua New Guinea as to ownership of land or rights in relation to land in the vicinity of the petroleum project in question, the results of social mapping and landowner identification studies that have been carried out in accordance with this Act, and submissions from affected Local-level Governments or affected Provincial Governments of the petroleum project in question or from any other person claiming an interest or to be affected by the decision of the Minister.

(3) Where, in the opinion of the Minister, having considered any agreements by persons who are or claim to be project area landowners, the decisions of the courts of Papua New Guinea as to ownership of land or rights in relation to land in the vicinity of the petroleum project in question, the results of any social mapping and landowner identification studies that have been carried out in accordance with Section 47, some project area landowners have a greater or more substantial occupation or right of occupation of the land referred to in the definition of "project area landowners" or are more adversely impacted by the petroleum project than other project area landowners, the Minister may, by instrument, determine that the sharing amongst project area landowners of equity benefits or royalty benefits in accordance with this section shall favour, on a per capita basis, those project area landowners who have that greater or more substantial occupation or right of occupation or are more adversely impacted by the petroleum project.

170. SHARING OF BENEFITS AMONGST PROJECT AREA LANDOWNERS.

(1) Any equity benefit or royalty benefit granted to project area landowners shall be shared amongst project area landowners in accordance with this section.

(2) Equity benefits and royalty benefits granted to project area landowners under this Act shall be shared among project area landowners or groups of project area landowners in proportions to be agreed by them in a development agreement, but in default of such agreement in the proportions determined by the Minister, by instrument.

(3) Where, in the opinion of the Minister, having considered the results of social mapping and landowner identification studies conducted in accordance with Section 47, some project area landowners have a greater or more substantial occupation or right of occupation of the land referred to in the definition of "project area landowners" or are more adversely impacted by the petroleum project that other project area landowners, the Minister may, by instrument, determine that the sharing amongst project area landowners of equity benefits or royalty benefits in accordance with this section shall favour, on a per capita basis, those project area landowners who have that greater or more substantial occupation or right of occupation or are more adversely impacted by the petroleum project.

(4) A trust deed implemented in accordance with Subsections 176(3) shall provide for the distribution of equity benefits and royalty benefits in accordance with this section.

171. OTHER PROJECT AREA LANDOWNER BENEFITS.

(1) Subject to Section 174 the State may, in a development agreement, reach agreement with project area landowners to provide and may provide to or for the benefit of project area landowners or the people of the project area or the people of the region, by way of grants out of consolidated revenue or otherwise, such other benefits in addition to those specified in this Part as the State sees fit.

(2) Nothing contained in this Part affects any agreement which might be reached between project area landowners and the developers of a petroleum project as to benefits to be provided or other commitments made to those project area landowners by those developers.

172. SHARING OF BENEFITS AMONGST AFFECTED LOCAL-LEVEL GOVERNMENTS AND AFFECTED PROVINCIAL GOVERNMENTS.

(1) If in respect of a petroleum project there is more than one affected Local-level Government, the equity benefit and royalty benefit granted to affected Local-level Governments by this Part shall, unless otherwise agreed in writing by the affected Local-level Governments and the State, be shared between those affected Local-level Governments in proportion to the number of project area landowners who receive those benefits in respect of that project who reside within the jurisdiction of each affected Local-level Government.
(2) If in respect of a petroleum project there is more than one affected Provincial Government, the royalty benefit granted to affected Local-level Governments by this Part shall, unless otherwise agreed in writing by the affected Local-level Governments and the State, be shared between those affected Provincial Governments in proportion to the number of project area landowners who receive a royalty benefit in respect of that project who reside within the jurisdiction of each affected Provincial Government.

173. PROJECT GRANTS.

(1) In addition to the other benefits granted to affected Local-level Governments and affected Provincial Governments under this Part, the State shall make grants to affected Local-level Governments and affected Provincial Governments of a petroleum project in accordance with this section.
(2) The State shall in a development agreement and may in any other agreement agree with the affected Local-level Governments and affected Provincial Governments of a petroleum project upon the amount and nature and timing of grants to be made by the State to those affected Local-level Governments and affected Provincial Governments in relation to the petroleum project.
(3) Grants made in accordance with this section may be in the form of monetary payments or in the form of provision of infrastructure or services or other benefits.
(4) The provision to an affected Local-level Government or an affected Provincial Government of a benefit in the form of infrastructure (or any other benefit) which is funded by the licensee in respect of the petroleum project pursuant to Section 219C of the *Income Tax Act 1959* shall be taken to be a grant made in accordance with this section.
(5) The State may, in addition to grants made to affected Local-level Governments or affected Provincial Governments under this section, make grants to project area landowners or customary owners of land in a petroleum project area.

174. LIMITATION ON PROJECT BENEFITS.

(1) The total benefits granted in accordance with this Act to project area landowners and affected Local-level Governments and affected Provincial Governments and any other persons or organisations shall not, when added to other costs incurred by the State in the course of the development or operation of a petroleum project, exceed 20% of the total net benefit to the State from that petroleum project as determined in a cost-benefit analysis under Section 116 of the *Organic Law on Provincial Governments and Local-level Governments*.
(2) No commitment shall be made by the State pursuant to Section 171 or 173 unless the Minister is satisfied that, following the provision of any benefits or grants which might be agreed under those sections, Subsection (1) is complied with.

175. ADDITIONAL INTERESTS IN PETROLEUM PROJECTS.

(1) Affected Provincial Governments, affected Local-level Governments and project area landowners of a petroleum project are at liberty to negotiate with a licensee to acquire from the

licensee, on freely negotiated commercial terms, a participating interest in a petroleum project, in addition to the participating interest in that project granted under Section 167.
(2) Where an affected Provincial Government or an affected Local-level Government or project area landowners seeks or seek to acquire an additional participating interest in accordance with Subsection (1), the State, through MRDC, shall assist that process by providing, to the extent permitted by law, information and technical advice to the affected Provincial Government, affected Local-level Government or project area landowners, as the case may be.
(3) Nothing contained in this section obliges–

(*a*) a licensee to sell a participating interest in a petroleum project, or an interest in any other asset; or
(*b*) the State to provide or procure finance for an acquisition in accordance with this section or to procure any agreement with a licensee.

176. PROJECT BENEFITS TRUSTS.

(1)[120] [121]The equity benefit granted by the State in accordance with Section 167 and royalty benefit granted by the State in accordance with Section 168 to project area landowners, and any additional participating interest in a petroleum project acquired by project area landowners in accordance with Section 175, shall be received and held upon trust for those project area landowners by a corporate trustee which is wholly owned by MRDC.
(2)[122] [123]Where by an act or agreement the State grants to project area landowners or other customary land owners any other benefit in relation to the petroleum project, whether by way of a beneficial interest in a licence or assets attributable to a licence, or payments based on production or profits of the petroleum project, or otherwise, that benefit shall be received and held upon trust for those persons by a corporate trustee which is wholly owned by MRDC.
(3) Where a benefit referred to in Subsection (1) or (2) is held by a trustee upon trust pursuant to Subsection (1) or (2)–

(*a*) the terms of the trust shall be set out in a deed approved by the Minister; and
(*b*) the board of directors of the trustee shall be comprised in the majority by representatives of the State (including the managing director of MRDC) and in the minority by representatives of the grantees of the benefit; and
(*c*) any equity interest or equivalent in a petroleum project held by the trustee shall not without the consent of the State be sold or transferred or charged, mortgaged or otherwise encumbered other than for the purpose of financing the activities of the trustee in that petroleum project or securing its joint venture obligations in that petroleum project; and
(*d*) the trustee and the trust funds and any assets held by the trustee shall be managed by MRDC; and
(*e*) the trustee and MRDC shall enter into a management agreement on terms approved by the Minister which agreement shall govern the management of the trustee and its assets and the amounts charged to the trustee for those management services; and
(*f*) unless otherwise agreed between the State and the grantees of the benefit or prescribed by law, the beneficiaries of the trust shall be incorporated land groups on behalf of the grantees; and
(*g*) where project area landowners entitled to an equity benefit in accordance with this section and who are equally entitled amongst themselves to share in that benefit are represented by more than one incorporated land group (or other representative if permitted in accordance with Paragraph (f)) the incorporated land groups or other representatives shall be allocated the benefit in proportion to the number of project area landowners each represents; and
(*h*) the terms of the trust shall prescribe:

(i) that 30%, or such greater proportion as may be agreed between the State and the project area landowners, of the net income of the trust fund after payment of all costs and expenses shall be held upon trust for future generations of project area landowners; and
(ii) subject to the terms of any agreement between the State and project area landowners in force at the commencement of this section, that 30%, or such greater proportion as may be agreed between the State and the project area landowners, of the net income of the trust fund after payment of all costs and expenses shall be accumulated in investments in accordance with the terms of the trust and, together with the income from those investments, applied by the trustee for the benefit of project area landowners existing during the term of the trust for any one or more of the following purposes:–

(A) the general health, welfare, education and well being of the project area landowners;
(B) the provision or maintenance of community projects in the area of the petroleum project;
(C) such other purpose for the benefit of the project area landowners as is approved by the Minister; and

> (*i*)[124] the grantees of the benefit shall be at liberty to share or distribute income received by them from the trust in accordance with any customary arrangements or agreements they have entered into with the customary land owners outside of the area of the petroleum project, but such other customary land owners shall have no entitlement to or claim upon any part of the trust funds.

(4) The equity benefit granted by the State in accordance with Section 167 of this Act to affected Local-level Governments or affected Provincial Governments, and any additional participating interest in a petroleum project acquired by an affected Local-level Government or an affected Provincial Government in accordance with Section 175, shall be received and held upon trust for those grantees by a corporate trustee which is wholly owned by MRDC.
(5) Subject to Subsection (6), where by an act or by agreement the State grants to a Local-level Government or Provincial Government any other benefit in relation to the petroleum project, whether by way of a beneficial interest in a licence or assets attributable to a licence, or payments based on production or profits of the petroleum project, or otherwise, that benefit shall be received and held upon trust for that government by a corporate trustee which is wholly owned by MRDC.
(6) Subsection (5) shall not apply to–

> (*a*) monetary grants made by the State to a Local-level Government or Provincial Government; or
> (*b*) any interest in buildings or other infrastructure provided to a Local-level Government or Provincial Government where the buildings or infrastructure are not dedicated project facilities of the petroleum project.

(7) Where a benefit referred to in Subsection (4) or (5) is held by a trustee upon trust pursuant to Subsection (4) or (5)–

> (*a*) the terms of the trust shall be set out in a deed approved by the Minister; and
> (*b*) the board of directors of the trustee shall be comprised in the majority by representatives of the State (including the managing director of MRDC) and in the minority by representatives of that government; and

(*c*) any equity interest or equivalent in a petroleum project held by the trustee shall not without the consent of the State be sold or transferred or charged, mortgaged or otherwise encumbered other than for the purpose of financing the activities of the trustee in that petroleum project or securing its joint venture obligations in that petroleum project; and
(*d*) the trustee and the trust funds and any assets held by the trustee shall be managed by MRDC; and
(*e*) the trustee and MRDC shall enter into a management agreement on terms approved by the Minister which agreement shall govern the management of the trustee and its assets and the amounts charged to the trustee for those management services.

(8)[125] [126]Notwithstanding any other provision of this Act, the royalty and equity benefits granted b ythe State to project area land owners who have been identified as grantees of such benefits in petroleum projects which were at the commencement date of this Act are in production or have commenced development, shall be received and held upon trust for those project area landowners by a corporate trustee which is wholly owned by MRDC in accordance with this section.

177. BENEFITS WHERE PIPELINE OR PETROLEUM PROCESSING FACILITY NOT PART OF PETROLEUM PROJECT.

[127]Where a pipeline or petroleum processing facility is constructed otherwise than as part of a petroleum project, customary land owners in the area in which the pipeline or petroleum processing facility is constructed shall be entitled only to such benefits as may be agreed between the licensee of the pipeline or petroleum processing facility and those customary land owners or between that licensee and the State.

178. EXPENDITURE ON BEHALF OF AFFECTED LOCAL-LEVEL GOVERNMENTS AND AFFECTED PROVINCIAL GOVERNMENTS.

(1) All grants made in accordance with Section 173, and all monies held on behalf of an affected Local-level Government or affected Provincial Government in accordance with Section 176 and available to be spent by the affected Local-level Government or affected Provincial Government, shall be administered in accordance with this section.
(2)[128] [129]The Minister shall establish, in respect of each petroleum project, an Expenditure Implementation Committee comprising –

(*a*) the Secretary of the Department of National Planning or the department responsible for national planning matters, who shall be the Chairman; and
(*b*) the Director; and
(*c*) the Secretary of the Department of Treasury or the department responsible for national government finances; and
(*d*) the Secretary of the Department of Works and Transport; and
(*e*) the Secretary of the Department of Provincial and Local level Government Affairs; and
(*f*) the Administrator responsible of each affected Provincial Government or District Administrator responsible for an affected Local level Government; and

(*g*) the chief executive of the Operator who shall respect the licensees of the petroleum project,

or their respresentatives.
(3) Expenditure of monies referred to in Subsection (1) by or on behalf of an affected Local-level Government or affected Provincial Government and the implementation of grants referred to in that subsection shall be made only–

(*a*) in accordance with development plans submitted by the relevant Local-level Government or Provincial Government; and
(*b*) in accordance with the approval of the Expenditure Implementation Committee for the petroleum project in question.

(4) The Expenditure Implementation Committee shall be responsible for–

(*a*) monitoring budgets and timetables for construction and implementation of grant and benefit expenditure on behalf of affected Local-level Governments and affected Provincial Governments, and approving such expenditure; and
(*b*) monitoring expenditure made pursuant to Section 219C of the *Income Tax Act 1959* to ensure that project funded pursuant to that section comply with the development plans submitted by the relevant Local-level Government or Provincial Government; and
(*c*) monitoring the program of ongoing projects for expenditure of monies in accordance with this section.

(5) Notwithstanding the provisions of Section 219C of the *Income Tax Act 1959*, no expenditure by a licensee in respect of a petroleum project shall fulfil the requirements of that section unless approved by the Expenditure Implementation Committee of the petroleum project in question.

179. NATIONAL GAS CORPORATION.

(1) The Provincial Governments of Papua New Guinea, acting jointly, shall be at liberty to incorporate under the *Companies Act 1997* a company to be called National Gas Corporation Limited.
(2) If National Gas Corporation is formed in accordance with Subsection (1)–

(*a*) each of the Provincial Governments shall be entitled to a shareholding in NGC in accordance with a shareholders' agreement, which they may enter into; and
(*b*) NGC shall act as a corporate trustee for the Provincial Governments or any of them and any project area landowners on whose behalf it holds assets, and it shall hold its assets upon the trusts for which they were acquired and it and its office holders shall be subject to the fiduciary obligations of a trustee in favour of those beneficiaries; and
(*c*) NGC shall have the purpose of managing participating interests of Provincial Governments and project area landowners in gas projects (including downstream processing of natural gas) in Papua New Guinea conducted pursuant to licences granted after the commencement date, whether such participating interests are granted under this Act or acquired on commercial terms; and
(*d*)[130] NGC shall have the legal capacity–

(i) to do all things necessary to implement the purpose referred to in Paragraph (a); and
(ii) to obtain petroleum processing facility licences for processing of natural gas and any permits

required for NGC to be a domestic gas operator or a domestic gas supplier or an owner or operator of facilities for the storage or transportation of cylinders containing compressed natural gas or liquefied petroleum gas; and
(iii)[131] to hold and enter into agreements with licensees to acquire by agreement on commercial terms participating interests in gas projects; and
(iv)[132] to acquire by agreement on commercial terms, a participating interest in the Hides petroleum project conducted pursuant to Petroleum Development Licence 1, irrespective of whether the State exercistes its rights under Section 165 or any other law; and
(v)[133] to acquire by agreement or commercial terms processed petroleum including all liquefied petroleum gas; and
(vi)[134] to acquire by agreement by agreement on commercial terms an interest in a gas project at such time as any participant in a gas project wishes to sell such an interest; and
(vii) to borrow money for the purpose of acquiring or developing assets held by it in accordance with this section, and for that purpose to charge its assets; and

(*e*) NGC shall for the purposes of this Part be deemed to be a corporate trustee referred to in Section 176, and the provisions of this Part applying to corporate trustees referred to in Section 176 shall apply to NGC; and
(*f*) NGC shall obtain competent and professional management and shall provide to the Minister fully detailed quarterly reports on all of its activities and half yearly audited financial statements; and
(*g*) NGC shall not engage in any activities other than those referred to in this subsection or activities incidental thereto.

(3) Provincial Governments and project area landowners shall not be liable for the debts of NGC, notwithstanding that they may be a beneficiary of a trust referred to in Subsection (2).
(4) Nothing contained in this section obliges–

> (*a*) a licensee to sell a participating interest in a gas project, or an interest in any other property; or
> (*b*) the State to provide or procure finance for an acquisition in accordance with this section or to procure any agreement with a licensee.

(5)[135] [136]Notwithstanding in this Section 179 affects, restricts or limits, or will be taken to affect, restrict or limit, in any way, any right or entitlement of any person (regardless of that source of that right or entitlement), including, without limitation, the rights and entitlements of the State under Section 165 and the rights and entitlements of the Company under this Act or the option agreement,

PART V. – MISCELLANEOUS.

180. INSPECTORS NOT TO HAVE ANY INTERESTS IN LICENCES, ETC.

The Minister, the Director, an inspector or an authorized officer appointed under this Act must not hold, or have any interest in, any licence, or hold shares in any company holding, or having any interest in, any licence under this Act.
Penalty: A fine not exceeding K1,000.00 or imprisonment for a term not exceeding two years or both.

181. POINTS, ETC., TO BE ASCERTAINED BY REFERENCE TO GEODETIC DATUM.

(1) Where for the purposes of this Act, or for the purpose of an instrument under this Act, it is necessary to determine the position on the surface of the Earth at a point, line or area, that position shall be determined by reference to a spheroid having its centre at the centre of the Earth and a major (equatorial) radius of 6,378,160 m and a flattening of 100/29825 and by reference to the position of the Bevan Rapids (AA 070) Geodetic Station in the Gulf Province of Papua New Guinea.
(2) The Bevan Rapids Geodetic Station shall be taken to be situated at 7 degrees 21 minutes 34.7974 seconds of south latitude and at 145 degrees 15 minutes 52.9878 seconds of east longitude and to have a ground level of 406.30 m above mean sea level.

182. REGULATIONS.

(1) The Head of State, acting on advice, may make regulations not inconsistent with this Act, prescribing all matters that by this Act are required or permitted to be prescribed or are necessary or convenient to be prescribed for carrying out or giving effect to this Act or for securing, regulating, controlling or restricting–

(*a*) the exploration for petroleum and the carrying on of operations, and the execution of works, for that purpose; and
(*b*) the recovery of petroleum and the carrying on of operations, and the execution of works, for that purpose; and
(*c*) the construction and operation of pipelines and any of the pipes or facilities referred to in Paragraphs (a) to (d) inclusive of the definition of "pipeline"; and
(*d*)[137] the construction and operation of petroleum processing facilities; and
(*e*)[138] limitation of project benefits granted in accordance with this Act.

(2) Without limiting the generality of Subsection (1), the regulations may–

(*a*) prescribe work practices and safety measures to–

(i) control the flow and prevent the escape of petroleum or water; and
(ii) prevent the escape of water or drilling fluid or the mixture of water or drilling fluid with petroleum or any other matter; and
(iii) prevent damage to petroleum-bearing strata in an area in respect of which a licence is not in force; and
(iv) keep separate each petroleum pool and each source of water discovered in a licence area; and
(v) prevent water or other matter entering a petroleum pool through wells; and
(vi) prevent the pollution of any water-well, spring, stream, river, lake, reservoir, estuary, harbour or area of sea by the escape of petroleum, salt water, drilling fluid, chemical additive or any other waste product or effluent; and

(*b*) prescribe areas where drilling for petroleum Is prohibited; and
(*c*) regulate the location and spacing of wells, and for this purpose provide for the establishment and designation of spacing units; and
(*d*) prescribe the methods, equipment and materials to be used in boring, drilling completing, plugging or operating wells; and
(*e*) regulate the construction, erection, maintenance, operation or use of installations or equipment; and
(*f*) prescribe measures to prevent the escape of petroleum or petroleum products or water from a

pipeline, water line, flow lines or gathering lines, pumping station, tank station or valve station; and
(*g*) require a licensee to maintain in good condition and repair all structures, equipment and other property used or intended to be used for or in connection with exploration for, or the recovery or conveyance or processing of, petroleum or petroleum products; and
(*h*) provide for the removal of structures, equipment and other property, brought into the country in connection with exploration for, or the recovery or conveyance or processing of, petroleum or petroleum products, that are not used or intended to be used in connection with that exploration, recovery or conveyance or processing; and
(*i*) regulate the pressure maintenance in, or the repressuring of, a petroleum pool and the recycling of petroleum; and
(*j*) regulate the secondary or tertiary recovery of petroleum from a petroleum pool and provide for the methods to be used in such recovery; and
(*k*) regulate the use of wells and the use of the subsurface for the disposal of petroleum, water and other substances produced in association with the exploration for or the recovery of petroleum; and
(*l*) prescribe the rates, or the method of setting the rates, at which petroleum and water may be recovered from any well or petroleum pool; and
(*m*) prescribe the methods to be used for the measurement of petroleum, water and other substances from a well; and
(*n*)[139] regulate or control the tariffs charged by pipeline licensees or petroleum processing licensees and the conditions of use of pipelines or petroleum processing facilities; and
(*o*) prescribe safety standards and provide for the health and safety of persons employed in or in connection with the exploration for or the recovery or conveyance of petroleum; and
(*p*) require licensees to take, preserve and furnish to the Director cores, cuttings and samples from wells and samples of petroleum and water; and
(*q*) require licensees to give to the Director reports, returns and other information; and
(*r*) require a tenement holder to take logs or directional surveys or make other down-hole investigations; and
(*s*) prescribe forms and other documents to be used in the administration of this Act, other than approved forms; and
(*t*) prescribe penalties of fines not exceeding K5,000.00 and default penalties of fines not exceeding K500.00 for offences against the regulations; and
(*u*) prescribe fees; and
(*v*) prescribe work practices and safety measures, including qualifications for persons in control of petroleum processing facilities; and
(*w*) regulate the siting of petroleum processing facilities; and
(*x*) prescribe the methods, equipment and materials to be used in the operation of petroleum processing facilities; and
(*y*) prescribe the methods, equipment and materials to be used in the operation of domestic utilisation facilities; and
(*z*) regulate the construction, erection, maintenance, operation or use of installations or equipment; and
(*aa*) require a petroleum processing facility licensee to maintain in good condition and repair all structures, equipment and other property used or intended to be used for or in connection with the processing of petroleum; and
(*bb*) provide for the removal of structures, equipment and other property, brought into the country in connection with the processing of petroleum that are not used or intended to be used in connection with that processing; and
(*cc*) prescribe standards for construction, maintenance, calibration and listing of metering and measurement devices; and
(*dd*) prescribe standards for pressure, purity and uniformity of calorific value of petroleum or petroleum products that is, or is intended to be, supplied for domestic utilisation or export; and
(*ee*) prescribe other standards with respect to the properties, condition and composition of

petroleum or petroleum products that is, or is intended to be, supplied for domestic utilisation or export; and
(*ff*) prescribe safety standards and provide for the health and safety of persons employed in or in connection with the processing or supply of petroleum or petroleum products for domestic utilisation; and
(*gg*) require petroleum processing facility licensees and domestic gas suppliers who are not petroleum processing facility licensees to give to the Director reports, returns and other information; and
(*hh*) prescribe requirements for access arrangements for third-party use of strategic pipelines or strategic petroleum processing facilities; and
(*ii*) prescribe the manner in which the State acquires interests in petroleum development licences, pipeline licences, and petroleum processing facility licences and the assets that are related to those licences.
(*jj*)[140] prescribe the powers, functions and duties of the Chief Warden and the Wardens; and
(*kk*)[141] prescribe the manner and scope of agreement between a licensee and the State in relation to the co-ordination of a development forum, and the amount of money that a licensee can contribute for purposes of co-ordinating a development forum, and how payment of such monies will be made.

183. PETROLEUM AGREEMENT.

[142]The Minister may, on behalf of the State, execute an agreement with a licensee, providing for–

(*a*) the definition of the extent of a particular petroleum project and operations for that petroleum project, for the purposes of this Act and any other law; and
(*b*) the transfer and assignment of State equity interest in that petroleum project to MRDC; and
(*c*) any other matters relating to that petroleum project or those operations, which are agreed to by the parties to such agreement, which, without limiting the generality of the foregoing, may include –

(i) the application of particular provisions of this Act to that petroleum project and those operations; and
(ii) where permitted by other Acts, the application of particular provisions of those other Acts to that petroleum project and those operations,

and such agreement will, once so executed, have effect in accordance with its terms and notwithstanding any other provision of this Act.

184. GAS AGREEMENT.

[143]The Minister may, on behalf of the State, execute an agreement with a licensee, providing for–

(*a*) the definition of the extent of a particular gas project and gas operation for the gas project, for the purposes of this Act and any other law; and
(*b*) the transfer and assignment of a State equity interest in that gas project to MRDC; and

(*c*) any other matters relating to that gas project or those operations, which are agreed to by the parties to such agreement, which, without limiting the generality of the foregoing, may include:

(i) the application of particular provisions of this Act to that gas project and those operations; and
(ii) where permitted by other Acts, the application of particular provision of those other Acts to that gas project and those operations,

and such agreement will, once so executed, have effect in accordance with its terms and notwithstanding any other provision of this Act.

185. AGREEMENTS BY THE STATE.

[144]Notwithstanding any other provision of this Act, or any other Act (but without limiting Sections 183 or 184) where in a written agreement with a licensee, whether entered into before or after the commencement of this Act, the State agrees that a discretion under this Act or any other Act or any regulations under this Act or any other Act will be exercised in a certain way, or that certain rights or consents or authorisations or licences under this Act or any other Act or any regulation under this Act or any other Act will be granted to the licensee, then that discretion shall be exercised and those rights or consents or authorisations or licences shall be granted in accordance with that written agreement.

186. REPEAL.

The following Acts are repealed:–

(*a*) *Petroleum Act* (Chapter 198); and
(*b*) *Petroleum (Amendment) Act* 1987; and
(*c*) *Petroleum (Amendment No. 2) Act* 1987.

PART VI. – TRANSITIONAL PROVISIONS.

187. LICENCES UNDER FORMER ACT.

(1) Where, on the commencement date–

(*a*) a petroleum prospecting licence issued under Division III.2 of the former Act; or
(*b*) a petroleum retention licence issued under Division III.3B of the former Act; or
(*c*) a petroleum development licence issued under Division III.4 of the former Act,

was in force, that licence shall continue in force and shall be deemed for all purposes under this Act to be a tenement issued under Division III.2, III.4 or III.7 of this Act, as applicable, commencing on the date on which such licence was issued under the former Act.
(2)[145] [146]A licence referred to in Subsection (1) shall be subject–

(*a*) in the case of a petroleum prospecting licence issued under Division III.2 of the former Act, to the conditions referred to in Section 31(2); or
(*b*) in the case of a petroleum retention licence issued under Division III.3B of the former Act, to the conditions referred to in Section 46(a)(ii) and (iii) and to the condition that the licensee will, if he has not already done so, carry out the proposals approved in respect of that licence under Sections 31E(2) or 31J(8) of the former Act; or
(*c*) in the case of a petroleum development licence issued under Division III.4 of the former Act, to the conditions referred to in Section 63(a)(ii) and (iii) and to the condition that the licensee will, if he has not already done so, carry out the proposals approved in respect of that licence under Subsection 35(2) of the former Act,

and, to the extent consistent with this Act, to the conditions to which it was subject immediately prior to the commencement date.

188. PIPELINE LICENCES UNDER FORMER ACT.

(1) Where, on the commencement date a pipeline licence issued under Division III.5 of the former Act was in force, that pipeline licence shall continue in force and shall be deemed for all purposes under this Act to be a pipeline licence issued under Division III.9 of this Act, commencing on the date on which such licence was issued under the former Act.
(2) A licence referred to in Subsection (1) shall be subject, to the extent consistent with this Act, to the conditions to which it was subject immediately prior to the commencement date.
(3) Where construction or operation of a pipeline has commenced under a pipeline licence issued under the former Act and in force on the commencement date, the pipeline in question shall for the purposes of this Act be a project pipeline, unless converted to a strategic pipeline under Section 81 or 82.

189. EXISTING OR PROPOSED PETROLEUM PROCESSING FACILITIES.

(1) Where prior to the commencement date a person has commenced construction of a petroleum processing facility which was not previously required to be licensed under the former Act, or the State has entered into an agreement with a person which provides for the construction of a petroleum processing facility or has granted to a person a licence or pipeline licence under the former Act which provides for the construction of a petroleum processing facility in circumstances where a separate petroleum processing facility licence is required under this Act, the Minister shall, upon request by that person and without the requirement for a formal application or an application fee, grant to that person a petroleum processing facility licence under this Act on terms consistent with any applicable existing agreement with or licence or pipeline licence granted under the former Act which is held by that person.
(2) Where a person referred to in Subsection (1) requests the Minister to grant a petroleum processing facility licence within six months of the commencement date, until that person is granted a petroleum processing facility licence as required by Subsection (1) the petroleum processing facility in question shall be deemed to be licensed under this Act and the person shall not be in breach of this Act only by reason of the fact that he is continuing to construct or is operating a petroleum processing facility without a petroleum processing facility licence in respect thereof.

190. REFERENCES TO FORMER ACT, ETC.

A reference in any law or in any instrument made under or in relation to the former Act or a provision of the former Act shall, on and after the commencement date, unless the context otherwise requires, be read and construed as a reference to this Act or to the corresponding provision of this Act.

SCHEDULE 1 – DETERMINATION OF VALUE OF PETROLEUM UNDER SECTION 158.

Sec. 158.

PART 1. – PRELIMINARY.

1. INTERPRETATION OF SCHEDULE.

In this Schedule–

"adjusted price" means net realisable price with any appropriate adjustment for sales margins or commissions;
"appropriate adjustment", in relation to any provision of this Schedule, means such adjustment for the purposes of the provision as is agreed on between the Minister and the licensee, or in default of agreement, as is reasonably determined by the Minister;
"domestic value" means a value to be determined under Section 158 for petroleum not intended for export;
"export value" means a value to be determined under Section 158 for petroleum intended for export;
"the guidelines" means the guidelines adopted under Part 3 of this Schedule;
"the licensee" means the holder of the licence from which the petroleum which is to be given a value under Section 158 is produced;
"relevant contract" means an agreement for the sale at an arms' length price of petroleum for delivery–

(*a*) by more than one shipment; and
(*b*) over a period of more than three months,

that was in force during the relevant period;
"the relevant period", in relation to the determination of a value for any petroleum, means the period of three months, or such longer period as in special circumstances is agreed on between the Minister and the licensee, before the date as at which the value is to be determined.

2. "SALE AT ARMS' LENGTH".

For the purposes of this Schedule, a sale is at arms' length where–

(*a*) the consideration expressed in the agreement for the sale is the sole consideration for the sale; and
(*b*) the terms of the sale are not affected by any commercial relationship (other than the relationship created by the agreement or sale) between the seller and the buyer or any person connected with the buyer; and
(*c*) neither the seller nor any person connected with him has any

direct or indirect interest in the subsequent re-sale or disposal of the petroleum or of any product of it,

and no other sale shall be taken to be at arms' length.

3. "ARMS' LENGTH PRICE".

(1) In this Schedule, **"arms' length price"**, in relation to a sale or an agreement for the sale of any petroleum, means–

(*a*) where the sale was, or was to be, at arms' length–the sale price; and
(*b*) where the sale was not, or was not to be, at arms' length–the price that, in the opinion of the Minister, the petroleum would have brought had the sale been at arms' length.

(2) Subject to Subsection (3), where in the opinion of the Minister it is not practicable in the circumstances of a particular sale that was not at arms' length, or of a particular agreement for such a sale, to determine what would have been the price referred to in Subsection (1)(b), the sale shall be disregarded for the purposes of any provision of this Schedule that relates to arms' length prices.
(3) For the purposes of any provision of this Schedule that refers to an average price based on sales at arms' length or arms' length prices, a sale that is not a sale at arms' length, or a price that is not an arms' length price, may be taken into account where the Minister is satisfied that a series of sales, or a number of related sales, of which the sale concerned was one, was or were such that the total of the prices paid amounted to, or was the equivalent of, an arms' length price for all the petroleum sold.

4. COMPARISON OF PETROLEUM.

Where it is necessary for the purposes of this Schedule to compare–

(*a*) petroleum of different qualities or grades; or
(*b*) prices of–

(i) petroleum of different qualities or grades; or
(ii) petroleum sold, or agreed to be sold, in significantly different quantities,

appropriate adjustments shall be made to reconcile or compensate for the difference.

5. COMPARISON OF PRICES.

Where it is necessary for the purposes of this Schedule to compare prices, appropriate adjustments shall be made for differences in any relevant costs, including the terms of any credit allowed and transport costs, In addition to any adjustments to be made in accordance with Schedule Section 4 to enable the prices to be related to comparable qualities, grades or quantities of petroleum.

PART 2. – NORM VALUES.

6. DETERMINATION OF VALUE BY REFERENCE TO RELEVANT CONTRACTS.

If the Minister is satisfied that there has been a sufficient number of relevant contracts for the sale–

(*a*) where the value to be determined is an export value–of locally produced petroleum for export; or
(*b*) where the value to be determined is a domestic value–of locally produced petroleum for refining or processing in Papua New Guinea,

to allow a norm price to be satisfactorily determined, the export value or the domestic value, as the case may be, shall be determined having regard to the weighted average of the comparable adjusted prices per barrel under the contracts to which Paragraph (a) or (b), as the case may be, relates.

7. DETERMINATION OF VALUE IN OTHER CASES.

In a case to which Schedule Section 6 does not apply, the Minister shall determine an export value or a domestic value, as the case requires, that in his opinion represents a fair arms' length price for the petroleum concerned, and in so doing he shall have regard to any appropriate marker price adopted under Schedule Section 9.

PART 3. – GUIDELINES.

8. REGULATIONS AS TO GUIDELINES.

Subject to Section 158 and to this Schedule, the regulations may make provision in respect of the adoption of guidelines to be followed in, and in relation to, the determination of the value of petroleum under that section.

9. MARKER PRICES.

(1) The guidelines may adopt or provide for the adoption of marker prices for the purposes of the guidelines and of this Schedule.
(2) In arriving at any decision or opinion, and in making any calculation or estimation, for the purposes of this Schedule the Minister shall, to the extent and in the manner provided in this Schedule and the guidelines, have regard to any appropriate marker price adopted under Subsection (1).

PART 4. – ARBITRATION.

10. REFERENCES TO ARBITRATION.

(1) Subject to Subsection (3), where there is a dispute between the Minister and the licensee as to the value that should, in accordance with this Schedule, be determined for any petroleum, the licensee may, by written notice to the Minister, require that any matter relating to the determination of the value, being a matter of a kind specified in Schedule Section 11, be referred to arbitration.
(2) Where a licensee makes a requirement under Subsection (1), the matter stands referred to arbitration in accordance with the *Arbitration Act*, and pending a decision on the reference, the determination by the Minister stands.
(3) This section does not apply unless the difference between the value determined by the Minister and the value claimed by the licensee exceeds 0.5% of the former.

11. MATTERS REFERABLE TO ARBITRATION.

The matters that may be referred to arbitration under Schedule Section 10 are–

(*a*) any question, whether the Minister has had proper regard to the matters to which, under this Schedule or the guidelines, regard is to be had; and
(*b*) any question, whether the Minister has properly followed the guidelines; and
(*c*) any question as to the comparability of petroleum or of sales or prices, or as to the appropriate adjustments to be made in any case; and
(*d*) any question as to the sufficiency, for any purpose of this Schedule or of the guidelines, of a number of sales or contracts; and
(*e*) any question, whether a sale was an arms' length sale, or a price was an arms' length price; and
(*f*) any question, whether an export value or a domestic value determined under Schedule Section 7 represents a fair arms' length price; and
(*g*) any relevant scientific or technical matter, or any relevant factual matter; and
(*h*) any other matter that is prescribed, or that is agreed on by the Minister and the licensee, for the purpose.

Office of Legislative Counsel, PNG

OIL AND GAS REGULATION 1999

MADE by the Head of State, acting with, and in accordance with, the advice of the National Executive Council under the Oil and Gas Act 1998.

PART I. – PRELIMINARY.

1. DEFINITIONS.

(1) In this Regulation, unless the contrary intention appears:

"API" means the American Petroleum Institute;
"approved" in relation to drilling equipment and materials, means approved by the American Petroleum Institute (hereinafter in this Regulation referred to as 'API'), or other testing agency or authority recognized by the Director;
"AS" means Standards Association of Australia Standard;
"ASEG-GDF" means the Australian Society of Exploration Geophysicists-General Data Format;
"authorized person" means a person appointed by the Person-in-Charge to carry out a specific duty;
"barrel" means 34.9726 imperial gallons or 42 US gallons at a temperature of 60ºF and an absolute pressure of 14.73 pounds per square inch or 158.988 litres under similar conditions of temperature and pressure;
"blooey line" in relation to air or gas drilling, means a system of pipes arranged to carry the air or gas returning to the surface away from the drilling rig;
"cable" means an electrical conductor or system of conductors for the transmission of electrical power or communications;
"Chief Inspector" means the Chief Inspector appointed under Section 151(1) of the Act;

"circulation" means the passing of fluid down the drill pipe, casing or tubing in a well and up to the surface or in the reverse direction;
"classifying authority" means an approved authority qualified to classify ships, barges or mobile platforms;
"clean oil" means oil free from water and sediment;
"condensate" means a mixture mainly of pentanes and heavier hydrocarbons that exists in a gaseous phase in its virgin reservoir state, but is a liquid in the conditions in which its volume is measured or estimated;
"construction platform" means a ship, barge or other vessel or floating structure from which construction or installation operations for or in connection with the exploration for or recovery of petroleum are or are to be carried out;
"contractor" means a person or body corporate engaged or appointed by the licensee to perform a specific work or service at a certain price or rate;
"cubic foot" means the amount of gas or liquid in one cubic foot of space at a temperature of 60° F and an absolute pressure of 14.73 pounds per square inch;
"date of completion" means the date on which a well is first ready to produce reservoir fluids or if planned for some other purpose, the date on which it is left in a suitable condition to fulfill that purpose;
"Deputy Person-in-Charge" means a person appointed by the Person-in-Charge in accordance with Section 6;
"derrick" means a fixed framework over a well used in supporting, hoisting and lowering operations;
"directional drilling" means the intentional changing of the direction of the well when drilling;
"Director" means the person appointed as Director under Section 11 of the Act;
"drilling rig" means machinery and ancillary equipment used for drilling wells and/or for working over wells;
"dynamic positioning" means the positioning or repositioning of a vessel in or to a chosen location by automatic means and without recourse to any physical mooring arrangements;
"enhanced recovery" means the increased recovery from a pool achieved by artificial means or by the application of energy extrinsic to the pool, which increases the recovery of petroleum to more than that obtainable by the action of natural reservoir energy, gravity or secondary recovery methods as commonly defined within the petroleum industry;
"enhanced recovery scheme" means a scheme designed to increase the recovery of petroleum to more than that obtainable by the action of natural reservoir energy, gravity or secondary recovery methods as commonly defined within the petroleum industry;
"explosive" means:

(*a*) any substance or articles capable of producing an explosive, incendiary or pyrotechnic effect; or
(*b*) any substances prescribed under the Explosives Act (Adopted); or
(*c*) any containers that–

(i) have contained a substance or articles referred to in Paragraph (a) or (b); and

(ii) have not been certified in the manner prescribed under the Explosives Act (Adopted) to be free from explosives;

"extra-low voltage" means voltage not normally exceeding 32 volts alternating current or 115 volts direct current;
"field" means the general surface area underlain by and including one or more pools of oil or gas or both;
"firewall" means a wall of concrete, earth or other material surrounding a tank or tanks that confines the spillage of petroleum and prevents the spread of fire or the passage of flammable liquids or vapours;

"fixed platform" means a structure (including a floating structure) fixed or connected to the sea-bed otherwise than only by a part of the structure lowered to the sea-bed for the purpose of supporting the structure, from which petroleum exploration operations or operations for the recovery of petroleum are or are to be carried out and that is not or is not to be capable of being readily moved from one position to another as such a structure;

"flame-type equipment" means any equipment that through its design or use is able to cause ignition to flammable materials, liquids and/or gases;

"flowing well" means a well from which oil, gas or water is produced naturally without artificial lifting equipment;

"gas" means any natural gas, either hydrocarbon or other, or any mixture thereof;

"gas oil ratio" means the ratio of total gas (expressed in cubic feet) to clean oil (expressed in barrels) concurrently produced during any stated period;

"geophysical exploration" means geophysical investigation by any generally recognized method including seismic, gravimetric, magnetic, electrical, radioactive and geochemical methods in the study of the subsurface;

"ghost hole" means an uncased section of a well that once drilled, is unable to be reentered due to mechanical or formation conditions;

"good oilfield practice" means practice generally accepted as good and safe within the petroleum industry;

"hazardous area" means an area in which flammable gases or vapors are, or may be, present in the air in sufficient quantities to produce explosive or ignitable mixtures;

"helideck" means a deck or platform designed to accept a helicopter for landing or take-off;

"helipad" means a surface designed to take a helicopter for landing or take-off;

"inspector" or "inspection company" means a person or corporation with recognized qualifications accurately to inspect and evaluate equipment as meeting its intended specifications and its requirements of use;

"licensee" means the registered holder of a licence;

"licence area" means the area constituted by the blocks that are the subject of a licence;

"licensed electrical worker" means a person holding a certificate of competency issued by the Papua New Guinea Electricity Commission;

"magazine" means a place for the storage or keeping of any explosive;

"main operational site" means a location at which work occurs for extended periods of time or a location at which continuous operations are carried out;

"mast" means a portable or collapsible framework over a well used in supporting, hoisting and lowering operations;

"mobile platform" means a construction platform, floating service platform or mobile drilling unit that is capable of being moved readily from one position to another;

"mobile drilling unit" means a ship, barge or other vessel or floating structure including a structure any part of which may be lowered to the sea-bed for the purpose of supporting the structure that carries or includes equipment for drilling or carrying out other operations on a well from the vessel or structure;

"MSDS" sheet means the manufacturer's safety data sheet for a product provided to the petroleum industry;

"mud" means a drilling fluid consisting of any suitable mixture of water, oil, clay or other material (or any admixture of all or any of such materials) commonly used in the petroleum industry which will remove the drill cuttings from the hole and which will also control rock and reservoir pressures, stabilize disturbed formation conditions and seal formations into which fluid from the hole is escaping;

"multiple completion well" means a well for the segregated production from, or injection to, more than one pool;

"NATA" means the National Association of Testing Authorities, Australia;

"permit to work" means a system of approving/monitoring of other than normal work operations in a restricted area by use of approval permits authorized by the person in charge;

"Person-in-Charge" means a person appointed by the Licensee in accordance with Section 5;

"Petroleum Inspector" means a person appointed to be an inspector pursuant to Section 115 of the Act;
"plant" includes drilling equipment, derricks and masts, power units, pumps, units, separators, storage tanks, pipelines, vehicles and all other equipment, materials and tools used in a field operation;
"platform" means a construction platform, fixed accommodation, process, production or shipping platform, service platform or mobile drilling unit;
"PNGS" means a National Technical Standard established under the National Institute of Standards and Industrial Technology Act 1993;
"pool" means a discrete underground accumulation of oil or gas or an admixture of such substances;
"process vessel" includes a heater, dehydrator, separator, treater or any vessel used in the processing or treatment of produced petroleum;
"production" means the volume of oil, gas or water produced;
"production facility" means a system or arrangement of surface equipment receiving the effluents of one or more wells prior to delivery to market or other disposition, and may include equipment or devices for separating the effluents into oil, gas condensate or water, and for measurement;
"production potential" means the capacity of a well to produce oil, gas or water, calculated or measured in accordance with generally accepted procedures;
"reservoir" means a porous and permeable rock capable of storing fluids and yielding them to a well;
"reservoir pressure" means the static or stabilized pressure existing or presumed to exist in a reservoir at a given datum;
"reservoir measurements" means measurements of reservoir pressure and temperature and of the movements of fluids and fluid interfaces within a reservoir;
"seismic source" means the energy source used to create shock waves in the earth, the reflections of which are recorded in investigating underground strata;
"separator" means an apparatus at the surface for separating fluids produced from a well;
"service platform" means a ship, barge or other vessel or floating or fixed structure that, in connection with petroleum exploration operations or operations for recovery of petroleum, provides a base from or on which service such as diving, fire fighting, accommodation, processing or storage are controlled, mounted or performed;
"service rig" means rig machinery and ancillary equipment specifically for the use of working over, completing, recompleting and/or servicing wells;
"shot hole" means a hole drilled for the purpose of firing an explosive charge as a seismic source;
"shot point" means the surface location and area immediately surrounding a shot hole or point of initiation of a seismic source;
"site person-in-charge" means a person appointed by the Person-in-Charge to manage an operation at a main operational site or area and is responsible to ensure approved, proper and safe procedures and programs are followed;
"spud date" means the date a new well has spudded or the date when commencement of drilling operations has begun for the sidetracking of a wellbore or the commencement of actual operations on a well for a workover, completion or abandonment;
"spudding in" means the commencement of drilling a well;
"standard handrail" means a permanent and substantial railing, smooth and free from protruding nails, bolts, or splinters, and consisting of a horizontal top rail not less than 900mm or more than 1,050mm above floor level, mounted on posts or uprights spaced not more than 2.5m apart centre to centre and with an intermediate rail spaced midway between the top rail and floor level or top of the toeboard if a toeboard is provided;
"storage tank" means a tank containing flammable fluids;
"suspend" means to discontinue operations temporarily;
"suspended well" means a well, previously used for production or injection, in which all operations have been suspended prior to recompletion or abandonment, for a considerable period of time, with, however, the intention of operations being resumed at a later date;

"swing well" means a well that is intermittently produced;
"toeboard" means a vertical guard, not less than 100mm in height and fastened to the outer edge of a platform in order to prevent tools and other objects from falling therefrom;
"velocity log" means a recording of the travel time of sound waves through the strata penetrated in the well;
"verifying body" means an approved body qualified to–

(*a*) verify the design, construction and installation of structures fixed or intended to be fixed to the sea-bed; and
(*b*) carry out such verification as the Director may require;

"waste" in addition to its ordinary meaning, means–

(*a*) the locating, spacing, drilling, equipping, completing, operating, or producing of a well in a manner that could be shown to result in reduction of the quantity of oil, gas or water ultimately recoverable from a pool under sound engineering and economic principles; or
(*b*) the locating, drilling, equipping, completing, operating or producing of a well in such a manner that excessive surface loss or destruction of oil, gas or water is caused; or
(*c*) any inefficient, excessive, or improper use or dissipation of reservoir energy; or
(*d*) the failure to use suitable and timely enhanced recovery methods in a pool where it is demonstrated on the basis of available information, that any of such methods would result in increasing the quantity of oil, gas or water ultimately recoverable from a pool under sound engineering and economic principles; or
(*e*) the escape or flaring of natural gas where the Director considers that by the application of sound engineering principles the natural gas could be gathered and, if necessary, processed so that the gas or its by-products could be marketed or stored for marketing or beneficially injected into an underground reservoir; and
(*f*) the inefficient and improper storing of oil, gas or water whether on the surface or underground; or
(*g*) the production of oil, gas or water in excess of proper storage facilities or transportation and marketing facilities or of marketing demand; or
(*h*) the use of natural gas for purposes other than gas lift re-pressuring, recycling, drilling, pressure maintenance, or for chemical manufacture, light and fuel, unless the Minister considers such use is efficient and beneficial in the public interest;

"well" means a hole in the ground made, being made or proposed to be made for the purposes of searching for or producing petroleum, for reservoir, for disposal of waste fluids resulting from production operations, or through which any petroleum is obtained or is obtainable, but does not include a water bore or seismic shot hole;
"well log" means a recording of one or more physical or stratigraphic measurements as a function of depth in a well;
"workover operation" means a maintenance operation carried out on a well in order to improve productivity or to remedy some defect.
"workover rig" means rig machinery and ancillary equipment specifically for the use of working over, completing, recompleting and/or servicing wells.

(2) In this Regulation, a reference to the relevant requirements or recommendations of any Act, PNGS, Standards Association of Australia Standard or Code, any API Standard, Bulletin or Recommended Practice is a reference to those current standards, requirements or recommendations.

PART II. – ADMINISTRATION.

2. RESPONSIBILITY OF LICENSEE.

(1) Subject to Subsection (2), a licensee shall ensure that all operations carried out in the licence area are in accordance with this Regulation and in the case of any operation in respect of which an operator has been appointed, that operator and the licensee shall be jointly and severally responsible for ensuring the observance of this Regulation.

(2) The liability of the licensee and the operator of a licence area shall be in addition to, and shall not affect or be affected by, the liability of any other person for any contravention or failure to comply with this Regulation.

3. EXEMPTION.

(1) Where the Director is satisfied that compliance with a provision of this Regulation is impracticable, or undesirable in any particular circumstances, or that a satisfactory alternative procedure, action or installation may be adopted, taken or installed, he may, at his discretion, exempt a person or class of persons from the duty to comply with such provision.

(2) An exemption under Subsection (1) may be granted subject to such conditions and limitations as the Director considers necessary.

(3) The Director may cancel an exemption under Subsection (1) where any condition thereof is contravened, or not complied with, or where he is satisfied that the circumstances under which it was granted have altered.

4. POSTING OF THE REGULATION.

A copy of this Regulation shall be kept on all drilling rigs, service rigs and at other main operational locations and shall be available at all reasonable times for perusal by employees, contractors and Petroleum Inspectors.

5. PERSON-IN-CHARGE.

(1) The licensee shall, before commencing operations, appoint a competent person, to be known as the Person-in-Charge, to be in charge of all operations in the licence area and shall forthwith give to the Director–

(*a*) notification of the name and address of the Person-in-Charge; and
(*b*) where the Person-in-Charge has not previously held a position of Person-in-Charge in Papua New Guinea, a copy of the curriculum vitae of the Person in Charge; and
(*c*) a copy of the acceptance by that person of the appointment.

(2) A written notification of a change in appointment under Subsection (1) shall be forwarded to the Director forthwith.

(3) The Person-in-Charge shall ensure to the best of his ability that he and all workmen in his charge know and comply with all relevant provisions of this Regulation, applicable current laws of Papua New Guinea and with any corporate operations or safety manual that is applicable to the operations under his control.

(4) The Person-in-Charge shall comply with any conditions and/or directions which the Director considers appropriate in regards to any operation, notice, program or application.

(5) It shall be the responsibility of the Person-in-Charge to ensure that the equipment, program of operations, procedures and the working conditions provide for the safety of the personnel engaged in the operations, for the protection of the environment and equipment, and for the conservation of resources.

6. DEPUTY PERSON-IN-CHARGE.

(1) The Person-in-Charge may delegate to a competent person who shall be known as the Deputy Person-in-Charge such specified duties (other than this power of delegation) as he may think fit.

(2) The Person-in-Charge shall notify the Director of the name and address of any Deputy Person-in-Charge, the duties so delegated to him, and the acknowledgment by that person thereof.

7. NAME OF SITE PERSON-IN-CHARGE TO BE DISPLAYED.

The name of the site person-in-charge, and/or deputy site person-in-charge, of any site operation shall be clearly displayed on the site of that operation.

8. ACCIDENT, INCIDENT AND EMPLOYMENT REPORTING.

(1) The licensee shall–

(*a*) report forthwith to the Director–

(i) all accidents which–

(A) cause loss of life; or

(B) are of a serious nature resulting in injuries requiring urgent attention by a medical practitioner; and

(ii) all incidents involving fire, explosion, blow-out, spillage of hydrocarbons in excess of 10 barrels (1,600 litres) and/or serious structural damage; and

(*b*) within seven days send a written report to the Director detailing the nature and cause of the accident or incident and of the injuries sustained by any person and any damage caused to plant, property or the environment; and
(*c*) within 30 days submit a written report to the Director detailing the preventative measures that have been instigated to prevent further accidents or incidents of a similar nature from occurring.

(2) Where a fatal, serious or potentially serious accident occurs, no person shall, except with the consent of a Petroleum Inspector, or for the purpose of–

(*a*) saving human life; or
(*b*) relieving human suffering; or
(*c*) rendering the well or site safe,

move, interfere with or destroy any article or thing at the place of, or connected with, the accident.

9. MONTHLY ACCIDENT AND EMPLOYMENT RETURN.

(1) The Person-in-Charge shall complete, or ensure the completion of, a monthly accident and employment return in a form acceptable to the Director to reach the Director by the tenth day of each month, covering the previous month.

(2) A monthly accident and employment return under Subsection (1) shall provide–

(*a*) the total number of man hours worked including operator, contractor and subcontractors employed on the project; and
(*b*) the total number and relevant details of lost time injuries; and
(*c*) the total lost time for the month including any cases carried over from previous month(s), and shall include details of any potentially serious accidents or incidents even if not involving lost time.

10. WASTE OR CONTAMINATION.

(1) Where, in the opinion of the Director, a possibility exists of waste or contamination of oil, gas or water, he may require that designated tests be made by the Person-in-Charge, to detect whether or not waste or contamination is present, and shall notify the Person-in-Charge accordingly, who shall forthwith carry out such tests.

(2) Where a test required under Subsection (1) establishes that there is waste or contamination, the licensee shall forthwith carry out such measures as may be necessary to remedy or prevent the waste or contamination.

(3) On completion of any measures taken under Subsection (2), to remedy or prevent any waste or contamination, the Director may require that such additional tests, as he may consider necessary, be made to establish the effectiveness of such remedial measures.

(4) The results of any additional test required under Subsection (3) shall be forwarded forthwith to the Director.

11. EVALUATION OF AN OCCURRENCE OF OIL OR GAS.

Where the Director considers that insufficient coring, logging or testing is being carried out to evaluate an occurrence of oil or gas in a well, a potential occurrence of oil or gas or demonstrate a stratigraphic correlation in a well, he may require the Person-in-Charge to carry out any specified coring, logging or testing operations which are practical and reasonable under the circumstances existing and are of a kind generally recognized and used in the petroleum industry.

12. ENTRY ONTO PRIVATE LAND.

(1) A licensee shall, before he or his agents or servants enter on any private land, submit a completed Form 24 to the Director notifying of the licensee's intentions at least two weeks prior to making such entry and the Director shall immediately inform the person appointed under Section 73 of the Organic Law on Provincial Governments and Local-level Governments in relation to the Province in which the subject of the licence is situated.

(2) The licensee, or his agent or servants, immediately prior to entering on private land, shall consult with the Senior District Official in the District in which the subject of the licence is situated to ensure that landowners are adequately informed of the type of operation to be undertaken, the approximate duration of the operation and potential damage that could be caused to property.

13. PROTECTION OF PUBLIC UTILITIES AND EXISTING PIPELINES.

Unless otherwise approved by the Director, no interference with any existing pipeline or with any road, airstrip, telephone or power transmission line or cable, radio mast or other public utility or facility shall take place during the performance of any operation in the search for and the production of petroleum.

14. INTERFERENCE WITH FACILITIES AND EQUIPMENT.

A person who interferes with any work, facility or item of equipment constructed, installed or used pursuant to a licence area, such that the integrity or utility of that work, facility or item of equipment is lessened, is guilty of an offence.

Penalty: A fine not exceeding K5,000.00.

Default penalty: A fine not exceeding K500.00.

15. RELEASE OF INFORMATION.

(1) Where a licence area is in force, or has been in force, the Director may make public any technical data, report, analysis, sample or material supplied to the Minister, Director or any Petroleum Inspector after a period as specified in the Act.

(2) An analyses of core or cuttings material and a reprocessing of seismic or other geophysical or geo-chemical surveys carried out on material or data obtained pursuant to Subsection (1) shall be reported to the Director within six months of substantial completion of the work, and the Director may make any such report available as specified in the Act.

PART III. – SAFETY.

Division 1.

General.

16. RESPONSIBILITIES OF SUPERVISORS.

Without affecting the responsibility of the Person-in-Charge, every supervisor, foreman, tool pusher, and driller shall so supervise the workmen under his supervision that such workmen are not working in an unsafe manner, in unsafe circumstances and/or without proper protective equipment, and all supervisors shall comply with the provisions of the Industrial Safety, Health and Welfare Act 1961.

17. RESPONSIBILITY OF WORKMEN.

(1) A person shall use the safeguards, safety appliances, personal protective equipment or devices required by this Regulation.

(2) A person shall not use any equipment, or behave in a manner, that endangers himself or any other person.

(3) A person shall comply with the provisions of the Industrial Safety, Health and Welfare Act 1961.

18. FIRST AID.

(1) A stretcher and at least one clean, lockable, adequate first-aid kit, containing sterile dressings, antiseptics, splints, tape, scissors, sling and wrapping material shall be readily available on all drilling rigs, service rigs, well testing operations, seismic field crews, geological and geophysical field crews, production facilities, construction sites and other operational locations and all associated camps.

(2) Personnel with recognized first aid training shall be available on all main operational sites while work is in progress at the specific site.

(3) A comprehensive first-aid kit, containing, as a minimum, that described in Subsection (1), including a stretcher, shall be available on remote locations where skilled medical attention is not readily available.

(4) Procedures shall be established at all main operational locations for the transportation of persons needing prompt medical attention.

(5) Wherever possible, a seriously injured person, while being transported, shall be accompanied by, in addition to the driver or pilot, at least one person having valid first aid qualifications.

(6) Each main operational location other than a geophysical, geological or related operations camp, shall maintain or readily have access to a clean room equipped as a First-Aid room, with an adequate supply of hot and cold water, bed, instruments, dressings, bandages, drugs, splints, stretchers, oxygen breathing apparatus and other requirements for administering first-aid.

(7) Effective and reliable safety showers and/or eye wash stations shall be located within immediate access to any area where personnel may come in contact with materials which are injurious to the skin and/or eyes.

(8) A First-Aid room referred to in Subsection (6) shall be manned by at least one person who is–

(*a*) a registered general nurse; or
(*b*) a member of, or qualified for membership of, the Institute of Ambulance Officers (Australia); or
(*c*) trained and currently certified by an approved institution as a paramedic.

19. CONTAMINATED ATMOSPHERE.

(1) A person shall not enter or remain in the vicinity of a work area where there is a deficiency of oxygen or a danger of exposure to gases, fumes or vapours in sufficient quantity to create a health hazard, unless appropriate precautions are taken, as stipulated in the licensee's operations/safety manual, including but not limited to the use of proper respiratory apparatus that provides protection from the hazard which exists.

(2) Where a person may be exposed to injurious gases, there shall be kept at a readily accessible place at the site of the operations, at least two units of appropriate respiratory apparatus which shall be maintained in good working order at all times.

(3) Where a person is, or may be, required to use respiratory protective equipment, it shall be ensured that he has been medically approved to use the equipment and has received instruction and practice in its use.

(4) It shall be ensured that the respiratory protective equipment required by this section is used as intended by the manufacturer and that it provides the user with the essential respiratory protection against the hazardous atmospheres which may be encountered.

(5) Approved respiratory protective equipment shall include–

(*a*) self-contained breathing apparatus; or
(*b*) oxygen-generating apparatus; or
(*c*) supplied-air apparatus; or
(*d*) filter-type respiratory protective equipment.

(6) Persons required to wear supplied air apparatus of the air-line type in an area as described in Subsection (1) shall be provided with and shall wear an auxiliary air supply, such supply to be of sufficient amount to allow the worker to escape from the area in an emergency.

(7) On all drilling and servicing rigs there shall be at least six sets of self-contained respiratory protective equipment in good working order and readily available at the well site.

(8) Filter-type respiratory protective equipment shall be used where the atmosphere is contaminated or in danger of being contaminated by solid particles of a type and in sufficient quantities that create a health hazard.

(9) There shall be available at every drilling or workover location, well servicing location, production facility and pipeline facility, two portable instruments capable of detecting flammable vapours and measuring their concentrations, and such instruments shall be used to test the atmosphere of any area where flammable vapours may be reasonably expected to be present before the site person-in-charge allows a workman to enter.

(10) Adequate detection and monitoring equipment, for hydrogen sulfide gas will be provided and used in any area where H2S may exist in concentrations exceeding 10 PPM and, at concentrations exceeding 20 PPM, full respiratory equipment shall be made available and used by all personnel working in the affected area.

20. FIRE FIGHTING EQUIPMENT.

(1) Adequate, easily accessible, properly maintained fire fighting equipment shall be provided at all operational locations where the potential of fire does or may exist.

(2) Only fire extinguishers that have been manufactured for the purpose intended shall be used and all units shall be maintained, tested and recorded according to manufacturer's specifications.

(3) The operator shall ensure that sufficient personnel are trained in the effective use of fire fighting equipment which they may be called upon to operate at their place of work.

(4) Fire fighting contingency procedures shall be published and displayed around the site and such procedures shall include the provision of a trained fire fighting team for first line action from each crew and the provision of muster points for those personnel not assigned to the fire fighting team.

(5) All extinguishers and other fire fighting equipment shall be maintained in good working condition in accordance with PNGS 1218 Parts 1 and 2.

21. COMMUNICATIONS.

(1) Reliable and continuously available communication facilities shall be provided at main operational locations and at all main tank farms, main pumping stations and main compressor stations.

(2) Reliable communication facilities shall be continuously available at all drilling rigs and all workover or well servicing rigs and at their associated camp facilities if not in proximity to the rig.

(3) Radio communications shall be provided at remote geophysical survey camps and fly-camps.

(4) Where helicopter transport is utilized to support operations, radio communication between the helicopter and the operational site shall be required.

(5) Where the camp site is situated more than 1km from the well site, a means of communication between the well site and the camp shall be installed.

22. CLOTHING.

(1) All personnel shall wear clothing and footwear suitable for the operational conditions and the work being performed.

(2) No person shall unnecessarily expose any part of the body to substances which are injurious to the skin.

(3) Where there is a danger of contact with moving parts of machinery or in any work process where a similar hazard exists–

(*a*) close fitting and close fastened clothing shall be worn; and
(*b*) head and facial hair shall be completely confined or cut short; and

(*c*) dangling neckwear, jewelry or other similar items shall not be worn.

(4) Where a person's clothing or skin becomes contaminated with any flammable or harmful substance, the clothing shall be removed at the first practical opportunity and the affected part of the body cleansed and, when necessary, medically treated as soon as possible.

23. PERSONAL PROTECTIVE EQUIPMENT.

(1) Industrial protective wear shall meet standards which are not less than the applicable requirements of–

(*a*) PNGS 1088 (industrial safety helmets); and
(*b*) PNGS 1092 (industrial eye protectors); and
(*c*) AS 1338 (protective filters against optical radiation in welding and allied operations); and
(*d*) PNGS 1089 (industrial safety gloves and mittens); and
(*e*) PNGS 1085 (safety footwear).

(2) Industrial protective headgear shall be worn by a person engaged in any operation at any location where potential hazards exist that could result in head injuries.

(3) Properly fitting goggles, face-shields or other eye protective equipment, appropriate to the work being done, shall be worn by a person who is or could be exposed to injury or irritation of the eyes.

(4) Industrial protective safety footwear shall be worn by all personnel engaged in any operation at any location where any hazard to the feet may exist.

(5) A person engaged in the handling of harmful substances which are injurious to the skin shall wear suitable protective clothing and equipment.

(6) All personal protective equipment and safety equipment, required by this Regulation, shall be kept in a safe and sanitary condition and maintained to properly perform the function for which it was designed.

24. NOISE LEVELS.

All personnel exposed to noise levels, which may be injurious to their hearing, shall be issued with appropriate hearing protection equipment, and/or the equipment shall be designed, modified or constructed in such a manner as to reduce noise levels to an acceptable level.

25. RADIOACTIVE SUBSTANCES.

All operations entailing the storage, handling and use of radioactive substances shall be carried out in accordance with current applicable regulations and in such a manner as to provide full protection against contamination of personnel, equipment and the environment.

26. NOTICES.

(1) The site person-in-charge shall cause to be displayed at an operational site, where appropriate, notices warning all personnel of any potential dangers that exist or may exist, and notices of the associated safety requirements needed for the protection of the personnel, equipment, environment and resources

(2) Notices under Subsection (1) shall be in accordance with PNGS 1086, and shall be in English and Tok Pisin and the prevalent common language of the area of operations or shall be of a type using internationally accepted pictorial formats and/or easily recognizable symbols.

27. PRESSURE VESSELS.

All boilers and unfired pressure vessels used in conjunction with petroleum operations shall be designed, manufactured, installed, tested, inspected and maintained in accordance with Part V of the Industrial Safety, Health and Welfare Act 1961.

28. MACHINERY.

(1) A workman assigned by his supervisor to operate any tool, machine or equipment, or to carry out any work, process, or procedure shall be competent to carry out the assignment in a safe manner.

(2) All equipment and drive assemblies used for the transmission of power, such as belts, ropes, chains, gears, sprockets, clutches, cranks, connecting rods and any other exposed moving part of machinery (except equipment operated from catheads and/or supported or driven by the rotary table) shall have guards installed of sufficient strength to withstand the breaking of said equipment and the guards shall be positioned such that personnel cannot unintentionally come in contact with the moving parts.

(3) Pinch points of all types of machines and the cutting edge of all power-driven tools shall, where practical, be guarded.

(4) Every abrasive wheel shall, where practical, be guarded.

(5) Where power-driven machinery is used, each machine shall have a stopping device located within easy reach of the workman operating the machinery.

(6) Every machine not individually motor-driven shall be equipped with a clutch or other efficient means of stopping the machine.

(7) Starting devices shall be arranged to prevent accidental starting.

29. WINCHING, LIFTING EQUIPMENT.

(1) The working load on winch mechanisms, lines, slings, hooks and fittings shall not exceed the safe working load recommended by the manufacturer and equipment shall be used only in the manner for which it is designed.

(2) Damaged, frayed or worn hoisting lines, slings and/or hooks shall be taken out of use immediately and replaced with new or competent replacements.

30. REPAIR AND MAINTENANCE OF MACHINERY.

In order to protect personnel from potential injury, the site person-in-charge shall ensure that safety procedures are in place, and used by all personnel, for the repair and maintenance of equipment in all operational areas under his control.

31. MOBILE EQUIPMENT.

All powered mobile equipment shall be suitably equipped to protect the operator, safely operate in the designated area, maintained in proper running order, and operated in such a manner as to prevent undue danger to personnel working in the same area.

32. RESPONSIBILITY OF DRIVER.

(1) The driver of any mobile equipment shall be directly responsible for the safe operation of his unit and its associated equipment.

(2) No person shall remain on or ride on any load or part of a load being raised or lowered.

(3) A tag line of sufficient length shall be used when required to ensure that any movement of the load cannot strike the person controlling the tag line.

(4) A person shall not work, stand or pass under or near a suspended load, or between a winch mechanism and a load being winched.

33. AIRCRAFT OPERATIONS.

(1) For the purposes of this section, "aircraft operations" means aircraft operations in connection with petroleum exploration operations or operations for recovery of petroleum.

(2) Except as provided in this section, all aircraft operations shall be conducted in accordance with existing laws of Papua New Guinea relating to civil aviation.

(3) An order given by a pilot of an aircraft–

(*a*) while the aircraft is airborne or moving shall be obeyed immediately by all passengers; and
(*b*) affecting the loading of the aircraft, the method of approaching the aircraft and the embarkation or disembarkation of the aircraft while the aircraft is stationary, shall be obeyed.

(4) All persons shall exercise extreme care when approaching a helicopter when its rotors are in motion.

(5) Whenever practicable, a pilot of a helicopter shall adopt a flight path which avoids over flying a rig, camp or field facility, production facility and/or petroleum processing facility.

(6) Where helicopters are used, the following procedures shall be adhered to:–

(*a*) one person shall be designated as responsible for hooking on or unhooking an externally slung suspended load;
(*b*) when the person referred to in Paragraph (a) has carried out his task, he shall stand clear and signal the pilot that his task has been completed;
(*c*) all other persons shall stand clear of the externally slung suspended load;
(*d*) at an onshore rig location where all transportation is by helicopter, a helipad shall be constructed at a safe distance from the rig so that personnel can be safely evacuated in case of an emergency;
(*e*) when not in use, a helipad shall be kept clear at all times;
(*f*) stocks of appropriate aviation fuel shall be maintained at a drilling location and shall be situated at a safe place;
(*g*) during well testing, helicopter operations shall be conducted in such a manner as to be consistent with flying safety and to minimize the effect of rotor down wash on any flare or heat shield;
(*h*) at an onshore rig location, each helipad shall be equipped with adequate fire fighting equipment so that a fire inside or outside the helicopter can be safely and effectively fought and so that rescue and other personnel can be effectively protected during such fire or helicopter evacuation.

34. DEBRIS CONSTITUTING A FIRE HAZARD.

(1) Rubbish, debris, or refuse that might constitute a fire hazard shall be removed to a safe distance of not less than 50m from all buildings, installations, wells or production facilities, and shall be expeditiously and safely disposed of in an environmentally acceptable manner.

(2) All hydrocarbon based refuse shall be collected in adequate containers and disposed of in an environmentally acceptable manner.

35. FLAME TYPE EQUIPMENT AND PROCESS VESSELS.

(1) No person shall create or cause to be created any unprotected flame or source of ignition within 50m of a well, oil storage tank or other source of flammable vapour unless under approved work permit conditions.

(2) No flame type equipment shall be placed or operated within 50m of any well, storage tank or process vessel unless the flame type equipment is fitted with an adequate flame arrester and air inlets are adequately flame proofed unless under approved work permit conditions.

(3) No process vessel containing flammable material shall be placed within 25m of any well or storage tank unless otherwise approved by the Director.

(4) Where the size of the location prevents the spacing specified in Subsections (1), (2), and (3), the distances may be reduced to the maximum attainable, but not so as to relieve the licensee from constructing a location of as adequate in size as practical.

36. VENTING OF FLAMMABLE VAPOURS.

(1) All process vessels, instruments and equipment, from which any flammable vapour may issue, shall be safely vented to atmosphere.

(2) All vent lines from process vessels or storage tanks which are vented to flare pits or flare stacks shall be provided with a flame arrester or other equivalent safety devices.

(3) When venting flammable vapours from a well, the operator shall ensure that any dedicated recovery tank/blow down tank is located–

(*a*) a minimum of 25 from the well centre; and
(*b*) so that vapours are carried off location by the prevailing winds of that area,

and where the provisions of Paragraphs (a) or (b) cannot be met, the tank shall be a closed type with a vent line that meets the conditions of Paragraphs (a) and (b) or is directed to a flare as specified under Section 40.

(4) In all cases of venting of flammable vapours, gas detection equipment shall be utilized to determine vapour levels with specific reference to possible ignition sources.

37. INTERNAL COMBUSTION ENGINES.

(1) An internal combustion engine within 50m of a well, process vessel, storage tank or other potential source of flammable vapour shall be fitted with effective spark-arresting equipment.

(2) An internal combustion engine, operated within 25m of a well, a process vessel, storage tank or other potential source of flammable vapour–

(*a*) shall be of the compression ignition type; and
(*b*) the engine and all ancillary components shall be rendered externally spark proof; and
(*c*) exhaust pipes, manifolds and turbo chargers shall be

insulated, cooled, and/or otherwise constructed so as to preclude the ignition of flammable vapours.

(3) A compression ignition engine within 25m of a well, separator, storage tank or other source of flammable vapour shall be provided with one of the following:–

(*a*) an air intake shut-off valve operated by engine overspeed, remotely controlled from the rig floor or readily accessible location;
(*b*) a system for injecting an inert gas into the cylinders operated by engine overspeed, remotely controlled from the rig floor or other readily accessible location;
(*c*) a duct so that air for the engine is obtained at least 25m from the source of flammable vapour;
(*d*) such other device as may be approved in writing by the Director; or
(*e*) temporary equipment powered by compression ignition engines that do not meet the requirements of Paragraphs (a), (b), and (c) may be used under a permit to work system as outlined in the approved operations manual.

(4) Where a system has been installed in accordance with Subsection (3)(a) or (b), no part shall be sited within 6m of the vertical centre-line of the well or in a hazardous area, and the operation of the shut down system shall be tested at the following times:–

(*a*) where the engine forms part of a drilling rig–before the surface casing shoe is drilled out and thereafter at intervals of not more than seven days;
(*b*) where the engine forms part of a well servicing /workover rig and/or associated equipment–before commencing operations on any well, and thereafter at intervals of not more than seven days;
(*c*) where the engine is part of a production facility–at the commencement of operations and thereafter at intervals not exceeding one calendar month.

(5) Tests specified under Subsection (4) shall be recorded–

(*a*) where the engine forms part of a drilling or well servicing/workover rig and/or associated equipment, on the tour report; or
(*b*) where the engine does not form part of a drilling or well servicing/workover rig and/or associated equipment, in the log book required to be kept pursuant to Section 43(7).

(6) Notwithstanding Subsections (2) and (3), a compression ignition engine, meeting the design requirements of Subsections (1), (2) and (3), may be used on permanent well pumping installation providing it is not within 6m of the wellhead, process vessel or storage tank and it is inspected on a regular basis.

38. SMOKING, NAKED LIGHTS, WELDING AND CUTTING.

(1) Subject to Subsection (3) smoking, open fires or naked lights shall not take place or be located within a distance of 50m from any well, separator, storage tank, temporary production facility, or other potential source of flammable vapour.

(2) Well site geological and/or mud logging units located closer than 25 from the well centre shall be suitably equipped for hazardous area use and where any electrical or gas fueled equipment, which does not meet hazardous area classification, is used inside these units, the units shall be pressurized and obtain their source of air supply at a distance greater than 25 from the well centre.

(3) Electrical and gas or other fuel circuits, to which unprotected equipment is connected, shall be controlled by a master switch or shut-off, readily accessible to the occupant of the caravan or unit, so that in the case of a hazard arising, the supply from any such circuit can immediately be shut off.

(4) In the case of routine operations or emergencies requiring the use of welding or flame cutting equipment, the site person-in-charge, using the permit to work procedures that have been outlined in the Operations Manual submitted to and approved by the Director, may authorize the use of such equipment within the limits stated in Subsection (1), providing that he has taken all reasonable precautions to ensure that the area is, and will remain, in a safe condition for such operations.

39. SITING OF PRODUCTION FACILITIES.

(1) Separators, tanks, heaters and other production facilities shall not be constructed within 50m of a preexisting non-associated surveyed road or building.

(2) Similar production facilities may be grouped, but dissimilar facilities shall not be located within 50m of each other unless otherwise approved by the Director.

(3) A separator shall not be enclosed within a bund or firewall surrounding a tank or group of tanks.

40. SITING OF FLARES.

(1) A flare pit or end of flare line shall not be located within a distance of 50m from any point on the outside of a well, separator, below ground pipeline, storage tank, temporary production facility or other unprotected source of flammable vapours and any exemptions from this minimum distance must be obtained from the Chief Inspector.

(2) A flare pit or end flare line shall not be located within a distance of 50m from a surveyed road, above ground pipeline or non-associated building, provided that topographical conditions allow for such distances and any exemptions from this minimum distance must be obtained from the Chief Inspector.

(3) The flare line shall be securely staked down and as free of bends, tees or elbows as possible.

(4) Where it is practicable to do so, a flare pit, of a sufficient size and design, shall be constructed to contain the produced fluids and protect the producing facility, property, natural vegetation and personnel from the flare and resulting heat.

(5) Where large volumes of gas and/or oil are to be burnt and topographic conditions do not allow the flare line to be extended further than the 50m referred to in Subsection (1), a flare shield shall be constructed in a manner and of a standard acceptable to the Chief Inspector.

(6) A safe, reliable and continuous method of igniting flares, acceptable to a Petroleum Inspector, shall be provided.

(7) All permanent flare installations shall be fenced off and surrounded by a low retaining wall.

(8) Adequate supervision and fire fighting equipment shall be provided to meet an emergency during flaring operations.

41. FUEL TANKS.

(1) Gasoline or other liquid fuel shall not be stored within 50m of a well unless it is stored in an appropriate operating storage tank with facilities in place to prevent any leakage or spillage from contacting the ground.

(2) Spillage or leakage referred to in Subsection (1) shall be directed away from the well location and disposed of in an environmentally acceptable manner.

42. LIGHTING.

Lights, that conform to the requirements of Part IV, shall be located at all operational sites so that adequate illumination provides for safe working conditions.

43. GENERAL SAFETY PRECAUTIONS.

(1) Any equipment, that does not afford reasonable safety from accidents, shall not be used.

(2) All work areas and pedestrian areas shall be kept reasonably clear of hazards.

(3) All hand tools shall be kept in a good state of repair and neatly stored when not in use.

(4) Fixed platforms, walkways, stairways and ladders shall conform with PNGS 1081.

(5) All buildings, structures, machinery and equipment shall be of sufficient size and strength to withstand safely the imposed loads and to perform safely the functions for which they are used.

(6) Inspections of all buildings, structures, machinery and equipment shall be made by a qualified person, as often as the character thereof and the type of operation being conducted requires, to ensure the safety of the unit and compliance with Regulations and relevant laws.

(7) The person performing the inspection shall make a written report of the inspection and shall forward a copy of a report to the Director and the site person-in-charge as soon as possible after its completion.

(8) A log-book shall be kept and there shall be recorded therein, in a form and manner acceptable to the Director, a report of each inspection under Subsection (6) and the result thereof, and such report shall be signed by the person performing the inspection and by the site person-in-charge.

(9) Any defective equipment or unsafe condition, found on an inspection, shall be corrected, repaired, or replaced, and each such correction, repair or replacement shall be noted on the report.

(10) A person having custody of a log book under Subsection (8) shall produce it on demand by a Petroleum Inspector, who may review it, make entries and give written instructions.

44. PROCEDURE MANUALS.

(1) The Operator shall–

(*a*) prepare a manual of instructions for the safety of operations; and
(*b*) prepare a manual of response to emergencies which may occur; and
(*c*) prepare a manual of procedures, equipment and instructions for the maintenance of well control; and
(*d*) when applicable, prepare a manual of procedures,

equipment, instructions and training for safe operations in any area where hydrogen sulfide gas may exist at dangerous concentration levels; and
(*e*) submit such manuals to the Director for his review and approval prior to the commencement of operations.

(2) A manual under Subsection (1)(a) shall–

(*a*) detail procedures to be taken to safeguard the health and safety of all personnel associated with all foreseen operations to be performed and to safeguard the environment in which the operations are situated; and
(*b*) contain provisions relating to special precautions at any operational site; and
(*c*) take into account any potential adverse condition arising from the operations.

(3) A manual under Subsection (1)(b) shall detail procedures to be followed and actions to be taken and shall identify the persons to be responsible for following these procedures and taking these actions in the event of an emergency arising during the operations by reasons of–

(*a*) the escape or ignition of petroleum; or
(*b*) serious injury to a person; or
(*c*) the failure of a vessel or aircraft to arrive at its destination when it is expected to arrive, unless a report has been made as to the reason for the non-arrival; or
(*d*) a vessel or aircraft sending a distress signal; or
(*e*) conditions requiring the evacuation and/or abandonment of an operational site or camp; or
(*f*) a person overboard; or
(*g*) damage to or failure of equipment that adversely affects the operations; or
(*h*) any other emergency associated with the operations.

(4) A manual under Subsection (1)(c) shall detail the procedures, equipment, personnel and facilities that will be utilized to maintain well control or regain well control in the event of a kick or blowout situation.

(5) All personnel at an operational site are to be made aware of the procedures detailed in the manuals and shall have access to copies of the manuals at all reasonable times, and the site person-in-charge shall be fully conversant with the procedures related to the operation under his control.

45. MEDICINAL AND THERAPEUTIC DRUGS.

(1) A person who brings onto an operational site any medicinal or therapeutic drug, whether prescribed or not, shall, on arrival, report to the person referred to in Section 18(8) the nature and quantity of each such drug in that person's possession or control and, where it is prescribed, by whom it was prescribed.

(2) The person referred to in Section 18(8) shall maintain a record of the information given to that person pursuant to Subsection (1).

(3) On each operational site, the person referred to in Section 18(8) shall maintain a register which records each use of medicinal or therapeutic drugs–

(*a*) the date and dosage of every such use known to that person; and
(*b*) the name of the person to whom the drug was administered; and
(*c*) the name of the person who authorized the use of the drug.

(4) Any person on an operational site who is taking medication, whether prescribed or not, which impairs his ability to safely perform his duties, shall not remain on duty.

46. UNAUTHORIZED USE OF DRUGS AND INTOXICANTS.

(1) A person on an operational site shall not (otherwise than in the course of his duties) have in his possession or control any drug (which he is prohibited by law from having in his possession or control) or any intoxicant.

(2) A person on an operational site, who (otherwise than in the course of his duties, or as a result of any medical treatment or therapy administered to him) has in his possession or control, or is adversely affected by, any intoxicant or drug, which he is by law prohibited from having in his possession or control, shall immediately be relieved of his duties and removed as soon as practical and a report of the incident shall be sent to the Director forthwith.

47. HELICOPTER OPERATIONS.

(1) When a helicopter is arriving at or departing from a manned site, there shall be a person or persons on the site who shall ascertain and advise the helicopter pilot whether all requirements as to safety have been complied with and provide other pertinent information to ensure safety of helicopter operations, personnel and the recording of manifest, load and flight data.

(2) A person shall not be on the helideck/helipad on which or from which a helicopter is about to land or take off except for the purpose of handling an external load on the helicopter prior to landing or take off.

(3) All personnel shall be advised and/or trained in the proper procedures of helicopter embarkation, disembarkation and flight procedures.

(4) When a helicopter is about to land on or take off from a helideck/helipad, a revolving crane on or near the helideck/helipad shall not be operated and the jib of any such crane shall be placed in such a position as not to interfere with the landing or taking off of a helicopter.

(5) A person operating a crane referred to in Subsection (4) shall be advised in advance of the landing or taking off of a helicopter.

48. OIL SPILLS.

(1) Where an escape or ignition of petroleum occurs, such action as is necessary to minimize the loss of petroleum, the pollution of the area and to protect persons and property shall be taken.

(2) No chemical dispersant shall be used on an oil spill without approval from the Director.

Division 2.

Offshore.

49. GENERAL.

(1) The provisions of Division 1 shall apply with equal force to operations both onshore and offshore.

(2) Where any minimal distances specified in Sections 34 to 41 (inclusive) are impractical on a marine facility, the site person-in-charge shall ensure that the intent of this Regulation is observed so that sources of ignition are kept as far as possible from potential sources of flammable liquids and/or gas.

(3) Where there is an inconsistency between the provisions of this Division and Division 1, the provisions of this Division shall prevail.

50. COMMUNICATIONS.

(1) Where there is a manned platform in the licence area, there shall, at all times, be maintained a shore station from which radio or telephone communication is made to and received from the platform.

(2) Radio or telephone communication shall be made from the shore station to the platform at least once in each period of eight hours, except when the site person-in-charge of the platform has ordered that, due to restrictive operations, such communication shall not be made.

(3) Where the site person-in-charge has made an order under Subsection (2) the shore station shall be informed before the order is put into effect.

(4) A stand-by vessel shall be stationed in the immediate vicinity of the platform and shall remain so stationed except if required for the purpose of dealing with a serious emergency.

(5) When communication cannot be made by radio or by telephone between the shore station and the platform or its stand-by vessel, arrangements shall be made forthwith for communication to the platform by sea or air methods.

(6) Each support vessel or aircraft, in use during operations, shall be controlled and monitored from a shore station and/or a platform.

51. RESCUE CRAFT.

(1) A suitable helicopter service shall be maintained between a platform and the shore station.

(2) Where it is not possible to maintain a suitable helicopter service, pursuant to Subsection (1), there shall, where weather conditions allow, be provided a suitable surface craft able to come to the assistance of that platform within a minimum amount of time.

(3) A surface craft referred to in Subsection (2) shall be so designed, equipped and crewed as to be able safely to retrieve all platform personnel from the sea under adverse sea and weather conditions and administer adequate first aid as necessary.

52. HELICOPTER OPERATIONS.

(1) Prior to a helicopter landing or taking off, the site person-in-charge shall ensure a fully trained fire fighting crew is mustered to the helideck.

(2) The fire fighting crew shall man the fire fighting equipment and one member of the crew shall wear a close proximity fire fighting suit.

(3) When a helicopter is about to land on or take off from a platform, any handrails on the helideck shall be folded onto the deck.

53. LIFE JACKETS AND BUOYANCY VESTS.

(1) Unless otherwise approved, a person shall wear a life jacket, certified by a recognized institution, when engaged in an emergency drill or when evacuating a platform.

(2) A person who is in an unguarded area over water shall wear an approved buoyancy vest.

(3) A person on an open deck of a fixed platform, which open deck is at a level close to the maximum wave height, shall be accompanied by at least one other person and both shall wear an approved buoyancy vest.

(4) A person being transferred between a platform and a vessel shall wear an approved buoyancy vest or life jacket.

(5) A person being transported to or from a platform, either by sea or by air, shall wear an approved life jacket as directed by the captain of the vessel.

54. VESSELS NEAR PLATFORMS DURING DIVING.

Where diving operations are being carried out from a platform, the person in command of a vessel shall not cause it to approach or depart from the platform, or cause its propellers or thrusters to be engaged, without notifying and receiving approval from the site person-in-charge of the diving operations.

55. OTHER OPERATIONS DURING DIVING.

Where diving operations are being carried out from a platform, a person shall not–

(*a*) weld on the platform, unless approved by the site person-in-charge, and such welding is carried out under a permit to work system as outlined in the Procedure Operations Manual, as detailed in Section 44, which has been forwarded to and approved by the Director; or
(*b*) carry our any activity at a place from which sparks or slag could fall upon any item of diving equipment being used for diving operations; or
(*c*) operate a crane or other equipment not associated with diving operations or carry out any activity where diving personnel or diving equipment engaged in or being used for the diving operations could be struck by any material moving or falling as a result of the use of the crane or other equipment or the carrying out of the activity; or
(*d*) transfer methanol, diesel fuel or other flammable or combustible substances between a supply vessel and the platform; or
(*e*) carry out any operations involving explosives on or near the platform; or
(*f*) carry out operations associated with de-pressurizing vessels or pipelines as a result of which hydrocarbons could be released on or near the platform.

56. EMERGENCY DRILL EXERCISES.

All persons on a platform shall participate in escape drill exercises and fire drill exercises, which shall be carried out under the control of the site person-in-charge, at random times not exceeding seven days between each time, and a record shall be kept of such drills.

57. NOTICES.

(1) All exits from the accommodation, office and other enclosed areas will be clearly marked.

(2) Emergency assembly location notices shall be prominently displayed on all platforms.

58. WASTE DISPOSAL.

(1) No waste materials other than food scraps, sanitary effluents, drilling fluid or formation water conforming to the requirements of Section 190 shall be released into the sea.

(2) All waste materials, other than those as stated in Subsection (1), shall be stored on the platform in a safe and environmentally suitable manner and returned to shore for proper disposal.

59. RECORD OF ARRIVALS AND DEPARTURES.

(1) A written record, relating to one platform, in accordance with this section shall contain–

(*a*) the name of each person traveling to or from the platform and the name of his employer; and
(*b*) the date and time at which each person arrives at, or leaves from, the shore station; and
(*c*) the date and time at which each person arrives at, or leaves from, the platform; and

(2) A record in accordance with Subsection (1) shall be kept at each platform and at each shore station.

60. RADIO OPERATORS.

A radio operator on a platform shall hold at least a restricted radiotelephone operator's certificate of proficiency or equivalent and shall have experience in radio operations associated with offshore operations and be proficient in the English language.

61. CUTTING, HEATING AND WELDING.

(1) No cutting, heating or welding shall be carried out on a platform unless–

(*a*) the operation is carried out in accordance with PNGS 1115 (Fire Precautions in Cutting, Heating and Welding Operations); and
(*b*) the site person-in-charge of the platform has determined that it is safe to carry out the cutting, heating or welding operation, and has issued a 'work permit' that complies with the procedures manual referred to in Section 44; and
(*c*) any shielding or screening used in the hot work operation is of a material which is combustion resistant.

(2) The safety manual referred to in Section 44 shall contain provisions relating to the special precautions to be taken during cutting, heating or welding near–

(*a*) drilling operations; and
(*b*) well-head and production areas; and
(*c*) tanks containing flammable or combustible liquids; and
(*d*) diving operations.

(3) Electric welding neutral returns shall be connected directly to the equipment being welded.

(4) The issue of a work permit shall take into account any adverse conditions arising from the ongoing operations.

62. STORAGE OF DANGEROUS SUBSTANCES.

(1) No flammable liquids with a flash point below 38° C, as determined by the method PNGS 1449 set out in "Standard Methods for Testing Petroleum and its Products" or any other approved specifications, shall be kept on a platform without approval.

(2) Drum stocks of fuel or lubricating oil on a platform shall be stored as far as reasonably possible from areas where drilling operations are being carried out.

(3) A gas cylinder on a platform shall be properly secured in an upright position.

(4) No gas cylinder shall be transferred between a platform and a vessel, unless that cylinder is contained within an approved container.

(5) Potassium and sodium nitrates shall be stored in leak-proof containers, away from combustible materials.

PART IV. – ELECTRICAL INSTALLATIONS.

63. WIRING RULES.

(1) Subject to the requirements of any other law, all electric wiring, earthing and installations used in the exploration and drilling for, and the production of petroleum, whether in or outside hazardous locations as described in Subsection (2), shall be in accordance with PNGS 1022 (Wiring Rules)or other codes or standards as approved by the Director.

(2) Hazardous locations in which the provisions of Class 1, Zone 1 and Class 1, Zone 2 of the S.A.A. Wiring Rules shall apply, shall be–

(*a*) Class 1, Zone 1–all areas classified as division 1 in API RP500B, "Classification of Areas for Electrical Installations at Drilling Rigs and Production Facilities on Land and on Marine Fixed and Mobile Platforms"; and
(*b*) Class 1, Zone 2–all areas within 20m of a wellhead, temporary or permanent production facility and all areas within 20m of an area classified as Class 1, Zone 1.

(3) Within an area classified as Class 1 Zone 2 as above–

(*a*) the Director may approve the use of electrical equipment of vapor tight construction that is totally enclosed and gasketed to exclude or resist the passage of vapor; and
(*b*) all electrical connectors such as plugs and sockets shall have a mechanical device acceptable to a Petroleum Inspector to prevent inadvertent breaking of any electrical circuit capable of producing arcing or sparking.

64. ELECTRICAL GENERATORS, ALTERNATORS AND MOTORS.

(1) Subject to Subsections (2) and (5), no permanent electrical generator or electrical alternator shall be operated within 25m of a wellhead, temporary or permanent production facility or within 25m of an area classified as Class 1, Zone 1, unless the generator or electrical alternator has approved flame protection.

(2) Temporary electrical generators or alternators without approved flame protection may be operated within 25m by use of a permit to work system, under control of the site person-in-charge, that is outlined in the company's Operation Manual which has been presented to and approved by the Director.

(3) Subject to Subsections (4) and (5), no cooling or purge air for an electrical motor shall be drawn from a point within 25m of a wellhead, temporary or permanent production facility or within 25m of an area classified as Class 1 Zone 1, unless the motor has approved flame protection.

(4) Temporary electrical motors without approved flame protection may draw cooling or purge air within 25m by use of a permit to work system under control of the site person-in-charge, as outlined in the company's Operation Manual which has been presented to and approved by the Director.

(5) An electrical motor or electrical alternator or electrical generator may be used on a permanent well pumping installation providing it is not within 6m of the wellhead, process vessel or storage tank, and it meets the requirements as set out in Subsection (1) and Subsection (3).

65. RIG ELECTRICAL SYSTEMS EQUIPMENT.

(1) All electrical equipment shall be maintained in accordance with the original design.

(2) Flexible electrical cables intended for hard usage shall have inherent resistance to dampness, abrasion and petroleum products.

(3) All power cables shall be installed so that they are protected, as much as practical, from damage.

(4) Cables shall be repaired or replaced when insulation damage is detected, and makeshift wiring components and installations shall not be used.

66. PROTECTION OF ELECTRICAL CIRCUITS.

(1) Every circuit shall be protected against overload and short circuit in accordance with the PNGS 10223 (Wiring Rules).

(2) Except where approved otherwise by the Director, circuits above extra-low voltage shall be protected against leakage of current to earth by the use of approved circuit breakers and such protection systems shall be provided with means by which a function test of the effectiveness may be made.

67. EARTHING AND LIGHTNING PROTECTION.

(1) The structure of permanent oilfield facilities for handling flammable liquids shall be protected against lightning in accordance with the ASI 768 "Lightning Protection" or other approved code of practice for the protection of such structures from damage by lightning.

(2) The structure of a temporary drilling rig need not be so protected against lightning if it is earthed so that the maximum resistance to earth is not greater than 10 ohms.

68. CONTROL OF STATIC ELECTRICITY.

(1) All metal parts of masts and rig substructures within a hazardous location shall be earthed for the safe removal of static electricity so that the maximum resistance to earth is less than 10 ohms.

(2) The well casing may be used in the case of masts, provided that it is electrically connected to all tools and other equipment being used in operations such as drilling, servicing and pulling.

(3) Metallic parts of containers of flammable liquids shall be earthed for the safe removal of charges of static electricity, but shall not be connected in such manner as to form part of the earth circuit.

(4) Where transferring flammable liquids or finely divided flammable or explosive materials from one container to another, the containers shall be in firm contact with each other or be

continuously electrically bonded throughout the transfer so as to prevent the accumulation of static charges.

(5) Where tanks, mixers or processing vessels are used for flammable or explosive liquids or compounds, they shall be electrically bonded and earthed while being filled or emptied.

69. PORTABLE LIGHTS AND TOOLS.

(1) Subject to Subsection (2), a portable light or tool used in a hazardous location shall be of flameproof construction.

(2) The Person-in-Charge, utilizing approved permit to work procedures, may authorize the use of a portable tool having a vapor tight or general purpose enclosure by ensuring that the area is, and remains, in a safe condition with the continual use of approved gas detection equipment.

(3) The voltage of a hand-held portable light and tool shall not exceed 32 volts unless there is installed and adequate system of earth leakage protection or other adequate protective device, and in such case the voltage of a hand held tool shall not exceed 250 volts.

(4) An electrically operated hand tool shall be tested and examined at regular intervals by a suitably qualified person, any defect shall be corrected and results recorded.

70. MAINTENANCE, REPAIR OR ALTERATIONS.

(1) Maintenance, repair or alteration of any conductor or apparatus shall not be carried out while such conductor or apparatus is alive.

(2) Switches opened to permit work on lines or equipment shall be prominently marked to warn against closure.

(3) Before any item of electrical equipment, except a portable lamp or tool, is moved, it shall be disconnected from the power supply.

(4) The rewiring and replacement of an electrical fuse may be carried out by an authorized person, but shall be checked as soon as possible thereafter by a licensed electrical worker.

(5) An electric welding return conductor shall be connected directly to the equipment being welded as well as to the earthing system of the rig or operational unit.

71. ELECTRICIANS AND INSPECTION OF ELECTRICAL EQUIPMENT.

(1) Subject to Subsections (2) and (3), a person other than a licensed electrical worker shall not, on any drilling rig, production facility or associated plant–

(*a*) install electrical apparatus or circuits; or
(*b*) maintain electrical apparatus or cables including any automatic or other protective device; or
(*c*) carry out a routine examination or test of any electrical apparatus or cables; or
(*d*) carry out a routine test of the effectiveness of the earthing system, the continuity of the earthing conductors or the conditions of the electrical insulation; or
(*e*) carry out an examination or test of electrical apparatus or cables newly connected, or dismantled and reconnected in a new position.

(2) Subsection (1)(c), (d) and (e) shall not apply to apparatus carrying voltages not exceeding extra low voltage.

(3) Subsections (1) and (2), shall not apply to any apparatus in and ancillary to electric logging units, gas detection units and electronically equipped production control and gauging installations.

(4) A test or examination referred to in Subsection (1) shall be carried out–

(*a*) in the case of a drilling rig–prior to spudding in each well and at intervals not exceeding two months thereafter; and
(*b*) in the case of a temporary installation–at intervals not exceeding two months; and
(*c*) in the case of a permanent installation–at intervals not exceeding six months.

(5) The results of a test or examination under Subsection (1) shall be recorded by the electrical worker on the tour report or in a log book provided for the purpose, shall be countersigned by the site person-in-charge, and a copy shall be maintained, and upon request by a Petroleum Inspector, made available for review.

72. CONTROL EQUIPMENT.

(1) Switch gear and starting equipment for motors shall include an isolating switch interlocked with the cover of the equipment so as to prevent the opening or removal of that cover whilst the apparatus within is alive or the isolator is in the closed position.

(2) All live parts within the switch gear and starting equipment, which are exposed when such equipment is opened, shall be effectively screened to the satisfaction of a Petroleum Inspector.

PART V. – EXPLOSIVES.

Division 1.

General.

73. APPLICATION OF DIVISION 1.

The provisions of this Division shall apply wherever explosives are used in connection with the exploration for and the production of petroleum, but compliance with this Division shall not excuse a person from compliance with the Explosive Act (Adopted).

74. COMPETENCE OF WORKMEN.

A person shall not use, handle, prepare or fire explosives unless he is–

(*a*) the holder of an appropriate permit issued under Section 7 of the Explosives Act (Adopted); or
(*b*) under the direct personal supervision and direction of a person referred to in Paragraph (a).

75. STORAGE OF EXPLOSIVES, MAGAZINES.

Explosives shall be stored in accordance with the provisions of the Explosives Act (Adopted) and be under the supervision of an authorized site person-in-charge and magazines shall be made intrinsically safe from potential sources of ignition.

76. DETONATORS.

Except where approved by the Director, detonators other than electric detonators shall not be used.

77. APPLICATION FOR USE OF EXPLOSIVES.

(1) Prior to an operator commencing a geophysical or geological program of operations, that utilizes explosives in Papua New Guinea, a manual shall be submitted to the Director for review which includes operational, procedural and safety issues including, but not limited to the following items:–

(*a*) storage;
(*b*) transportation–land, marine and/or air;
(*c*) handling;
(*d*) personnel safety;
(*e*) detonating near surface facilities;
(*f*) loading shot holes;
(*g*) misfires;
(*h*) training of personnel;
(*i*) environmental issues.

(2) The Person-in-Charge shall submit the manual as outlined in Subsection (1) to the Director with the current notice of intention of a survey and shall update the manual as required for following surveys.

78. ELECTRICAL FIRING IN THE VICINITY OF A RADIO TRANSMITTER.

Electrical firing shall not take place in the vicinity of a live radio broadcasting transmitter unless the distance from the shot point to the base of the nearest mast is not less than that set out in the following table of minimum distances based on the power of the transmitter:

Transmitter Power (WATTS)	Minimum Distance (m)
5 - 25	50
25 - 50	70
50 - 100	100
100 - 500	220
500 - 1,000	300
1,000 - 5,000	700
5,000 - 10,000	1,000
10,000 - 50,000	2,200
50,000 - 100,000	3,000

79. PRE-LOADING.

(1) Where in seismic prospecting in populated areas, shot holes are pre-loaded, the detonator wires shall be short-circuited and concealed until they are connected to the firing circuit, and notices in accordance with Section 26 shall be displayed warning people of danger from explosives.

(2) All pre-loaded holes shall be fired as soon as practicable after charging.

Division 2.

Use of explosives in wells.

80. APPLICATION OF DIVISION 2.

The provisions of this Division shall apply where explosives are used in a well for the exploration for or production of petroleum, and where there is an inconsistency between the provisions of this Division and the provisions of Division 1, the provision of this Division shall prevail.

81. PERSONNEL HANDLING EXPLOSIVES.

The use, handling, preparation and firing of explosives for the purposes specified in Section 80 and the disposal of any misfires resulting therefrom shall be done by or under the direct personal supervision of a competent person, experienced in the use of explosives for such purposes.

82. SAFETY OF RIG PERSONNEL.

During rig floor operations involving equipment charged with explosives, only work that is essential to that operation shall take place utilizing only those persons necessary to carry out that work and all other persons shall remain at a safe distance.

83. SAFETY FROM ACCIDENTAL DETONATION.

The site person-in-charge is responsible for ensuring the safety of the operation against accidental detonation from all sources that may include stray electrical currents, electrical charges and radio transmissions.

PART VI. – EXPLORATION.

Division 1.

General.

84. APPLICATION OF PART VI.

Unless otherwise specified to the contrary, the provisions of Part VI shall apply to geophysical, geological and/or their related operations carried out in the search for petroleum.

85. NOTICE OF INTENTION TO COMMENCE OPERATIONS.

(1) No operation referred to in Section 84 shall commence without the written approval of the Director.

(2) The Director may impose conditions of approval and any such conditions shall be observed.

86. NOTICE OF INTENDED SURVEY.

(1) At least 14 days before commencing a geophysical, geological and/or a related exploration program, the Person-in-Charge shall submit to the Director, in duplicate, a Notice of Intention to carry out the program.

(2) A Notice of Intention submitted under Subsection (1) shall include, but not be restricted to, the following information:–

(*a*) licence area;
(*b*) name of the licensee;
(*c*) name of survey;
(*d*) objective of survey;
(*e*) prime survey method and techniques;
(*f*) any secondary survey method;
(*g*) name and address of contractor;
(*h*) details of equipment to be used;
(*i*) estimated commencement date;
(*j*) estimated duration;

(*k*) line kilometres;
(*l*) estimated cost;
(*m*) line plans in duplicate, one at 1:250,000, one on A4 size paper;
(*n*) notice of Intended Entry on Land;
(*o*) name and address of site person-in-charge.
(*p*) manual, if required, as outlined in Section 77, unless previously submitted.

87. OPERATIONS NEAR MINES AND QUARRIES.

(1) No seismic operations shall take place within 300m of any operating mine or quarry, unless the Person-in-Charge notifies the Director accordingly and has received permission in writing from the Person-in-Charge of the said mine or quarry, a copy of which shall be forwarded to the Director.

(2) The operations to which Subsection (1) refers shall be conducted according to any special requirements as outlined by the Person-in-Charge of the mine or quarry and/or the Director.

88. OPERATIONS ON ROADS AND IN INHABITED AREAS.

(1) Where shot hole drilling or other geophysical or geological exploration is to be carried out on a road or track used by the public, or in the vicinity of an inhabited area, the site person-in-charge shall consult with the senior officer at the District or Sub-district Office nearest to the area of intended operations, or if in a township declared under the Town Boundaries Act 1951, the commander of the nearest Police Station.

(2) A wooden stake, spike, pin or other pointed metal object shall not, in the performance of any exploration program, be driven into the carriageway of any road or track.

(3) Where a seismic survey is conducted in the vicinity of buildings or public utilities, all practical precautions shall be taken to ensure that no damage or inconvenience is caused by the operation.

89. MARKING SEISMIC LINES.

A permanent marker shall be set in place at points of intersection of survey lines, at intersections of a survey line with any road which has been formed or graded and at intervals on each survey line of not more than 5km.

90. SHOT POINTS NEAR BUILDINGS AND PUBLIC UTILITIES.

(1) Unless otherwise approved by the Director in writing, a shot point shall not be located within the following distance of a building, a public utility of any description or a water well–

(*a*) 150m–in the case of shot holes;
(*b*) 100m–in the case of vibratory or other surface seismic sources.

(2) The site person-in-charge, if he considers it impracticable to fire a shot hole outside the distances specified in Subsection (1), may make application to the Director to fire a shot within such distances and the Director may grant such permission.

91. TEMPORARY SHOT HOLE PLUGS.

Where a drilling crew is in advance of a firing crew to the extent that a shot hole will not be fired on completion of drilling, a temporary plug or cover shall be placed in or over the shot hole until the firing crew is ready to fire the charge.

92. PERMANENT SHOT HOLE PLUGS.

Unless otherwise approved by the Director, a shot hole shall be suitably plugged with earth after firing and the disturbed area shall be restored, as far as practical, to the original state.

93. UNCONTROLLED FLOW OF WATER.

Where a flow of artesian water is encountered in the course of drilling operations, or detected subsequently, it shall be controlled, and the site person-in-charge shall report forthwith the flow of water to the Director advising him of the steps taken to control it.

94. SIX MONTHLY REPORTS ON OPERATIONS.

(1) A licensee shall submit to the Director a report on operations carried out within the area subject to a petroleum prospecting licence during each six monthly period after the date of issue of the licence, within one month after the end of the period to which the report relates.

(2) A report under Section 31(2)(c) of the Act shall include, in addition to a general review of the operations which have been carried out during the previous period, the following:–

(*a*) where there is an intention to carry out major geological or geophysical surveys during the next six monthly period, the notice of that intention;
(*b*) regional interpretation of the subsurface structure in all areas over which any combination of geophysical, geological, geochemical surveys and special studies have been conducted during the past period and any revised interpretations of adjacent areas resulting from the exploration in question.

(3) Each alternate such six monthly report is to be of a more comprehensive nature, and to include a general discussion of operations carried out, the conclusions derived therefrom and the main results obtained, mention of reports submitted during the year and an outline of work plans for the next year.

(4) Each second such six monthly report shall include seismic maps of key horizons at appropriate scales and details of annual expenditure covering time periods as agreed to by the Director.

(5) Where no operations are carried out in any six monthly period, a statement to this effect is to be submitted to the Director.

95. SUBMISSION OF DATA.

(1) The licensee shall submit to the Director, within four months of completion of any seismic, gravimetric or airborne geophysical survey operation, a report, in duplicate, in a form and content acceptable to the Director.

(2) A report submitted under Subsection (1)–

(*a*) shall contain, but shall not be restricted to, the topics listed in Section 238; and
(*b*) where so recorded, basic geophysical field data shall be

supplied in digital form and in a format agreed to between the licensee and the Director.

(3) The licensee shall submit to the Director within four months of completion or any other type of geophysical survey, geochemical survey of any major geological survey, a full report on the findings of such survey including geological maps, measured sections and other basic data obtained by such survey.

(4) The licensee shall submit to the Director at weekly intervals during the course of any geophysical survey progress reports including, as soon as they are available, preliminary plots of data, such as shot hole location plans, cross-sections, gravity profiles and magnetic profiles.

(5) As part of a completion report submitted under Subsections (1) or (3), there shall be supplied either a film negative (35mm) or other transparent copy of each plan larger than 380mm by 250mm or 8mm tape of the seismic sections in SEGY format.

96. SUBMISSION OF DATA ON RELINQUISHMENT.

(1) The licensee shall submit to the Director within 30 days of relinquishment of any portion of a petroleum prospecting licence all basic data derived from field operations on the relinquished area which have not previously been submitted to the Director.

(2) Data submitted under Subsection (1) shall include but not be restricted to the field records, aerial photography negatives, magnetic tapes (or any other digital information storage system), seismograms, film of final record sections, surveyor's notes, plane table sheets, shot-point location map, observers' tickets and shot hole logs.

(3) Where results of geological surveys are submitted under this section, they shall include all maps, sections and other data.

Division 2.

Offshore.

97. GENERAL.

The provisions of Sections 84, 85, and 86 (with the exception of Subsection (2)(n)), 94, 95 and 96 and of this Division shall apply to offshore exploration.

98. NOTICE OF INTENDED GEOPHYSICAL SURVEY OFFSHORE.

Where it is intended to carry out a geophysical survey offshore, in addition to the information required by Section 86 there shall also be submitted–

(*a*) a copy of current vessel classification; and
(*b*) evidence that the vessel and crew comply with the requirements of the Merchant Shipping Act 1975.

99. COMMENCEMENT OF SURVEY OFFSHORE.

A survey offshore shall not commence unless at least 48 hours notice of the date and time of commencement, the survey duration, the survey area coordinates and, in the case of a seismic survey, the length of streamers to be towed by the survey vessel has been given to–

(*a*) the Director or a Petroleum Inspector nominated by the Director; and
(*b*) the Department responsible for administering legislation relating to fisheries in the licence area; and

(*c*) Marine Search and Rescue Division of the Department of Transport, Port Moresby.

100. SEISMIC ENERGY SOURCES.

(1) Explosives shall not be used for an offshore seismic survey without the approval of the Director.

(2) An energy source used in a seismic survey shall be operated in accordance with good safety practices, the manufacturer's recommendations, and the requirements of Subsections (4), (5), (6) and (7), as applicable.

(3) A charge shall not be detonated underwater within–

(*a*) one nautical mile of the platform; and
(*b*) five nautical miles of the platform where diving operations are in progress;

unless adequate notification to the person in charge of the diving operations has been given of–

(*c*) the type of energy source to be used, its frequency and intensity; and
(*d*) the times at which the energy source is to be used; and
(*e*) any other pertinent information.

(4) Where an air gun is used in a seismic survey, system components shall be maintained in a clean and safe condition to comply with the manufacturers' specifications and safety procedures shall be implemented to ensure the proper and safe maintenance, testing and operation of the system and its associated components.

(5) Where gas exploders are used in a seismic survey full safety precautions shall be implemented to prevent accidental ignition and/or explosion of the gas and gas cylinders due to heat, electrical charges, open flame or other sources of ignition.

(6) Where steam sources are used in a seismic survey, high pressure and high temperature valves, lines and vessels shall be adequately protected and shall be clearly marked with warning signs and testing of the source shall be only done when the gun is fully immersed in water.

(7) Where sparker and boomer electrical systems are used in a seismic survey, circuits shall be equipped with circuit breakers, electrical cables shall be protected, adequately insulated and grounded and the operation of the sparker or boomer shall be only tested when the gun is fully immersed in water.

PART VII. – DRILLING, COMPLETION, RECOMPLETION, SIDETRACK, MAJOR REPAIR, SUSPENSION AND ABANDONMENT OF WELLS.

Division 1.

General.

101. NOTIFICATION BEFORE DRILLING A WELL.

(1) Subject to Subsection (2) and Section 104, the Person-in-Charge shall not commence to drill a well before–

(*a*) he has submitted to the Director a proposed well program for that well; and (*b*) he has received written approval of the proposed well program from the Director.

(2) Where–

(*a*) the Person-in-Charge has submitted a proposed well program to the Director under Subsection (1); and
(*b*) the Director has failed to reply concerning the proposed well program to the Person-in-Charge within 15 working days of the receipt by the Director of the proposed well program,

the Person-in-Charge may carry out the proposed well program without approval.

102. NOTIFICATION BEFORE DEEPENING, REDRILLING, ETC.

(1) Subject to Subsections (2) and (3) and Section 103, the Person-in-Charge shall not commence to deepen, sidetrack, complete, re-complete, workover, plug back or materially alter an existing approved well program or suspend or abandon, before–

(*a*) he has given a proposed program of operations to the Director; and
(*b*) he has received written approval from the Director to carry out the program.

(2) Where–

(*a*) the Person-in-Charge has given a program to the Director under Subsection (1); and
(*b*) the Director has failed to reply concerning the program of operations within 72 hours of the receipt of the program of operations,

the Person-in-Charge may carry out the work specified in the program of operations without approval.

(3) Where, for any unforeseen reason, minor changes in the approved well program are required to be made to reach the well objective, approval for such changes is not required, but a notice of intention to carry out the necessary work shall be sent to the Director at the earliest opportunity.

103. EMERGENCY ACTION.

The site person-in-charge shall, in the case of emergency, take such immediate action as is necessary to protect a well, personnel and/or the environment under the prevailing conditions, and shall, as soon as possible thereafter, notify the Director of the action taken.

104. PROPOSED WELL PROGRAM.

A Proposed Well Program shall include the following information as applicable:–

(*1*) Drilling Program:–

(a) licence area;
(b) licensee;
(c) operator;

(d) well name and number;
(e) location coordinates and graticular block number;
(f) elevation, ground and KB or DF;
(e) water depth (if applicable);
(g) total depth;
(h) estimated spud-in date;
(j) estimated completion date;
(k) geologic prognosis (accompanied by appropriate maps and cross-sections);
(l) drilling contractor;
(m) drilling rig designation;
(n) hole sizes and depths, complete with directional drilling program and well trajectory plot;
(o) casing sizes, weights, grades, coupling types and setting depths complete with design parameter assumptions, rationale and calculations based on Section 122 requirements;
(p) cementing program;
(q) mud program;
(r) sampling and mud logging program;
(s) coring program;
(t) logging program;
(u) testing program including surface equipment descriptions and its working pressure, placement of equipment relative to hazardous areas;
(w) service companies to be employed together with a brief description of the equipment to be provided;
(x) communication facilities;
(y) transportation facilities;
(z) medical facilities, including provisions made for evacuating sick or injured persons;
(aa) estimated costs;
(ab) a well control program and details of financial cover for regaining lost control and the clean up of any oil spills or damage caused;
(ac) names of well site supervisors and copies of current well control certification;
(ad) copy of water use permit;
(ae) plans for any potential flaring;

(2) A Rig Supported Completion/Workover Program shall include the following information as applicable:–

(a) licence area;
(b) licensee;
(c) operator;
(d) well name and number;
(e) location coordinates;
(f) elevation, ground and KB or DF;
(g) water depth (if applicable);
(h) total depth;
(i) estimated spud date;
(j) estimated completion date;
(k) current and/or proposed perforation details, measured depth and depth SS;
(l) existing top of cement behind casing and details on how determined;
(m) well deviation data over zones of interest;
(n) well completion diagrams of existing status and proposed completion/workover status;
(o) details of planned operations and equipment to be used;
(p) listing of contractors and services;
(q) estimated well cost;
(r) details of procedure to kill the well prior to workover;
(s) details for venting/flaring of vapors;

(t) well history, present producing status and workover justification with emphasis on maximization of recovery of hydrocarbons;
(u) for each reservoir to be worked over-petroleum in place, estimated ultimate recovery from workover, estimated cumulative recovery from zone, original and current pressures, original and present fluid contacts;

(*3*) Non Rig Supported Workover Program shall include such items as listed in Subsection (2) as may be applicable to the operation.

105. NOTICE OF INTENTION TO ABANDON.

A notice of intention to abandon a well shall give full details of the method of abandonment, withdrawal of casing, placement and confirmation of quality and position of plugs and capping, and a copy of electric or other type of log, not previously supplied to the Director, shall be supplied with the notice of the intention to abandon a well.

106. LOCATION SURVEY.

(1) As soon as practicable after the location of any well has been established, either on or offshore, and not later than three months after the well has been spudded, the location and elevation of the well shall be determined by a person and method that meets current Papua New Guinea legislation requirements and is approved by the Director.

(2) As soon as practicable, and not later than one month after completion of the survey for the location and elevation of a well, the licensee shall submit to the Director a plan certified as to accuracy by the person who made the survey.

(3) A plan under Subsection (2) shall, as applicable–

(*a*) show the location of the well relative to the control point; and
(*b*) show the well name and number; and
(*c*) show the control point and bench mark together with particulars thereof; and
(*d*) show any other wells, roads, public utilities and any substantial structures or buildings within 300m of the well; and
(*e*) indicate the coordinates of the well in the Papua New Guinea Map Grid and the latitude and longitude of the well computed within the accuracy limits of the survey previously specified, the direction of true north, the elevation of the natural surface and any permanent reference marks established in accordance with this Regulation; and
(*f*) shall be accompanied by a copy of the field notes and other data pertinent to the survey, unless the Director otherwise approves.

107. SUSPENSION OF OPERATIONS.

(1) A Person-in-Charge, who has commenced drilling, completing or working over a well, shall not suspend operations nor move major drilling items from the well without first having completed operations as approved by the Director.

(2) A program detailing the suspension operations and justification for the suspension shall be forwarded to the Director for his approval if prior approved well programs cannot be completed due to mitigating circumstances.

(3) All wells that have previously been active producers and/or injection wells–

(*a*) may be shut-in/suspended for a period of time not exceeding six months upon approval of the suspension program and justification forwarded to the Director; and
(*b*) applications for extension to the suspension period, including justification, shall be forwarded to the Director, by the Person-in-Charge, prior to the expiry date of the previous period.

(4) The Person-in-Charge shall forward a list of all shut-in and/or suspended wells to the Director on a yearly basis and include the reason for well status, suspension period dates for each well and forward plans for each well.

(5) The Person-in-Charge shall be responsible for ensuring the safety and integrity of all shut-in or suspended wells and shall abide by Section 139(1) of the Act.

108. FAILURE TO FULFILL CONDITIONS.

Where a program of operations is not carried out as approved by the Director, he may cause the program to be carried out in accordance with his requirements.

109. RESTORATION OF SITE.

On the completion, suspension or abandonment of a well, the Person-in-Charge shall, as soon as possible, restore the well site and any surrounding area or areas giving access, as near to the original state as can reasonably be done, unless he has already reached a mutually acceptable agreement in writing with the owner or occupier of the land affected (a copy of which must be forwarded to the Director), in accordance with the provisions of the Act and of this Regulation.

110. OIL OR GAS LOST OR USED DURING WELL OPERATIONS.

Unless otherwise approved by the Director, the quantities of all oil or gas lost by burning, venting to atmosphere, flaring or admixture with other circulating fluids in the course of any well completion, recompletion, or workover operations, shall be reported forthwith to the Director.

111. WELL RECORDS.

Careful and accurate records, relative to the drilling, completing, workover, re-completing, stimulating, suspending or abandoning of every well, shall be kept.

112. DAILY REPORTS.

(1) The site person in charge shall prepare an accurate daily report on each well being drilled, suspended, completed, repaired, tested, stimulated, recompleted or abandoned and dispatch a copy of each report to the Director as soon as practicable after its preparation.

(2) A report under Subsection (1) shall include those items as indicated in Section 239.

113. REPORTS ORIGINATING AT THE WELL SITE.

(1) Typed copies of the operator's daily drilling reports, leak off test reports, BOP test reports and casing pressure test reports shall be forwarded to the Director weekly to reach the Director within one week of the period covered.

(2) Tour reports in a form as specified by the International Association of Drilling Contractors (IADC) shall be retained by the operator or licensee and submitted to the Director upon request or upon expiration, relinquishment or other termination of the licence in which the well was drilled and/or worked over.

114. WELL COMPLETION REPORT.

(1) Within two months from the date of rig release of a well, there shall be forwarded to the Director–

(*a*) a completion report, or end of well report, in duplicate; and
(*b*) an electronic copy of that report on computer disc in a format agreed to by the Director.

(2) A completion report under Subsection (1) shall include, where applicable, but not be limited to, items listed in Section 240, but where those items involve third party analysis and final preparation they can be submitted under separate cover within three months.

(3) In the case of a well repair, recompletion or other operation in which the previous completion of the well is in any way modified, a revised down hole drawing detailing the final well and well equipment status shall be delivered to the Director within one month of the completion of the operation.

(4) On completion or recompletion of a well, transparent and/or computer retrievable (in a format approved by the Director)copies of all logs obtained from the well shall be delivered to the Director as soon as possible.

115. SPECIAL STUDIES.

A report of technical studies on samples and cores obtained from wells including, but not limited to, paleontology, permeability, porosity, fluid saturation, relative permeability, capillary pressure, fluid analysis and well test analysis shall, where for any reason not included in the completion report, be delivered to the Director as soon as they are available.

116. PROHIBITED DRILLING AREAS.

(1) A well shall not be drilled within 75m of any road, pipeline or flowline, high voltage power line, or other right of way, dwelling, industrial plant, aerodrome, building, school or church, unless otherwise approved in writing by the Director.

(2) A licensee who drills near an aerodrome shall comply with the requirements of the Department responsible for civil aviation matters.

(3) A well shall not be drilled within 3 km of known subsurface mine workings without the prior approval of the Director and then only under the conditions determined by the Director.

117. OPERATIONS CLOSE TO COMMUNITIES.

(1) Where drilling operations are to be carried out close to communities, the Person-in-Charge shall advise the Local-level Government, in whose area such operations are to be carried out or whose area is likely to be affected by such operation, of his intention to carry out such work.

(2) In the case of a serious blowout occurring during drilling operations in an area referred to in Subsection (1), the Person-in-Charge shall advise the police in that area so that proper measures can be taken to safeguard the general public.

118. DEVIATION SURVEY.

(1) Unless otherwise approved by the Director, surveys on a well being drilled shall be taken in sufficient number and at appropriate intervals to provide an accurate deviation profile of the wellbore from surface to total depth.

(2) Where the vertical projection to the surface of the point at which a well intersects a producing zone is nearer to a licence area boundary than 300m, the well shall not be brought into production without the prior approval of the Director.

Division 2.

Operational Requirements.

119. EQUIPMENT TO COMPLY WITH CERTAIN STANDARDS.

(1) Unless otherwise authorized by the Director, materials and equipment used in the drilling or rig assisted workover operations in a licence area shall conform to such current standards as are listed in this section.

(2) Masts and sub-structures shall be in accordance with the relevant requirements of API Specifications for Drilling and Well Service Structures, Spec. 4E.

(3) Rotary drilling equipment shall be in accordance with the relevant requirements of API Specification for Rotary Drilling Equipment, Spec. 7.

(4) Well casing and tubing, (other than structural or drive casing and high strength casing and tubing) and drill pipe shall be in accordance with the relevant requirements of API, Specification for Casing and Tubing, Spec. 5CT, and for drill pipe, Spec. 5D.

(5) High strength well casing and tubing shall be in accordance with the relevant requirements of API Specification for High Strength Casing and Tubing, Spec. 5CT.

(6) Wellhead equipment shall be in accordance with the relevant requirements of API Specification of Wellhead Equipment, Spec. 6A.

(7) Hoisting equipment shall be in accordance with the relevant requirements of API Specification for Drilling and Production Hoisting Equipment, Spec. 8A.

(8) The recommendations of API Recommended Practice for Hoisting Tool and Maintenance Procedures, RP 8B, shall be observed in the operation and maintenance of hoisting equipment.

(9) Wire rope shall be in accordance with the relevant requirements of API, Specification for Wire Rope, Spec. 9A.

(10) The recommendations of API, Recommended Practice for Application, Care and Use of Wire Rope for Oil Field Service, RP 9B, shall be observed in the operation and maintenance of wire rope.

120. INSPECTION OF DRILLING EQUIPMENT.

(1) In the case of the first well to be drilled or worked over by a unit in Papua New Guinea, the drilling or workover rig and associated equipment shall be inspected by a qualified inspection company, approved by the Director, and the subsequent inspection report shall be forwarded to the Chief Inspector for review.

(2) Any deficiencies in the equipment, as highlighted by inspection report under Subsection (1), shall be remedied prior to spud or start of operations on the well.

(3) Following the remedying of deficiencies, the rig and associated equipment shall be re-inspected and approved by a Petroleum Inspector appointed under the Act, prior to the commencement of drilling.

121. CASING OF WELLS.

(1) The design and placement of all casing strings shall take into account known or predicted formation characteristics and strength, temperature, known or predicted formation pore-fluid type and pressures, kick influx volumes, required anticipated maximum mud weights,

estimated maximum circulating pressures formation fracture and propagation pressures, lost circulation and loads exerted by other casing strings, wellhead and blowout prevention equipment.

(2) The maximum performance properties used in the design of casing strings shall be those indicated as minimum performance properties in API Bulletin 5C2 on Performance Properties of Casing, Tubing and Drill Pipe.

(3) Where practical, surface casing (which is defined as that casing which is set subsequent to the conductor pipe or casing) shall be set 25m into a competent formation and sufficient casing shall be run to cover shallow aquifers, prevent the release of well fluids to the environment and be set at the approximate depth as set out in the approved program.

(4) All casing and liner strings shall be designed to withstand the maximum anticipated burst, collapse and tensile loads at the temperatures and wellbore environments expected to be encountered.

(5) Where a casing liner is run in a well, there shall be an overlap of at least 30m between the top of the liner and the shoe of the previously run string of casing.

122. PRESSURE TESTING OF CASING STRINGS.

(1) Prior to drilling the plug after cementing, all casing strings, except the conductor casing, shall be pressure tested to either 70% of the programmed design burst pressure or 70% of the manufacturer's minimum internal yield pressure, whichever is lower, but no less than the pressures as shown in the following table:–

(2) A test under Subsection (1) shall not exceed the rated working pressure of the casing and well head equipment, and where the pressure declines more than 10% in 15 minutes, or where there is other indication of a leak, corrective measures shall be taken until a satisfactory test is obtained prior to drilling out the shoe.

(3) The results of a test under Subsection (1) shall be entered in the daily drilling report and the tour report.

(4) Casing recovered from a well shall not be reused in another well unless–

(*a*) it has been inspected in accordance with API RP 5C1, "Recommended Practice for Care and Use of Casing and Tubing"; and
(*b*) its physical characteristics established by such inspection ensure compliance with Subsection (1).

(5) Unless otherwise approved by the Director, a well completed to produce oil or gas or to inject any fluid shall have the annulus between the second casing string and the surface casing vented to atmosphere.

123. CEMENTING OF CASING.

(1) The conductor and surface casings shall be cemented to surface or as indicated in the drilling program that has been approved by the Director.

(2) All ensuing casing strings shall be cemented with sufficient cement of sufficient compressive strength to ensure that all aquifers and zones containing movable hydrocarbons are competently covered and/or isolated by cement and that the top of cement is at least 150m above the cementing point.

(3) The overlap between a liner and the next larger casing previously set shall be cemented with sufficient cement to fill at least 30m of the annular space between the liner and the next larger casing, or the overlap is sealed in some other approved manner.

(4) If the cementing requirements of this section have not been achieved, the site person-in-charge shall meet those requirements by remedial cementing, unless otherwise approved by the Director.

(5) Drilling shall not be commenced until a time lapse of–

(*a*) 24 hours; or
(*b*) 8 hours under pressure for all other casing strings or until surface cement samples are set.

(6) For the purposes of Subsection (5), the cement is considered to be under pressure if it is restrained from movement by the use of float valves or surface valves in the casing string.

124. FORMATION INTEGRITY TESTS.

(1) Unless otherwise approved by the Director, a formation integrity test shall be conducted after drilling out the casing shoe of surface and intermediate casing strings to ensure well integrity during the subsequent drilling operations.

(2) The results of a test under Subsection (1) shall be reported in the daily report and entered on the tour report and where the result of a test requires that the drilling and casing programs previously approved by the Director be amended, any such amendments will be submitted to the Director for approval.

125. SAMPLES.

(1) Unless the prior approval of the Director has been obtained the site person-in-charge shall, where applicable, take, preserve and maintain a series of cutting samples of not less that 100g (dry weight) of the various formations which the drill penetrates in drilling the well, taken every 3m or at intervals as required by or approved by the Director.

(2) The samples referred to in Subsection (1) shall be washed, dried and packed, and labeled with the name of the well and interval of depth and shall be delivered as soon as practicable, but within one month of rig release, to the Director at the licensee's expense.

126. CORES.

(1) Cores shall be placed in core boxes, or other suitable containers, accurately labeled as to the well number, number of core, top and bottom of core, interval cored and percentage recovery of core and shall be suitably stored until delivered at the licensee's expense, within one month of the date of completion of the well, to the Director.

(2) Where vertical splitting of a core is required by the Director, a continuous section comprising at least a half slice of the core will be provided, but otherwise the core shall be apportioned into representative sections.

(3) In either case referred to in Subsection (2), the core shall be divided as follows:–

(*a*) licensee–50%, if desired;
(*b*) State–50%.

(4) Notwithstanding anything in Subsections (2) and (3), the licensee may retain all cores from productive intervals, potential or actual, providing that–

(*a*) the Director may, if he so desires, require that 25% of such cores be delivered to the Core Library of the Department of Petroleum and Energy; and
(*b*) the core retained by the licensee shall be used for reservoir or other allied investigations, and shall not be in any other way disposed of or destroyed; and
(*c*) all results of such investigations shall be reported promptly by the Person-in-Charge to the Director; and
(*d*) when the licensee desires to send such cores out of Papua New Guinea for any purpose whatsoever, he shall advise the Director of his intention so that the provisions of Paragraph (a) may be invoked.

127. AGE DATING OF SAMPLES.

The licensee shall, as early as practicable, use his best endeavours to ascertain, by palaeontological, radiometric or other suitable means, the ages of all undated rocks penetrated by the well.

128. FLUID SAMPLES.

(1) Recovery from formation tests shall, when practicable, be sampled in accordance with API RP44 "Recommended Practice for Sampling Petroleum Reservoir Fluids".

(2) A sample under Subsection (1), shall be labeled and analyzed and liquid samples shall be preserved for at least six months.

(3) Analyses of a sample under Subsection (1) shall be forwarded to the Director as soon as possible.

(4) Where required by the Director, a one litre portion of each sample under Subsection (1), shall be forwarded to the Director suitably labeled as to well number, condition of well when sampled, date, productive interval, type of test, nature of sample and sampling point, and such samples shall be supplied in sealed containers that meet all appropriate regulations of the Civil Aviation Act 2000, Harbours Board Act 1963 and Inflammable Liquid Act 1953 for the product it contains and the form of transport of such sample.

129. FORMATION AND INFLOW TESTS.

(1) The site person-in-charge shall make every reasonable effort to advise the Director of his intention to conduct a formation test or inflow test.

(2) The site person-in-charge shall notify the Director as soon as possible of the results of a formation test and shall not make public the results until the Director has been so notified.

(3) The site person-in-charge shall, where requested by the Director, supply to him as soon as possible, a copy of the relevant operational report, fluid recovery rates, choke sizes, pressure and temperature readings and pressure recorder charts for each drill stem test or other test taken at the well and an interpretation and analysis of the test.

130. ELECTRIC OR OTHER WELL LOGS.

(1) The site person-in-charge shall, before a drilling well is cased (other than surface casing), completed, suspended or abandoned, ensure that a suite of open hole wire line logs, as considered necessary by the licensee and approved by the Director, is run and recorded.

(2) Cased hole logs for well evaluation, as required by the Director, shall be run and recorded.

(3) Copies, stable base transparencies, magnetic tapes or other digital log data of all logs run, and computer processed interpretive logs made, shall be dispatched forthwith to the Director.

131. PROTECTION OF AQUIFERS.

During operations on a well, every practical precaution shall be taken to prevent communication between, leakage from or pollution to aquifers that are or may be used for any purpose.

132. ABANDONMENT PRINCIPLES.

Where a well or portion of a well is to be abandoned, the following provisions shall be observed:–

(*a*) the operator shall submit an abandonment program to the Director and said program shall not be carried out prior to receiving approval from the Director;
(*b*) abandonment programs shall be designed so as to ensure zonal isolation of any or all aquifers, lost circulation zones and other zones capable of fluid production and the programs shall specifically address the prevention of inter-zonal pressure transfer, pressure transfer from formations to the wellbore or tubulars and operational safety;
(*c*) ghost holes shall be abandoned or isolated by use of cement plugs unless otherwise approved by the Director;
(*d*) abandonment plugs shall be tested for quality and placement as directed by the Director;
(*e*) a steel well marker plate, having the well name and operator's name bead-welded onto it, shall be installed 2m above ground level and permanently affixed to the abandoned well equipment;
(*f*) where at some future time, in the opinion of the Director, the abandonment has proven to be ineffectual, the licensee at the time of abandonment, shall be operationally and financially responsible for rectifying the situation as directed by the Director.

133. WELL COMPLETION.

(1) A completed well shall be completed in such a manner as to allow measurement of pressure and temperature under static or dynamic well conditions.

(2) The surface equipment shall be provided with sampling connections.

(3) The Person-in-Charge of a well shall, on completion of such well, keep and make readily available to a Petroleum Inspector an accurate record of all subsurface equipment and junk in the well.

(4) Before opening a well to production or injection and after every major repair, recompletion or workover, the well head and christmas tree shall be adequately pressure tested and the flow line shall be inspected to ensure satisfactory makeup.

(5) All produced and injected fluids shall be through tubing unless prior approval is received from the Director.

134. DISPOSAL OF PRODUCED OIL AND GAS.

(1) All oil or gas, that is circulated out of, or produced from a well during a drilling, testing or repair operation and that is not flowed via the well's flowline to a gathering facility, shall be flowed to a vented storage tank or flare on location.

(2) Clean up operations or testing of a well using temporary well site facilities may be continued during the hours of darkness subject to the condition where oil and gas are being produced together, they shall be flowed through a separator and the gas flowed to a flare.

(3) The flare referred to in Subsections (1) and (2), shall be equipped with a reliable, continuous ignition source.

135. DISPOSAL OF OTHER LIQUID WASTE.

(1) All waste liquids, used during the drilling or workover of a well, or that have been produced from a well as it cleans up, shall be drained to a waste sump or otherwise disposed of in a manner approved by the Director.

(2) A waste sump referred to in Subsection (1) that is permanently maintained on any location shall be adequately fenced or otherwise protected.

(3) Every practicable precaution shall be taken to prevent pollution of the environment by a waste sump referred to in this section.

136. DISPOSAL OF OTHER WASTE.

(1) All worn drilling equipment, damaged or surplus drilling supplies and other rubbish shall be removed from site to an approved waste disposal site and no drilling waste of any description is to be buried on site.

(2) All food scraps and kitchen waste are to be disposed of in an environmentally and hygienically acceptable manner.

(3) Effluent from the toilet facilities provided at the rig and camp is to be treated or discharged in an environmentally and hygienically acceptable manner.

137. REPLACEMENT OF WELL SITE FENCING.

Where installed, the well site fencing protecting the wellhead from outside interference shall be replaced upon completion of a repair operation.

138. PENETRATION RATE.

Every drilling rig shall be equipped to provide continuous recording of the rate of penetration.

139. DETECTION OF PETROLEUM.

(1) Suitable equipment shall be continuously available and/or installed on or near every drilling rig, prior to the drilling out of the surface casing, to permit the detection of hydrocarbons in cuttings, cores and mud.

(2) Equipment shall be readily available for adequate formation testing and sampling, both in open hole and through perforated casing.

Division 3.

Safety in Drilling and Workover Operations.

140. OPERATIONS.

Operations carried out at or about a well site and the associated equipment shall be in general accordance with API RP 54.

141. MASTS AND DERRICKS.

(1) All masts and derricks exceeding 30m above ground level shall be equipped with a mast head light.

(2) No structural change or addition to a derrick or mast shall be made unless approved beforehand by the Director, who shall require a written submission from the manufacturer or a qualified professional engineer as to the effects of such structural change or addition.

142. SPUDDING-IN.

A well shall not be spudded or a rig assisted well reentry shall not start until the rig and its associated equipment are completely rigged up and reliable communications have been established as required in Section 21.

143. BLOWOUT PREVENTION.

(1) The site person-in-charge of a well that is being drilled, tested, completed or worked over shall, at all times, employ adequately designed blowout prevention equipment.

(2) Prior to drilling below the surface casing string, or before re-entering a completed well, hydraulically operated blowout prevention equipment shall be installed, operated and tested, generally in accordance with the relevant requirement of API RP 53, "Recommended Practices for Blowout Prevention Equipment System for Drilling Wells", and shall be maintained ready for use subject to Section 147 until abandonment, completion or recompletion operations have been completed.

(3) The blowout prevention equipment referred to in Subsection (2) shall comprise a minimum of–

(*a*) three remotely controlled hydraulically actuated blowout preventers each with a working pressure which exceeds the maximum anticipated surface pressure and which preventers consist of–

(i) one set of pipe rams appropriate for the size of pipe being run in the hole; and
(ii) one set of blind rams; and
(iii) one annular preventer; and
(iv) extension hand wheels or hydraulic locks on all ram type preventers; and

(*b*) a drilling spool with side outlets for the attachment of choke and kill lines, or side outlets in the blowout preventer body, for choke and kill lines, which side outlets shall be connected to pipe lines which have a pressure rating not less than the blowout preventer assembly to which they are connected, except that part of the choke line which is down stream of the last valve on the choke manifold; and
(*c*) one kill pump facility connected to the kill line; and
(*d*) one fill up line.

(4) Where the pressure rating of the blowout preventers is–

(*a*) less than 2000 PSI, both the choke and kill lines shall contain related fittings of a minimum diameter of 2 inches and shall be equipped with at least one control valve; or
(*b*) greater than 2000 PSI, the choke line shall contain related fittings of a minimum diameter of 3 inches, and both kill and choke line outlets on the blowout preventer stack shall be equipped with two control valves, one of which on the choke line shall be hydraulically controlled.

(5) Where the Director has approved the setting of deep surface casing, he may require the installation of an adequate diverter system to the conductor in accordance with API RP 53.

(6) All valves, fittings and lines between the closing unit and the blowout prevention stack shall be of steel construction.

(7) Approved fire resistant hose with a rated working pressure at least equal to the working pressure rating of the stack may be used on equipment rated at 5000 PSI or less.

(8) Where manual controls for blowout preventers are provided they shall be located outside the rig substructure at a maximum practicable distance from the well-head.

(9) An inside blowout preventer assembly and a full opening safety valve in the open position, with crossovers as needed to fit all tool joints in the drill or tubing string, shall be maintained on the rig floor while drilling or work-over operations are being conducted.

(10) An upper kelly cock shall be installed below the swivel and, where high pressures are anticipated, another at the bottom of the kelly of such design that it can be run through the blowout preventers.

(11) Choke and kill lines of flange, weld or clamp connected steel or approved fire resistant hose shall be fitted and equipped generally in accordance with API RP 53 and apart from the choke there shall be no reduction in diameter from the primary choke line to the flare.

(12) The choke manifold shall be fitted with not less than two adjustable chokes and it is recommended that a hydraulically controlled choke be fitted as one such choke, where the pressure rating of the blowout preventer equipment exceeds 3000 PSI.

(13) Each choke manifold shall have the following equipment clearly visible to the choke operator when standing in his normal operating position for either of the adjustable chokes–

(*a*) a pressure gauge which indicates the drill pipe pressure at the drilling floor; and
(*b*) a pressure gauge which indicates the casing/drill pipe annulus pressure at a known point upstream of the choke.

(14) The choke manifold shall be sited away from the rig substructure so that the choke and flare lines contain a minimum number of bends and, so far as is practicable, the driller has a clear view of a person operating chokes and monitoring pressures.

(15) An adequately constrained flare line shall extend at least 50m from the well, oil storage tank, separator, temporary production facility or other unprotected source of flammable vapors.

144. BLOWOUT EQUIPMENT CERTIFICATION.

All drilling contractors shall have their blowout preventer stacks inspected by a qualified inspection organization or tested and certified by a qualified facility that is authorized by the manufacturer and such inspections or certifications shall be performed according to the manufacturer's recommended procedure and schedule, but not less than once every five years.

145. BLOWOUT PREVENTER CLOSING UNITS.

(1) Blowout preventer activating accumulator units generally in accordance with the requirements of API RP 53, shall be located a minimum of 20m from the wellhead and, without accumulator pump assistance, shall have sufficient capacity to–

(*a*) open or close the hydraulically operated choke line valve; and
(*b*) close or open the annular type blowout preventer; and
(*c*) close or open all blowout preventer pipe rams.

(2) After the functions specified in Subsection (1) have been carried out, the accumulator pump shall be capable of rebuilding fluid pressure in the accumulator within a period of three minutes to a sufficiently high level to–

(*a*) open the hydraulically operated choke line valve; and
(*b*) close the annular type blowout preventer.

(3) Accumulators shall be connected to the blowout preventers with lines of safe working pressure at least equal to the working pressure of the accumulator, and where these lines are located adjacent to and within the substructure they shall be of steel construction unless completely sheathed with adequate fire resistant material, installed and maintained to the manufacturer's specifications.

(4) Accumulator pumps shall have two independent sources of power which shall not be connected to the same circuit.

(5) During drilling and work-over operations there shall be a control manifold for operating the blowout preventers accessible to the driller on the rig floor and another located at least 20m from the well, so that where the rig floor controls are rendered inoperable the distant master control unit shall be able to operate all blowout preventer functions.

146. TESTING BLOWOUT PREVENTION EQUIPMENT.

(1) The blowout prevention equipment shall be tested in the manner and at the times set out in Subsections (2), (3), (4), (5) and (6) in the event that a test indicates that the equipment is not operating correctly, the equipment shall be made serviceable before operations are recommenced.

(2) The ram type preventers, the annular preventer, the choke and kill lines and valves, the choke manifold and the kelly cock shall be pressure tested on installation and following the setting of each string of casing in the wellhead, prior to drilling out or commencing completion operations or at any time any part of the BOP stack has been altered in any way that compromises the pressure integrity results of the preceding test.

(3) A test under Subsection (2) is to be conducted using water and to pressure consistent with the rating of the equipment, the recommendations of the manufacturer and the casing installed in the well, and the results of any such test shall be reported in the daily report and entered on the tour report.

(4) Under normal operating conditions, at least once every two weeks, the blowout preventers and choke manifold shall be pressure tested and the results shall be recorded in the daily report and on the tour report.

(5) Where well conditions preclude the safe testing of the BOP stack and manifold, the pressure test may be postponed until normal operating conditions are regained, at which time the test shall be immediately carried out and the reasons for the postponement shall be entered into the daily report and the tour report on the day the test was originally due.

(6) The blowout preventers are to be inspected or checked on a daily basis and the rams operated as required to ensure functional competence and such function tests shall be recorded in the daily report and the tour report.

(7) Every closing of the blowout preventer system and the reasons for the closing shall be included in the daily report and the tour report.

147. INSTALLATION AND REMOVAL OF BLOWOUT PREVENTION EQUIPMENT.

During the period of operations when blowout prevention equipment is installed and maintained it shall not be removed until proper plans to safely seal the wellbore, approved by the Director, have been carried out.

148. WELL CONTROL RECORDS.

(1) All on-site supervisors and rig personnel holding the position of driller or above, shall maintain valid well control certification.

(2) A certificate issued under Subsection (1) is to be produced when so requested by the Director or a Petroleum Inspector.

(3) Blowout prevention drills shall be conducted weekly for each crew to ensure that crews are properly trained to carry out emergency procedures and the response times shall be recorded in the tour reports and the daily drilling report.

(4) Proper trip sheet records shall be maintained until rig release date of the well, and shall be produced when requested by the Director or a Petroleum Inspector.

(5) Detailed well control procedures shall be displayed at the location.

(6) A well kill work sheet shall be maintained current with respect to the drilling conditions.

149. DRILLING FLUID FACILITIES.

(1) Drilling fluid facilities, materials and procedures shall be established and maintained to minimize the potential of a blowout on any well.

(2) The drilling fluid facilities system shall include–

(*a*) recording and alarmed mud pit/tank level indicators; and
(*b*) an appropriate sized trip tank; and
(*c*) a mud return or full hole indicator; and
(*d*) pump stroke counters; and
(*e*) mud degasser.

(3) When pulling drill pipe or tubing from an uncased or perforated well, the annulus shall be filled with a fluid of appropriate density before the change in the fluid level decreases the hydrostatic pressure by 75 PSI, or every five stands of tubular, whichever gives the lower decrease in hydrostatic pressure.

150. WELL TESTING.

(1) Any formation test in which formation fluids are produced into the test string shall have–

(*a*) provision to avoid pulling the test string full of produced fluids; and
(*b*) provisions to kill the well in case of an emergency; and
(*c*) any other provision as may be prescribed by the Director.

(2) During formation testing, or the removal of pipe after a formation test, a competent supervisor shall remain at the rig site to supervise the operations.

(3) During formation testing flow periods, motors engines and lights not required in the operation shall be shut off and water sprays, fitted to the exhausts of the engines that are required to be run, shall be turned on during all flow periods.

(4) During formation testing flow periods, no motor vehicle shall be operated with 25m of the well bore.

(5) During formation testing, the testing string annulus shall contain sufficient fluid of a density adequate to control formation pressure.

(6) Produced fluids at surface shall be safely routed through an appropriate independent test manifold and choke facility.

(7) Blowout prevention equipment shall not be used for flow control during a formation test.

(8) The site person-in-charge during an open hole formation test shall–

(*a*) make every endeavour to estimate the rates of flow of oil and/or gas and/or water produced; and
(*b*) ensure that the volumes of liquids contained in the dill pipes at the conclusion of a test are measured; and
(*c*) ensure that samples are taken of all fluids produced or recovered from the drill pipe.

(9) Unless otherwise approved by the Director, all formation flowing tests shall utilize appropriate equipment located to accurately measure both flowing and shut in pressures and temperatures of the formation being tested.

(10) During a production test, the fluid flow shall be diverted through an adequate separator and the resultant flows of oil, gas and water shall be measured.

151. SWABBING.

(1) While swabbing operations are being conducted, all engines, motors, and other possible sources of ignition, not essential to the operation, shall be shut down.

(2) During swabbing operations the fluids shall be routed through a closed flow system to a production facility or tank located not less than 25m from the well bore and any flare/vent line from the tank shall incorporate a flame arrester.

(3) Swabbing operations shall not be conducted during the hours of darkness.

152. EQUIPMENT AND PROCEDURES.

Equipment used on a rig, whether permanently attached or temporarily installed, and all working procedures shall be designed such that the safety of personnel, equipment, resources and the environment is assured.

Division 4.

Rig and Associated Equipment.

153. DRILLING AND WORKOVER RIGS–GENERAL.

(1) Where practical, three exits from the floor of a rig shall be provided.

(2) All work areas and walkways that are elevated by more than 1.8m, and stairs, shall be provided with secure and safely designed handrails or other appropriate safety facilities and shall comply with PNGS 1081 "Code for Fixed Platforms, Walkways, Stairways and Ladders".

(3) Unless otherwise approved by the Director, the substructure of a rig shall not be enclosed.

154. DERRICK AND MAST PLATFORMS.

Every derrick and mast shall have a safely designed, secured and adequately sized landing platform level with each principal working platform of the derrick.

155. LADDERS AND STAIRWAYS.

Ladders and stairways shall comply with PNGS 1081 "Code for Fixed Platforms, Walkways, Stairways and Ladders".

156. HOISTING LINES.

(1) A wire-line service record shall be kept on all drilling and workover rigs and shall be in accordance with the provisions of API RP9B or such other form as may be acceptable to the Director and shall be produced to a Petroleum Inspector when required.

(2) All hoisting lines and hoisting line equipment shall be designed, operated and maintained in safe and serviceable condition.

(3) All overhead sheaves or pulleys shall be securely fastened to their support.

(4) All hooks used in single point hoisting shall be equipped with a device to prevent the accidental release of the load.

157. PRESSURE LINES AND HOSES.

All fluid system pressure hoses, high pressure pneumatic flexible lines, high pressure pipe used in fluid pumping systems including those fitted with flexible joints shall be equipped with restraint devices of sufficient strength, secured to an adequate support, to effectively prevent dangerous movement in the case of coupling or near coupling failures.

158. SAFETY VALVES AND PUMPS.

(1) A pressure relief device shall be installed on all power driven high pressure fluid pumps and there shall be no valve between the pump and the pressure relief device.

(2) The pressure relief device shall be set to discharge at a pressure not in excess of the manufacturer's recommended maximum working pressure of the pump and all connecting pipes and fittings.

(3) Shear pins used in pressure relief devices shall be of a design and strength specified by the manufacturer.

(4) A guard shall be placed around the shear pin and spindle of a pressure relief device.

(5) The fluids discharged from a pressure-relieving safety device shall be directed to a place where they will not endanger any person.

(6) There shall be no valve of any kind in the discharge opening of a pressure-relieving safety device or in the discharge pipe connected to it.

(7) The pipe connected to the pressure side and discharge side of a pressure-relieving safety device shall not be smaller than that of the normal pipe size openings of the pressure-relieving safety device.

(8) The piping on the discharge side of a pressure-relieving safety device shall be secured.

Division 5.

Offshore Operations.

159. GENERAL.

(1) Certain minimal distances specified in Part VII may be impractical on a marine facility, but the Person-in-Charge shall ensure that the intent of the provisions of Part VII is observed.

(2) A provision in respect of casing, blow-out preventers, blow-out preventer closing units, and abandonment in Part VII shall apply with equal force to operations both onshore and offshore

160. MOBILE DRILLING UNIT.

(1) Any mobile offshore drilling unit shall be in possession of a current MODU certification and a current certification of seaworthiness from a recognized and authorized classifying authority such as the American Bureau of Shipping.

(2) In the case of the first well to be drilled or worked over by a unit offshore Papua New Guinea, the mobile offshore drilling unit and associated equipment shall be inspected by a qualified inspection company, approved by the Director, and the subsequent inspection report shall be forwarded to the Chief Inspector for review.

(3) Any deficiencies in the equipment, as highlighted by this inspection report, under Subsection (2) shall be remedied prior to spud or start of operations on the well and the rig and associated equipment shall then be re-inspected and approved by a Petroleum Inspector appointed under the Act, prior to the commencement of drilling.

161. OFFSHORE DRILLING PROGRAM.

An offshore drilling proposal shall address the following items (drilling unit applicable) prior to or in conjunction with the details as stated in Section 104:–

(*a*) anchoring of the drilling unit;
(*b*) shallow gas drilling procedures for conductor and surface holes; and
(*c*) site pull off plans during drilling and/or completion operations in case of emergency;
(*d*) site repositioning and well reconnect;
(*e*) disposal of drilling fluid and drill cuttings;
(*f*) initial site survey and seafloor evaluation for bottom supported drilling units;
(*g*) details for the containment of hydrocarbon spills into the sea, complete with a copy of the financial responsibility;
(*h*) details of the chemicals to be used in the drilling fluid, copies of the MSDS sheets and the treatment procedure for rendering the drilling fluids harmless prior to disposal to the sea;
(*i*) details of safety facilities contracted for offshore personnel safety.

162. OFFSHORE CASING DESIGN.

(1) For drilling operations carried out from a mobile offshore drilling unit, except for the conductor hole, all casing or subsea equipment shall be designed to return drilling fluids to the drilling unit and such design shall take into account all lateral loads that may be exerted on the casing or riser system.

(2) For the design of casing strings used in offshore wells, the design shall be governed by Section 121.

163. OFFSHORE BLOWOUT PREVENTERS.

(1) Prior to drilling below the surface casing string, blowout prevention equipment as generally recommended in API RP 53, shall be installed and tested.

(2) The blow-out preventer assembly shall include at least one blind/shear ram and one annular type.

(3) A sub-sea blowout preventer shall be provided with duplicate sets of control lines, designed to allow for sub-sea disconnect at the stack.

164. OFFSHORE BLOWOUT PREVENTER CLOSING UNITS.

In the case of a well drilled from a mobile drilling unit (other than a jack-up platform), the accumulator unit shall be capable of opening the riser connector in addition to the requirements specified in Section 145.

165. DISPOSAL OF DRILLING FLUIDS OFFSHORE.

Offshore disposal of water based drilling fluids and cuttings into the sea shall be in accordance with the prevailing laws of Papua New Guinea, and drilling fluids and cuttings containing oil or other hydrocarbons shall meet the requirements of Section 190.

166. ABANDONMENT OF OFFSHORE WELLS AND PLATFORMS.

All casing strings and pilings from offshore wells or platforms being permanently abandoned shall be severed at least 5m below the seabed and removed, and the sea floor surrounding the well location, to an area extent as determined by the Director, shall be surveyed to determine debris and obstructions and cleared as directed.

Division 6.

Air Drilling.

167. GENERAL.

The provisions of this Division shall apply whenever air is used as a circulating fluid in rotary drilling operations in the search for and production of petroleum and where there is any conflict between any of the provisions of this Division and of any other provision of this Regulation, the provisions of this Division shall prevail.

168. DELIVERY LINES.

(1) The main air supply line shall be located so that it does not interfere with pedestrian or vehicular movement.

(2) A check valve shall be installed on the delivery line at or near the standpipe.

(3) All high pressure air lines on the drilling location shall be suitably marked or posted with warning notices and a supervisor shall ensure that all workmen working under his supervision are aware of the method of marking of the high pressure lines.

(4) All main valves in the supply system that may require quick closure in the event of an emergency shall be clearly labeled and shall be readily accessible.

169. MOTOR VEHICLES.

Every vehicle that is not directly engaged in operations on the well shall not approach within a distance of 50m from the well.

170. FIRE PRECAUTIONS.

(1) Adequate fire extinguishing equipment, properly positioned at or under the substructure, safely and effectively to fight a fire or at least one mud gun shall Adequate fire extinguishing equipment, properly positioned at or be permanently mounted under the substructure pointing directly at the rotating blowout preventer assembly, and the line between the mud pump and that mud gun shall be controlled by a single valve situated at the pump end of the line.

(2) Where the mud pump referred to in Subsection (1) is not kept in continuous operation, pump starting controls shall be located at the pump and at the driller's control panel.

171. SITING OF COMPRESSORS.

(1) Where practical, compressors and boosters used for drilling shall be sited at least 25m away from the rig and the gas separator, and shall be placed so as to be visible from the driller's position.

(2) Oil and diesel fuel storage shall be sited at least 25m away from the compressors.

172. BLOOEY LINE.

(1) Blooey and bleed-off lines shall extend at least 50m from the wellhead and shall, where practical, be laid downwind of the well or at a right angle to the direction of the prevailing wind.

(2) A geological sample catcher installed on a blooey line shall be designed to avoid flashback and to provide protection to personnel from dust.

(3) Sufficient space shall be cleared around the end of the blooey line to prevent ignition of vegetation.

(4) Where dust discharged by drilling causes a hazard to health on the drilling location, provision shall be made to inject water into the blooey line to suppress such dust.

(5) Any gas discharged from the blooey line shall be immediately ignited by a reliable, safe and continuous method acceptable to a Petroleum Inspector.

173. SUPPLY LINE VALVES.

At least two valves shall be installed in the main air supply line, of which one shall be on the standpipe accessible from the derrick floor and one shall be at a distance of at least 25m from the well.

174. DRILL STRING FITTINGS.

A downhole float valve shall be installed in the drill string and both top and bottom kelly cocks shall be employed in a manner similar to that provided for in Section 143(9) and (10).

175. MUD STOCKS.

Drilling fluid, readily available and in adequate volume to fill and circulate the hole, shall be maintained on location in satisfactory condition at all times.

176. GAS DETECTION EQUIPMENT.

Sufficient gas detection equipment, of a type and number acceptable to a Petroleum Inspector, shall be provided and used at all drilling locations when air drilling is in progress.

Division 7.

Special Services.

177. DEFINITION.

Special services are those usually provided by a contractor other than the drilling contractor and shall comprise all logging, formation testing, formation stimulation, cementing and other services of a like nature that are carried out in support of the drilling, completion, abandonment, suspension and workover of a well.

178. OPERATIONS.

(1) Special services shall be conducted in accordance with this Regulation and the applicable recommended practices set forth in API RP 54 "Oil and Gas Well Drilling and Servicing Operations".

(2) All safety and operating requirements contained in this Regulation are applicable.

179. STIMULATION OPERATIONS.

In any stimulation operation in which high pressure pumping equipment is used–

(*a*) all equipment shall be pressure tested to a pressure greater than the maximum anticipated treating pressure; and
(*b*) where crude oil is to be used in such operations, it shall be weathered in a facility for a sufficient period to ensure that the more volatile components have escaped before the crude is so used and, for any operation using petroleum based products, sufficient fire protection shall be available on site to contain any fire and provide personnel protection; and
(*c*) pump vehicles and other pumping equipment shall be located at least 25m from the well, whenever possible, and shall be stationed in such a position as to provide the persons operating such vehicles with a clear view of the wellhead; and
(*d*) injection lines or manifolds shall not be laid beneath vehicles or pumping equipment; and
(*e*) all unnecessary electrical equipment shall be shut down during a stimulation operation that uses petroleum based fluids; and
(*f*) only persons, vehicles and equipment necessary for the operation shall be permitted within 50m of the well; and
(*g*) in any acidization, an adequate source of fresh water shall be available for personnel safety purposes; and
(*h*) before pumping flammable liquids, all components of the system shall be grounded.

PART VIII. – PRODUCTION.

180. IDENTIFICATION OF WELLS AND PRODUCTION FACILITIES.

The licensee shall mark each well and production facility with a notice in large, legible letters, of a type and size acceptable to a Petroleum Inspector, stating the name of the field and the well or production facility number.

181. PROTECTION OF COMPLETED WELLS.

All completed wells shall be reasonably protected and a notice, in accordance with Section 26, warning persons of the danger that exists, shall be prominently displayed.

182. CONSTRUCTION APPROVAL.

The licensee shall not commence the construction of a facility without the written approval of the Director.

183. APPLICATION FOR APPROVAL.

(1) An application for approval of the location, construction and operation of a production facility shall include the following information:–

(*a*) the name, location and coordinates of the facility;
(*b*) a listing of the well names and pools planned to be producing to the facility complete with a listing of petroleum in place, ultimate recovery and remaining reserves for each pool;
(*c*) estimated minimum, maximum and average oil, gas and water rates for each well and justification for these rates in respect to the maximum ultimate recovery to be achieved at these rates in comparison to maximum recovery of alternate rates;
(*d*) a plan showing the intended location of all gathering lines forming part of the production facility, together with pipe sizes;
(*e*) a statement of the main specifications to which the facilities have been designed and are planned to be constructed and operated, and a statement of the proposed operating pressures;
(*f*) the specifications of the separation equipment including pressure rating, minimum and maximum flow capacities and operating pressures and temperatures;
(*g*) a discussion of–

(i) the well testing frequency and duration intended; and
(ii) the measurement capabilities of the facility; and
(iii) any off-lease disposal;

(*h*) a list of the common flow lines intended and the method of testing the wells on each common line;
(*i*) a schematic flow diagram showing–

(i) the location of all major equipment including separation, dehydration, treating and storage facilities if any; and
(ii) the location and type of measurement equipment with each measurement point properly identified; and
(iii) emergency relief valves, lines, tanks or emergency shut down system; and
(iv) location and size of pits, dikes, flare lines and flare stacks; and
(v) location and capacity of pumps or

compressors delivering oil, gas or water to a
pipe line or injection;

(*j*) a sample set of field production reports for the facility with each entry explained using the identified measurement points from the schematic flow diagram;
(*k*) a plan showing the land surface contours, type of vegetation, bodies of water and surface improvements within 200m of the facility and the size and location of the facility site;
(*l*) operational and equipment details of any trucking facilities;
(*m*) where production from more than one pool is received at the facility, a statement of the method intended for allocating production between pools.

(2) An application for approval to modify a production facility shall be accompanied by the applicable information required by Subsection (1) where the modification affects the general measurement and flow capability aspects of the production facility.

(3) Where maintenance or preventative maintenance is carried out that does not affect the existing flow capability, an informational notice that does not require approval, is requested to be submitted to the Director.

(4) An approval for the location and construction or modification of a production facility shall be subject to any conditions set out in the approval.

184. GAUGING AND METERING FACILITIES.

(1) Tanks or meters shall be provided to measure continuously the quantities of oil, condensate, water, and gas from each producing field.

(2) Unless otherwise approved by the Director, the oil, gas and water production rate of every uniquely completed zone on extended production, in every well, shall be determined by test at intervals not exceeding one month during such production.

(3) A test referred to in Subsection (2) shall be–

(*a*) of sufficient duration so that–

(i) the volume of gas and liquid produced can be metered within the manufacturer's specified accuracy tolerance for the measurement devices in use; and
(ii) the rate of production determined for the test period is representative of the producing characteristics of the well; and

(*b*) normally once per month except in the case where the oil rate, GOR or WOR vary significantly from that of the previous test, in which case two or more tests per month shall be performed at reasonably consistent time intervals and the results of said tests shall be submitted to the Director as soon as practical.

(4) In the case of a swing well, the same test requirements apply although the variation parameters may differ.

(5) Unless otherwise approved by the Director, the production rate of every gas well on extended production shall be measured separately and continuously from each flowing string in each well.

(6) All meters and devices used to measure production of oil, water and gas shall be proved and certified as to accuracy in a manner and frequency acceptable to the Director.

185. MEASUREMENT OF PRODUCTION FOR ROYALTY PURPOSES.

(1) The Director may, for the purposes of measuring production for royalty, seal with a metallic seal, a valve or meter selected by him and installed at a well or on a pipeline, tank or other receptacle used for the storage or transportation of oil, gas or other fluid produced or withdrawn from the well.

(2) The site person-in-charge shall be notified orally in advance by a Petroleum Inspector of his intention to affix a seal under Subsection (1) stating his reasons therefor and such oral notification shall be confirmed in writing.

(3) Except in case of emergency, a seal affixed under Subsection (1) shall not be tampered with or removed without written permission from the Director.

186. PRODUCTION LINES AND EQUIPMENT.

Production lines and equipment shall be in accordance with relevant Australian or API Standards, or to specifications acceptable to the Director.

187. MONITORS, CONTROL MECHANISMS AND SAFETY DEVICES.

(1) A monitor and control mechanism, whose specifications are acceptable to the Director, shall be used to–

(*a*) control the rate of recovery of petroleum or water from a well; and
(*b*) control the pressure in pressure vessels and associated piping so that the safe working pressure of the vessels and piping is not exceeded; and
(*c*) prevent the escape of petroleum; and
(*d*) shut down an artificial lift device and close in a well in the event of–

(i) a break in a pressure vessel or associated piping receiving or conveying petroleum or water flowing to or from the well; or
(ii) a failure of any control mechanism associated with the well which might result in an unsafe condition being caused by the escape of petroleum or water; or
(iii) a fire or explosion in the vicinity of the well; and

(*e*) activate fire control mechanisms in the event of the outbreak of fire or an explosion.

(2) A well that is capable of producing petroleum by natural flow or by gas lift shall be equipped with a surface controlled subsurface safety device whose specification is acceptable to the Director.

(3) A surface controlled subsurface safety device shall be–

(*a*) designed so that it closes off automatically the flow of petroleum or water from the well where the wellhead or production equipment is damaged in such a way that would allow the escape of petroleum or water from the well; and
(*b*) operated at regular intervals not exceeding six months and tested at intervals according to manufacturer's recommendations; and
(*c*) where a test indicates that it may not operate correctly, repaired or replaced forthwith.

(4) An existing wireline retrievable, non-surface controlled subsurface safety device that was installed and in service prior to the coming into operation of this Regulation shall be–

(*a*) pulled, serviced and tested during all planned wireline operations on the well; and
(*b*) replaced with a surface controlled subsurface safety device during the first rig assisted workover operation on the well after the coming into operation of this Regulation.

(5) A surface controlled subsurface safety valve or injection valve that is capable of preventing back flow from a well shall be installed in all injection and/or disposal wells, operated at regular intervals not exceeding six months and tested at intervals according to manufacturer's recommendations, unless the Person in Charge can prove that the well is incapable of flowing.

188. INITIAL PRODUCTION TESTS.

(1) Each newly completed, recompleted or stimulated flowing oil well shall, prior to being put on production, or within 14 days thereof, be subjected to a production test, which shall include where practical, bottom hole pressure measurements, for not less than four consecutive hours and the Person-in-Charge shall, as soon as practicable after the completion of the test, send to the Director a report showing–

(*a*) completion interval and details of perforations; and
(*b*) oil, water and gas production with gas/oil ratio; and
(*c*) the choke size; and
(*d*) the API gravity of the oil; and
(*e*) casing and tubing pressures; and
(*f*) separator temperature and pressure; and
(*g*) duration of test; and
(*h*) interpretation of the test.

(2) Each newly completed, recompleted or stimulated non-naturally flowing oil well, being artificially lifted shall, prior to being put on production, or within 14 days thereof, be subjected to a production test that shall include bottom hole pressure measurement if practical for not less than eight consecutive hours, and the Person-in-Charge shall, as soon as is practicable after the completion of the test, send to the Director a report showing–

(*a*) completion interval and details of perforations; and
(*b*) oil, water and gas production with gas/oil ratio; and
(*c*) the API gravity of the oil; and
(*d*) casing pressures and fluid levels where applicable; and
(*e*) method of artificial lift, depth of device, and operational parameters; and

(*f*) duration of test; and
(*g*) interpretation of the test.

(3) Each newly completed, recompleted or stimulated gas well shall, before being placed on production or within three months of its completion, recompletion or stimulation, be subjected to a flow potential test using a multi-point back pressure method, isochronal method, or any other method approved by the Director, and the Person-in-Charge shall, as soon as is practicable after the completion of the test, send a report to the Director showing–

(*a*) completion interval and details of perforation; and
(*b*) the choke size or sizes; and
(*c*) gas, oil and water production rate or rates; and
(*d*) gas/oil ratio; and
(*e*) the API gravity of the oil or condensate; and
(*f*) casing and tubing pressures; and
(*g*) separator temperature and pressure; and
(*h*) duration of test; and
(*i*) any further relevant details; and
(*j*) interpretation of the test.

(4) Each newly completed, recompleted or stimulated water or gas injection well, prior to being put on line, or within seven days thereof, shall be subjected to an injectivity test for not less than four consecutive hours and the Person-in-Charge shall, as soon as practicable after the completion of the test, send to the Director a report inclusive of–

(*a*) completion interval and details of the perforations; and
(*b*) water and/or gas injection rate; and
(*c*) casing and tubing pressures; and
(*d*) pump or compressor outlet pressure; and
(*e*) interpretation of the test.

(5) On each well where equipment installation permits, closed in and flowing bottom hole pressures shall be measured during the tests specified in Subsections (1), (2), (3) and (4), unless otherwise approved by the Director.

(6) The Person-in-Charge shall notify the Director as early as is practicable, but in any case prior to the commencement of the test, of his intention to conduct a production or injectivity test, as required by this Regulation.

189. MULTIPLE COMPLETION WELL.

(1) A well shall not be allowed to produce oil, gas or water from different pools at the same time from the same string unless the production from each individual pool can be independently tested and measured or approval in writing has been obtained from the Director.

(2) The Person-in-Charge shall, when required by the Director, conduct interference tests between the various zones of a multiple completion well to ensure that isolation of the various zones is being maintained to his satisfaction.

(3) Within one month of the completion of each test required by this section a report of the test containing all relevant data and an analysis and interpretation of the test proving or confirming segregation shall be forwarded to the Director.

(4) Where at any time a test required by this section or the production characteristics of the well indicate that segregation between the zones is ineffective–

(*a*) a diligent attempt to establish segregation shall be made; and
(*b*) where required by the Director, one of the zones shall be sealed off or abandoned.

(5) Where proof of segregation of zones is not submitted to the Director as required by this section, the well shall be shut in or produced in such manner as instructed by the Director.

(6) At least three days notice shall be given to a Petroleum Inspector of the intention to carry out a test required by this section.

190. DISPOSAL OF PRODUCED LIQUIDS.

(1) All formation water and other waste liquids produced from a well or refuse from tanks shall be disposed of by a method that is environmentally acceptable and does not constitute a health or safety hazard.

(2) The concentration of petroleum in any formation water discharged into the sea shall not exceed the limits set by the current Papua New Guinea environmental legislation.

(3) Produced formation water shall not be discharged into the sea unless–

(*a*) there is approved equipment which monitors, records and ensures that the concentration of petroleum in the discharged formation water specified in Subsection (2) is not exceeded; and
(*b*) an approved test is conducted at intervals not less frequently than weekly to check the performance of the equipment referred to in Paragraph (a), and the test results are recorded; and
(*c*) the records referred to in Paragraphs (a) and (b) are available to a Petroleum Inspector for a period of at least six months from the date on which the record is made.

191. PRODUCTION RATE RESTRICTION.

(1) The Director may restrict the amount of oil or gas or both that may be produced from a pool by limiting, where such limitation appears to him necessary, the total daily amount of oil and/or gas that may be produced from a pool, having regard to the efficient use of gas for the production of oil, the demand for oil or gas from the pool and/or the ultimate recovery of the oil or gas.

(2) Where the Director is satisfied that the licensee is not complying with any conditions imposed by him, or any requirement of this Part with respect to any pool, he may vary the rate at which petroleum is being recovered from that pool.

192. ENHANCED RECOVERY.

(1) In order to enhance reserves recovery, and after due consideration of the economic feasibility thereof, the Director may, by written direction to the licensee–

(*a*) require enhanced recovery operations in any pool or portion thereof, and for or incidental to such purpose, require the introduction or injection of a fluid into any pool or portion thereof; and
(*b*) require that any produced gas be gathered and processed where necessary, and the gas or products therefrom marketed or injected into an underground reservoir for storage or for any other purpose.

(2) No scheme for–

(*a*) enhanced recovery, including gas cycling in any field or pool; or
(*b*) the disposal of any fluid or other substance to an underground formation through a well,

shall be proceeded with unless the Director has approved the scheme upon such terms and conditions as he may prescribe.

193. USE OF CONSUMPTION OF GAS BY THE LICENSEE.

The licensee shall not use, flare or consume gas produced from a well, for a purpose other than–

(*a*) for pressuring, cycling or reservoir pressure maintenance; or
(*b*) for light or as process fuel,

until he has filed, with the Director, particulars concerning such use, flaring or consumption, in such detail as the Director may require and the Director may, by written direction, require the licensee to use, flare or consume the gas in a particular manner within set rates.

194. USE OF DIRECT WELL PRESSURE.

Direct well pressure shall not be used other than for the operation of gas operated valves or regulators, chemical injection pumps, pressure testing of wireline blowout preventers and lubricators, to aid in unloading fluid to restore production from an adjacent well, equalizing the pressure differential across a subsurface safety device or such other purposes as may be approved in writing by the Director.

195. TANKS AND STORAGE.

(1) Oil shall not be stored in unprotected earthen sumps except as an emergency measure.

(2) All permanent tanks for petroleum liquids, or batteries of tanks, shall be designed and constructed in accordance with the applicable API Standard for design and construction, and PNGS 1503, the Flammable and Combustible Liquids Code for installation, or such other Standards or Codes or Specifications as the Director may from time to time approve in writing.

(3) An oil storage tank shall not be placed within 50m of any well or building, unless otherwise approved by the Director.

(4) An oil storage tank of a capacity greater than 1,000 barrels shall be surrounded by a bund wall capable of holding 150% of the capacity of the tank.

196. TANK BATTERY CONTROL VALVES.

All field tank battery installations shall be so arranged and provided with control valves as to permit the ready shut off of oil or gas in the event of fire.

197. ENTERING TANKS OR OTHER PRODUCTION VESSELS.

(1) A tank or other closed vessel shall not be entered by any person until the tank or vessel has been declared free of hazardous substances by an authorized person and the vessel shall have sufficient oxygen present to sustain human life.

(2) All lines leading to a tank or vessel referred to in Subsection (1) shall be depressured and either disconnected or isolated prior to the entry of any person.

(3) Where in an emergency it is necessary for a tank or vessel which previously contained flammable or toxic substances to be entered by a person, such person shall–

(*a*) wear breathing apparatus; and
(*b*) shall be supplied with a life-line held by some responsible person outside each tank or vessel, who shall have a breathing apparatus at hand to effect rescue if required; and
(*c*) shall not enter the vessel without being attached to a rescue line that is being held by another responsible person.

198. MONTHLY PRODUCTION REPORT.

(1) The licensee, in respect of any well that during a given month, produced or was capable of producing crude oil or gas, or into which crude oil, gas, natural gas liquids, water, air or other substance was injected or disposed of during the preceding month, shall not later than the last day of the following month, submit to the Director, in form and content acceptable to him, a full report for the preceding month of the following applicable items–

(*a*) the amounts of crude oil, condensate, gas water or other substance produced from the well; and
(*b*) the amounts of crude oil, gas, natural gas liquids, water, air or other substance injected or disposed of into the well; and
(*c*) the average separator or treater pressure and temperature if a separator or treater was in use; and
(*d*) the wellhead pressure and temperature; and
(*e*) the choke size; and
(*f*) the number of hours during which the well produced, was injected into, or was used for disposal purposes; and
(*g*) where the well is producing from more than one reservoir, the data required in Paragraphs (a) to (f) in respect of each reservoir; and
(*h*) particulars of the disposition and deliveries of the crude oil, condensate, gas, water or other substance produced from the well; and
(*i*) cumulative production of oil, condensate, gas and water produced from the well; and

(2) Where a well is shut in, the licensee shall, unless otherwise approved by the Director, each month submit a return so stating until production is resumed or the well is abandoned.

199. ROUTINE PRODUCTION OPERATIONS.

(1) The Director shall be notified of all routine down hole well operations in a supplement to the monthly production report.

(2) A supplement under Subsection (1) shall indicate only the well number, type of operation or treatment and the date it was carried out.

200. ANNUAL PRODUCTION REPORT.

An annual report on total production from a field, in an acceptable form, shall be submitted by the licensee to the Director.

201. RESERVOIR DATA.

(1) Unless otherwise approved by the Director, routine reservoir measurements, conforming to normally accepted practices of producing a field in a sound and efficient manner, shall be taken, and the results shall, within one month thereafter, be reported to the Director.

(2) Routine reservoir measurements under Subsection (1) shall include–

(*a*) for gas wells in a producing field–

(i) water production from each zone through a separator half yearly; and
(ii) salinity of water produced from each zone half yearly; and
(iii) a yearly flowing or static bottom hole pressure survey that includes static pressure gradient surveys; and
(iv) gas and condensate analyses every two years; and

(*b*) for oil wells in a producing field–

(i) a flowing or static bottom hole pressure survey with static pressure gradient survey yearly; and
(ii) salinity of water produced from each zone yearly; and
(iii) an oil analysis every two years.

(3) Unless otherwise approved by the Director, an annual reserves report, in a form acceptable to the Director, shall be prepared for a Petroleum Development Licence by the licensee.

(4) The Director may require that other reservoir measurements, necessary to ensure the establishment of efficient reservoir control, shall be carried out and reported to him.

(5) All available reservoir data, the results of associated studies and petroleum reserve estimates of a pool or a field, shall be submitted without delay to the Director.

202. REPORT ON AN ENHANCED RECOVERY PROJECT.

(1) Where approval has been given for an enhanced recovery project, reports in accordance with Subsections (2) and (3) and any variation to those requirements that may be specified by the Director from time to time, shall be submitted to the Director.

(2) During the first two years, or such other period as the Director may specify, from the date of commencement of the enhanced recovery project, a report detailing the progress and performance, at regular intervals as approved by the Director, shall be submitted to the Director within two months of the expiration of the approved interval.

(3) A report required by this section shall set out the following information for the approved interval covered by the report:-

(*a*) the daily average rate during each month of oil production of each producing well, and of the whole scheme;
(*b*) the average gas/oil and water/oil ratios during each month of each production well, and of the whole scheme;

(*c*) the monthly cumulative gas, oil and water production for each producing well, and of the whole scheme;
(*d*) for each type of fluid being injected, the average rate of injection per operating day during each month to each injection well, and to the whole scheme;
(*e*) for each type of fluid being injected, the average wellhead injection pressure during each month for each injection well, and for the whole scheme;
(*f*) for each type of fluid being injected, the monthly cumulative volume of fluid injected to each injection well and to the whole scheme;
(*g*) the area-weighted formation pressure for the whole scheme;
(*h*) for each type of fluid being injected, the average injectivity index during each month for each injection well, and for the whole scheme, which index shall be determined as the daily average injection rate divided by the difference between the sand face pressure and the average formation pressure;
(*i*) the date and type of any well treatment or workover which shall be indicated, in the case of injection wells, on the report of the injectivity index and, in case of producing well, on the report of the daily average oil production rate;
(*j*) calculations on a monthly and cumulative basis of the balance between fluids injected to and fluids withdrawn from the part of the pool subject to the scheme;
(*k*) calculations on a monthly and cumulative basis of the balance between fluids injected to and fluids withdrawn from each injection pattern area or sector specified in the approval;
(*l*) such other interpretive information as the licensee considers necessary to evaluate adequately the progress and performance of the scheme.

(4) Subsequent to the first two years of the scheme or period as specified by the Director, the report required by this section may be submitted annually in a form acceptable to the Director.

PART IX. – MARINE FACILITIES.

203. MOBILE PLATFORM.

A floating structure, tender barge or construction barge forming part of a fixed platform shall be deemed for the purposes of Sections 204 and 205 to be a mobile platform when it is disconnected from the fixed platform.

204. MOBILE PLATFORM APPROVAL.

(1) A mobile platform shall not be used unless–

(*a*) either it complies with such provisions of the Merchant Shipping Act 1975 as apply to it by virtue of that Act or it meets the requirements of that Act relating to the safety and operation of a vessel or structure performing the functions of the mobile platform; and
(*b*) it is currently certified, and maintains its certification, by a recognized and authorized classifying authority for mobile platforms of its class; and
(*c*) all equipment and facilities have been inspected and

approved by a qualified inspection company; and
(*d*) the Director has given consent to the use of the mobile platform.

(2) The documents issued from time to time by the classifying authority under its rules which relate to the use and maintenance of a mobile platform shall be produced when required by the Director or a Petroleum Inspector.

(3) Except in an emergency, a mobile platform and its associated facilities shall not be materially altered or reconstructed without approval of and verification by the appropriate classifying authority.

(4) An emergency alteration or reconstruction shall, as soon as practicable, be reported to the appropriate classifying authority.

205. MOVEMENT OF MOBILE PLATFORM.

(1) Subject to Subsection (4), a mobile platform shall not, without approval of the appropriate Authority under the Merchant Shipping Act 1975 and the Director, be moved–

(*a*) into the licence area; or
(*b*) from a particular place in the licence area to another place in the licence area; or
(*c*) to a place outside the licence area.

(2) An application for approval under the Merchant Shipping Act 1975 to move a mobile platform shall be lodged directly with the appropriate Authority under that Act.

(3) An application for approval by the Director to move a mobile platform shall, unless the Director allows in exceptional circumstances, be made in writing at least seven days before the proposed move and shall include particulars of–

(*a*) the dates and times at which the move is proposed to be carried out, and the locations concerned; and
(*b*) any buoy or underwater obstruction proposed to be left at a location from which the mobile platform is to be moved.

(4) Notwithstanding Subsection (1), a person may, in the case of an emergency, make any change in the location of a mobile platform necessary to protect personnel and property.

(5) The movement of a mobile platform made in accordance with Subsection (4) shall, as soon as practicable after that movement has taken place, be reported to the Director and to the Marine Search and Rescue Division of the Department of Transport, Port Moresby.

(6) Before a mobile platform is moved to another location, details of the move, including the present and new locations, the time of departure from the present location, and the estimated time of arrival and expected duration of stay at the new location, shall be reported to the Director and to the Marine Search and Rescue Division of the Department of Transport, Port Moresby.

(7) When a mobile platform has arrived at a new location the actual time of arrival shall be reported to the Director and to the Marine Search and Rescue Division, Port Moresby.

206. ANCHORING VESSELS NEAR PIPELINES.

A vessel associated with operations in a title area shall not, without approval from the Person-in-Charge of a pipeline, drop anchor within one nautical mile of that pipeline in the licence area.

207. CONSENT TO CONSTRUCT OR INSTALL A FIXED PLATFORM.

(1) A fixed platform, prefabricated parts or sections, for installation in the licence area, shall not be constructed or installed unless the consent of the Director has been obtained in writing.

(2) Prior notice, acceptable to the Director, shall be given of the commencement of construction and the commencement of installation of the platform.

(3) Arrangements acceptable to the Director shall be made to enable a Petroleum Inspector to examine the platform at any time during its construction or installation.

208. APPLICATION FOR CONSENT TO CONSTRUCT OR INSTALL A FIXED PLATFORM.

An application for consent to the construction and installation of a fixed platform shall include particulars of–

(*a*) the location at which it is intended to construct and install the fixed platform; and
(*b*) the reason, including the geological evidence, for the selection of that location; and
(*c*) copies of reports and recommendations made by persons responsible for ascertaining the criteria determining the design; and
(*d*) design criteria including–

(i) the depth of the sea and the nature of the sea-bed and subsoil at the intended location; and
(ii) the maximum and minimum air and sea temperatures likely to occur at that location; and
(iii) the characteristics of the waves (including heights, periods and directions, and their probable distribution) at that location; and
(iv) the relevant water current information; and
(v) the maximum wind speeds and the direction of winds and the estimated maximum three second gust speed at that location; and
(vi) details of estimated marine growth on the fixed platform; and
(vii) the worst combination of dead and live loads likely to be applied to the fixed platform; and

(*e*) specifications for the construction and installation of the fixed platform; and
(*f*) drawings of the structure and of the equipment installed or to be installed on the structure; and
(*g*) the parts or sections constructed or proposed to be constructed before installation in the licence area; and
(*h*) standards and codes followed or to be followed in the construction and installation; and
(*i*) the fire protection and fire extinguishing equipment installed or to be installed on the platform; and
(*j*) the communication equipment; and

(*k*) the life saving equipment; and
(*l*) plans and specifications for the periodic inspection of the fixed platform
(*m*) a certificate of the verification of design given by a verifying body in accordance with Section 210(1) and a copy of the contract for that verification.

209. CONSENT TO USE A FIXED PLATFORM.

(1) A fixed platform shall not be used unless the Director has given consent in writing to the use of the fixed platform.

(2) An application for consent to the use of a fixed platform shall be made in writing and shall be accompanied by a certificate of verification of construction and installation of the platform, given by a verifying body in accordance with Section 210(2) and a copy of the contract for that verification.

(3) The structure of an installation on a fixed platform of other than the drilling and production equipment, personnel emergency facilities and accommodation shall not be altered or reconstructed without approval and, where applicable, verification by the verifying body.

210. CERTIFICATE OF VERIFICATION OF DESIGN, CONSTRUCTION AND INSTALLATION OF A FIXED PLATFORM.

(1) A certificate of verification of design of a fixed platform referred to in Section 208(I) is a certificate given by a verifying body certifying that the body is satisfied in relation to the design of the fixed platform that–

(*a*) the basic structural concept and configuration are appropriate for the conditions in which the fixed platform is proposed to be used; and
(*b*) a structural analysis has been made for critical loading with particular attention to the interaction between the structure and the piling; and
(*c*) a fatigue analysis has been made of critical joints; and
(*d*) an assessment of steel grades has been made in relation to stress levels, minimum service temperature and other significant parameters; and
(*e*) from an examination of the plans of the structure and the installations, the primary and secondary structures are suitable for the overall and local loading to be imposed and the design is in accordance with good practice; and
(*f*) the welding procedures used or proposed to be used are satisfactory and the design of the principal welds is satisfactory; and
(*g*) such other matters, as the Director has required, have been taken into account.

(2) A certificate of verification of construction and installation of a fixed platform referred to in Section 209(2) is a certificate given by the verifying body that verified the design, certifying that the body is satisfied in relation to the construction of the fixed platform and its installation in the licence area, that adequate and satisfactory inspection was carried out during the construction and installation and that all construction and installation was carried out as per the specifications.

211. INSPECTIONS OF A FIXED PLATFORM.

(1) Where the Director has consented to the use of a fixed platform, an inspection shall be carried out from time to time to ascertain whether the structure of and installations on the platform are being maintained in a safe working condition.

(2) An inspection under Subsection (1) shall be carried out by qualified personnel, in the manner and at the intervals at which the Director approves, and shall be certified on completion.

212. TESTS ON A FIXED PLATFORM.

Where the Director requires that a test in relation to the structural integrity of a fixed platform be carried out, that test shall be carried out in such a manner as will enable the results to be recorded and certified in an endorsed test document within the meaning of the By-laws of the National Association of Testing Authorities, Australia.

213. RECORDS OF TESTS ON A FIXED PLATFORM.

Records of or relating to an inspection, survey, examination or quality surveillance in relation to a fixed platform shall be forwarded forthwith to the Director.

214. ADDITIONAL REQUIREMENTS FOR A PLATFORM.

(1) A platform to be used or constructed or installed in the licence area shall have–

(*a*) around the unprotected perimeter of the floor or deck areas of, and openings on, the platform (other than a helideck), safety devices, guards or rails properly designed to prevent personnel from falling from the deck; and
(*b*) the perimeter of the helideck protected with a device of sufficient strength and size to provide an effective safeguard against a person falling from the helideck; and
(*c*) suitable access ways to helidecks which will ensure the safety of all embarking and disembarking passengers; and
(*d*) suitable transfer facilities sufficient to ensure safe movement of persons onto and off boats; and
(*e*) on any deck where there are survival craft, at least two adequately sized walkways running either the full length or the full width of the deck leading to those craft; and
(*f*) at least two separate stairways between decks; and
(*g*) on any deck, at least two adequately sized walkways running either the full length or the full width of the deck and leading to the stairways referred to in Paragraph (f); and
(*h*) stairways which comply with PNGS 1081 Code for Fixed Platform, Walkways, Stairways, and Ladders; and
(*i*) an appropriately equipped first aid facility for the care of sick or injured persons unless otherwise approved.

(2) In this section "survival craft" means survival craft complying with Section 221.

215. HELIDECK.

A helideck on a platform shall be designed, constructed and lighted in accordance with the requirements of the Civil Aviation Act 2000.

216. WARNING LIGHTS.

(1) A platform other than–

(*a*) a construction platform; or
(*b*) a mobile drilling unit that is being moved from one place to another,

shall show white warning lights in accordance with Subsection (2) and red warning lights in accordance with Subsection (3).

(2) White warning lights referred to in Subsection (1) shall–

(*a*) be not less than 6m and not more than 30m above mean high water; and
(*b*) be of such a number and (subject to this subsection) so placed that from any position in the vicinity of the platform at least one light is visible; and
(*c*) have an apparent intensity in the horizontal direction of not less than 1,400 candelas and shall be such that they are visible for a distance of not less than 10 nautical miles from all points more than 5m above sea level when the meteorological visibility is not less than 10 nautical miles; and
(*d*) be operated in unison to show the letter "U" in Morse Code at intervals of not more than 30 seconds.

(3) A red warning light referred to in Subsection (1) shall–

(*a*) be carried in such a position on the highest point of the equipment on the platform as to be visible for not less than two nautical miles from all points more than 5m above sea level when the meteorological visibility is not less than 10 nautical miles; and
(*b*) unless the extremity of the platform carried a white light in accordance with Subsection (2), be carried on each extremity in such a position as to be visible as required by Paragraph (a); and
(*c*) have an apparent intensity in all directions, at and above the horizontal, of not less than 10 candelas.

(4) Each obstruction (other than a buoy) associated with operations carried on in the licence area shall be marked by a buoy unless otherwise approved.

(5) There shall be–

(*a*) a flashing yellow light showing the letter "U" in Morse Code at intervals of not more than 30 seconds and visible for a distance of not less than four nautical miles from all points more than 5m above sea level when the meteorological visibility is not less than 10 nautical miles; and
(*b*) a radar reflector-on each buoy (other than a mooring buoy or buoy marking a mooring associated with a platform).

217. SOUND SIGNALS.

(1) A platform shall be equipped with a device capable of emitting sound signals which satisfies the requirements of the International Association of Lighthouses Authorities (IALA) for two nautical miles usual range fog signals.

(2) The device referred to in Subsection (1) shall be operated at all times, when the meteorological visibility is less than 0.5 nautical miles, to sound the letter "U" in Morse Code at intervals of not more than 30 seconds.

218. EMERGENCY ENERGY SOURCE FOR SIGNALS.

(1) The warning lights and sound signals referred to in Sections 216 and 217 on a platform shall have a reserve source of energy–

(*a*) that enables them to be operated for a period of four days in the event of the failure of the main energy supply on the platform; and
(*b*) that automatically comes into operation on the failure of the main energy supply.

(2) A platform shall be equipped with a device–

(*a*) that indicates whether the lights and signals referred to in Subsection (1) are operating on the main energy supply or the reserve source of energy; and
(*b*) that is readily observable by the site person-in-charge of the platform or, in the case of an unmanned platform, by a person at a shore station.

219. MARKING OF PLATFORMS.

(1) A platform shall be marked with a name not less than 600mm high such that it can be readily identified during day and night when approached from any direction.

(2) A platform helideck shall be marked so that it can be identified from an airborne helicopter.

220. LIFE JACKETS AND LIFEBUOYS.

(1) A platform shall carry life jackets:

(*a*) in number 150% of the number of persons on the platform; and
(*b*) complying with the provisions of Merchant Shipping Act 1975; and
(*c*) kept in approved places that are readily accessible and prominently indicated; and
(*d*) available for inspection at least once in each year by an approved qualified person.

(2) A platform shall carry at least eight lifebuoys of a type complying with the provisions of the Merchant Shipping Act 1975.

221. SURVIVAL CRAFT.

(1) In this section and in Section 222, "normal complement" means the number of persons who are normally present on a platform.

(2) Unless otherwise determined by the Director, a platform other than a construction platform or a service platform shall carry survival craft with an aggregate capacity sufficient to accommodate twice the normal complement.

(3) The survival craft referred to in Subsection (2) shall include–

(*a*) rigid totally enclosed, motor propelled and fire protected survival craft that will accommodate the normal complement; and
(*b*) other survival craft that will accommodate the normal complement which are capable of floating free and/or breaking free in the event of an emergency.

(4) Unless otherwise determined by the Director, a construction platform or service platform shall carry survival craft, capable of floating free and breaking free in the event of the platform becoming submerged, that will accommodate twice the normal complement.

(5) Survival craft shall be constructed and equipped so as to comply with the provisions of the Merchant Shipping Act 1975.

(6) Survival craft shall be prominently marked with an identifying name or number.

(7) Survival craft referred in Subsections (3)(b) and (4) shall be provided on at least two opposite sides of the platform.

(8) Each person on a platform shall be informed, and prominent notices shall show, which survival craft that person is to occupy in the event of an emergency.

(9) Survival craft carried on a platform shall be inspected at least once in each year by an approved qualified inspector.

222. EXCEEDING THE NORMAL COMPLEMENT.

The normal complement–

(*a*) may, in approved circumstances, be exceeded by 25%; and
(*b*) may be exceeded by more than 25% for a period not exceeding three hours during which there is a rostered shift change and there is a standby vessel, so situated, that if summoned, would arrive at the platform within 15 minutes.

223. ALTERNATIVE EVACUATION FACILITIES.

Alternative evacuation facilities, other than the fixed stairways, ladders or walkways shall be provided on at least two opposite sides of the platform.

224. FIRE FIGHTING EQUIPMENT.

A platform shall be provided with items of fire fighting equipment in such number, of such types and capacity and in such locations to safely and effectively to fight any fire that could occur on the platform.

225. COMMUNICATION EQUIPMENT.

(1) A platform shall be equipped with communication facilities which enable contact to be made at all times with the shore station referred to in Section 51 and with vessels and helicopters in transit between the platform and the shore.

(2) The equipment referred to in Subsection (1) shall include equipment which enables operation of an international distress frequency.

(3) There shall be a communication systems available on a platform to enable communications to a person or persons anywhere on the platform.

(4) All communication equipment referred to in this section shall have a source of energy that enables it to be immediately and continuously operated for a period of four days in the event of the failure of the main electricity supply on the platform.

226. BUOYS.

(1) A buoy, including a buoy referred to in Section 216, shall be painted yellow and shall be marked with the name of its owner.

(2) Where a buoy comes adrift from its moorings, steps shall be taken to recover it as soon as possible.

227. ELECTRICAL INSTALLATIONS.

(1) The classification of hazardous areas, electrical installations, wiring and fittings on a platform shall comply with PNGS 1022, PNG Wiring Rules or other approved code.

(2) A platform shall not be used for neutral returns from electrical installations.

(3) There shall be installed an earthing system connected to the structure at one or more points, all of which are effectively equipotential by nature of the structure or by bonding, and there shall be connected to the system–

(*a*) earth conductors from electrical equipment; and
(*b*) the frames of motors and generators; and
(*c*) metallic housings of all other electrical apparatus; and
(*d*) armoring of cables.

(4) The earth resistance or impedance of the earthing system shall be such as will permit the passage of a current from any pint in a circuit at which a fault may occur equal to three times the current required to operate the circuit protective device or in the case of insulated neutral system, to operate an alarm device.

(5) Provisions shall be made for the dissipation of static charges in accordance with PNGS 1458 Static Electricity Code or other approved code.

(6) Provision shall be made for lightning protection in accordance with PNGS 1288 Lighting Protection or other approved code.

228. FURNITURE AND FURNISHINGS.

In fixed platform offices and accommodation–

(*a*) all furniture shall be constructed, as much as possible, of non-combustible and/or fire retardant materials; and
(*b*) all suspended textile materials, upholstery covers and floor coverings shall have flame retardant qualities; and
(*c*) all combustible materials in Paragraphs (a) and (b) shall be of material that does not give off toxic fumes upon ignition.

229. FLAMMABLE AND TOXIC GASES.

(1) Any area in which operations could lead to the emission or accumulation of flammable or toxic gases shall be provided with suitable means of ventilation.

(2) A drilling or workover installation shall have approved degassing equipment installed in the mud system.

(3) A drilling, workover or production installation on a platform shall have continuous flammable gas detection equipment installed in any enclosed area containing petroleum handling equipment, open parts of the mud system or internal combustion engines.

(4) An operation where an emission of flammable gases can result in hydrogen sulfide gas concentrations of greater than 20ppm shall not be carried out unless continuous hydrogen sulfide gas detection equipment has been installed and is functioning.

(5) The monitoring devices referred to in Subsection (3) or (4), and the control mechanisms referred to in Subsection (7) shall be so arranged that functional tests of the separate components and of the whole system can be carried out efficiently.

(6) The functional tests referred to in Subsection (5) shall be carried out by a qualified person–

(*a*) at approved intervals; and
(*b*) immediately after any event indicating that the system or any part of the system is not operating correctly, and the results of any such test shall be recorded in an approved manner.

(7) The central control for the gas detection system required by Subsection (3) or (4) shall–

(*a*) be capable of giving an alarm at a point not higher than 60% of the lower explosive limit; and
(*b*) automatically activate shut-in sequences at a point not higher than 70% of the lower explosive limit; and
(*c*) in the case of hydrogen sulfide detection, be capable of giving an alarm before the concentration exceeds 20ppm.

(8) An internal combustion engine on a platform, other than an engine operating a fire pump, shall be provided with an emergency shutdown device which is automatically activated when flammable gas is detected in the air intake or, where such an engine is installed in pressurized housings, in the air intake of these housings and which is, where necessary, equipped with remote control equipment that is–

(*a*) accessible to the driller on a drilling or workover rig; and
(*b*) at some readily accessible point on a production platform.

(9) The exhaust piping of an internal combustion engine located on a platform shall be adequately lagged with approved material to prevent the ignition of any hydrocarbons accidentally coming into contact with the exhaust and shall be fitted with an approved spark arresting device.

(10) At least two approved portable explosimeters shall be provided on a platform.

230. PROGRESS REPORT OF CONSTRUCTION AND INSTALLATION.

(1) There shall be submitted to the Director not later than the 15th day of each month a report on progress made during the preceding calendar month in the construction and/or installation of facilities in the licence area.

(2) A report referred to in Subsection (1) shall contain all relevant information including progress reports of a verifying body, deviations from approved specifications for design, construction or installation, and proposed alternative courses of action.

PART X. – PIPELINES.

231. COMPLIANCE WITH CODES.

(1) Except where this Regulation otherwise requires, the construction and operation of a pipeline, as defined in the Act, (including design, manufacture, testing, maintenance, repair thereof and alterations and additions thereto) shall be in accordance with the Act and–

(*a*) AS 2885; or
(*b*) or such other code as the Director may from time to time approve in writing.

(2) Wherever the codes and specifications referred to in Subsection (1) require certified test reports to be submitted, such certification shall be in the form of Australian National Association of Testing Authorities endorsed test certificates.

(3) Before construction is commenced, the licensee shall supply to the Director the names of all testing authorities and other inspection services or contractors to be employed in quality surveillance of materials and fabrication and shall confirm that such testing authorities and inspection services meet the requirements of the Australian National Association of Testing Authorities or such other requirements as the Director may approve.

(4) Where a test is required to be carried out, under this Regulation or the Pipeline Licence issued under the Act, that is not included in a class of test in respect of which an endorsed test document of the kind referred to in this section can be given, the result of the test shall be recorded and certified to the satisfaction of the Director.

(5) Where practical, at least seven days notice shall be given to the Director of any proposed hydrostatic or flow efficiency tests.

(6) All test certificates referred to in this section and all radiographs shall at all times be readily available to a Petroleum Inspector and shall not be destroyed or otherwise disposed of except with the permission in writing of the Director.

(7) Unless otherwise agreed to by the Director, two copies of construction plans, including the location of all power lines and their voltages, oil and/or gas pipelines and their operating pressures, roads, stream and river crossings, engineering drawings, specifications and material lists shall be submitted to the Director before construction commences.

232. SIGNS.

(1) Signs or markers, in accordance with the standards nominated in Section 231, shall be erected and maintained–

(*a*) at each abrupt change of direction of the pipeline; and
(*b*) at each point where a pipeline crosses the boundary of a road; and
(*c*) at each side of a river or stream crossing; and
(*d*) at intervals not exceeding 500m where the pipeline parallels a road, within or immediately adjacent to the road easement; and
(*e*) at each point at which the pipeline crosses a significant service including, but not limited to, telecommunications and electric power cables, major pipelines, including water pipelines, and sewers and buried storm water drains; and
(*f*) at intervals not exceeding 2 km.

(2) The Director may approve variations to the requirements of Subsection (1).

(3) Where aerial markers are to be installed along a pipeline route, the signs required in Subsection (1) may be incorporated in such markers.

233. CONSTRUCTION AND OPERATIONAL REPORTING.

(1) The licensee shall submit to the Director a written report–

(*a*) on the construction of the pipeline during each six-monthly period ending on the 30 June and the 31 December; and
(*b*) upon completion of construction for each year a yearly ending on the 31 December, on the operation of the pipeline.

(2) Reports referred to in Subsection (1), shall be submitted within one month of the end of the period to which the report relates.

(3) A report under Subsection (1) shall give–

(*a*) such information on the construction and operation of the pipeline as the Director may require; and
(*b*) particulars of all persons employed by the licensee or his contractors in the construction or operation of the pipeline.

(4) During the construction of the pipeline, the site person-in-charge shall submit a progress report to the Director at regular intervals as approved by the Director.

234. COMMISSIONING OF PIPELINE.

A pipeline shall not commence operation unless the Director has approved pipeline safety, operating, commissioning and emergency procedures and has given his consent to the commencement of operations.

235. DISCONTINUATION OF OPERATIONS.

Where in the opinion of a Petroleum Inspector a condition which may endanger life or property exists in any section of a pipeline, he may direct in writing that the section be taken out of operation or that such other precautions be taken as are approved by him to ensure safety, and the Person-in-Charge of the section shall forthwith obey the direction.

236. ESCAPE OF SUBSTANCES FROM PIPELINES.

(1) Where any substance escapes from a pipeline, the Person-in-Charge shall take such steps as are necessary–

(*a*) to safeguard human life; and
(*b*) to minimize the loss of the substance from the pipeline; and
(*c*) to minimize the pollution of the surrounding environment by such substance,

and shall, as soon as possible, report the escape to the Director.

(2) After an escape of any fluid from a pipeline has been stopped and any necessary repairs completed, the Person-in-Charge shall forthwith submit a written report, complete with photographs, to the Director containing information upon–

(*a*) the time and place of the escape; and
(*b*) the approximate quantity of fluid lost; and
(*c*) the damage to equipment and/or the environment that resulted from the escape and/or ignition of the fluid; and
(*d*) the conditions that caused or contributed to the escape or

ignition; and
(*e*) the methods adopted to carry out repairs; and
(*f*) the circumstances generally relating to the escape, its control and any necessary repairs; and
(*g*) steps taken to minimize the chances of such circumstances recurring.

237. PIPELINE OR FLOWLINE ABANDONMENT.

(1) Abandonment of a buried pipeline or flowline shall meet the following requirements:–

(*a*) the line shall be depressured and purged of all produced fluids;
(*b*) the line shall be filled with clean fresh water;
(*c*) operations shall be performed to prevent the entrapment of fluid pressure within the line whether from hydrostatic head or other causes;
(*d*) all risers shall be cut off at the line burial level;
(*e*) all open accesses into the line shall be covered with a material that will prevent access to the line internals.

(2) Abandonment of a surface pipeline or flowline shall meet the following requirements:–

(*a*) the line shall be depressured and purged of all produced fluids using fresh water;
(*b*) the line and associated equipment shall be deconstructed, removed and disposed of in a safe manner as approved by the Director;
(*c*) the right of way shall be cleaned of debris and returned to as close to original condition as possible.

(3) Abandonment of an offshore pipeline or flowline shall meet the following requirements:–

(*a*) an offshore line may be abandoned in place if, in the opinion of the Director and the governing marine body of Papua New Guinea, the line will not present a hazard to marine navigation, fishing and other marine uses;
(*b*) the line shall be depressured, flushed and filled with sea water;
(*c*) any riser cut off at the sea floor and the ends of the line shall be properly plugged;
(*d*) where a line comes to shore, the line will be cut off at a distance from the shore or at a depth below sea level as directed by the Director.

PART XI. – REPORTING REQUIREMENTS.

238. SUBMISSION OF DATA.

Completion reports, in a style and format as approved by the Director, as required by Section 95 shall include–

(*a*) for seismic surveys–

(i) operations report; and
(ii) interpretation report; and
(iii) processing report; and
(iv) surveyor's report; and
(v) shot-point location maps on stable-base transparencies and in digital UKOOA format; and
(vi) processed seismic record sections on stable-base transparencies or digitally in SEGY format; and
(vii) seismic horizon structural contour maps (paper prints); and
(viii) elevation maps (paper prints); and
(ix) weathering maps or profiles on paper prints and digital ASCII format; and
(x) refraction records or record sections with shot-to-geophone distance shown on paper prints and in digital format; and
(xi) velocity analysis data on paper prints or digital ASCII format; and
(xii) experimental data (e.g. filter/noise analyses) (paper prints); and
(xiii) any other data relevant to the evaluation or interpretation of the survey; and
(xiv) magnetic data tapes in any acceptable format of–

(A) location data in A.M.G. plus latitudes and longitudes; and

(B) basic field data; and

(C) final data; and

(*b*) for gravimetric surveys–

(i) operations report; and
(ii) interpretation report; and
(iii) processing report; and
(iv) gravity profiles on paper prints and digital ASCII format; and
(v) bouguer anomaly maps with calculation methods explained; and
(vi) station location and line maps on stable-base transparencies or in digital ASCII format; and
(vii) elevation data (paper prints); and
(viii) meter calibration, drift and lis; and
(ix) of base station values, and locations with detailed descriptions; and
(x) surveying records as required for corrections to observations; and
(xi) tables of principal facts including station number, station coordinates, elevation and observed gravity plus copies of actual field data books; and
(xii) for digitally recorded data, magnetic data tapes in ASEG-GDP format or ER-Mapper format; and

(*c*) for an airborne geophysical survey

(i) operations report, including calibrations, test flight data, and
(ii) flight log copies; and
(iii) navigation, recovery and processing report; and
(iv) analogue records of magnetics or other parameters, terrain clearance, position, diurnal/storm monitor; and
(v) flight path plots; and
(vi) stacked profiles; and
(vii) contour maps of T.M.I. or other parameters; and
(viii) contour maps of depth-to-magnetic basement or of other parameters; and
(ix) magnetic data tapes in ASEG-GDF or ER-Mapper format of–

(A) grid data; and

(B) located data; and

(C) any other data relevant to the evaluation or interpretation of the survey.

239. DAILY REPORT.

The daily report as required under Section 112, shall include–

(*a*) the well name and number; and
(*b*) the report number and, if drilling, days from the spud date; and
(*c*) the depth of the well, current operation progress for the previous 24 hour period, bottom hole assembly and bit performance details; and
(*d*) the contractor carrying out operations; and
(*e*) details of any casing string run including size, weight, grade, type of coupling and accessories; and
(*f*) details of any cementing operations including quantity, additives, slurry density, anticipated top of cement and waiting on cement time; and
(*g*) blowout preventer tests, closures and reasons for closure, BOP drills and response times; and
(*h*) core recovery, core and cuttings description together with a statement of evidence of gaseous and liquid hydrocarbons in cores and cuttings; and
(*i*) results of deviation surveys; and
(*j*) mud properties, rates of penetration and loss of circulation; and
(*k*) details of formation or other tests carried out including production at the surface, drill pipe recovery, recorded pressures (field readings), bottom hole temperatures, flow and shut-in periods, surface choke size, API gravity of liquid hydrocarbons recovered and resistivity of water recovered; and
(*l*) evidence of high formation pressures encountered; and
(*m*) details of shooting, fracturing, acidizing, or other stimulation treatment; and
(*n*) details of plugging operations; and
(*o*) details of well logs run; and
(*p*) details of fishing or repair operations; and
(*q*) details of completion fluids, the depth of all perforations and the type of guns used; and
(*r*) details of well completion including well head, packers, tubing string and any artificial lift equipment installed; and
(*s*) details of liquid evaluation tests, multi-point and single point back pressure tests, subsurface pressure surveys, flow potential tests, separator tests and pre-and post-stimulation tests; and
(*t*) details of all formation integrity tests.

240. WELL COMPLETION REPORT.

The well completion report required under Section 114 shall include–

(*a*) the well name and number; and
(*b*) surveyed location in accordance with Section 106 and location relative to the nearest shot line and shot point; and
(*c*) surveyed elevation of ground level and kelly bushing; and
(*d*) the operating company, the interest holders and comprehensive details of the drilling rig used; and
(*e*) the spud date, date of completion of drilling and date of rig release, with driller's and logger's total depths; and
(*f*) a description of the stratigraphic units penetrated; and
(*g*) a composite well log containing bit record, penetration rate, casing record, formation tops giving name and age, sonic and gamma ray logs, core intervals, sidewall cores with age, hydrocarbon shows, test intervals and results, log analyses

intervals and results and a film or other transparent copy of each plan or composite log that is larger than A3 paper size submitted under this section shall also be supplied; and
(*h*) core and sidewall sample descriptions; and
(*i*) petrologic reports; and
(*j*) palaeontological and palynological reports; and
(*k*) fluid analyses (hydrocarbons and water); and
(*l*) core analyses; and
(*m*) formation test reports, charts and interpretation; and
(*n*) log interpretation; and
(*o*) full details of hole size, deviation surveys, casing string and cementing summaries; and
(*p*) details of the well completion where applicable, including well head, valves and choke assemblies, flow recorders, tubing string(s) and all down hole items and any down hole and surface artificial lift equipment; and
(*q*) details of the abandonment procedure where applicable; and
(*r*) maps of the structure horizons used to locate the well with post-drill intersections; and
(*s*) well velocity survey details where carried out; and
(*t*) a summary sheet giving brief details of the drilling, any problems encountered, coring, testing, casing, cementing and geological interpretations of the well; and
(*u*) details of any drillstem tests or production tests performed complete with preliminary interpretation of the test; and
(*v*) complete directional drilling data in tabular format including a final trajectory plot; and
(*w*) bit record in IADC format; and
(*x*) drilling fluid summary report for each hole section; and
(*y*) final wellbore schematic; and
(*z*) final wellhead schematic; and
(*aa*) perforating summaries; and
(*ab*) well stimulation summaries; and
(*ac*) cased hole logging summaries.

241. ADDRESSES TO WHICH NOTICES TO BE SENT.

(1) Reports required under this Regulation shall be addressed to the following address–

"The Director of Petroleum
"Department of Petroleum & Energy
"PO Box 1993
"PORT MORESBY
"PAPUA NEW GUINEA.
"Telephone: 322-4200
"Fax: 322-4222"

(2) If reports are sent by courier, the report shall be addressed to the following address–

"The Director of Petroleum,
"Department of Petroleum & Energy
"Elanese Street,
"Newtown,
"PORT MORESBY
"PAPUA NEW GUINEA."

(3) Cores and cuttings shall be sent to the address as listed in Subsection (2).

PART XII. – PENALTIES.

242. OFFENCES.

(1) A person who fails to comply with a Direction given under this Regulation or who contravenes a provision of this Regulation is guilty of an offence.

(2) Where a person–

(*a*) is performing the functions of a Licensee, whether as an employee or agent of or contractor to the Licensee, or as an employee or agent or subcontractor of a contractor to the Licensee, or otherwise; and
(*b*) in carrying out those functions commits an offence under this Regulation,

the licensee is guilty of an offence.

243. PENALTIES.

A person who commits an offence against this Regulation, for which a penalty is not otherwise provided for that offence, is liable–

(*a*) where he is the licensee, Person-in-Charge, deputy Person-in-Charge or other person giving directions relating to the carrying on of any petroleum prospecting development or production operations in a licence area–to a penalty of a fine not exceeding K5,000.00 and where the offence is a continuing one, to a default penalty of a fine not exceeding K500.00 per day for each and every day during which the offence continues; and
(*b*) where he is a person other than a person described in Paragraph (a)–to a penalty of a fine not exceeding K500.00 and where the offence is a continuing one, to a default penalty of a fine not exceeding K100.00 per day for each and every day during which the offence continues.

244. DEFENCE OF IMPRACTICABILITY.

It is a defence to a charge of a contravention of, or non-compliance with, any provision of this Regulation or a special instruction for the time being applicable under this Regulation that observance of or compliance with such Regulation or special instruction as the case may be was not reasonably practicable in the circumstances.

245. DEFENCE OF HAVING TAKEN RESPONSIBLE STEPS TO COMPLY.

It is a defence to a charge of a contravention of, or non-compliance with, any provision of this Regulation or a special instruction for the time being applicable under this Regulation if the person charged proves that he took all reasonable steps to comply with the requirements of the Regulation or special instruction.

IMPORTANT OPPORTUNITIES AND CONTACTS

PETROLEUM IN PNG

There has been a marked increase in the number of Petroleum Prospecting Licenses (PPL) issued in recent years and currently there are 40 PPLs blanketing most of Papuan and North New Guinea Basins.

Exploration drilling has increased commensurably with this growth and has already produced some notable successes including the gas/condensation discoveries at the Douglas well in the Western Province and Elk well in the Gulf Province. Exploration expenditure is expected to top US$100 million per annum in the near future. There will be a significant increase in the number of Foreland exploration wells drilled in the next few years.
Aggressive drilling will continue in the Fold Belt proper to prove up further oil reserves and to further appraise known gas resources.

PNG Oil Production has stabilised around 30,000bopd with input from the SE Mananda and NW Moran fields. Gas output from Hides average 14-15mmscf per day which is utilised for power generation for the Porgera mine. Gas commercialisation is the current driving force in the PNG petroleum sector and there are three separate LNG proposals being mooted. Other gas commercialisation projects under consideration include Dimethylether (DME), methanol and urea/fertilisers.

It is envisaged that this downstream industries would be developed in the Konebada Petroleum Park to be established on the west side of the Port Moresby Harbour, adjacent to InterOil's oil refinery or at suitable locations on the west coast of Port Moresby. Any development would be based on a gas pipeline sourcing gas from the existing producing fields or from stranded gas fields in the Foreland.

CHAMBER OF MINES AND PETROLEUM

The Chamber Secretariat is the administrative arm of the organisation and is headed by an Executive Director.

Office Location
Port Moresby, Papua New Guinea

Courier Address
First Floor, The Lodge, Bampton Street,
Port Moresby, National Capital District,
Papua New Guinea

Postal Address
PO Box 1032, Port Moresby, National
Capital District, 121, Papua New Guinea

Telephone
(675+) 321 2988 / 321 3827 / 321 0546

Facsimile
(675+) 321 7107

Email: info@pngchamberminpet.com.pg

STAFF

Greg Anderson FAusIMM Executive Director
ga@pngchamberminpet.com.pg

Jacinta Towamwesi Admin/Finance Officer
jdt@pngchamberminpet.com.pg

Leah Warupi Projects Officer
proj@pngchamberminpet.com.pg

Women in Mining Project

Lesley Bennett Project Manager | wim@pngchamberminpet.com.pg

PETROLEUM DIVISION

Department of Petroleum & Energy
PO Box 1993
Port Moresby
Papua New Guinea

Telephone: (+675) 322 4200
Facsimile: (+675) 322 4222
E-mail: Stanley_Pono@petroleum.gov.pg

Department of Petroleum & Energy
PO Box 1993
Port Moresby
Papua New Guinea

Telephone: (+675) 322 4207
Facsimile: (+675) 322 4222
E-mail: Peter_Woyengu@petroleum.gov.pg

Department of Petroleum & Energy
PO Box 1993
Port Moresby
Papua New Guinea

Telephone: (+675) 322 4299
Facsimile: (+675) 322 4222
E-mail: Iati_Ai@petroleum.gov.pg

Department of Petroleum & Energy
PO Box 1993
Port Moresby
Papua New Guinea

Telephone: (+675) 322 4245
Facsimile: (+675) 322 4222
E-mail: Rendle_Rimua@petroleum.gov.pg

Department of Petroleum & Energy
PO Box 1993
Port Moresby
Papua New Guinea

Telephone: (+675) 322 4282
Facsimile: (+675) 322 4222
E-mail: Peter_Kogl@petroleum.gov.pg

Department of Petroleum & Energy
PO Box 1993
Port Moresby
Papua New Guinea

Telephone: (+675) 322 4207
Facsimile: (+675) 322 4222
E-mail: Joe_Kuatowa@petroleum.gov.pg

For general enquiry's, contact us at: enquiry@petroleum.gov.pg or if you wish to send us electronic correspondence, please forward to: registrar@petroleum.gov.pg.

Mr. Stanley Pono
DIRECTOR

Mr. Peter Woyengu
a/ Assistant Director
Exploration Branch
Mr. Iati Ai
REGISTRAR
Licence Administration
Branch
Mr. Rendle Rimua
Assistant Director
Policy Branch
Mr. Peter Kogl
Assistant Director
Engineering Branch
Mr. Joe Kuatowa
Assistant Director
Co-ordination Branch

PAPUA NEW GUINEA DEPARTMENT OF MINING

The functions of the Department of Mining are:

- Develop the mining industry by actively encouraging socially, environmentally and technically responsible private sector exploration and development of mineral resources
- Expedite rural development by promoting and facilitating small-scale mining
- Provide background data, advice and services in the fields of exploration, geotechnical engineering, hydrogeology, volcanology and seismology aimed at facilitating development and identifying, monitoring and mitigating geological hazards
- Negotiate mining agreements and carry out related research and policy analysis
- Provide services to standing or *ad hoc* organisations relating to the functions of the Department

DEPARTMENT OF MINES CONTACTS

DEPARTMENT OF MINES
PMB PO,
Port Moresby 121
Konedobu
Port Moresby,
NCD
Papua New Guinea
Fax: (+675) 321 3701
General Enquiries: (+675) 322 7600

DoM STAFF

Ms Isabella **Abiari**	Regional Geologist
Telephone:	321 5888 Ext 612
email:	-
Mineral District Survey Section	Geol Survey, Headquarters, Newtown

Mr Jack **Abrahams**	Engineering Geologist
Telephone:	3224 620
email:	jack_abrahams@mineral.gov.pg
Geotechnical & Hydrogeological Survey Branch (GHS)	Geol Survey, Headquarters, Newtown

Ms Janet **Amean**	Director
Telephone:	322 7648
email:	janet_amean@mineral.gov.pg
Corporate Services Division	Headquarters, Konedobu

Mr Lawrence **Anton**	Chief Seismologist
Telephone:	321 3976 Ext 15
email:	-
Geophysical Observatory Branch (GPS)	Geol Survey, Headquarters, Newtown

Ms Rori **Arua**	Revenue Officer
Telephone:	322 7652

email:	-
Finance & Accounts Branch	Headquarters, Konedobu

Mr John **Arumba**	Sysmin Co-ordinator
Telephone:	322 7680
email:	john_arumba@mineral.gov.pg
Office Of The Secretary	Headquarters, Konedobu

Mr Ken **Aua**	General Labourer
Telephone:	-
email:	-
Reception Section	Headquarters, Konedobu

Mr Kuma **Aua, OBE**	Secretary
Telephone:	322 7675 (Direct Line 321 1961)
email:	kuma_aua@mineral.gov.pg
Office Of The Secretary	Headquarters, Konedobu

Ms Sharon **Bagi**	Secretary/KBO
Telephone:	322 7606
email:	-
Tenements Administration Branch	Headquarters, Konedobu

Mr Malcolm **Baibuni**	Co-ordinator (Porgera)
Telephone:	322 7620
email:	malcolm_baibuni@mineral.gov.pg
Mining Co-ordination Branch	Headquarters, Konedobu

Mr Daniel **Baine**	Senior Programmer (Hardware)
Telephone:	322 7669
email:	daniel_baine@mineral.gov.pg
Information Services Branch	Headquarters, Konedobu

Mr Fafaeg **Bibin**	Liaison Officer
Telephone:	852 1706
email:	-
Ramu Liaison Office	Headquarters, Konedobu

Ms Hedwig **Bob**	Executive Secretary
Telephone:	322 7629
email:	hedwig_bob@mineral.gov.pg
Mining Division	Headquarters, Konedobu

Mr John **Bosco**	Manager, Technical Services
Telephone:	982 1004 Ext 20
email:	-
Electronics Section (Technical Support) Branch	Rabaul Volcanological Observatory

Mr Joe **Buleka**	Chief Government Geologist (Director)
Telephone:	321 1973
email:	joe_buleka@mineral.gov.pg
GEOLOGICAL SURVEY DIVISION	Geol Survey, Headquarters, Newtown

Mr Tom **Charlton**	Geologist / Database Admnistrator
Telephone:	-
email:	palunkit@hotmail.com
TerraSearch	Headquarters

Ms Judy **Daniel**	Branch Clerk
Telephone:	322 7608
email:	-
Mining Co-ordination Branch	Headquarters, Konedobu

Mr Justin **Edimani**	Mining Engineer
Telephone:	474 6214
email:	-
Wau Office	Headquarters, Konedobu

Ms Marisah **Egara**	Secretary/KBO
Telephone:	321 3976 Ext 10
email:	-
Geophysical Observatory Branch (GPS)	Geol Survey, Headquarters, Newtown

Mr Simon **Egara**	Hydrogeologist
Telephone:	321 1360 Ext 222
email:	-
Geotechnical & Hydrogeological Survey Branch (GHS)	Geol Survey, Headquarters, Newtown

Mr Jason **Elemunop**	Geologist
Telephone:	321 1360 Ext 224
email:	-
Geotechnical & Hydrogeological Survey Branch (GHS)	Geol Survey, Headquarters, Newtown

Mr Kawa **Eva**	Security
Telephone:	-
email:	-
Wau Office	Headquarters, Konedobu

Dr Robert H. **Findlay**	Assistant Director
Telephone:	Ext 205
email:	gspng@mineral.gov.pg
Geological Mapping and Mineral District Survey Branch (GM	Geol Survey, Headquarters, Newtown

Ms Fresli **Fone**	General Labourer
Telephone:	321 1360 Ext 223
email:	-
Geotechnical & Hydrogeological Survey Branch (GHS)	Geol Survey, Headquarters, Newtown

Mr Kerry **Gadua** | Assets Manager
Telephone: 322 7653
email: -
Assets Section | Headquarters, Konedobu

Mr Vance **Gaoro** | Lands Officer
Telephone: 986 4100
email: -
Lihir Liaison Office | Headquarters, Konedobu

Mr Boge **Gari** | Senior Examiner
Telephone: 322 7650
email: -
Finance & Accounts Branch | Headquarters, Konedobu

Mr Vele **Gavu** | Mining Warden
Telephone: 322 7635
email: -
Tenements Administration Branch | Headquarters, Konedobu

Mr Ron **Gawi** | Assistant Director
Telephone: 322 7622
email: ron_gawi@mineral.gov.pg
Mining Co-ordination Branch | Headquarters, Konedobu

Mr Lawrie **Giwi** | Technical Officer
Telephone: 321 1360 Ext 215
email: -
Technical Staff | Geol Survey, Headquarters, Newtown

Mr Rausi **Guba** | Driver
Telephone: -
email: -
Mining Co-ordination Branch | Headquarters, Konedobu

Mr Ipi **Hailaeavila** | Assistant Director
Telephone: 322 7657
email: ipi@mineral.gov.pg
Human Resources Management Branch | Headquarters, Konedobu

Dr Graeme **Hancock** | Director
Telephone: 321 0466
email: graeme_hancock@mineral.gov.pg
Project Co-ordination & Implementation Unit ? Wbta (pciu) | Headquarters, Konedobu

Ms Margaret **Haoda** | Office Manageress (Executive Secretary)
Telephone: 321 0466

email: pciu@mineral.gov.pg
Project Co-ordination & Implementation Unit ? Wbta (pciu)
Headquarters, Konedobu

Mr Peter **Harou** — Expenditure Manager
Telephone: 322 7659
email: -
Finance & Accounts Branch — Headquarters, Konedobu

Mr Nagnining **Hawak** — General Labourer
Telephone: -
email: -
Wau Office — Headquarters, Konedobu

Miss Rachel **Heaven** — World Bank Consultant
Telephone:
email: reh@bgs.ac.uk
Geological Survey — Geophysics

Mr Shadrach **Himata** — Snr Co-ordinator (Misima/Simberi)
Telephone: 322 7623
email: shadrach_himata@mineral.gov.pg
Mining Co-ordination Branch — Headquarters, Konedobu

Ms Tova **Hou** — Paying Officer
Telephone: 322 7646
email: -
Finance & Accounts Branch — Headquarters, Konedobu

Mr Kennis **Ikilik** — Branch Clerk
Telephone: 982 1004 Ext 12
email: -
RVO DIVISION Branch — Rabaul Volcanological Observatory

Mr Robert **Imuli** — Security (Back Gate)
Telephone: 322 7664
email: -
Reception Section — Headquarters, Konedobu

Mr Ima **Itikarai** — Assistant Director
Telephone: 982 1699 Ext 11
email: hgurial@global.net.pg
RVO DIVISION Branch — Rabaul Volcanological Observatory

Mr Valu **Ivoa** — Systems Administration
Telephone: 322 7649
email: -
Finance & Accounts Branch — Headquarters, Konedobu

Ms Nellie **James**	Registrar
Telephone:	322 7615 (Direct Line 321 7981)
email:	nellie_james@mineral.gov.pg
Tenements Administration Branch	Headquarters, Konedobu

Ms Patricia **Japhlom**	Executive Secretary
Telephone:	322 7660
email:	patsony_japh@mineral.gov.pg
Corporate Services Division	Headquarters, Konedobu

Mr Lasark **Joseph**	Senior Economic Geologist
Telephone:	322 7634
email:	lasark_joseph@mineral.gov.pg
Mineral Project Assessment Branch	Headquarters, Konedobu

Ms Serah **Kais**	Secretary/KBO
Telephone:	474 6214
email:	-
Wau Office	Headquarters, Konedobu

Mr Pius **Kami**	Senior Liaison Officer
Telephone:	548 9087
email:	-
Tabubil Liaison Office	Headquarters, Konedobu

Mr Walo **Karona**	Chief Accountant
Telephone:	322 7662
email:	-
Finance & Accounts Branch	Headquarters, Konedobu

Mr Leo **Kasa**	Senior Mining Engineer
Telephone:	322 7603
email:	leo_kasa@mineral.gov.pg
Mineral Project Assessment Branch	Headquarters, Konedobu

Mr Paul **Kiu**	Regional Geologist
Telephone:	Ext 214
email:	-
Geological Mapping and Mineral District Survey Branch (GM	Geol Survey, Headquarters, Newtown

Mr Pokana **Kila**	Training & Staff Development Manager
Telephone:	322 7693
email:	-
Personnel Section	Headquarters, Konedobu

Mr Terry Win **Kilya**	Senior Regional Geologist
Telephone:	Ext 609

email: geosurvl@daltron.com.pg
Geological Mapping and Mineral District Survey Branch (GM
Geol Survey, Headquarters, Newtown

Mr Kessie **Kimbek** — Personnel Officer (Wages)
Telephone: 322 7642
email: -
Personnel Section — Headquarters, Konedobu

Mr Gwaibo **Kopi** — Senior Exploration Geologist
Telephone: 321 1360 Ext 208
email: -
Mineral District Survey Section — Geol Survey, Headquarters, Newtown

---

Mr Timonty **Kota** — Chief Mining Warden
Telephone: 322 7635
email: -
Tenements Administration Branch — Headquarters, Konedobu

Mr Gideon **Kouoru** — Senior Registry Clerk
Telephone: 322 7644
email: -
Registry Section — Headquarters, Konedobu

Mr Jonathan **Kuduon** — Senior Technical Officer
Telephone: 982 1004 Ext 18
email: -
Seismology Section — Rabaul Volcanological Observatory
Branch

Mr Gabriel **Kuna** — Assistant Director
Telephone: 321 1360 Ext 218
email: ghs@mineral.gov.pg
Geotechnical & Hydrogeological Survey Branch (GHS) — Geol Survey, Headquarters, Newtown

---

Mrs Gege **Kwapena** — Executive Secretary
Telephone: 322 7686
email: gege_kwapena@mineral.gov.pg
Office Of The Secretary — Headquarters, Konedobu

Mr Kwapena **Kwapena** — Assistant/Driver
Telephone: -
email: -
Project Co-ordination & Implementation Unit ? Wbta (pciu)
Headquarters, Konedobu

Ms Tania **Kwaragu** — Secretary/KBO
Telephone: Ext 213
email: -

Geological Mapping and Mineral District Survey Branch (GM
Geol Survey, Headquarters, Newtown

Ms Maxine **Lahan** — Acting Mining Warden
Telephone: 322 7606
email: -
Tenements Administration Branch — Headquarters, Konedobu

Mr Peter **Laka** — Contract Geologist
Telephone: 322 7606
email: -
Tenements Administration Branch — Headquarters, Konedobu

Ms Daisy **Lele** — General Labourer
Telephone: -
email: -
Mineral Project Assessment Branch — Headquarters, Konedobu

Ms Helen **Lohai** — Secretary/KBO
Telephone: 322 7678
email: -
Mineral Project Assessment Branch — Headquarters, Konedobu

Mr Howard **Lole** — Senior Mines Inspector
Telephone: 322 7616
email: min_lole@datec.com.pg
Inspection & Engineering Branch — Headquarters, Konedobu

Ms Nancy **Lolya** — Secretary/KBO
Telephone: 322 7677
email: -
Human Resources Management Branch — Headquarters, Konedobu

Mr Jim **Lytham** — Chief Hydrogeologist
Telephone: 321 1360 Ext 219
email: -
Geotechnical & Hydrogeological Survey Branch (GHS) — Geol Survey, Headquarters, Newtown

---

Ms Bernadette **Mararan** — Secretary/KBO
Telephone: 982 1004 Ext 26
email: -
RVO DIVISION Branch — Rabaul Volcanological Observatory

Mr John **Marcus** — Senior Mines Inspector
Telephone: 322 7614
email: john_marcus@mineral.gov.pg
Inspection & Engineering Branch — Headquarters, Konedobu

Mr Chris **McKee**	Assistant Director
Telephone:	321 3976 Ext 12 (Direct Line 321 4500)
email:	pmgo@daltron.gov.pg
Geophysical Observatory Branch (GPS)	Geol Survey, Headquarters, Newtown

Ms Helen **McKenzie**	General Labourer
Telephone:	-
email:	-
Tenements Administration Branch	Headquarters, Konedobu

Mr Mathew **Moihoi**	Geophysicist
Telephone:	321 3976 Ext 15
email:	-
Geophysical Observatory Branch (GPS)	Geol Survey, Headquarters, Newtown

Mr James **Mokepwesi**	Geophysicist
Telephone:	321 1360 Ext 216
email:	james_mokepwesi@mineral.gov.pg
Geophysics Section	Geol Survey, Headquarters, Newtown

Ms Evelyn **Mopafi**	Resource Scientist
Telephone:	322 7668
email:	emopafi@hotmail.com
Mineral Project Assessment Branch	Headquarters, Konedobu

Mr Nathan **Mosusu**	Principal Geophysicist
Telephone:	321 1360 Ext 216
email:	nathan_mosusu@mineral.gov.pg
Geophysics Section	Geol Survey, Headquarters, Newtown

Ms Judy **Muliap**	Assistant Accountant
Telephone:	-
email:	judy_muliap@mineral.gov.pg
Project Co-ordination & Implementation Unit ? Wbta (pciu)	
	Headquarters, Konedobu

Mr Kila **Mulina**	Senior Volcanologist
Telephone:	982 1004 Ext 18
email:	-
Volcanology Section	Rabaul Volcanological Observatory
Branch	

Mr Anselm **Mulungu**	Internal Auditor
Telephone:	322 7661
email:	-
Office Of The Secretary	Headquarters, Konedobu

Mr Jerry **Naime**	Co-ordinator (Tolukuma/Ramu/H. Valley)
Telephone:	322 7625
email:	jerry_naime@mineral.gov.pg

Mining Co-ordination Branch	Headquarters, Konedobu

Ms Noelyn **Naisen Lakl**	Executive Secretary
Telephone:	Ext 201
email:	noelyn_naisen@mineral.gov.pg
GEOLOGICAL SURVEY DIVISION	Geol Survey, Headquarters, Newtown

Mr Neka **Nansia**	General Labourer
Telephone:	-
email:	-
Wau Office	Headquarters, Konedobu

Mr Steven **Narawen**	Co-ordinator (Kainantu)
Telephone:	322 7630
email:	-
Mining Co-ordination Branch	Headquarters, Konedobu

Mr Stan **Nekitel**	Deputy Registrar
Telephone:	322 7633
email:	snekitel@mineral.gov.pg
Tenements Administration Branch	Headquarters, Konedobu

Mr Stevie T.S **Nion**	Deputy Secretary
Telephone:	322 7618 (Direct Line 321 2945)
email:	steve_nion@mineral.gov.pg
Office Of The Secretary	Headquarters, Konedobu

Mr John **Nohou**	Technical Officer
Telephone:	982 1004 Ext 31
email:	-
Survey Section	Rabaul Volcanological Observatory
Branch	

Mr James **Passmore**	World Bank Consultant
Telephone:	-
email:	jpass@bgs.ac.uk
British Geological Survey	Geol Survey and DoM HQ

Mr Herman **Patia**	Chief Seismologist
Telephone:	982 1004 Ext 17
email:	-
Seismology Section	Rabaul Volcanological Observatory
Branch	

Mr Firoz **Patwa**	Chief Mines Inspector
Telephone:	322 7607
email:	firoz_patwa@mineral.gov.pg
Inspection & Engineering Branch	Headquarters, Konedobu

Ms Patricia **Pepena**	Senior Resource Scientist
Telephone:	322 7695
email:	pat_pepena@mineral.gov.pg
Mineral Project Assessment Branch	Headquarters, Konedobu

Mrs Carol **Peter**	Executive Secretary
Telephone:	322 7687
email:	carol_peter@mineral.gov.pg
Office Of The Secretary	Headquarters, Konedobu

Ms Naomi **Peter**	Secretary/KBO
Telephone:	322 7688
email:	-
Mining Co-ordination Branch	Headquarters, Konedobu

Ms Mary **Pino?on**	Librarian
Telephone:	321 1360 Ext 217
email:	-
Technical Staff	Geol Survey, Headquarters, Newtown

Ms Ikanau **Pohu Aumi**	Receptionist (Switchboard Operator)
Telephone:	Ext 202/200
email:	-
GEOLOGICAL SURVEY DIVISION	Geol Survey, Headquarters, Newtown

Ms Kila **Pokana**	Secretary/KBO
Telephone:	322 7604
email:	-
Information Services Branch	Headquarters, Konedobu

Mr Igua **Robert**	Project Accountant
Telephone:	321 0466
email:	igua_robert@mineral.gov.pg
Project Co-ordination & Implementation Unit ? Wbta (pciu)	
	Headquarters, Konedobu

Ms Gepsy **Salala**	General Labourer
Telephone:	Ext 202
email:	-
GEOLOGICAL SURVEY DIVISION	Geol Survey, Headquarters, Newtown

Mr Steve **Saunders**	Chief Geodetic Surveyor
Telephone:	982 1004 Ext 30
email:	-
Survey Section	Rabaul Volcanological Observatory
Branch	

Mr Sigu **Sivok**	General Labourer
Telephone:	321 3976 Ext 10
email:	-

Geophysical Observatory Branch (GPS) — Geol Survey, Headquarters, Newtown

---

Ms Mary **Soi** — Senior Personnel Officer
Telephone: 322 7643
email: -
Personnel Section — Headquarters, Konedobu

Mr Robin **Suami** — General Labourer
Telephone: 321 1360 Ext 215
email: -
Technical Staff — Geol Survey, Headquarters, Newtown

Mr Douglas **Swalili** — Assistant Librarian (Engineering)
Telephone: 321 1360 Ext 223
email: -
Geotechnical & Hydrogeological Survey Branch (GHS) — Geol Survey, Headquarters, Newtown

---

Mr Peter **Taboko** — Technical Officer
Telephone: 982 1004 Ext 21
email: -
Electronics Section (Technical Support) Branch — Rabaul Volcanological Observatory

---

Mr Sonic **Taguse** — Supervising Draftsman
Telephone: 322 7632
email: -
Drafting Section (terra Search Ltd) — Headquarters, Konedobu

Mr Felix **Taranu** — Seismologist
Telephone: 982 1004 Ext 18
email: -
Seismology Section Branch — Rabaul Volcanological Observatory

---

Mr William **Tau-Vali** — Assistant Director
Telephone: 322 7638
email: willy_tauvali@mineral.gov.pg
Information Services Branch — Headquarters, Konedobu

Mr Husain **Tawakkul** — Deputy Mines Inspector
Telephone: 322 7602
email: tawakkul_husain@mineral.gov.pg
Inspection & Engineering Branch — Headquarters, Konedobu

Mr Graham **Taylor** — Sustainable Development Advisor
Telephone: 321 0466
email: graham_taylor@mineral.gov.pg
Project Co-ordination & Implementation Unit ? Wbta (pciu) — Headquarters, Konedobu

Mr Simon **Tohui**	Chief Technical Officer
Telephone:	982 1004 Ext 20
email:	-
Electronics Section (Technical Support) Branch	Rabaul Volcanological Observatory

Mr Gideon **Tongo**	Senior Mining Engineer
Telephone:	474 6353
email:	-
Wau Office	Headquarters, Konedobu

Ms Ani **Topurua**	Senior Policy Officer
Telephone:	322 7604
email:	atopurua@mineral.gov.pg
Mineral Project Assessment Branch	Headquarters, Konedobu

Mr Tony **Torea**	Office Assistant
Telephone:	322 7600 Ext. 9
email:	-
Reception Section	Headquarters, Konedobu

Mr Augustine **Tukas**	Liaison Officer
Telephone:	-
email:	-
Lihir Liaison Office	Headquarters, Konedobu

Mr Gabriel **Tukas**	Senior Liaison Officer
Telephone:	986 4059
email:	-
Lihir Liaison Office	Headquarters, Konedobu

Ms Nisal **Turbarat**	Secretary/KBO
Telephone:	322 7692
email:	-
Mining Co-ordination Branch	Headquarters, Konedobu

Ms Morea **Varuko**	Secretary/KBO
Telephone:	322 7611
email:	-
Mineral Project Assessment Branch	Headquarters, Konedobu

Mr Adrian **Walker**	World Bank Consultant
Telephone:	Ext 204
email:	-
WBTA Project	Geol Survey, Headquarters, Newtown

Ms Jessie **Wama**	Exploration Geologist
Telephone:	321 5888 x 611

email:	-
Mineral District Survey Section	Geol Survey, Headquarters, Newtown
Mr James **Wanjik**	Assistant Director
Telephone:	322 7628
email:	james_wanjik@mineral.gov.pg
Mineral Project Assessment Branch	Headquarters, Konedobu
Mr Sylvester **Wapea**	Staff Development Officer
Telephone:	322 7676
email:	-
Personnel Section	Headquarters, Konedobu
Mr Aaron **Watan**	Security (Front Gate)
Telephone:	322 7664
email:	-
Reception Section	Headquarters, Konedobu
Mr Anthony **Williamson**	Director
Telephone:	322 7624 (Direct Line 321 3093)
email:	anthony_williamson@mineral.gov.pg
Mining Division	Headquarters, Konedobu
Mr Joseph **Wukawa**	Geodetic Surveyor
Telephone:	982 1004 Ext 31
email:	-
Survey Section	Rabaul Volcanological Observatory
Branch	
Mr James **Yako**	General Labourer
Telephone:	322 7660
email:	-
Finance & Accounts Branch	Headquarters, Konedobu
Mr Thomas **Yetuin**	Senior Programmer (Software)
Telephone:	322 7670
email:	yetuin@mineral.gov.pg
Information Services Branch	Headquarters, Konedobu
Mrs Columbana **Ziksieh**	Secretary/KBO
Telephone:	-
email:	-
Lihir Liaison Office	Headquarters, Konedobu

List generated on: Friday 26 March 2004

BUSINESS TRAVEL

US STATE DEPARTMENT SUGGESTIONS

COUNTRY DESCRIPTION: Papua New Guinea is a parliamentary democracy and a member of the British Commonwealth. The country consists of the eastern half of New Guinea Island, the Bismarck Archipelago, the D'Entrecasteaux Islands, the Louisiade Archipelago, and the islands of Buka and Bougainville. Good tourist facilities exist in the capital of Port Moresby and in major towns such as Lae and Madang. The quality of tourist facilities in other areas varies and may be below U.S. standards, particularly in remote areas. Crime is a serious concern throughout Papua New Guinea (see paragraph on crime below).

ENTRY REQUIREMENTS: A valid passport, onward/return ticket, and proof of sufficient funds for the intended visit are required. Tourist visas are required for stays up to 60 days. (Visas are issued upon arrival at Jacksons International Airport in Port Moresby). Business visas require passport validity of at least one year from the date the visa is issued, two application forms, two photos, a company letter, biographic data, a recent annual report of the parent company and a fee for multiple entries. An AIDS test is required for work and residency permits (U.S. test accepted).

American citizens who remain in Papua New Guinea beyond the period authorized by immigration authorities may face fines and penalties. Papua New Guinea collects a departure tax. The departure tax is normally incorporated into airline fares at the time of ticket issuance.

For more information about entry and exit requirements, travelers may contact the Embassy of Papua New Guinea, 1615 New Hampshire Ave., NW, Suite 300, Washington DC 20009, Tel. 202-745-3680, or visit the Embassy's website at http://www.pngembassy.org.

Travelers may also wish to obtain entry permission from the Government of Australia for transit or other purposes (see section on Medical Facilities) before traveling to Papua New Guinea. American citizens no longer need a visa to travel to Australia as tourists but must obtain an Electronic Travel Authority (ETA) through their travel agent. For further information about Australian visas or the ETA, contact the Embassy of Australia in Washington, D.C., at 1-800-242-2878 or at the Embassy of Australia's website at http://www.austemb.org.

SAFETY AND SECURITY: Before traveling to Bougainville, the largest island in the North Solomons province, it is recommended that visitors obtain updated security information from the U.S. Embassy in Port Moresby. Despite a peace agreement between the government and dissidents, law enforcement is weak on Bougainville, there are no tourist facilities on the island and transportation facilities are limited.

An Indonesian secessionist group remains active along the largely inaccessible Papua New Guinea/Indonesia border on the island of New Guinea.

The Southern Highlands Province is also an area of instability. Incidents of ethnic violence have occurred near urban centers and tourist sites. American citizens considering travel to the region should consult with their tour operator and the American Embassy prior to doing so.

The town of Rabaul, on the island of New Britain, is located near two active volcanoes that buried half of the town during eruptions in September 1994. Volcanic activity continues, and travelers should be aware of the potential for further eruptions. Persons with respiratory problems may find that airborne ash exacerbates their conditions.

CRIME: Papua New Guinea has a high crime rate. Crime and personal security are serious concerns throughout Papua New Guinea. Carjackings, armed robberies, and stoning of vehicles are a problem in Port Moresby, the capital. Pickpockets and bag-snatchers frequent crowded public areas. Hiking in rural areas and visiting isolated public areas such as parks, golf courses, beaches, or cemeteries can be dangerous. Persons traveling alone are at greater risk for robbery or gang rape than those who are part of an organized tour or under escort. Visitors to Papua New Guinea should avoid using taxis or buses, known as public motor vehicles, and should rely instead on their sponsor or hotel to arrange for taxi service or a rental car.

Travel outside of Port Moresby and other major towns at night can be hazardous, as criminals set up roadblocks. Visitors should consult with the U.S. Embassy or with local law enforcement officials concerning security conditions before driving between towns. Travel to isolated places in Papua New Guinea is possible primarily by small passenger-aircraft; there are many small airstrips throughout the country. Security measures at these airports are rare. Organized tours booked through travel agencies remain the safest means to visit attractions in Papua New Guinea. The Embassy recommends that prospective visitors consult "A Primer on Personal Security for Visitors to Papua New Guinea," available from the Bureau of Consular Affairs homepage at http://travel.state.gov.

The loss or theft abroad of a U.S. passport should be reported immediately to the local police and the nearest U.S. Embassy or Consulate. U.S. citizens may refer to the Department of State's pamphlet *A Safe Trip Abroad* for ways to promote a more trouble-free journey. The pamphlet is available by mail from the Superintendent of Documents, U.S. Government Printing Office, Washington, D.C. 20402, via the Internet at http://www.access.gpo.gov/su_docs, or via the Bureau of Consular Affairs home page at http://travel.state.gov.

MEDICAL FACILITIES: Medical facilities in Papua New Guinea vary from hospitals in Port Moresby and the larger towns to aid posts (including some missionary stations) in remote areas. Medical facilities vary in quality, but those in the larger towns are usually adequate for routine problems and some emergencies. Equipment failures and sudden shortages of common medications can mean, however, that even routine treatments and procedures (such as X-rays) may become unavailable. A hyperbaric recompression chamber for diving emergencies is available in Port Moresby. Pharmacies in Papua New Guinea are small and may be inadequately stocked. They are found only in urban centers and at missionary clinics. Doctors and hospitals often expect immediate cash payment for medical services.

Medical conditions arising as a result of diving accidents will almost always require medical evacuation to Australia. More sophisticated medical facilities are located in Australia. The most commonly used facilities are in Brisbane and Cairns, both in the Australian state of Queensland. Travelers who anticipate the need for ongoing medical treatment should obtain entry permission for Australia in advance. Entry permission for Australia can be granted by the Australian Embassy in Port Moresby, but it is easier to obtain prior to leaving the United States.

MEDICAL INSURANCE: U.S. medical insurance is not always valid outside the United States. U.S. Medicare and Medicaid programs do not provide payment for medical services outside the United States. Doctors and hospitals often expect immediate cash payment for health services. Uninsured travelers who require medical care overseas may face extreme difficulties.

Check with your own insurance company to confirm whether your policy applies overseas, including provision for medical evacuation, and for adequacy of coverage. Serious medical problems requiring hospitalization and/or medical evacuation to the United States can cost tens of thousands of dollars. Ascertain whether payment will be made to the overseas hospital or doctor or whether you will be reimbursed later for expenses you incur. Some insurance policies also include coverage for psychiatric treatment and for disposition of remains in the event of death.

Useful information on medical emergencies abroad, including overseas insurance programs, is provided in the Department of State's Bureau of Consular Affairs brochure *Medical Information for Americans Traveling Abroad*, available via the Bureau of Consular Affairs home page or autofax: (202) 647-3000.

OTHER HEALTH INFORMATION: Information on vaccinations and other health precautions may be obtained from the Centers for Disease Control and Prevention's hotline for international travelers at 1-877-FYI-TRIP (1-877-394-8747); fax 1-888-CDC-FAXX (1-888-232-3299), or via CDC's Internet site at http://www.cdc.gov.

TRAFFIC SAFETY AND ROAD CONDITIONS: While in a foreign country, U.S. citizens may encounter road conditions that differ significantly from those in the United States. The information below concerning Papua New Guinea is provided for general reference only, and may not be totally accurate in a particular location or circumstance.

Safety of Public Transportation: Poor
Urban Road Conditions/Maintenance: Poor to Good
Rural Road Conditions/Maintenance: Poor
Availability of Roadside Assistance: Not Available

Traffic in Papua New Guinea moves on the left. Travel on highways outside of major towns can be hazardous. Motor vehicle accidents, especially where passengers are sitting in the open bed of a pickup truck, are one of the more common causes of serious injury in Papua New Guinea. Drivers and passengers are urged to wear seatbelts whenever possible. There is no countrywide road network, roads are generally in poor repair, and flat tires occur routinely as a result of debris on the roadways. Landslides can be a problem on some stretches of the Highlands Highway between Lae and Mount Hagen during the rainy season. Criminal roadblocks have occurred during the day on the Highlands Highway and more widely after dark. Travelers should consult with local authorities or the U.S. Embassy before traveling on the Highlands Highway.

Reactions by crowds after road accidents in Papua New Guinea can be emotional and violent. Crowds form quickly after an accident and may attack those whom they hold responsible, stoning and/or burning their vehicles. Friends and relatives of an injured party may demand immediate compensation from the party they hold responsible for injuries, regardless of legal responsibility. Persons involved in accidents usually find it prudent to proceed directly to the nearest police station rather than stopping at the scene of an accident.

For additional general information about road safety, including links to foreign government sites, see the Department of State, Bureau of Consular Affairs home page at http://travel.state.gov/road_safety.html. For specific information concerning Papua New Guinea driving permits, vehicle inspection, road tax and mandatory insurance, contact the Papua New Guinea Tourism Promotion via the Internet at http://www.paradiselive.org.pg.

AVIATION SAFETY OVERSIGHT: As there is no direct commercial air service by local carriers at present, or economic authority to operate such service, between the U.S. and Papua New Guinea, the U.S. Federal Aviation Administration (FAA) has not assessed Papua New Guinea's Civil Aviation Authority for compliance with international aviation safety standards.

For further information, travelers may contact the Department of Transportation within the U.S. at 1-800-322-7873, or visit the FAA's Internet website at http://www.faa.gov/avr/iasa/. The U.S. Department of Defense (DOD) separately assesses some foreign air carriers for suitability as official providers of air services. For information regarding the DOD policy on specific carriers, travelers may contact DOD at (618) 229-4801.

CUSTOMS REGULATIONS: Papua New Guinea customs authorities may enforce strict regulations concerning temporary importation into or export from Papua New Guinea of items such as firearms, certain prescription drugs and sexually explicit material. Other products may be subject to quarantine. It is advisable to contact the Embassy of Papua New Guinea in Washington for specific information regarding customs requirements.

CRIMINAL PENALTIES: While in a foreign country, a U.S. citizen is subject to that country's laws and regulations, which sometimes differ significantly from those in the United States and may not afford the protections available to the individual under U.S. law. Penalties for breaking the law can be more severe than in the United States for similar offenses. Persons violating the Papua New Guinea law, even unknowingly, may be expelled, arrested or imprisoned. Penalties for possession, use, or trafficking in illegal drugs in Papua New Guinea are strict, and convicted offenders can expect severe jail sentences and fines.

CONSULAR ACCESS: U.S. citizens are encouraged to carry a copy of their U.S. passports with them at all times, so that, if questioned by local officials, proof of identity and U.S. citizenship are readily available.

DISASTER PREPAREDNESS: Papua New Guinea is located in an area of high seismic activity. Although the probability of a major earthquake occurring during an individual trip is remote, earthquakes can and will continue to happen. In addition, there are two active volcanoes near the town of Rabaul on New Britain. General information regarding disaster preparedness is available via the Internet from the U.S. Federal Emergency Management Agency (FEMA) home page at http://www.fema.gov.

CHILDREN'S ISSUES: For information on international adoption of children or international parental child abduction, please refer to our Internet site at http://travel.state.gov/children's_issues.html or telephone (202) 736-7000.

REGISTRATION/EMBASSY LOCATION: U.S. citizens are encouraged to register at the Consular Section of the U.S. Embassy in Port Moresby and obtain updated information on travel and security within Papua New Guinea. The U.S. Embassy is located at Douglas Street, Port Moresby, Papua New Guinea. This address should be used for courier service deliveries. The Embassy is located adjacent to the Bank of Papua New Guinea. The mailing address is P.O. Box 1492, Port Moresby, N.C.D. 121, Papua New Guinea. The U.S. Embassy's telephone number is (675) 321-1455; fax (675) 321-1593. Americans may submit consular inquiries via e-mail to: consularportmoresby@state.gov.

BUSINESS CUSTOMS

The workday is 8:00 a.m. to 4:30 p.m. Monday to Friday for most people. Banks are open from 9:00 a.m. until 2:00 p.m. from Monday to Thursday and from 9:00 a.m. to 5:00 p.m. on Fridays. Most business and government offices do not open on the weekends.

Business dress is moderately casual, befitting PNG's tropical climate. Work attire usually consists of shirt and tie or sport shirt for men, and light business suit or dress for women. In most areas, lightweight clothing is appropriate year round, but warmer clothes may be necessary in the Highlands, especially in the evening.

IMPORTANT INFO FOR TRAVEL

TRAVEL ADVISORY AND VISAS

Entry Requirements: Tourists may obtain a 60-day visa for K10 (about US$ 7.50) at a Papua New Guinea diplomatic mission or for K25 (less than US$ 20) upon arrival at Port Moresby International Airport. The visa can only be obtained upon presentation of an onward air ticket and evidence of funds sufficient for the proposed stay. Business travellers must apply at a Papua New Guinea diplomatic mission to obtain a business visa. The one-year visa allows multiple entries not exceeding 60 days per visit and costs K250 (about US$ 190).

Travellers may also wish to obtain a visa for Australia before travelling to PNG. Australia began participating in the Visa Waiver Pilot Program with the U.S. in July 1996. However, depending on the carrier, Australian visas may be required for U.S. citizens whose travel to Australia originates in PNG. Travellers who anticipate the need for on-going, routine, or other forms of medical treatment in Australia are advised to obtain visas for Australia before leaving the United States. Australian visas are issued in Port Moresby, but in a case involving medical treatment the Australian visa authorities will require a referral from a local doctor, proof of acceptance by an Australian doctor, and proof of the patient's ability to pay for treatment. For information on Australian visa requirements, contact an Australian diplomatic mission.

Information on Crime: Crime and personal security are serious concerns in PNG. Armed robberies and carjackings are a problem in Port Moresby and other urban areas. Armed robbery is sometimes accompanied by gratuitous violence. Criminals often target persons who are part of large crowds. There is a danger of rape, including gang rape, in many urban and rural areas of PNG. Women should not walk alone in PNG, especially at night. Travellers to PNG should avoid using taxis or buses and should rely instead on a sponsor or on a rented car for transportation. Travel outside of Port Moresby by car at night can be hazardous. Holdups at roadblocks have been known to occur day or night on the Highlands Highway. Reactions to road accidents involving fatalities or serious injuries can be emotional and violent, regardless of legal responsibility. Persons involved in accidents should proceed to the police station in the provincial capital.

STATUTORY HOLIDAYS

New Year's Day January 1
Good Friday variable
Easter Saturday variable
Easter Monday variable
Queen's Birthday mid-June
Provincial Government Day July 19
Remembrance Day July 23
(observed 7/21/97)
Independence Day September 16
Christmas Day December 25
Boxing Day December 26
Business Infrastructure

Language: English is the official language of government and commerce and will be spoken by almost all people with whom the business traveller is likely to deal. However, the language understood by the majority of Papua New Guineans is Melanesian Pidgin.

Currency: No restrictions are placed on bringing U.S. dollars into or out of PNG. Letters of credit, travellers' checks, U.S. currency, and personal checks drawn on U.S banks are freely negotiable. PNG uses a decimal currency system; the units are kina and toea (100 toea = 1 kina).

Health: Most serious endemic diseases are not a problem in PNG. Malaria, however, is endemic to the area and includes coroquine-
resistant strains. Seek medical advice prior to arrival for recommended precautions. There are hospitals in Port Moresby and in the larger towns. Medical facilities vary in quality, but in the larger towns generally are adequate for routine problems and some emergencies. Equipment failures, shortages of common medications, and reductions in services due to lack of government funding can mean, however, that even routine treatments and procedures are sometimes unavailable. The nearest reliable medical facilities are located in the Australian town of Cairns in North Queensland, a 1 1/2 hour flight from Port Moresby. Medevac flight services are available.

Communications: International telephone, telegraph, telex, internet, and facsimile services are available. International telecommunications and postal services are reasonably reliable.

Transportation: PNG is served by an international airport at Port Moresby and over 400 other airports and airstrips throughout the country. Air Niugini, the national carrier, operates scheduled domestic cargo and passenger services within PNG and international services to Australia, Indonesia (Jayapura, Irian Jaya), Solomon Islands, Manila, Singapore and Hong Kong. Several smaller carriers offer scheduled domestic service and charters. Qantas flies regularly to Port Moresby from Sydney, Brisbane and Cairns. Milne Bay Air recently inaugurated a passenger service from Port Moresby to Cairns and Townsville, Australia. Rental cars are available in the major towns. Traffic moves on the left, as in the United Kingdom. Bus service exists in the few areas where there are connecting roads but is not recommended. The longest road is the Highlands Highway from Lae to Mendi. There are no railroads.

Housing: There are hotels of moderate to good quality in Port Moresby and other major towns. Suitable Western-style residential and business premises are available in urban areas. Rental rates are high due to the shortage of land available for lease.

Food: Supermarkets stock a wide variety of fresh foods and groceries. There are several good restaurants in Port Moresby and other major towns.

IMPORTANT INFORMATION: VISAS

ENTRY PERMITS (FOR EMPLOYMENT PURPOSES)

These procedures are a guide to all employers recruiting non-citizens for employment purposes and for prospective employees who wish to obtain an entry permit for employment.

PNG position Approval and Work Permit Requirement

The Employment of Non Citizen's Act Chapter 374 and Fourth Edition Work Permit Guidelines prescribe that subject tot he receipt of a satisfactory Training and Localization Programme in the context of a Three Year training plan, approval will be granted to a company or an employer to recruit non-citizens to fill certain positions.

The approval by the Department of Industrial Relations (DIR) of a position to be held by a non-citizen is valid for up to three years.

The non-citizen also must obtain a valid work permit from the DIR before entry to PNG.

Immigration Requirements for Entry to PNG for Employment

In addition to DIR requirements the prospective employee must meet immigration requirements. To enter PNG the employee must obtain a valid and appropriate entry permit.

How to Obtain a Entry Permit for Employment: What the Employer Has to Do

The employee must provide:

a written sponsorship letter to the ICD indicating the job offer to the employee highlighting person's name, position number, position title, period of contract approved by the DIR, salary range and a company guarantee of accommodation and transportation for the employee and dependents.
an original maintenance guarantee bond/s for the employee/applicant and dependents.
copy of the work permit approval letter from the DIR for employment of the applicant in the approved position.
an Immigration Fee for an entry permit for employment purposes and appropriate dependent entry permit fees are to be paid by the employer/agent in PNG. Fees are to be paid tot he Department of Finance Cash Office, Bureau of Management Services or nearest Customs Office and receipts are to be given as evidence of payment to ICD. See Schedule 1 for appropriate fees.
the overseas Mission at which the applicant will apply for the entry permit.
What the Employee Has To Do

The prospective employee is to complete an entry permit application and forward/deliver it to the nearest PNG Overseas Mission or if there is no PNG presence the nearest Australian Overseas Mission.

The Entry Permit Application will require the applicant to provide full personal particulars of the applicant and his/her dependents (if any, whether travelling/not travelling as below:

Full Name
Date of Birth
Marital Status
Citizenship Status during last ten (10) years
What Does It Cost?

A fee of K50 (US$52.00) is also payable to cover facsimile and telephone costs incurred in facilitating issue of the permit.

Processing of the Application

Once the employee completes the entry permit application, details of the application will be sent to the Immigration and Citizenship Division (ICD) in Port Moresby who will consider issue of an entry Permit for the non-citizen.

At the same time, the DIR in Port Moresby will consider the employer's application to employ the applicant against the approved position. If the DIR accepts the application, a work permit approval will be sent to the employer and notification to ICD.

Once the overseas Mission has the ICD approval to issue an Entry Permit, an entry permit with work permit number included will be issued. The permit will be issued for a maximum of three (3) years subject to the applicant's passport also being valid for the three year period. Should the passport expire before the three year period, the entry permit will only be issued for the period of validity of the passport. When the applicant obtains a new passport, ICD Port Moresby will issue an entry permit for the balance of the three year period. This new entry permit will be issued without charge.

An extension to a work permit beyond the three year limit is also possible. Please read the procedures for entry permit extension.

CHANGE OF STATUS

From/To Dependant's entry Permit (Foreign Employee)

A dependant spouse of a foreign employee ma be allowed to work in PNG after the DIR has assessed the labor market situation and upon receipt of authentic documents in relations o the qualifications and experience of the dependent.

In order to work, a work permit is required from the DIR and the status of the spouse's entry must be changed from "Employment Prohibited" to an employment entry permit. ICD will issue an employment entry permit for the applicant for the period of contract regardless of whether the principal applicant's entry permit expires at an earlier date. It is possible for the principal applicant, at the expiry of his/her contract/entry permit, to seek change of status from "employment" to "dependant" and remain in PNG with his/her spouse.

Persons arriving in PNG on visitor and business entry permits are not permitted to change status to employment.

How to Apply

To change entry permit status from dependant to employment the dependant must complete a Request For Entry Permit Extension form with a copy of the DIR work permit. To change entry permit status from employment to dependant, the application must also complete the relevant sections of a Request for Entry permit Extension form, submit details of the employment of his/her spouse and provide his/her passport and also that of the spouse.

Dependant of Citizen

A dependant (with foreign nationality) of a PNG citizen may engage in employment in PNG if:

he/she has a DIR work permit and
the appropriate change of status fee and employment entry permitfee are paid (change of status refers to change of status from dependant to working resident).
Change of Marital Status

A person who whilst in PNG changes marital status detailed on their entry permit is required to apply for change of entry permit status. The applicant must provide ICD with proof of marital status change i.e. marriage or divorce papers and ICD will re-issue the entry permit accordingly.

What is the fee?

The cost for a change of marital status is K500 (US$512.50)

Change of Name/Change of Employer Name

Where a person changes his/her name by Deed Pole etc or where the name of the company which employs the person changes, the Immigration Regulations require that a change of name be effected on the entry permit. Details of the change of name have to be furnished to ICD and the entry permit will be reissued accordingly.

What is the fee?

The cost for a change of name/change of employer name is K500 (US$512.50)

Change of Contractual Commitment/Status

Persons in the following categories must seek a change of entry permit status:

who resign from their position and find alternative employment.
whose contract expires and find alternative employment.
People whose contracts expire and are extended in their current position or in another position in the same company do not require a change of status.

The above change of status is usually undertaken in conjunction with an application for an entry permit extension. See entry permit extension guidelines.

What does it cost?

The cost for a change of contractual commitment/status is K500 (US$512.50)

Penalties

A penalty of K5,000 (US$5,125.00)is payable in respect of failure to obtain an appropriate entry permit for employment and residence purposes and failure to apply for appropriate change of status.

ENTRY PERMIT EXTENSION FOR EMPLOYMENT PURPOSES

These procedures are a guide to all employers, agents and/or non-citizen employees requesting entry permit extension for employment or defendants purposes.

When Does An Entry Permit Need Extension?

An Entry Permit needs to be extended if the employee is required to continue in the same position beyond the expiry date of his/her initial (entry permits are usually issued for three years) and the DIR issues the necessary work permit.

Entry permits also need to be extended where the employee changes positions in the company or finds alternative employment i.e. changes employers.

When Can't An Entry Permit Be Extended?

Entry permits cannot be extended where:

the DIR has not issued the appropriate work permit for the position occupied.
for an unmarried child with a dependant entry permit reaches the age of sixteen (6) years. When the child attains sixteen year of age he/she must leave PNG unless he/she is enrolled in academic study in PNG. If the child is enrolled in academic study in PNG, then a student entry permit will be issued. For children over 16 years and not enrolled in study in PNG, future visits would normally occur under sixty day Tourist Entry Permit arrangements.
How To Obtain An Entry Permit Extension

What The Employer Has To Do

The Employer must provide to ICD:

the job offer to the employee highlighting person's name, position number, position title, period of contract approved by the DIR, salary range and a company guarantee of accommodation and transportation for the employee and defendants.
copy of the DIR work permit approval letter for the person to be employed in the position.
an original maintenance guarantee bond/s for the employee/applicant and defendants.
a copy of the changeof status (if appropriate) and entry permit extension fee receipt is to be attached.

What the Employee Has To Do

The applicant must complete a "Request to Extend Period of Validity of an Entry Permit Form" and submit it to ICD together with his/her passport and those of any defendants.

Rates For Entry Permit Extensions

The cost for extension of an Entry Permit for Employment is K500 (US$512.50). It should be noted that a fee for change of status is also applicable where the applicant changes employers of class/types e.g. from dependant to working resident.

The fee for each dependant entry permit extended is K20 (US20.50)

What Penalties Apply?

A penalty of K500 (US$512.50) applies to late application for entry permit extension. Breaches on the Migration Act attract a penalty of K5,000 (US$5,125.00).

BUSINESS PERSON/INVESTOR ENTRY PERMIT

These procedures are a guide to all persons who wish to invest in PNG establish companies and seek an entry permit as an owner/operator or senior executive.

How To Obtain A Entry Permit For Business Person/Investor

What the Investor Has To Do

The investor has to invest a minimum of K150,000 (US$153,750) in PNG in a company or business. The K150,000 (US$153,750) must be transferred into PNG and not derived through loans raised with PNG banks. The investment may be by way of cash investment in plant and equipment or a combination of plant/equipment and annual salaries (including annual superannuation) of PNG staff and approved expatriate staff salaries/fees/superannuation paid to the investor or his/her immediate family cannot be included as part of the K150,000 (US$153,750) investment.

The investor also has to seek a position and work permit from the DIR.

The investor must:

provide a letter to ICD indicating his/her name, position number, position title, period of contract approved by the DIR and salary range.
documentary evidence that the K150,000 (US$153,750)investment has been transferred into the country and a copy of the Investment Promotion Authority (IPA) approval letter and share/registration certificate.
copy of work permit approval letter in respect of the position from the DIR.
For entry permits for employment purposes and dependant, K250.00 (US$256.25) and K10.00 (US$10.25) are respectively required.
Fees are to be paid to the Department of Finance Cash Office. Bureau of Management Services or nearest Customs Office and receipts are to be given as evidence of payment to ICD.
complete an Entry Permit Application form and forward it to the ICD of the Department of Foreign Affairs and Trade.
Processing of the Application

The ICD in Port Moresby will consider issue of an Entry Permit for the non-citizen. If the applicant meets the criteria and a work permit has been issued by the DIR, any entry permit will be issued.

The applicant need not depart PNG in order to receive the entry permit i.e. a change of status in entry permit category may be effected in PNG at a cost of K500 (US$512.50). An extension of the entry permit beyond an initial three year limit is also possible. Please read the procedures for entry permit extension.

Dependant Entry Permits

Entry permits for defendants are also available in the same manner as permits are issued to defendants of applicants for employment entry permits.

Extension of Entry Permits

An entry permit extension can be obtained in accordance with the fees and procedures outlined for Entry Permit Extension for Employment purposes.

BUSINESS ENTRY PERMIT

These procedures are a guide to all business people and agents requesting business entry permits.

What is a Business Entry Permit?

A Business Entry Permit permits a person to enter PNG to conduct business as a distinct from undertaking employment. Business Entry Permits are valid for a maximum of sixty (60) days per entry and are valid for twelve (12) months from date of issue. As such, business entry permits are multiple entry.

When is a Business Entry Permit Required?

Business activity encompasses such things as checking on investments, investigating business opportunities, holding meetings with suppliers/buyers, signing contracts, attending board meetings, etc. If a person engages in any of the above activities, a maximum entry business permit is required. A Tourist Entry Permit is not appropriate if the above activities are undertaken. Heavy penalties apply for engaging in business without having a business entry permit.

Where To Apply

Application for permits may be made at PNG Overseas Missions or if there is no PNG presence, the nearest Australian Overseas Mission. Application may also be made on arrival at Jackson's International Airport in Port Moresby.

How To Apply

The procedures below are to obtain multiple entry business permits for Papua New Guinea. These procedures apply both to applications lodged overseas and those lodged on arrival in Port Moresby.

The application must complete a "Request for entry Permit" (Form 1).
A covering letter from the sponsor detailing why the applicant is coming to Papua New Guinea and the expected number and length of visits is to be provided. Note that a sponsor letter is required in order to obtain a business entry permit on arrival.
Evidence of return tickets from Papua New Guinea must be supplied.
Payment of the Migration Service Fee of K250 (US$256.25) must be made.
An extension of up to thirty (30) days maybe granted in exceptional cases to the sixty (60) days entry period by application to the Minister of the Department of Foreign Affairs and Trade and payment of K200 (US$205.00). Such applications must provide:
documentary evidence that the applicant still has business to complete in Papua New Guinea.
reasons why it could not be completed within the sixty (60) days period.
A dependant of the applicant may enter PNG under a visitor entry permit upon payment of the fee listed in Schedule 1.
What Penalties Apply?

A penalty of K1,000 (US$1,025.00)applies to any breach of conditions and requirements for business entry permits.

SHORT TERM ATTACHMENT ENTRY PERMITS

These procedures are a guide to persons seeking short term attachment entry permits for Papua New Guinea.

What is a Short Term Attachment?

A Short Term Attachment refers to situations where a person wishes to enter PNG for a period of not more than three months and undertake a work assignment.

What are the Restrictions on Such Employment?

Entry to PNG for short term attachment is only possible in respect of positions approved by the DIR. Short term attachments include, such activities as performing short work assignments (e.g. conduct a company audit, performance reviews, repair/commission equipment, train staff in new systems/procedures, etc) and relief duties.

Entry is only possible where there is a valid reason for the short term attachment. In this respect, employers are not permitted to employ non-citizens on a temporary basis while the permanent occupant is absent on either sick leave or recreation leave without first obtaining the written approval of the DIR. Approval will only be given by DIR where the occupation is classed as professional i.e. doctors, accountants, managers, lawyers, engineers, etc. In all other cases national employees who are qualified and experienced, or understudying non-citizen counterparts, are to assume full responsibilities for such positions during temporary absences of nominal occupants.

Are Dependant Entry Permits Available?

Dependant Entry Permits are not issued for short term attachments. Dependants may enter PNG as visitors and receive a 60 day entry permit. Visitor permits are available from PNG Missions overseas or on arrival at Jacksons International Airport in Port Moresby at the cost K25 (US$25.63). A visitor entry permit may be extended for a further 30 days upon application to the Minister of Foreign Affairs and Trade and payment of K50 (US$51.25).

What are the Procedures for Application?

The applicant must complete an Application for Entry Permit detailing the reason for requesting a short term entry and have a confirmed return air ticket.
The employer must submit details of the DIR approved position to the Immigration and Citizenship Division in Port Moresby.
Where can Applications be Lodged?

Applications may be lodged at any PNG Overseas Mission or where there is no PNG presence, the nearest Australian Mission.

How is the Application Processed?

The PNG Overseas Mission will refer details of the application to ICD for decision. ICD will consider the application and advise the Mission of approval or rejection. The Mission will then issue the necessary entry permit.

What is the Fee?

The fee for a short term attachment entry permit is K250 (US$256.25).

What Penalty Applies for Overstay?

Heavy penalties apply for overstay of entry permits. It is the responsibility of the permit holder to ensure that he/she leaves the country on or before the date that his/her entry permits expires. If the permit holder is unable to leave on/before the due date it is his/her responsibility to contact the Director of Entries, ICD to explain the circumstances.

If the permit holder fails to contact the ICD and he/she overstays the entry permit, a penalty of K5,000 (US$5,125.00) applies.

CONSULTANT/SPECIALIST ENTRY PERMIT

These procedures are a guide for consultants/specifies wishing to enter PNG.

What is a Consultant/Specialist Entry Permit?

A Consultant/Specialist Entry Permit allows entry of a person to PNG for consultancy/specialist work for not more than three months.

What Restrictions Apply on Such Employment?

Persons entering under this category of entry permit are permitted to enter PNG only once per calendar year. The consultant/specialist must have a PNG sponsor.

What are the Procedures for Application?

The applicant must complete an Application for Entry Permit detailing the reason for requesting a permit and have a confirmed return air ticket.
The PNG sponsor must submit details of the requirement for the consultancy/specialist assistance in writing to the ICD in Port Moresby.
Are Dependant Entry permits Available?

Dependant Entry Permits are not issued in respect of this category of entry permit. Dependants may enter PNG as visitors and receive a 60 day entry permit. Visits permits may be obtained overseas or on arrival at Jacksons International Airport in Port Moresby for the costs of K10 (US$10.25). A visitor entry permit may be extended for a further 30 days upon application to the Minister of Foreign Affairs and Trade and payment of K50 (US$51.25).

Where can Applications be Lodged?

Applications may be lodged at any PNG Overseas Mission or where thee is no PNG presence, the nearest Australian Mission.

How is the Application Processed?

The PNG Overseas Mission will refer details of the application to ICD for decision. ICD will consider the application and advise the Mission of approval or rejection. The Mission will then issue the necessary entry permit.

What is the Fee?

The fee for a consultancy/specialist entry permit is K250 (US$256.25).

What Penalty Applies for Overstay?

Heavy penalties apply for overstay of entry permits. It is the responsibility of the permit holder to ensure that he/she leaves the country on or before the date that his/her entry permit expires. If the permit holder is unable to leave on/before the due date, it is his/her responsibility to contact the Director of Entries, ICD to explain the circumstances.

If the permit holder fails to contact ICD and he/she overstays the entry permit, a penalty of K5,000 (US$5,125.00).

DEPENDANTS OF PNG CITIZENS

Dependants of citizens may enter PNG and reside as non-working or working residents.

Where to Apply?

Application for entry permits may be made at PNG Overseas Mission or where there is no PNG presence or the nearest Australian overseas Mission.

How to Apply

To reside in PNG as a non working resident, the following information must be provided to ICD or the PNG Mission.

a letter from the applicant's spouse (i.e. the PNG citizen) outlining the personal particulars of the applicant and providing a copy of the marriage certificate (or birth certificate for children).
payment of a landing bond (equivalent tot he cost of return airfare for the dependant/s) and a copy of the receipt.
payment of the appropriate immigration fee of K10 (US$10.25).
To resident in PNG as a working resident, the following information must be provided to ICD or the PNG Mission.

information/receipts as per a non-working resident.
a work permit from the DIR. See procedures for obtaining an employment entry permit. In certain circumstances, a spouse can obtain a letter from the Minister for the DIR exempting him/her from the provisions of the Employment of Non-Citizens Act i.e. exempting the person from the need to obtain a work permit. This letter is accepted by ICD in lieu of a work permit.
payment of an immigration fee for an employment entry permit (instead of a dependant of citizen entry fee).
It should be noted that dependants of citizens who initially enter PNG as non working spouses and subsequently seek employment are required to pay not only the fee for an employment entry permit but also pay for a change of status.

TOURIST ENTRY PERMITS

These procedures are a guide to all tourist requesting tourist entry permits.

Where to Apply

Application for permits may be made a PNG Overseas Missions or where there is no PNG presence, the nearest Australian Overseas Mission or Jacksons International Airport, Port Moresby. Tourist Entry Permits are valid for sixty (60) days.

How to Apply

The procedures below are to be followed to obtain tourist entry permits for Papua New Guinea.

The applicant must complete a "Request for Entry Permit" (Form 1).
Evidence of return tickets from Papua New Guinea must be supplied.
Payment of the Migration Service Fee of K10 (US$10.25) must be made if the application is lodged at a PNG or Australian Overseas Mission. where an entry permit application is made on arrival at Jacksons International Airport in Port Moresby, payment of K25 (US$25.63), in local currency, is required. It should be noted that while entry permits for visitors will be issued on arrival, this process obviously takes more time than for passengers with permits. For this reason, it is advisable to obtain entry permits before arrival in PNG.
What is the Fee?

The cost for a Tourist Visa is K10.00 ($ 10.25)

Tourist Entry Permit Extensions

The sixty (6) days entry permit may be extended by a maximum of thirty (30) days by application tot he Minister of Foreign Affairs and Trade. The procedure is as follows:

The Applicant must complete a Request to Extend Period of Validity of an Entry Permit, Form 3.
The applicant must provide evidence of payment of the Migration Service Fee of K50 (US$51.25) for Permit Extensions i.e. a copy of the receipt paid to the Department of Finance Cash Office, Bureau of Management Services or nearest Customs Office.

TOURIST YACHTSMAN ENTRY PERMIT

Special entry permits are issued for yachtsmen (owner/captain of yacht) and are valid for 60 days. an extension of 30 days is possible upon application tot he Minister for Foreign Affairs and Trade.

The crew of yachts are treated as visitors and are provided with Tourist Entry Permits valid for 60 days. An extension of 30 days is possible upon application to the Minister of Foreign Affairs and Trade.

Where Can Entry Permits for Yachtsmen be Obtained?

They can be obtained at PNG Overseas Missions or where there is no PNG presence, the nearest Australian Overseas Mission, on arrival in PNG from any Customs Office or at the ICD in Port Moresby.

How Much Do they Cost?

The costs for Entry Permits for Yachtsmen (owner/captain) is K100.00 (US$103.00) whilst the Crew of Yacht is K10.00 (US$10.25)

What Penalties Apply?

A penalty of K500 (US$512.50) applies to late application for entry permit renewals and a penalty of K5,000 (US$5,125.00) applies for breaches of the Migration Act.

ENTRY PERMITS FOR OTHER CATEGORIES

JOURNALIST/REPORTERS

Special entry permits are necessary for journalists/reporters wishing to enter PNG and are valid for 60 days.

How to Apply

The applicant must complete an entry permit application and attach a letter of confirmation from the Institute of Papua New Guinea Studies.

Where to Apply

Application may be made through a PNG overseas Mission or where thee is no PNG presence, the nearest Australian overseas Mission. Applicants may also be made direct with the ICD of the Department of Foreign Affairs and Trade.

Are Dependant Entry Permits Available?

Dependent Entry Permits are not issued in respect of this category of entry permit. Dependants may enter PNG as visitors and receive a 60 day entry permit. Visitor Permit costs K10.00 (US$10.25). A visitor entry permit may be extended for a further 30 days upon submission of application to the Minister of Foreign Affairs and Trade and payment of K50.00 (US$51.25) is applied.

How Much Do Entry Permits Costs?

Costs for Entry Permits for journalists/reporters is K100.00 (US$103.00). A thirty day extension will cost K200 (US$205.00).

ENTERTAINERS

Entry Permits for commercial entertainers for 60 days are available at a cost listed by category as follows: Comedian (Commercial) K250.00 (US$256.25); Musician (Commercial) K250.00 (US$256.25).

Applicants must complete an entry permit application and have a letter from the event organizer providing details of the event and expected length of stay. Entry Permits for dependants are issued under visitor entry permit provisions.

FILM MAKERS (COMMERCIAL)

Entry Permits are available for commercial filmmakers for 60 days at the cost of K500 (US$512.50).

The applicant must complete an entry permit application and produce a letter from the Institute of PNG Studies indicating its approval tot he project and expected length of stay. Entry permits for dependants are issued under visitor entry permit provisions.

GOSPEL AND CULTURAL EXCHANGE GROUPS

Entry Permits are available to the above groups at the cost of K10 (US$ 10.25) for Gospel Group (Charity), K10 (US$ 10.25) for Cultural Exchange (Charity) and K10 (US$ 10.25) for Dependant (considered as tourist)

Gospel groups require a letter from the sponsoring religious organization or performance event organizer providing details of the event and the expected length of stay. Cultural groups require a letter from the Institute of PNG Studies indicating its agreement to the exchange or a letter from the event organizer providing details of the exchange and expected length of stay. In either case, an entry permit application must be completed.

OCCUPATIONAL TRAINEES

Entry Permits for foreign cadets and trainees are available at the cost of K10 (US$10.25). Applicants must complete an entry permit application and have a letter from the educational institution or sponsoring organization providing details of the course of study and the expected length of stay. A maintenance guarantee for the costs of repatriating the trainee at the end of their course must also be provided by the sponsoring organization.

STUDENT/FORMAL EDUCATION

Entry Permits will be issued to student applicants undertaking full time study in Papua New Guinea. The fee for this type of entry permit is K10 (US$10.25). Student applicants must complete an entry permit application and present a copy of a letter from the educational institution or sponsoring organization providing details of the course of study and the expected length of stay. Confirmation of acceptance into the course must be provided.

Penalties Applicable to the Above Categories

A penalty of K5,000 (US$5,125.00) applies to breaches of the Migration Act in respect of the above categories.

SPECIAL EXEMPTION ENTRY PERMITS

Multiple Entry Permits for periods of one to five years may be granted to the following categories of persons. The cost of an entry permit is K10 (US$10.25) with the exception of the Melanesian Spearhead Group (MSG) member countries category which is gratis and the diplomatic category which is gratis if the country in question reciprocates for PNG diplomatic staff:

resident or accredited diplomats of foreign governments and international organizations.
nationals of MSG countries (Solomon Islands, Vanuatu, and FLNKS) and Fiji nationals.
church workers engaged in pastoral duties and Mission volunteers not engaged in business activities of a church. Such workers are required to be employed in positions approved by the DIR for foreign occupancy.
volunteers/aid workers from overseas agencies working directly with the PNG community. These volunteers require a sponsor letter detailing work to be performed and the expected length of stay. They are required to be employed in positions approved by the DIR.
Volunteers from overseas on secondment to PNG agencies. These volunteers require a sponsor letter and are required to be employed in positions approved by the DIR. In addition they must obtain a work permit from the DIR.
foreign aid personnel from approved organizations as per the aid Status Act.
personnel from approved research or educational institutions from abroad. Foreign academics working in PNG are required to be employed in positions approved by the DIR for foreign employment.

employees of foreign governments.
researchers/film makers (non commercial).
dependants of the above categories of exempt persons.

Where to Apply

Application may be made through any PNG Overseas Mission or where there is no PNG presence, the nearest Australian Overseas Mission. Applications may also be made direct with the ICD of the Department of Foreign Affairs and Trade.

Papua New Guinea Citizens

Download Current Immigration Guidelines
Application for New Papua New Guinea Passport
Renewal of Papua New Guinea Passport

Non-Papua New Guinea Citizens

Entry Requirements for Business Visa
Requirements for Short-Term Visas (other than tourism and business)
Entry Requirements for Tourist/Visitors Visa
Visa on Arrival
Visa obtained on Post
Long-Term Entry Requirements

APPLICATION FOR NEW P.N.G PASSPORT

Please send the following:

Completed new passport application forms (2)
Processing fee of $31.00 per applicant
Three (3) Passport size photographs
Mailing fee to/from Papua New Guinea via Express Mail $44.00
Birth Certificate
Marriage Certificate (if applicable)
Note:
Your application will be sent to the Department of Foreign Affairs Immigration and Citizenship Division.
Your new Papua New Guinea passport will be sent directly to your home address after it is processed.

RENEWAL OF PAPUA NEW GUINEA PASSPORT

Please send the following:

Expired Papua New Guinea passport
Completed new passport application forms
Processing fee of $31.00 per applicant
Passport size photographs (3)
Return stamped address envelope (Federal Express, Express Mail or Certified Mail)
Note:

Processing time is 3 - 5 days upon receipt of application.

ENTRY REQUIREMENTS FOR BUSINESS VISA

Valid passport (must be valid at least one year from the date visa is issued)
Application form with 1 passport photo.
Brief report on PNG-based company or on-going Business in Papua New Guinea;
Recent annual report of parent company.
Complete bio-data of the applicant.
Self-addressed stamped envelope either certified, express mail or Federal Express (if visa is obtained by mail)
Company letter (endorsing/indicating exact purpose of business).
Travel itinerary or copy of ticket.
Visa Fee: multiple entry - $256.25
(Money order or company check payable to the Embassy of Papua New Guinea)

PERSONAL CHECKS OR CASH NOT ACCEPTABLE

Multiple entry visa is valid for one (1) year, with eight (8) weeks maximum stay each visit.

(*)Extension to period of each visit not exceeding thirty (30) days may be granted upon production of supporting documents and subject to Ministerial approval. Fee: $205.00

Dependent of Business Visitor Fee: $10.25

Extension to period of visit for Dependent of Business visitor may be granted subject to (*) above. Fee: $51.25

Upon receipt of all the required documents your visa will be processed within three (3) to seven (7) working days.

All items on the application form must be completed/signed. Failure to do so will result in return of your visa application.

Revised Migration & Citizenship Policies
Effective March 5, 1996

REQUIREMENTS FOR SHORT-TERM VISAS OTHER THAN TOURISM AND BUSINESS

All applicants for Medical Elective, Research, Short Term Consultancy, Volunteer,(see separate section for Journalist & media) are advised to take note of the following important information.

It is very important that approval for all above categories of visas are obtained from Immigration in Port Moresby before visas are issued at this Embassy.

This is necessary to ensure that integration into the rural people of researchers is done with the knowledge of the local authorities to avoid indiscriminate interference with the people's lives.

It is also to ensure that visitors into the country have a genuine interest in the lives and culture of the traditional life of Papua New Guinea in carrying out their programme.

Journalist and Film Makers

All applications for the above two (2) categories require the approval of the Secretary of Foreign Affairs, through the Assistant Secretary, Media and Information Branch, Department of Foreign Affairs, P.O. Wards Strip, Waigani.

Telephone: (675) 271260
Fax: 254467
Telex: NE 22136 FOREIGN
NE 22194 FOREIGN

The request for approval to enter Papua New Guinea should be sought in advance of the request for visa being presented at the Embassy.Any tourist writers travelling on the invitation of a tourist agent in Papua New Guinea, or on behalf of a tour agent in the United States or Canada, must submit the letter of invitation and their itinerary for consideration.

Procedures

When visas for above are requested, they should be done with a knowledge of an agency in Papua New Guinea. The agency in Papua New Guinea having established where the visit will take place and the purpose of the visit, should formally request for the visa from the Immigration Division, Department of Foreign Affairs, Waigani, PNG. Telex: NE 22377. On the basis of this request from the local authority, approval will then be telexed to the Embassy to issue the visa.

It is also advisable that applications should be accompanied by a copy of their research or programme proposal, as well as a copy of the letter to the Immigration Division from a local authority. This is necessary for the Embassy staff to know if approval for visa requests are delayed.

Important

It is therefore important for all interested persons to ensure that a copy of a letter from the Papua New Guinea agency is submitted with the passport and the applications for visa, for speedy processing and to avoid unnecessary delays.

The process of request and approval for visas sometimes takes up to 6 months if members of the public are not familiar with the procedures.

VISA FEES:

Entertainer (Commercial) $256.25/passport
Film Maker (Commercial) $512.50/passport
Journalist/Reporter $102.50/passport
(Extension of 30 days) $205.00/passport

ENTRY REQUIREMENTS FOR TOURIST/VISITORS VISA

VISA ON ARRIVAL

Citizens of the following countries intending to travel to PNG for tourism purposes may be issued with a maximum of 60 days visa on arrival.

Australia Cyprus Japan Portugal
Austria Denmark Netherlands Switzerland
Belgium France Norway Sweden
Canada Germany New Zealand United States
United Kingdom

Entry is subject to the following conditions:

one is not adversely recorded by PNG authorities;
have sufficient funds;
in possession of return/onward tickets to country for which entry rights are assured; (ticket may not be purchased at Jackson Airport)
in possession of 1 completed request for entry permit form
passports bear automatic returnability;
total stay of 60 days;
entry is made at Jacksons Airport, Port Moresby

VISA FEE : K25 = $25.63
VISA OBTAINED ON POST

Following are the short term entry requirements for applicants travelling to Papua New Guinea for the purpose of tourism (maximum of sixty (60) days visa)

Application to be lodged at Embassy of PNG Washington D.C.
Applicant must submit a valid passport at least 6 months from the time application is submitted;)
application form with 1 passport photo;
evidence of return or onward ticket;
self-addressed stamped envelope either certified, express mail or Federal Express (if visa is obtained by mail)
VISA FEE - $10.25 per passport (company check or money order payable to the Embassy)
PERSONAL CHECK OR CASH NOT ACCEPTABLE.

All items on the application form must be completed/signed. Failure to do so will result in return of your visa application)

Upon receipt of all the required documents your visa will be processed within three (3) to seven (7) working days.

Revised Migration & Citizenship Policies
Effective: March 5, 1996

LONG TERM ENTRY REQUIREMENTS

Following are the long term entry requirements for applicants travelling to Papua New Guinea (PNG) for the purposes of; Employment and all other applications other than the Tourist/Business/Official Business.

Valid Passport
1 application form
1 passport size photograph
Full medical check
Certificate of AIDS check results from a U.S. Government Health Agency

Chest X-ray results/reports (do NOT send the X-ray film)
Security (police) checks from local place of residence
Character reference from competent authorities
Letter of confirmation from sponsoring organisation or employer
Visa Fee in money order or company check payable to the Embassy of Papua New Guinea.
self-addressed envelope, stamped either certified, Federal express, DHL, UPS, Airborne or Express Mail
PERSONAL CHECKS OR CASH NOT ACCEPTABLE.

MULTIPLE EMPLOYMENT

Period of 3 months to 3 years $256.25/passport
Extension to Employment Entry Permit $512.50/passport
Dependents $ 10.25/passport
Volunteer church workers/researchers/missionaries $ 10.25/passport

Children under the age of 16 and accompanying their parent(s) are exempted from requirements 6 to 9.

The medical X-ray reports will be returned to the applicants, who will hand carry together with the X-ray film for presentation to the Immigration Office, Waigani, Port Moresby (PNG)

The Immigration Division of the Department of Foreign Affairs in Papua New Guinea authorises long term entry visas. Employers and sponsoring organisations liaise with Immigration Division to authorise Papua New Guinea Diplomatic Missions and Posts to issue the appropriate visa.

The foregoing are the requirements of the Government of Papua New Guinea.

SUPPLEMENTS

PAPUA NEW GUINEA LAWS AND REGULATIONS: ALPHABETICAL LISTING

A

Accountants Act 1996
Accountants Registration and Practice Regulation 1998
Admiralty Court Act 1840 (United Kingdom, adopted)
Admiralty Court Act 1861 (United Kingdom, adopted)
Admiralty Rules (United Kingdom, adopted)
Adoption of Children Act (Chapter 275)
Adoption of Children Regulation (Chapter 275)
Adultery and Enticement Act 1988
Aerodrome (Business Concessions) Act 2000
Agents for Natives Regulation (TNG) (Chapter 298)
Agriculture Bank Regulation (Chapter 139) [Rural Development Bank Regulation (Chapter 139)]
Aid Status (Privileges and Immunities) Act (Chapter 345)
Anatomy Act (Chapter 227)
Anatomy Regulation (Chapter 227)
Anglican Church of Papua New Guinea Property Trust Act 1993
Animal Disease and Control Act (Chapter 206)
Animal Disease and Control Regulation (Chapter 206)
Animals Act (Chapter 329)
Animals Regulation (Chapter 329)
Apprenticeship and Trade Testing Act 1986
Apprenticeship and Trade Testing Regulation 1991
Appropriation (National Development Expenditure 2001) Act 2000
Arbitration Act (Chapter 46)
Architects (Registration) Act 1989
Architects (Registration) Regulation 1992
Arrest Act (Chapter 339)
Arrest Regulation (Chapter 339)
Asian Development Bank Act (Chapter 82)
Asian Development Bank (Privileges and Immunities) Regulation (Chapter 87)
Assemblies of God in Australia (New Guinea) Mission Act (Chapter 1002)
Associations Incorporation Act (Chapter 142)
Associations Incorporation Regulation (Chapter 142)
Attorney-General Act 1989
Attorney-General Regulation 1990
Auctioneers Act (Chapter 90)
Auctioneers Regulation (Chapter 90)
Audit Act 1989
Australian Churches of Christ Overseas Mission Board Act (Chapter 1003)

B

Baby Feed Supplies (Control) Act (Chapter 365)
Baby Feed Supplies (Control) Regulation (Chapter 365)
Bail Act (Chapter 340)
Bail Regulation (Chapter 340)

Bamu River Mission Act (Chapter 1005)
Banking Corporation Act (Chapter 136)
Banks and Financial Institutions Act 2000
Banks and Financial Institutions Regulation (Chapter 137)
Bills of Exchange Act (Chapter 250)
Boards (Fees and Allowances) Act (Chapter 299)
Bodies Corporate (Joint Tenancy) Act (Chapter 143)
Bookmaking Act (Chapter 265)
Bookmaking Regulation (Chapter 265)
Bougainville (International Assistance Groups) (Privileges and Immunities) Act 1997
Boxing and Wrestling Control Act (Chapter 300)
Bread Act (Chapter 283)
Bread Regulation (Chapter 283)
British and Foreign Bible Society Act (Chapter 1006)
Broadcasting Corporation Act (Chapter 149)
Building Act (Chapter 301)
Building Regulations 1994
Business Groups Incorporation Act (Chapter 144)
Business Groups Incorporation Regulation (Chapter 144)
Business Names Act (Chapter 145)
Business Names Regulation (Chapter 145)

C

Calendar Act (Chapter 3)
Carriage of Goods by Sea Act 2000
Catholic Diocesan Joint Ventures Agency Act 1994
Catholic Diocese of Kundiawa Act 1994
Catholic Diocese of Wabag Act 1994
Cemeteries Act (Chapter 302)
Cemeteries Regulation (Chapter 302)
Central Bank (Prescribed Liabilities) Regulation (Chapter 138)
Central Bank (Statutory Appointees' Provident Fund) Regulation (Chapter 138)
Central Banking Act 2000
Central Banking (Foreign Exchange and Gold) Regulation (Chapter 138)
Child Welfare Act (Chapter 276)
Child Welfare Regulation (Chapter 276)
Cities Act (Chapter 4)
Cities (Official Styles and Precedence) Regulation (Chapter 4)
Citizenship Act (Chapter 12)
Citizenship Regulation (Chapter 12)
Civil Aviation Act 2000
Civil Aviation (Aircraft Charges) Regulation 2000
Civil Aviation (Aircraft Operators' Liability) Act (Chapter 292)
Civil Aviation Regulation (Chapter 239)
Civil Registration Act (Chapter 304)
Civil Registration Regulation (Chapter 304)
Claims By and Against the State Act 1996
Classification of Publication (Censorship) Act 1989
Classification of Publication (Censorship) Regulation 1990
Cocoa Act (Chapter 388)
Cocoa Regulation (Chapter 388)
Coffee Industry Corporation (Statutory Functions and Powers) Act 1991
Colonial Courts of Admiralty Act 1890 (United Kingdom, adopted)

Commerce (Trade Descriptions) Act (Chapter 284)
Commercial Advertisement (Protection of Local Industry) Act (Chapter 407)
Commercial Advertisement (Protection of the Public) Act (Chapter 352)
Commissions of Inquiry Act (Chapter 31)
Companies Act 1997
Companies Regulation 1998
Companies Rules (Chapter 146)
Compensation (Prohibition of Foreign Legal Proceedings) Act 1995
Congregation of the Passion of Jesus Christ Act 1995
Conservation Areas Act (Chapter 362)
Constitution of the Independent State of Papua New Guinea
Constitutional Commission Act (Chapter 21A)
Constitutional Commission (Interim Provisions) Act (Chapter 21)
Constitutional Development Commission Act 1997
Constitutional Documents (Manner of Proof) Act (Chapter 5)
Constitutional Office-Holders Retirement Benefits Act 1986
Consumer Affairs Council Act 1993
Co-operative Societies Act (Chapter 389)
Copra Act (Chapter 211)
Copra Inspection Regulation (Chapter 211)
Copra Marketing Board Act (Chapter 212)
Copra Marketing Board Regulation (Chapter 212)
Copyright and Neighbouring Rights Act 2000
Coroners Act (Chapter 32)
Coroners Regulation (Chapter 32)
Correctional Service Act 1995
Correctional Service Regulation 1995
Creditors' Remedies Act (Papua) (Chapter 47)
Criminal Code Act (Chapter 262)
Criminal Code (Chapter 262)
Criminal Justice (Sentences) Act 1986
Criminal Law (Bail) Act (Chapter 413)
Criminal Law (Compensation) Act 1991
Criminal Law (Compensation) Regulation 1992
Criminal Law (Miscellaneous Provisions) Act (Chapter 263)
Criminal Practice Rules 1987
Crocodile Trade (Protection) Act (Chapter 213)
Crocodile Trade (Protection) Regulation (Chapter 213)
Curfew Act 1987
Customs Act (Chapter 101)
Customs (Ad Valorem Duties) Regulation 1987
Customs Duty (Automotive Diesel Fuel Rebate) (Repeal) Regulation 1986
Customs Duty (Rebate) Act (Chapter 390)
Customs (Personal Effects) Regulation 1995
Customs (Prohibited Exports) Regulation (Chapter 101)
Customs (Prohibited Imports) Regulation (Chapter 101)
Customs (Prohibition of Trade with South Africa) Regulation (Chapter 101)
Customs Recognition Act (Chapter 19)
Customs Regulation (Chapter 101)
Customs Tariff Act 1990
Customs Tariff (Dumping and Subsidies) (Repeal) Act 2000

D

Dangerous Drugs Act (Chapter 228)
Dangerous Drugs Regulation (Chapter 228)
Defamation Act (Chapter 293)
Defence Act (Chapter 74)
Defence (Aid to Civil Power) Regulation (Chapter 74)
Defence (Aid to Civil Power) Regulation 1988
Defence (Australian Forces) Act (Chapter 75)
Defence (Boards of Inquiry) Regulation (Chapter 74)
Defence Force Retirement Benefits Act (Chapter 76)
Defence Force Retirement Benefits Regulation (Chapter 76)
Defence Forces (Presence Abroad) Act (Chapter 372)
Defence (Member's Defence Force History) Regulation (Chapter 74)
Defence (Period of Service) Regulation (Chapter 74)
Defence (Prescribed Offices) Regulation (Chapter 74)
Defence (Transitional) Regulation (Chapter 74)
Defence (Visiting Forces) Act (Chapter 77)
Defence (Visiting Forces) Vehicles Regulation (Chapter 77)
Dental Charges Act (Chapter 104)
Dental Charges Regulation (Chapter 104)
Departure Tax Act (Chapter 387)
Departure Tax Regulation (Chapter 387)
Deserted Wives and Children Act (Chapter 277)
Diplomatic and Consular Privileges and Immunities Act (Chapter 83)
Disaster Management Act (Chapter 403)
Disciplined Forces Canteen Organization (Repeal) Act 1998
Discriminatory Practices Act (Chapter 269)
Distillation Act (Chapter 305)
District Courts Act (Chapter 40)
District Courts Regulation (Chapter 40)
Divine Word University Act 1999
Drugs Act (Chapter 229)
Drugs Regulation (Chapter 229)
Dumping of Wastes at Sea Act (Chapter 369)

E

Education Act (Chapter 163)
Education (Boards of Studies) Regulation 1986
Education (International Education Agency Schools) Regulation 1985
Education Regulation (Chapter 163)
Electricity Commission Act (Chapter 78)
Electricity Commission (Productive Use of Land) Act (Chapter 181)
Electricity Commission Regulation (Chapter 78)
Electricity Supply (Government Power Stations) Act (Chapter 306)
Emergency (Bougainville) (General Powers) Act 1989
Emergency (Bougainville) (General Powers) Regulation 1989
Emergency Committees Act (Chapter 33A)
Emergency (Custody of Members of Parliament) Act (Chapter 33B)
Emergency (General Powers No 2) Regulation 1998
Employment Act (Chapter 373)
Employment of Non-citizens Act (Chapter 374)
Employment of Non-citizens Regulation (Chapter 374)
Employment Placement Service Act (Chapter 172)
Employment Regulation (Chapter 373)

Environment Act 2000
Environmental Planning Act (Chapter 370) [To be repealed when the Environment Act 2001 commences - see Repealed Legislation Library for copy of Act]
Environmental Contaminants Act (Chapter 368) [To be repealed when the Environment Act 2001 commences - see Repealed Legislation Library for copy of Act]
Evangelical Lutheran Church of New Guinea Property Trust Act (Chapter 1007)
Evangelical Lutheran Church of Papua New Guinea Act 1992
Evidence Act (Chapter 48)
Evidence (Foreign Tribunals) Act (Chapter 335)
Evidence (Prescribed Officers) Regulation (Chapter 48)
Excise Act (Chapter 105)
Excise (Beer) Act (Chapter 106)
Excise (Beer) Regulation (Chapter 106)
Excise Regulation (Chapter 105)
Excise Tariff Act (Chapter 107)
Explosives Act (Adopted) (Chapter 309)
Explosives Act (Chapter 308)
Explosives Areas Regulation (Adopted) (Chapter 309)
Explosives Regulation (Adopted) (Chapter 309)
Explosives Regulation (Chapter 308)
Export (Desiccated Coconut) Regulation (Chapter 101)
Export (Fish) Regulation (Chapter 101)
Exports (Control and Valuation) Act (Chapter 108)
Exports (Control and Valuation) Regulation (Chapter 108)
Extradition Act (Chapter 49)
Extradition (Commonwealth Countries) Regulation (Chapter 49)

F

Fairness of Transactions Act 1993
Fauna (Protection and Control) Act (Chapter 154)
Fauna (Protection and Control) Bagiai Wildlife Management Area Rules (Chapter 154)
Fauna (Protection and Control) Balek Wildlife Sanctuary Rules (Chapter 154)
Fauna (Protection and Control) Crown Island Wildlife Sanctuary Rules (Chapter 154)
Fauna (Protection and Control) Garu Wildlife Management Area Rules (Chapter 154)
Fauna (Protection and Control) Maza Wildlife Management Area Rules (Chapter 154)
Fauna (Protection and Control) Mojirau Wildlife Management Area Rules (Chapter 154)
Fauna (Protection and Control) Pokili Wildlife Management Area Rules (Chapter 154)
Fauna (Protection and Control) Ranba Wildlife Management Area Rules (Chapter 154)
Fauna (Protection and Control) Ranba Wildlife Sanctuary Rules (Chapter 154)
Fauna (Protection and Control) Regulation (Chapter 154)
Fauna (Protection and Control) Sawataitai Wildlife Management Area Rules (Chapter 154)
Fauna (Protection and Control) Siwi-Utame Wildlife Management Area Rules (Chapter 154)
Fauna (Protection and Control) Tonda Wildlife Management Area Rules (Chapter 154)
Fire Service Act (Chapter 64)
Fire Service (Amendment) Act 1993
Fire Service Regulation (Chapter 64)
Firearms Act (Chapter 310)
Firearms Regulation (Chapter 310)
Fiscal Year (Change) Act (Chapter 350)
Fisheries Management Act 1998
Fisheries Management Regulation 2000
Fisheries (Torres Strait Protected Zone) Act (Chapter 411)
Fisheries (Torres Strait Protected Zone) Regulation 1987

Fluoridation of Public Water Supplies Act (Chapter 230)
Fluoridation of Public Water Supplies Regulation (Chapter 230)
Food Sanitation Act 1991
Forestry Act 1991
Forestry Regulation 1998
Forsayth Prize Fund Trust Act (Chapter 164)
Frauds and Limitations Act 1988
Free Trade Zones Act 2000

G

Gaming Act (Chapter 270)
Gaming Machine Act 1993
Gaming Machine Regulation 1993
Gaming Regulation (Chapter 270)
Gazelle Restoration Authority Act 1995
Geneva Conventions Act (Chapter 84)
Girl Guides Association Act (Chapter 1008)
Goods Act (Chapter 251)

H

Harbours Board Act (Chapter 240)
Harbours Board (General) By-laws (Chapter 240)
Harbours Board (Inflammable Liquid and Dangerous Goods) By-laws (Chapter 240)
Higher Education Act (Chapter 397)
Hire-purchase Act (Chapter 252)
Hire-purchase Regulation (Chapter 252)

I

IDA (Agricultural Development) Credit Agreements Ratification Act (Chapter 122)
Income Tax Act 1959
Income Tax, Dividend (Withholding) Tax and Interest (Withholding) Tax Rates Act (Chapter 111)
Income Tax (International Agreements) Act 1987
Income Tax (New Fiscal Year-Transitional Provisions) Act (Chapter 110A)
Income Tax (Rates) Act 1975
Income Tax (Rates) Act (Consolidated) 1976
Income Tax Regulations 1959
Income Tax (Salary or Wages Tax) (Rates) Act 1979
Income Tax (Specific Gains Tax) (Rates) Act 1982
Independence Fellowship Trust Act (Chapter 1040)
Indonesian Border Agreement Act (Chapter 85)
Industrial Centres Development Corporation Act 1990
Industrial Development (Incentives to Pioneer Industries) (Repeal) Act 1998
Industrial Development (Wage Subsidy) Act (Chapter 110B)
Industrial Development (Wage Subsidy) Regulation (Chapter 110B)
Industrial Organizations Act (Chapter 173)
Industrial Organizations Regulation (Chapter 173)
Industrial Relations Act (Chapter 174)
Industrial Relations Regulation (Chapter 174)
Industrial Safety (Building Works) Order (Chapter 175)
Industrial Safety (Chemical Treatment of Timber) Order (Chapter 175)
Industrial Safety (Excavation Works, Shafts and Tunnels) Order (Chapter 175)

Industrial Safety (Explosive-powered Tools) Order (Chapter 175)
Industrial Safety (Lifts) Order (Chapter 175)
Industrial Safety (Monocrotophos) Order (Chapter 175)
Industrial Safety (Tractors and Earthmoving and Mobile Construction Equipment) Order (Chapter 175)
Industrial Safety, Health and Welfare Act (Chapter 175)
Industrial Safety, Health and Welfare Regulation (Chapter 175)
Industry Assistance Board Act 1985
Infants Act (Chapter 278)
Infants (Clarification of Application) Act (Chapter 278A)
Inflammable Liquid Act (Chapter 311)
Inflammable Liquid Regulation (Chapter 311)
Insolvency Act (Chapter 253)
Institute of Medical Research Act (Chapter 166)
Instruments Act (Chapter 254)
Instruments Regulation (Chapter 254)
Insurance Act 1995
Insurance Corporation Act (Chapter 366)
Insurance (Miscellaneous Provisions) Act (Chapter 256)
Integrity of Political Parties and Candidates Regulation 2001
Inter-group Fighting Act (Chapter 344)
Interim Provincial Governments Tax Act 1996
Internal Security Act 1993
International Bank (Ramu Hydroelectric Project) Loan Agreement Act (Chapter 125)
International Bank (Telecommunications) Loan Agreement Ratification Act (Chapter 123)
International Bank/IDA (Highway Project) Loan and Credit Agreements Act (Chapter 124)
International Financial Organizations Act (Chapter 86)
International Organizations (Privileges and Immunities) Act (Chapter 87)
International Organizations (Privileges and Immunities) Regulation (Chapter 87)
International Trade (Fauna and Flora) Act (Chapter 391)
International Trade (Fauna and Flora) (Fauna) Regulation (Chapter 391)
Interpretation Act (Chapter 2)
Investment Corporation Act (Chapter 140)
Investment Disputes Convention Act (Chapter 346)
Investment Promotion Act 1992
Investment Promotion Regulation 1992

J

Judges' Pensions Act 1997
Judicial Proceedings (Interest on Debts and Damages) Act (Chapter 52)
Judicial Proceedings (Regulation of Reports) Act (Chapter 51)
Juvenile Courts Act 1991

K

Koki Market-Place Trust (Repeal) Act 1986
Kwato Church Corporation Act (Chapter 1036)

L

Land Act 1996
Land Disputes Settlement Act (Chapter 45)
Land Disputes Settlement Regulation (Chapter 45)
Land Groups Incorporation Act (Chapter 147)
Land Groups Incorporation Regulation (Chapter 147)
Land (Ownership of Freeholds) Act (Chapter 359)
Land (Ownership of Freeholds) Regulation (Chapter 359)
Land Registration Act (Chapter 191)
Land Registration Regulation 1999
Land Regulation 1999
Land (Tenure Conversion) Act 1963
Land (Tenure Conversion) Regulations 1964
Land Titles Commission Act 1962
Land Transport Board Act (Chapter 245)
Landlord and Tenant (Miscellaneous Provisions) Act (Chapter 189)
Law of Property (Execution of Powers) Act (Chapter 290)
Law Reform Commission Act (Chapter 18)
Laws Adoption and Adaptation Act (Chapter 20)
Lawyers Act 1986
Lawyers Admission Rules 1990
Lawyers' Conveyancing Costs Rules (Chapter 91)
Lawyers (Examination) Regulation 1992
Lawyers (Prescribed Rate) Regulation 1990
Lawyers (Trust Account) Regulation 1990
Leaders (Benefits) Act 1987
Leadership Code (Alternative Penalties) Act (Chapter 1A)
Legislative Drafting Service Act (Chapter 80)
Levien Memorial Act (Chapter 167)
Licences Regulation (TNG) (Chapter 112)
Licences (TNG) Act (Chapter 112)
Licensing of Heavy Vehicles Act (Chapter 367)
Licensing of Heavy Vehicles Regulation (Chapter 367)
Life Insurance Act 2000
Life Policies Protection Act (Chapter 257)
Liquor (Licensing) Act (Chapter 312)
Liquor (Licensing) Regulation (Chapter 312)
Liquor Licensing (Trading Hours) Rules (Chapter 312)
Liquor (Miscellaneous Provisions) Act (Chapter 313)
Liquor (Panguna Canteen) Regulation (Chapter 312)
Loan (Arawa Town Works) Act (Chapter 126)
Loan (Bougainville Copper Agreement) Act (Chapter 127)
Loan (Electricity) Act (Chapter 128)
Loan (Works and Services) Act (Chapter 129)
Loan (Works, Services and Electricity) Act (Chapter 130)
Loan (Works, Services and Government Instrumentalities) Act (Chapter 131)
Loans and Assistance (International Agencies) Act (Chapter 132)
Loans and Assistance (International Agencies) (Prescribed Body) Regulation (Chapter 132)
Loans and Assistance (International Finance Agencies) Regulation (Chapter 132)
Loans (Overseas Borrowing) (No 2) Act (Chapter 133A)
Loans (Overseas Borrowings) Act (Chapter 133)
Loans Securities Act (Chapter 134)
Loans Securities Regulation (Chapter 134)
Loans (Works, Services and Other Purposes) Act (Chapter 347)
Loans (Works, Services and Other Purposes) Act (Chapter 376)

Local Courts (Repeal) Act 2000
Local Government Service Act (Chapter 58)
Local-level Government System (Interim and Transitional Arrangements) Act 1995
Local-level Governments Administration Act 1997

M

Magisterial Service Act (Chapter 43)
Maintenance Orders Enforcement Act (Chapter 279)
Maintenance Orders Enforcement Regulation (Chapter 279)
Marine Insurance (Adopted) Act (Chapter 258)
Maritime College Act (Chapter 355)
Maritime College (Levy) Regulation (Chapter 355)
Marking of Weight on Heavy Packages Act (Chapter 241)
Marriage Act (Chapter 280)
Marriage Regulation (Chapter 280)
Married Women's Property Act (Chapter 281)
Matrimonial Causes Act (Chapter 282)
Matrimonial Causes Rules (Chapter 282)
Medical Registration Act (Chapter 398)
Medical Registration By-laws (Chapter 398)
Medicines and Cosmetics Act 1999
Melbourne Bible Institute Act (Chapter 1009)
Mercantile Act (Chapter 260)
Merchant Shipping Act (Chapter 242)
Merchant Shipping (Coasting Trade) Regulation (Chapter 242)
Merchant Shipping (Committee of Advice) Regulation (Chapter 242)
Merchant Shipping (Crewmen) Regulation (Chapter 242)
Merchant Shipping (Navigational Aids) Regulation (Chapter 242)
Merchant Shipping (Pilotage) Regulation (Chapter 242)
Merchant Shipping (Registration) Regulation (Chapter 242)
Merchant Shipping (Safety) Regulation (Chapter 242)
Migration Act (Chapter 16)
Migration (Fees) Regulation (Chapter 16)
Migration Regulation (Chapter 16)
Mineral Resources Development Company Pty Limited (Privatisation) Act 1996
Mineral Resources Stabilization Fund (Repeal) Act 2000
Minimum Age (Sea) Act (Chapter 176)
Mining Act 1992
Mining (Bougainville Copper Agreement) Act (Chapter 196)
Mining Development Act (Chapter 197)
Mining Development Regulation (Chapter 197)
Mining (Ok Tedi Agreement) Act (Chapter 363)
Mining (Ok Tedi Agreements) (Amendment) Act 1986
Mining (Ok Tedi Fifth Supplemental Agreement) Act (Chapter 363E)
Mining (Ok Tedi Fourth Supplemental Agreement) Act (Chapter 363D)
Mining (Ok Tedi Restated Eighth Supplemental Agreement) Act 1995
Mining (Ok Tedi Second Supplemental Agreement) Act (Chapter 363B)
Mining (Ok Tedi Seventh Supplemental Agreement) Act 1986
Mining (Ok Tedi Sixth Supplemental Agreement) Act 1986
Mining (Ok Tedi Supplemental Agreement) Act (Chapter 363A)
Mining (Ok Tedi Third Supplemental Agreement) Act (Chapter 363C)
Mining Regulation 1992
Mining (Safety) Act (Chapter 195A)

Mining (Safety) Regulation (Chapter 195A)
Mining (Transitional Provisions) Regulation 1992
Ministers (Delegation) Act (Chapter 35)
Ministers (Delegation) Regulation (Chapter 35)
Motor Car Dealers Act (Chapter 353)
Motor Car Dealers (Price of Vehicles) Regulation (Chapter 353)
Motor Traffic Act (Chapter 243)
Motor Traffic (Amendment) Regulation 1989
Motor Traffic Regulation (Chapter 243)
Motor Vehicles Insurance (PNG) Trust (Administrative Arrangements) Act 1996
Motor Vehicles (Third Party Insurance) Act (Chapter 295)
Motor Vehicles (Third Party Insurance) (Basic Protection Compensation) Act (Chapter 296)
Motor Vehicles (Third Party Insurance) (Basic Protection Compensation) Regulation (Chapter 296)

N

National Agricultural Research Institute Act 1996
National Agriculture Quarantine and Inspection Authority Act 1997
National AIDS Council Act 1997
National Airline Commission Act (Chapter 244)
National and Local-level Government Electoral Regulation 1997
National Capital District Commission Act 1990
National Capital District Commission (Building Board) Regulation 1991
National Capital District Commission (Delegated Committees) Regulation 1991
National Capital District Commission (Electoral Provisions) Regulation 1990
National Capital District Commission (Land Tax) Regulation 1991
National Capital District Commission (Legislative Procedures) Regulation 1991
National Capital District Commission (Motu-Koitabu Village Development Committees) Regulation 1992
National Capital District Commission (Sales and Service Tax) Regulation 1991
National Capital District Commission (Ward Committees) Regulation 1991
National Capital District (Transfer of Assets, etc) Act 1996
National Capital District Water Supply and Sewerage Act 1996
National Council of Women Incorporation Act (Chapter 1041)
National Court Act (Chapter 38)
National Court Assessors Act (TNG) (Chapter 42)
National Court Assessors Regulation (TNG) (Chapter 42)
National Court (Number of Judges) Act (Chapter 404)
National Court Rules (Chapter 38)
National Cultural Centre Trust Act (Chapter 155)
National Cultural Commission Act 1994
National Cultural Property (Preservation) Act (Chapter 156)
National Cultural Property (Preservation) Regulation (Chapter 156)
National Economic and Fiscal Commission Act 1996
National Health Administration Act 1997
National Housing Corporation Act 1990
National Identity Act (Chapter 9)
National Identity Regulation (Chapter 9)
National Institute of Standards and Industrial Technology Act 1993
National Intelligence Organization Act (Chapter 405)
National Judicial Staff Service Act 1987
National Land Registration Act (Chapter 357)
National Library and Archives Act 1993

National Library and Archives (National Library and Archives Board) Regulation 1998
National Museum and Art Gallery Act 1992
National Name (Protection) Act (Chapter 10)
National Narcotics Control Board Act 1992
National Parks Act (Chapter 157)
National Parks Regulation (Chapter 157)
National Provident Fund Act (Chapter 377)
National Provident Fund Rules (Chapter 377)
National Provident Fund (Financial Reconstruction) Act 2000
National Research Institute Act (Chapter 165) [formerly Institute of Applied Social and Economic Research Act]
National Research Institute (Election of Staff Representative) Regulation (Chapter 165)
National Revival Church Mission Act (Chapter 1010)
National Road Safety Council Act 1997
National Seal Act (Chapter 11)
National Seas Act (Chapter 361)
National Training Council Act 1991
National Volunteer Service Act 1990
National Water Supply and Sewerage Act 1986
National Youth Commission Act 1999
Native Administration Regulation (TNG) (Chapter 315)
Native Regulation (Papua) (Chapter 316)
Nursing Registration By-Laws (Chapter 398)

O

Oaths, Affirmations and Statutory Declarations (Chapter 317)
Offences (Overseas) Act (Chapter 406)
Official Personal Staff Act (Chapter 383)
Offshore Seas Proclamation 1978
Oil and Gas Act 1998
Oil Palm Industry Corporation Act 1992
Order in Council made under the Colonial Courts of Admiralty Act 1890 (United Kingdom, adopted)
Organic Law on Certain Constitutional Office-holders
Organic Law on Immediate and Transitional Constitutional Provisions
Organic Law on National and Local-level Government Elections
Organic Law on Provincial Boundaries
Organic Law on Provincial Governments and Local-level Governments
Organic Law on Residence
Organic Law on the Advisory Committee on the Power of Mercy
Organic Law on the Boundaries of the National Capital District
Organic Law on the Calling of Meetings of the Parliament
Organic Law on the Duties and Responsibilities of Leadership
Organic Law on the Guarantee of the Rights and Independence of Constitutional Office-holders
Organic Law on the Integrity of Political Parties and Candidates
Organic Law on the Internment Tribunal
Organic Law on the Judicial and Legal Services Commission
Organic Law on the Nomination of the Governor-General
Organic Law on the Number of Ministers
Organic Law on the Ombudsman Commission
Organic Law on the Public Services Commission (Repeal)
Organic Law on the Relief of Members of Disciplined Forces from the Responsibility for the Consequences of Carrying out a Lawful Order

Organic Law on the Terms and Conditions of Employment of Judges
Organic Law on the Terms and Conditions of Employment of the Governor-General
Overseas Trade (Shipping) Act (Chapter 399)

P

Pacific Adventist University Act 1997
Packaging Act (Chapter 285)
Packaging Regulation (Chapter 285)
Palm Oil Industry (Biala Project Re-organization) Act (Chapter 364)
Palm Oil Industry (New Britain Agreement) (Repeal) Act 1994
Palm Oil Industry Stabilization Funds Act (Chapter 400)
Papua New Guinea Institute of Public Administration Act 1993
Papua New Guinea Law Society Rules 1987
Papua New Guinea National Service Corps (Repeal) Act 1992
Papua New Guinea Red Cross Society Incorporation Act (Chapter 1042)
Papua New Guinea Science and Technology Council Act 1992
Papua New Guinea Sports Commission Act 1992
Papua New Guinea Sports Commission (Charges and Penalties) By-Law 1999
Papua New Guinea University of Technology Act 1986
Parliamentary Members' Compensation Act (Chapter 23)
Parliamentary Members' Personal Staff Act 1988
Parliamentary Members' Retirement Benefits Act 1997
Parliamentary Powers and Privileges Act (Chapter 24)
Parliamentary Service Act 1997
Parole Act 1991
Parole Regulation 1992
Partnership Act (Chapter 148)
Passports Act (Chapter 17)
Passports Regulation (Chapter 17)
Patents and Industrial Designs Act 2000
Pawnbrokers Act (Chapter 93)
Peace and Good Order Act 1991
Permanent Parliamentary Committees Act 1994
Personal Tax Act (Chapter 113)
Personal Tax Regulation (Chapter 113)
Petroleum Agreements (Currency Provisions) Act (Chapter 348)
Petroleum (Gulf of Papua) Agreements Act (Chapter 199)
Petroleum (Submerged Lands) Act 1967-1968, Section 11 (Australia, Adopted)
Physical Planning Act 1989
Physical Planning Regulation 1990
Place Names Act (Chapter 318)
Place Names Regulation (Chapter 318)
Places of Entertainment Act (Papua) (Chapter 319)
Places of Entertainment Regulation (Papua) (Chapter 319)
Places of Entertainment Regulation (TNG) (Chapter 319)
Plant Disease and Control Act (Chapter 220)
Plant Disease and Control Regulation (Chapter 220)
PNG Co-operative Investments Act (Chapter 412)
Poisons and Dangerous Substances Act (Chapter 231)
Poisons and Dangerous Substances Regulation (Chapter 231)
Police Act 1998
Port Charges Act (Chapter 114)
Port Charges Regulation (Chapter 114)

Postal Services Act 1996
Post-graduate Legal Training Act (Chapter 168)
Post-graduate Legal Training (Allowances) Regulation (Chapter 168)
Prevention of Pollution of the Sea Act (Chapter 371)
Prevention of Pollution of the Sea Regulation (Chapter 371)
Prices Regulation Act (Chapter 320)
Prices Regulation (Chapter 320)
Prime Minister Act (Chapter 27)
Printers and Newspapers Act (Chapter 151)
Printers and Newspapers Regulation (Chapter 151)
Printing of the Laws Act (Chapter 333)
Privatization Act 1999
Probation Act (Chapter 381)
Probation (Forms) Regulation 1991
Professional Boxing Control Board Act 1991
Professional Conduct Rules 1989
Professional Engineers (Registration) Act 1986
Professional Engineers (Registration) Regulation 1988
Protection of Private Communications Act (Chapter 272)
Provincial Government (Constituencies) Regulation (Chapter 56)
Provincial Government (Electoral Provisions) Regulation (Chapter 56)
Provincial Governments Administration Act 1997
Provisional Collection of Taxes Act (Chapter 115)
Public Curator Act (Chapter 81)
Public Curator Regulation (Chapter 81)
Public Employment (Non-citizens) Act (Chapter 342)
Public Finances (Management) Act 1995
Public Finances (Management) Regulation 1996
Public Health Act (Chapter 226)
Public Health (Barbers' Shops) Regulation (Chapter 226)
Public Health (Dairy Farms) Regulation (Chapter 226)
Public Health (Drinking Water) Regulation (Chapter 226)
Public Health (Infectious Diseases) Regulation (Chapter 226)
Public Health (Mental Disorders) Regulation (Chapter 226)
Public Health (Paint) Regulation (Chapter 226)
Public Health (Sanitation and General) Regulation (Chapter 226)
Public Health (Septic Tanks) Regulation (Chapter 226)
Public Health (Sewerage) Regulation (Chapter 226)
Public Health (Underground Water Tanks) Regulation (Chapter 226)
Public Holidays Act (Chapter 321)
Public Hospitals Act 1994
Public Hospitals (Charges) Act (Chapter 116)
Public Hospitals (Charges) Regulations (Chapter 116)
Public Officers Superannuation Fund Act 1990 [formerly State Services and Statutory Authorities Superannuation Fund Act 1990]
Public Prosecutor (Office and Functions) Act (Chapter 338)
Public Service (Oversea Agencies) Act (Chapter 68)
Public Services Conciliation and Arbitration Act (Chapter 69)
Public Services Conciliation and Arbitration Regulation (Chapter 69)
Public Services (Management) Act 1995
Public Solicitor (Charges) Act (Chapter 337)
Public Works Committee Act (Chapter 28)
Public Works Committee Regulation (Chapter 28)

Q

Quarantine Act (Chapter 234)
Quarantine Regulation (Chapter 234)

R

Radio Spectrum Act 1996
Radio Spectrum Regulation 1997
Rationalisation of the Public Service (Budget Provisions) Act 1995
Reciprocal Enforcement of Custody Orders Act (Chapter 336)
Reciprocal Enforcement of Judgements Act (Chapter 50)
Resource Contracts Fiscal Stabilization Act 2000
Revised Edition of the Laws Act 1976
Revised Laws (Commencement) Act 1981
Roads Maintenance Act (Chapter 246)
Roads Maintenance Regulation (Chapter 246)
Roads Regulation (TNG) (Chapter 221)
Roman Catholic Archdiocese of Rabaul Act (Chapter 1012)
Roman Catholic Archdiocese (Port Moresby) Act (Chapter 1011)
Roman Catholic Congregation (Handmaids of Our Lord) Act (Chapter 1013)
Roman Catholic Congregation of the Missionaries of the Sacred Heart Act (Chapter 1014)
Roman Catholic Diocese (Alotau) Act (Chapter 1015)
Roman Catholic Diocese of Bereina Act (Chapter 1037)
Roman Catholic Diocese of Bougainville Act (Chapter 1016)
Roman Catholic Diocese of Goroka Act (Chapter 1038)
Roman Catholic Diocese of Kerema Act (Chapter 1039)
Roman Catholic Diocese of Lae Act (Chapter 1046)
Roman Catholic Diocese of Mendi Act (Chapter 1017)
Roman Catholic Divine Word Mission (Goroka) Act (Chapter 1018)
Roman Catholic Hospitaller Order of St John of God Act (Chapter 1019)
Roman Catholic Mission of Marianhill Lae Act (Chapter 1021)
Roman Catholic (Mission of the Divine Word) Act (Chapter 1025)
Roman Catholic (Mission of the Holy Ghost) Act (Chapter 1022)
Roman Catholic Mission of the Holy Trinity Act (Chapter 1023)
Roman Catholic Mission of the Order of Friars Minor Act (Chapter 1024)
Roman Catholic Mission, Kavieng Property Trust Act (Chapter 1020)
Roman Catholic Missionaries of the Sacred Heart (American Province) Act (Chapter 1027)
Roman Catholic Mission-Vanimo Act (Chapter 1026)
Roman Catholic Montfort Catholic Mission Act (Chapter 1028)
Roman Catholic Society of Mary of Bougainville Incorporation Act (Chapter 1029)
Roman Catholic Society of the Divine Word Mission Act (Chapter 1030)
Rubber Act (Chapter 222)
Rubber Regulation (Chapter 222)
Rules Respecting the Use of the National Flag and the National Emblem (Chapter 9)
Rural Development Bank Act (Chapter 139)
Rural Development Bank Regulation (Chapter 139) [Agriculture Bank Regulation (Chapter 139)]

S

Salaries and Conditions Monitoring Committee Act 1988
Salaries and Remuneration Commission Act 1988

Sale of Human Blood Act (Chapter 236)
Sale of Stolen Cattle Prevention Act (Chapter 223)
Salvation Army (Papua New Guinea) Property Trust Act (Chapter 1031)
Sarto Secular Institute Trust Act (Chapter 1044)
Savings and Loan Societies Act (Chapter 141)
Savings and Loan Societies Regulation (Chapter 141)
Scout Association of Papua New Guinea Incorporation Act (Chapter 1032)
Sea-carriage of Goods Act (Chapter 261)
Seamen (Foreign) Act (Chapter 177)
Seamen (Unemployment Indemnity) Act (Chapter 178)
Search Act (Chapter 341)
Search Regulation (Chapter 341)
Second-hand Dealers Act (Chapter 322)
Second-hand Dealers Regulation (Chapter 322)
Securities Act 1997
Securities Regulation 1999
Sheriff Act (Chapter 55)
Sheriff Regulation (Chapter 55)
Shipping Act (Chapter 395)
Shipping (Freight Rate) Regulation (Chapter 395)
Simultaneous Deaths Act (Chapter 332)
Sir Donald Cleland Swimming-pool Trust (Repeal) Act 1987
Sir Hubert Murray Stadium Trust (Repeal) Act 1987
Slaughtering Act (Chapter 238)
Slaughtering Regulation (Chapter 238)
Small Business Development Corporation Act 1990
Sorcery Act (Chapter 274)
South Pacific Forum Fisheries Agency (Privileges and Immunities) Regulation (Chapter 87)
Spice Industry Act 1989
St John Council Incorporation Act (Chapter 1043)
Stamp Duties Act (Chapter 117)
Stamp Duties Regulation (Chapter 117)
Standard Rules for Savings and Loan Societies (Chapter 141)
Standard Time Act (Chapter 7)
Standing Orders of the National Parliament
Statistical Services Act (Chapter 386)
Statute Law Revision Machinery Act (Chapter 29)
Street Closing Act (Chapter 201)
Submarine Cables and Pipelines Protection Act (Adopted) (Chapter 247)
Summary Ejectment Act (Chapter 202)
Summary Ejectment Regulation (Chapter 202)
Summary Offences Act (Chapter 264)
Summer Institute of Linguistics Act (Chapter 1033)
Superannuation (General Provisions) Act 2000
Supreme Court Act (Chapter 37)
Supreme Court Rules 1984
Survey Act (Chapter 95)
Survey Co-ordination Act (Chapter 203)
Survey Co-ordination Regulation (Chapter 203)
Survey Regulation (Chapter 95)
Swiss Evangelical Brotherhood Mission Act (Chapter 1034)

T

Takeovers Code 1998
Teaching Service Act 1988
Teaching Service (Auxiliary Members) Act (Chapter 72)
Teaching Service (Auxiliary Members) (Disciplinary Procedures) Regulation 1988
Teaching Service (Auxiliary Members) Regulation (Chapter 72)
Teaching Service Conciliation and Arbitration Act (Chapter 73)
Teaching Service Conciliation and Arbitration Regulation (Chapter 73)
Teaching Service Regulation 1994
Telecommunications Act 1996
Telephone Tax (Repeal) Act 1992
Television (Prohibition and Control) Act 1986
Telikom PNG Limited Act 1996
Tobacco Products (Health Control) Act 1987
Tourism Promotion Authority Act 1993
Town Boundaries Act (Chapter 8)
Trade Licensing Act (Chapter 96)
Trade Licensing Regulation (Chapter 96)
Trade Marks Act (Chapter 385)
Trade Marks Regulation (Chapter 385)
Trade Measurement Act (Chapter 286)
Trading Act (Chapter 324)
Trading Regulation (Chapter 324)
Transport (Collection of Information) Act (Chapter 248)
Treasury Bills Act (Chapter 135)
Trust Accounts Act (Chapter 287)
Trust Accounts (Lawyers) Regulation (Chapter 287)
Trustee Companies Act (Chapter 288)
Trustee Companies Regulation (Chapter 288)
Trustees and Executors Act (Chapter 289)

U

Unclaimed Goods Act (Chapter 325)
Unclaimed Moneys Act (Chapter 326)
Unclaimed Moneys Regulation (Chapter 326)
Underlying Law Act 2000, The (*certified by the Speaker on 18 August 2000)
United Church in Papua, New Guinea and the Solomon Islands Incorporation Act (Chapter 1035)
United Nations and Specialized Agencies (Privileges and Immunities) Act (Chapter 88)
University of Goroka Act 1997
University of Papua New Guinea Act (Chapter 169)
University of Vudal Act 1997

V

Valuation Act (Chapter 327)
Valuation Regulation (Chapter 327)
Value Added Tax Act 1998
Value Added Tax Regulation 1999
Value Added Tax Revenue Distribution Act 1998
Veterinary Surgeons Act (Chapter 98)
Veterinary Surgeons Regulation (Chapter 98)
Vice-Ministers Act 1994
Village Courts Act 1989
Village Courts Regulation (Chapter 44)

W

War Cemeteries and Graves Act 1986
War Deaths Registration Act (Chapter 414)
War Surplus Material Act (Chapter 331)
War Surplus Material Regulation (Chapter 331)
Water Resources Act (Chapter 205) [To be repealed when the Environment Act 2001 commences - see Repealed Legislation Library for copy of Act]
Water Resources Regulation (Chapter 205) [To be repealed when the Environment Act 2001 commences - see Repealed Legislation Library for copy of Regulation]
Weights and Measures Regulation (Chapter 286)
Whaling Act (Chapter 225)
Wills, Probate and Administration Act (Chapter 291)
Workers' Compensation Act (Chapter 179)
Workers' Compensation Regulation (Chapter 179)
Wrongs (Miscellaneous Provisions) Act (Chapter 297)

X

There is no legislation beginning with the letter X

Y

Y2K Fairness in Litigation Act 1999

US AND COUNTRY CONTACTS

U.S. GOVERNMENT CONTACTS

Ambassador: Arma Jane Karaer
Deputy Chief of Mission: Edward J. Michal
Economic/Commercial Officer: Beatrice P. Soila (September 1997: Edward P. Arrizabalaga)
Commercial Assistant: Crescentia K. Anderson
Consular Officer: Robert Waldrop

Tel: 675-321-1455
Fax: 675-321-3423

International Address:

U.S. Embassy
P.O. Box 1492
Port Moresby, N.C.D. 121
Papua New Guinea

Via U.S. Postal Service:

Port Moresby
Department of State
Washington, DC 20521-4240

U.S. Agricultural Trade Office
541 Orchard Road #08-03
Liat Towers
Singapore 0923

Tel: 65-737-1233
Fax: 65-732-8307

Office of Pacific Island Affairs
EAP/PIA
Room 5317, N.S.
U.S. Department of State
Washington, DC 20520-6310

Tel: 202-647-3546
Fax: 202-647-0118

Office of Pacific Basin
International Trade Administration
U.S. Department of Commerce
Washington, DC 20230

Tel: 202-482-2954
Fax: 202-482-5330

Department of Agriculture
Foreign Agricultural Service
Trade Assistance and Promotion Office
Washington, DC 20250

Tel: 202-720-7420

TPCC Trade Information Center
Tel: 1-800-USA-TRADE

Office of the Coordinator for Business Affairs
U.S. Department of State

Tel: 202-647-1625
Fax: 202-647-3953

MULTILATERAL DEVELOPMENT BANK CONTACTS

U.S. Department of Commerce
Liaison to the U.S. Executive Director's Office
International Bank for Reconstruction and Development
Room D-13004
1818 H Street, NW
Washington, DC 20433

Tel: 202-458-0118
Fax: 202-477-2967

Cantwell Walsh
Senior Commercial Officer
ADB Liaison Office
U.S. Embassy, Manila
APO AP 96440

Fax: 632-816-7684
e-mail: cwalsh@doc.gov

Janet Thomas, Acting Director
Multilateral Development Bank Office
U.S. Department of Commerce
14th and Constitution, NW
Washington, DC 20007

Phone: 202-482-3399
Fax: 202-482-5179

PNG TRADE AND INDUSTRY ASSOCIATIONS

PNG Chamber of Mines and Petroleum
PO Box 1032
Port Moresby, N.C.D. 121

Tel: 675-321-2988
Fax: 675-321-7107

PNG GOVERNMENT OFFICES

Embassy of Papua New Guinea
1615 New Hampshire Ave. NW
Washington, DC 20009

Tel: 202-745-3680
Fax: 202-745-3679

Investment Promotion Authority
PO Box 5053
Boroko, N.C.D. 111

Tel: 675-321-7311
Fax: 675-321-2819

Department of Mining & Petroleum
PO Box 352
Konedobu, N.C.D. 125

Office of the Secretary: Ph 675-321-7600/Fax 321-7958
Mining Division: Ph 675-322-7624/Fax 321-3701

Department of Mining & Petroleum
Petroleum Division
PO Box 778
Port Moresby, N.C.D. 121

Tel: 675-322-4200/321-2422
Fax: 322-4222

Internal Revenue Commission
Customs and Excise Operations
PO Box 777
Port Moresby, N.C.D. 121

Tel: 675-322-6600
Fax: 675-321-4249/321-3484

PNG National Fisheries Authority
PO Box 2016
Port Moresby, N.C.D. 121

Tel: 675-321-2643
Fax: 675-320-2074

Papua New Guinea Forest Authority
PO Box 5055
Boroko, N.C.D. 111

Tel: 675-327-7800
Fax: 675-325-4433

Country Market Research Firms

IMPS Research Pty Ltd
PO Box 986
Port Moresby, N.C.D. 121

Tel: 675-321-3283
Fax: 675-321-7360

Publishes "Petroleum & Minerals Industry Directory" and "The Governments of PNG" (directory of Government Ministries, Departments, etc.)

The CAM Group Pty Ltd
P.O. Box 7312
Cairns, Qld 4870
Australia

Tel: 61-70-521-999
Fax: 61-70-313-661

Publishes "Papua New Guinea Oil and Gas" (monthly report on developments in petroleum industry) and offers mining and petroleum research materials and services

PAPUA NEW GUINEA BASIC TITLES

All publications are updated annually!
Please contact IBP, Inc. at ibpusa3@gmail.com for the latest ISBNs and additional information

title
Papua New Guinea A "Spy" Guide
Papua New Guinea A Spy" Guide"
Papua New Guinea Banking & Financial Market Handbook
Papua New Guinea Banking & Financial Market Handbook
Papua New Guinea Business and Investment Opportunities Yearbook
Papua New Guinea Business and Investment Opportunities Yearbook
Papua New Guinea Business and Investment Opportunities Yearbook Volume 1 Strategic Information and Opportunities
Papua New Guinea Business and Investment Opportunities Yearbook Volume 1 Strategic Information and Opportunities
Papua New Guinea Business Intelligence Report
Papua New Guinea Business Intelligence Report
Papua New Guinea Business Law Handbook
Papua New Guinea Business Law Handbook
Papua New Guinea Business Law Handbook
Papua New Guinea Business Law Handbook
Papua New Guinea Country Study Guide
Papua New Guinea Country Study Guide
Papua New Guinea Country Study Guide Volume 1 Strategic Information and Developments
Papua New Guinea Diplomatic Handbook
Papua New Guinea Diplomatic Handbook
Papua New Guinea Ecology & Nature Protection Handbook
Papua New Guinea Ecology & Nature Protection Handbook
Papua New Guinea Ecology & Nature Protection Laws and Regulation Handbook
Papua New Guinea Economic & Development Strategy Handbook
Papua New Guinea Economic & Development Strategy Handbook

title
Papua New Guinea Energy Policy, Laws and Regulation Handbook
Papua New Guinea Energy Policy, Laws and Regulations Handbook
Papua New Guinea Energy Policy, Laws and Regulations Handbook
Papua New Guinea Foreign Policy and Government Guide
Papua New Guinea Foreign Policy and Government Guide
Papua New Guinea Investment and Business Guide
Papua New Guinea Investment and Business Guide
Papua New Guinea Investment and Business Guide
Papua New Guinea Investment and Business Guide
Papua New Guinea Mineral & Mining Sector Investment and Business Guide
Papua New Guinea Mineral & Mining Sector Investment and Business Guide
Papua New Guinea Mining Industry Business Opportunities Handbook
Papua New Guinea Mining Industry Business Opportunities Handbook
Papua New Guinea Mining Laws and Regulations Handbook
Papua New Guinea Oil & Gas Sector Business & Investment Opportunities Yearbook
Papua New Guinea Oil & Gas Sector Business & Investment Opportunities Yearbook
Papua New Guinea Oil & Gas Sector Business and Investment Opportunities Yearbook Volume 2
Papua New Guinea Oil & Gas Sector Energy Policy, Laws and Regulations Handbook
Papua New Guinea Oil & Gas Sector Energy Policy, Laws and Regulations Handbook
Papua New Guinea Oil & Gas Sector Oil & Gas Sector Business & Investment Opportunities Yearbook
Papua New Guinea Oil & Gas Sector Oil & Gas Sector Business & Investment Opportunities Yearbook
Papua New Guinea Oil & Gas Sector Oil and Gas Exploration Laws and Regulation Handbook
Papua New Guinea Oil and Gas Exploration Laws and Regulation Handbook
Papua New Guinea Recent Economic and Political Developments Yearbook
Papua New Guinea Taxation Laws and Regulations Handbook

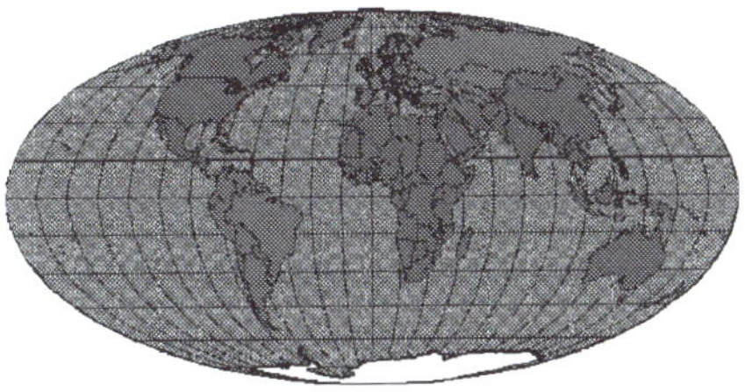

TITLE
Cape Verde Business Law Handbook Volume 1 Strategic Information and Basic Laws
Cayman Islands Business Law Handbook Volume 1 Strategic Information and Basic Laws
Central African Republic Business Law Handbook Volume 1 Strategic Information and Basic Laws
Chad Business Law Handbook Volume 1 Strategic Information and Basic Laws
Chile Business Law Handbook Volume 1 Strategic Information and Basic Laws
China Business Law Handbook Volume 1 Strategic Information and Basic Laws
Colombia Business Law Handbook Volume 1 Strategic Information and Basic Laws
Comoros Business Law Handbook Volume 1 Strategic Information and Basic Laws
Congo Business Law Handbook Volume 1 Strategic Information and Basic Laws
Congo, Democratic Republic Business Law Handbook Volume 1 Strategic Information and Basic Laws
Cook Islands Business Law Handbook Volume 1 Strategic Information and Basic Laws
Costa Rica Business Law Handbook Volume 1 Strategic Information and Basic Laws
Cote d'Ivoire Business Law Handbook Volume 1 Strategic Information and Basic Laws
Croatia Business Law Handbook Volume 1 Strategic Information and Basic Laws
Cuba Business Law Handbook Volume 1 Strategic Information and Basic Laws
Cyprus Business Law Handbook Volume 1 Strategic Information and Basic Laws
Czech Republic Business Law Handbook Volume 1 Strategic Information and Basic Laws
Denmark Business Law Handbook Volume 1 Strategic Information and Basic Laws
Djibouti Business Law Handbook Volume 1 Strategic Information and Basic Laws
Dominica Business Law Handbook Volume 1 Strategic Information and Basic Laws
Dominican Republic Business Law Handbook Volume 1 Strategic Information and Basic Laws
Ecuador Business Law Handbook Volume 1 Strategic Information and Basic Laws
Egypt Business Law Handbook Volume 1 Strategic Information and Basic Laws
El Salvador Business Law Handbook Volume 1 Strategic Information and Basic Laws
Equatorial Guinea Business Law Handbook Volume 1 Strategic Information and Basic Laws
Eritrea Business Law Handbook Volume 1 Strategic Information and Basic Laws
Estonia Business Law Handbook Volume 1 Strategic Information and Basic Laws
Ethiopia Business Law Handbook Volume 1 Strategic Information and Basic Laws
Falkland Islands Business Law Handbook Volume 1 Strategic Information and Basic Laws
Faroes Islands Business Law Handbook Volume 1 Strategic Information and Basic Laws
Fiji Business Law Handbook Volume 1 Strategic Information and Basic Laws
Finland Business Law Handbook Volume 1 Strategic Information and Basic Laws
France Business Law Handbook Volume 1 Strategic Information and Basic Laws
Gabon Business Law Handbook Volume 1 Strategic Information and Basic Laws
Gambia Business Law Handbook Volume 1 Strategic Information and Basic Laws
Georgia Business Law Handbook Volume 1 Strategic Information and Basic Laws
Germany Business Law Handbook Volume 1 Strategic Information and Basic Laws
Ghana Business Law Handbook Volume 1 Strategic Information and Basic Laws
Gibraltar Business Law Handbook Volume 1 Strategic Information and Basic Laws
Greece Business Law Handbook Volume 1 Strategic Information and Basic Laws
Greenland Business Law Handbook Volume 1 Strategic Information and Basic Laws
Grenada Business Law Handbook Volume 1 Strategic Information and Basic Laws
Guam Business Law Handbook Volume 1 Strategic Information and Basic Laws
Guatemala Business Law Handbook Volume 1 Strategic Information and Basic Laws
Guernsey Business Law Handbook Volume 1 Strategic Information and Basic Laws
Guinea Business Law Handbook Volume 1 Strategic Information and Basic Laws

TITLE
Guinea-Bissau Business Law Handbook Volume 1 Strategic Information and Basic Laws
Guyana Business Law Handbook Volume 1 Strategic Information and Basic Laws
Haiti Business Law Handbook Volume 1 Strategic Information and Basic Laws
Honduras Business Law Handbook Volume 1 Strategic Information and Basic Laws
Hungary Business Law Handbook Volume 1 Strategic Information and Basic Laws
Iceland Business Law Handbook Volume 1 Strategic Information and Basic Laws
India Business Law Handbook Volume 1 Strategic Information and Basic Laws
Indonesia Business Law Handbook Volume 1 Strategic Information and Basic Laws
Iran Business Law Handbook Volume 1 Strategic Information and Basic Laws
Iraq Business Law Handbook Volume 1 Strategic Information and Basic Laws
Ireland Business Law Handbook Volume 1 Strategic Information and Basic Laws
Israel Business Law Handbook Volume 1 Strategic Information and Basic Laws
Italy Business Law Handbook Volume 1 Strategic Information and Basic Laws
Jamaica Business Law Handbook Volume 1 Strategic Information and Basic Laws
Japan Business Law Handbook Volume 1 Strategic Information and Basic Laws
Jersey Business Law Handbook Volume 1 Strategic Information and Basic Laws
Jordan Business Law Handbook Volume 1 Strategic Information and Basic Laws
Kazakhstan Business Law Handbook Volume 1 Strategic Information and Basic Laws
Kenya Business Law Handbook Volume 1 Strategic Information and Basic Laws
Kiribati Business Law Handbook Volume 1 Strategic Information and Basic Laws
Korea, North Business Law Handbook Volume 1 Strategic Information and Basic Laws
Korea, South Business Law Handbook Volume 1 Strategic Information and Basic Laws
Kosovo Business Law Handbook Volume 1 Strategic Information and Basic Laws
Kurdistan Business Law Handbook Volume 1 Strategic Information and Basic Laws
Kuwait Business Law Handbook Volume 1 Strategic Information and Basic Laws
Kyrgyzstan Business Law Handbook Volume 1 Strategic Information and Basic Laws
Laos Business Law Handbook Volume 1 Strategic Information and Basic Laws
Latvia Business Law Handbook Volume 1 Strategic Information and Basic Laws
Lebanon Business Law Handbook Volume 1 Strategic Information and Basic Laws
Lesotho Business Law Handbook Volume 1 Strategic Information and Basic Laws
Liberia Business Law Handbook Volume 1 Strategic Information and Basic Laws
Libya Business Law Handbook Volume 1 Strategic Information and Basic Laws
Liechtenstein Business Law Handbook Volume 1 Strategic Information and Basic Laws
Lithuania Business Law Handbook Volume 1 Strategic Information and Basic Laws
Luxembourg Business Law Handbook Volume 1 Strategic Information and Basic Laws
Macao Business Law Handbook Volume 1 Strategic Information and Basic Laws
Macedonia Business Law Handbook Volume 1 Strategic Information and Basic Laws
Madagascar Business Law Handbook Volume 1 Strategic Information and Basic Laws
Madeira Business Law Handbook Volume 1 Strategic Information and Basic Laws
Malawi Business Law Handbook Volume 1 Strategic Information and Basic Laws
Malaysia Business Law Handbook Volume 1 Strategic Information and Basic Laws
Maldives Business Law Handbook Volume 1 Strategic Information and Basic Laws
Mali Business Law Handbook Volume 1 Strategic Information and Basic Laws
Malta Business Law Handbook Volume 1 Strategic Information and Basic Laws
Man Business Law Handbook Volume 1 Strategic Information and Basic Laws
Marshall Islands Business Law Handbook Volume 1 Strategic Information and Basic Laws

TITLE
Mauritania Business Law Handbook Volume 1 Strategic Information and Basic Laws
Mauritius Business Law Handbook Volume 1 Strategic Information and Basic Laws
Mayotte Business Law Handbook Volume 1 Strategic Information and Basic Laws
Mexico Business Law Handbook Volume 1 Strategic Information and Basic Laws
Micronesia Business Law Handbook Volume 1 Strategic Information and Basic Laws
Moldova Business Law Handbook Volume 1 Strategic Information and Basic Laws
Monaco Business Law Handbook Volume 1 Strategic Information and Basic Laws
Mongolia Business Law Handbook Volume 1 Strategic Information and Basic Laws
Montserrat Business Law Handbook Volume 1 Strategic Information and Basic Laws
Montenegro Business Law Handbook Volume 1 Strategic Information and Basic Laws
Morocco Business Law Handbook Volume 1 Strategic Information and Basic Laws
Mozambique Business Law Handbook Volume 1 Strategic Information and Basic Laws
Myanmar Business Law Handbook Volume 1 Strategic Information and Basic Laws
Nagorno-Karabakh Republic Business Law Handbook Volume 1 Strategic Information and Basic Laws
Namibia Business Law Handbook Volume 1 Strategic Information and Basic Laws
Nauru Business Law Handbook Volume 1 Strategic Information and Basic Laws
Nepal Business Law Handbook Volume 1 Strategic Information and Basic Laws
Netherlands Business Law Handbook Volume 1 Strategic Information and Basic Laws
New Caledonia Business Law Handbook Volume 1 Strategic Information and Basic Laws
New Zealand Business Law Handbook Volume 1 Strategic Information and Basic Laws
Nicaragua Business Law Handbook Volume 1 Strategic Information and Basic Laws
Niger Business Law Handbook Volume 1 Strategic Information and Basic Laws
Nigeria Business Law Handbook Volume 1 Strategic Information and Basic Laws
Niue Business Law Handbook Volume 1 Strategic Information and Basic Laws
Northern Cyprus (Turkish Republic of Northern Cyprus) Business Law Handbook Volume 1 Strategic Information and Basic Laws
Northern Mariana Islands Business Law Handbook Volume 1 Strategic Information and Basic Laws
Norway Business Law Handbook Volume 1 Strategic Information and Basic Laws
Oman Business Law Handbook Volume 1 Strategic Information and Basic Laws
Pakistan Business Law Handbook Volume 1 Strategic Information and Basic Laws
Palau Business Law Handbook Volume 1 Strategic Information and Basic Laws
Palestine (West Bank & Gaza) Business Law Handbook Volume 1 Strategic Information and Basic Laws
Panama Business Law Handbook Volume 1 Strategic Information and Basic Laws
Papua New Guinea Business Law Handbook Volume 1 Strategic Information and Basic Laws
Paraguay Business Law Handbook Volume 1 Strategic Information and Basic Laws
Peru Business Law Handbook Volume 1 Strategic Information and Basic Laws
Philippines Business Law Handbook Volume 1 Strategic Information and Basic Laws
Pitcairn Islands Business Law Handbook Volume 1 Strategic Information and Basic Laws
Poland Business Law Handbook Volume 1 Strategic Information and Basic Laws
Polynesia French Business Law Handbook Volume 1 Strategic Information and Basic Laws
Portugal Business Law Handbook Volume 1 Strategic Information and Basic Laws
Qatar Business Law Handbook Volume 1 Strategic Information and Basic Laws
Romania Business Law Handbook Volume 1 Strategic Information and Basic Laws
Russia Business Law Handbook Volume 1 Strategic Information and Basic Laws
Rwanda Business Law Handbook Volume 1 Strategic Information and Basic Laws
Sahrawi Arab Democratic Republic Volume 1 Strategic Information and Developments

TITLE
Saint Kitts and Nevis Business Law Handbook Volume 1 Strategic Information and Basic Laws
Saint Lucia Business Law Handbook Volume 1 Strategic Information and Basic Laws
Saint Vincent and The Grenadines Business Law Handbook Volume 1 Strategic Information and Basic Laws
Samoa (American) A Business Law Handbook Volume 1 Strategic Information and Basic Laws
Samoa (Western) Business Law Handbook Volume 1 Strategic Information and Basic Laws
San Marino Business Law Handbook Volume 1 Strategic Information and Basic Laws
Sao Tome and Principe Business Law Handbook Volume 1 Strategic Information and Basic Laws
Saudi Arabia Business Law Handbook Volume 1 Strategic Information and Basic Laws
Scotland Business Law Handbook Volume 1 Strategic Information and Basic Laws
Senegal Business Law Handbook Volume 1 Strategic Information and Basic Laws
Serbia Business Law Handbook Volume 1 Strategic Information and Basic Laws
Seychelles Business Law Handbook Volume 1 Strategic Information and Basic Laws
Sierra Leone Business Law Handbook Volume 1 Strategic Information and Basic Laws
Singapore Business Law Handbook Volume 1 Strategic Information and Basic Laws
Slovakia Business Law Handbook Volume 1 Strategic Information and Basic Laws
Slovenia Business Law Handbook Volume 1 Strategic Information and Basic Laws
Solomon Islands Business Law Handbook Volume 1 Strategic Information and Basic Laws
Somalia Business Law Handbook Volume 1 Strategic Information and Basic Laws
South Africa Business Law Handbook Volume 1 Strategic Information and Basic Laws
Spain Business Law Handbook Volume 1 Strategic Information and Basic Laws
Sri Lanka Business Law Handbook Volume 1 Strategic Information and Basic Laws
St. Helena Business Law Handbook Volume 1 Strategic Information and Basic Laws
St. Pierre & Miquelon Business Law Handbook Volume 1 Strategic Information and Basic Laws
Sudan (Republic of the Sudan) Business Law Handbook Volume 1 Strategic Information and Basic Laws
Sudan South Business Law Handbook Volume 1 Strategic Information and Basic Laws
Suriname Business Law Handbook Volume 1 Strategic Information and Basic Laws
Swaziland Business Law Handbook Volume 1 Strategic Information and Basic Laws
Sweden Business Law Handbook Volume 1 Strategic Information and Basic Laws
Switzerland Business Law Handbook Volume 1 Strategic Information and Basic Laws
Syria Business Law Handbook Volume 1 Strategic Information and Basic Laws
Taiwan Business Law Handbook Volume 1 Strategic Information and Basic Laws
Tajikistan Business Law Handbook Volume 1 Strategic Information and Basic Laws
Tanzania Business Law Handbook Volume 1 Strategic Information and Basic Laws
Thailand Business Law Handbook Volume 1 Strategic Information and Basic Laws
Timor Leste (Democratic Republic of Timor-Leste) Business Law Handbook Volume 1 Strategic Information and Basic Laws
Togo Business Law Handbook Volume 1 Strategic Information and Basic Laws
Tonga Business Law Handbook Volume 1 Strategic Information and Basic Laws
Trinidad and Tobago Business Law Handbook Volume 1 Strategic Information and Basic Laws
Tunisia Business Law Handbook Volume 1 Strategic Information and Basic Laws
Turkey Business Law Handbook Volume 1 Strategic Information and Basic Laws
Turkmenistan Business Law Handbook Volume 1 Strategic Information and Basic Laws
Turks & Caicos Business Law Handbook Volume 1 Strategic Information and Basic Laws
Tuvalu Business Law Handbook Volume 1 Strategic Information and Basic Laws
Uganda Business Law Handbook Volume 1 Strategic Information and Basic Laws
Ukraine Business Law Handbook Volume 1 Strategic Information and Basic Laws

TITLE
United Arab Emirates Business Law Handbook Volume 1 Strategic Information and Basic Laws
United Kingdom Business Law Handbook Volume 1 Strategic Information and Basic Laws
United States Business Law Handbook Volume 1 Strategic Information and Basic Laws
Uruguay Business Law Handbook Volume 1 Strategic Information and Basic Laws
Uzbekistan Business Law Handbook Volume 1 Strategic Information and Basic Laws
Vanuatu Business Law Handbook Volume 1 Strategic Information and Basic Laws
Vatican City (Holy See) Business Law Handbook Volume 1 Strategic Information and Basic Laws
Venezuela Business Law Handbook Volume 1 Strategic Information and Basic Laws
Vietnam Business Law Handbook Volume 1 Strategic Information and Basic Laws
Virgin Islands, British Business Law Handbook Volume 1 Strategic Information and Basic Laws
Wake Atoll Business Law Handbook Volume 1 Strategic Information and Basic Laws
Wallis & Futuna Business Law Handbook Volume 1 Strategic Information and Basic Laws
Western Sahara Business Law Handbook Volume 1 Strategic Information and Basic Laws
Yemen Business Law Handbook Volume 1 Strategic Information and Basic Laws
Zambia Business Law Handbook Volume 1 Strategic Information and Basic Laws
Zimbabwe Business Law Handbook Volume 1 Strategic Information and Basic Laws

Made in United States
Orlando, FL
04 November 2026

90207773R00199